Historical Memory of Central and East European Communism

Every political movement creates its own historical memory. The communist movement, though originally oriented toward the future, was no exception: The theory of human history constitutes a substantial part of Karl Marx's and Friedrich Engels's writings, and the movement inspired by them very soon developed its own strong historical identity, combining the Marxist theory of history with the movement's victorious milestones such as the October Revolution and later the Great Patriotic War, which served as communist legitimization myths throughout almost the entire twentieth century. During the Stalinist period, however, the movement's history became strongly reinterpreted to suit Joseph Stalin's political goals. After 1956, this reinterpretation lost most of its legitimating power and instead began to be a burden. The (unwanted) memory of Stalinism and subsequent examples of violence (the Gulag, Katyn, the 1956 Budapest uprising and the 1968 Prague Spring) contributed to the crisis of Eastern European state socialism in the late 1980s and led to attempts at reformulating or even rejecting communist self-identity. This book's first section analyzes the post-1989 memory of communism and state socialism and the self-identity of the Eastern and Western European left. The second section examines the state socialist and post-socialist memorial landscapes in the former German Democratic Republic, Czechoslovakia/Czech Republic, Poland, Lithuania, Ukraine and Russia. The final section concentrates on the narratives the movement established, when in power, about its own past, with the examples of the Soviet Union, Poland, Romania and Czechoslovakia.

Agnieszka Mrozik is Assistant Professor at the Institute of Literary Research of the Polish Academy of Sciences.

Stanislav Holubec is Associate Professor at the University of České Budějovice and University of Hradec Králové, Czech Republic.

Routledge Studies in Cultural History

The Romantic Idea of the Golden Age in Friedrich Schlegel's Philosophy of History
Asko Nivala

Student Revolt, City, and Society in Europe
From the Middle Ages to the Present
Edited by Pieter Dhondt and Elizabethanne Boran

Respectability as Moral Map and Public Discourse in the Nineteenth Century
Woodruff D. Smith

The British Anti-Psychiatrists
From Institutional Psychiatry to the Counter-Culture, 1960–1971
Oisín Wall

Cultural Histories of Crime in Denmark, 1500 to 2000
Edited by Tyge Krogh, Louise Nyholm Kallestrup and Claus Bundgård Christensen

Fascism and the Masses
The Revolt Against the Last Humans, 1848–1945
Ishay Landa

The Irish and the Origins of American Popular Culture
Christopher Dowd

The Medieval and Early Modern Garden in Britain
Enclosure and Transformation, c. 1200–1750
Edited by Patricia Skinner and Theresa Tyers

Historical Memory of Central and East European Communism
Edited by Agnieszka Mrozik and Stanislav Holubec

For more information about this series, please visit: www.routledge.com/Routledge-Studies-in-Cultural-History/book-series/SE0367

Historical Memory of Central and East European Communism

Edited by Agnieszka Mrozik and
Stanislav Holubec

NEW YORK AND LONDON

First published 2018
by Routledge
711 Third Avenue, New York, NY 10017

and by Routledge
2 Park Square, Milton Park, Abingdon, Oxon OX14 4RN

Routledge is an imprint of the Taylor & Francis Group, an informa business

© 2018 Taylor & Francis

The right of the editors to be identified as the authors of the editorial material, and of the authors for their individual chapters, has been asserted in accordance with sections 77 and 78 of the Copyright, Designs and Patents Act 1988.

All rights reserved. No part of this book may be reprinted or reproduced or utilized in any form or by any electronic, mechanical, or other means, now known or hereafter invented, including photocopying and recording, or in any information storage or retrieval system, without permission in writing from the publishers.

Trademark notice: Product or corporate names may be trademarks or registered trademarks, and are used only for identification and explanation without intent to infringe.

Library of Congress Cataloging-in-Publication Data
A catalog record for this book has been requested

ISBN: 978-1-138-54226-6 (hbk)
ISBN: 978-1-351-00928-7 (ebk)

Typeset in Sabon
by Apex CoVantage, LLC

Contents

List of Tables …… vii
Acknowledgments …… viii

Introduction: Historical Memory of European Communisms Before and After 1989 …… 1
STANISLAV HOLUBEC AND AGNIESZKA MROZIK

PART I
Memory of the Left in Post-Socialist Europe …… 19

1 "Of the Past Let Us Make a Clean Slate": The Lack of a Left-Wing Narrative and the Failure of the Hungarian Left …… 21
CSILLA KISS

2 Communist Successors and Narratives of the Past: Party Factions in the German PDS and the Russian CPRF, 1990–2005 …… 41
THORSTEN HOLZHAUSER AND ANTONY KALASHNIKOV

3 The Memory and Identity of the Western European Left in the Light of European Integration: View from Inside …… 74
WALTER BAIER

PART II
Memorial Landscapes in Central and Eastern Europe …… 99

4 Dissonant Heritage: Soviet Monuments in Central and Eastern Europe …… 101
ALEKSANDRA KUCZYŃSKA-ZONIK

5   Lenin, Marx and Local Heroes: Socialist and
    Post-Socialist Memorial Landscapes in Eastern
    Germany and Czechoslovakia—The Case Study of
    Jena and Hradec Králové   122
    STANISLAV HOLUBEC

6   The Politics of Oblivion and the Practices of Remembrance:
    Repression, Collective Memory and Nation-Building in
    Post-Soviet Russia   141
    EKATERINA V. KLIMENKO

PART III
Communist Politics of Memory Before 1989   163

7   What Happened in 1980? Memory Forging and the Official
    Story of Martial Law in the Polish United Workers' Party   165
    JAKUB SZUMSKI

8   "We Must Reconstruct Our Own Past": 1960s Polish
    Communist Women's Memoirs—Constructing the
    (Gender) History of the Polish Left   192
    AGNIESZKA MROZIK

9   Romanian Communists Under Gheorghiu-Dej: Legitimation
    Before 1965 and Its Memory as Opposition to Ceaușescu   221
    MONICA CIOBANU

10 Constructing New Friends and Enemies: Rewriting
    Czechoslovak History After the Communist Takeover   242
    DARINA VOLF

11 Constructing Memoirs of the October Revolution in the 1920s   260
    OKSANA KLYMENKO

    Contributors   274
    Index   278

Tables

7.1 PUWP Membership 1980–1981   173
7.2 PUWP Membership 1982–1985   178

Acknowledgments

We are grateful to Routledge—in particular to our editors Jennifer Morrow and Max Novick—for their encouragement, assistance and technical support. We are grateful for the helpful comments of the two anonymous reviewers.

The contributions were coordinated by Dagmar Švendová and proofread by Eric Canepa with the support of transform! europe, the European network for alternative thinking and political dialogue. This project was partially financed through a subsidy from the European Parliament.

The proofreading was also partly financed by the Association for Left Theory SOK (Czech Republic), by the University of South Bohemia in České Budějovice (Czech Republic) and by the Institute of Literary Research of the Polish Academy of Sciences (Poland).

Introduction

Historical Memory of European Communisms Before and After 1989

Stanislav Holubec and Agnieszka Mrozik

George Orwell wrote in his famous *1984* that history was continuously changed in fictional Oceania by decision of its rulers. The past activities of current leaders were magnified and celebrated; their defeated opponents either disappeared from the pages of history or were demonized as eternal traitors, and allies called eternal friends suddenly became archenemies. Orwell's book, written between 1945 and 1948, was clearly meant to reflect the politics of history under Joseph Stalin, familiar to Orwell since the Spanish Civil War. His image of the communist movement as systematically fabricating its own history became influential during the Cold War and was taken over by anti-communists. One of the posters of the Civic Forum, the leading force of the Czech Velvet Revolution in 1989, depicted two pupils saying, "Ms. Teacher, you do not need to lie to us anymore."[1] Not only was the communist term "comrade" (*soudružka*) used by children to address their teachers, replaced by the civic version "Ms." (*paní*), but also the poster text as a whole evidenced one of the most important aspects of Czechoslovak public anger in the 1980s: that the regime constantly lied about history—at school, in the media and in official speeches. People expressed their demand to hear the "truth" about Vladimir Lenin, Stalin, Tomáš Garrigue Masaryk, Klement Gottwald, 1948, 1968, etc. The official interpretation of history was perceived as one big lie. It was believed that the state authorities had to lie about their own history to prevent their power from collapsing.

We first need to consider how it was that the communist movement, which from its origins focused on the creation of the future world, turned into a movement heavily focused on its own history, creating extensive commemorative rituals and developing and protecting an official interpretation of history; how the meaning of history for the labor movement changed over time; and how the narrative of history produced first by communist movements and later by the ideological apparatuses of post-World War II Eastern Bloc countries was developed and transformed. In the last decade, historiography and other disciplines have paid much attention to the question of how communism is remembered, particularly in terms of its crimes, but also as nostalgia for state socialism, its memorial landscapes, etc.[2] Much less attention has been paid to the question of how communism was and is remembered by various political organizations, politicians and other social actors who call themselves "communist(s)." In this volume, we hope to compensate this lack. We are aware, however, that there are several different communist identities, principally around the axis of reform communism and Stalinism. Space does not permit us to examine other sectors of the left, such as social democracy or democratic socialism, although these developed their historical identities as well. Nor can we focus on the historical narratives developed by marginal factions of the communist movements in Europe such as Trotskyists or Maoists.

Every modern political movement creates its own historical memory and narratives in order to reinforce its identity and legitimize its goals. This narrative generally involves the story of the movement's birth and early development, life stories of its leaders, important events in its history, etc. Modern political movements also look for older historical movements or personalities that can be interpreted as predecessors and absorbed into their own stories, with the current movement seen as their inheritor or developer.[3] Marxism differed from other movements in the sense that its founders not only formulated a certain politics of history but also developed an extensive and intellectually highly attractive grand narrative of European and global history, which explained in a scientific manner that capitalism would be overturned by a revolution and replaced by a more socially progressive communist society. Social uprisings and revolts occupied a special place in this narrative: "The history of all hitherto existing society is the history of class struggles"—Karl Marx and Friedrich Engels wrote in their famous *Communist Manifesto* in 1848. What particularly interested them were slave uprisings in antiquity, most importantly the Spartacus revolt, and medieval and early modern peasants' and artisans' uprisings, with special attention to the sixteenth-century German Peasants' War. They also admired modern "bourgeois" revolutions, called by Marx "the locomotives of history," and the historical role of their alleged agent, the bourgeoisie. The French Revolution and revolutions of 1848 seemed to confirm the expectations that communist revolution led by the industrial proletariat would one day arrive on the scene. The focus of Marx and Engels on the economic processes and particularly on the roots of modern capitalism and the Industrial Revolution, as well as their desire to discover economic laws of the future collapse of capitalism, gave the impression that the communist movement had the force of history on its side.[4]

Despite the general importance of the laws of history emphasized by the labor movement throughout the nineteenth century, it actually had little interest in the politics of history, in historical identity, rituals and commemorations. This changed in 1871 when it politically rose to the level of world history for the first time. The Paris Commune, interpreted by Marx and his followers both as the first serious attempt of the working class to seize power and as a moment of martyrdom because of its defeat, became an important *lieu de mémoire* of the movement. Its commemoration began in socialist circles right after its defeat.[5]

The next occasion came with the communist founding fathers' death. Their biographies were written, dates of birth and death commemorated and Marx's grave visited frequently (his birth house in Trier much later, only during the 1920s and after 1945).[6] Engels, outliving Marx for more than a decade, actively contributed to these practices through the publishing of nonfinalized manuscripts such as the second and third volumes of *Capital*, published, respectively, in 1884 and 1894. He decided to have his own ashes thrown into the sea in order to leave nothing that "detracts from the glory of Marx: no Highgate headstone or family tomb, no public memorial."[7]

In this period, the labor movement organized an annual celebration, which overshadowed the Day of the Commune and the commemorations of Marx's birth and death. This was the May Day celebrated on the First of May ever since the 1890s. The date was chosen in an attempt to displace the traditional religious festivities, and only later, it was projected as a commemoration of the 1886 Haymarket affair in Chicago. As this definitely was not the bloodiest event in the history of nineteenth-century class struggle, memory of it unsurprisingly disappeared from later May Day celebrations.[8]

Besides cultivating May Day, the labor movement was involved in women's rights, and the idea of International Women's Day was developed in the early 1900s in German and American socialist movements. In this case, there was no historical event suitable for commemoration. The first celebration took place in Germany and Austria-Hungary on March 18, 1911. Some considered the date a commemoration of the victims of the March 1848 revolution, while others regarded it as commemorating the founding of the 1871 Paris Commune, but neither event explicitly involved women's issues. March 8 was introduced only in 1921 by the Comintern as a commemoration of the female workers' strike in Saint Petersburg in 1917, which led to the outbreak of the February Revolution. Up until World War II, only the communist movement celebrated it, and after 1945, it became a state holiday in Eastern Europe. Western social democracies and feminist movements adopted it only during the 1970s. It is a mere legend that the day commemorates the strike of female textile workers in the US in 1857—an event that in fact never took place. The legend appeared in the 1950s in French communist circles seeking to legitimize March 8 in Western societies by demonstrating its, allegedly, US roots, just as happened with May Day.[9] Interestingly, all of the commemorations mentioned earlier were truly international, as before 1914, the workers' movements were reluctant to include any national traditions.

When the Bolsheviks took power in Russia in 1917, they faced a new situation. The movement's historical memory had to be transformed into the official memory of the new proletarian state, and the memory of the recently established international communist movement had to be formulated as well. The solution was to take the traditions of the socialist movement and combine them with recent political events and the life stories of the revolution's leaders: first of all with Lenin, but also with his faction in Russian social democracy, 1905 revolution, the October Revolution and the subsequent victorious Civil War. For the German communists, representing the second paramount party within the Comintern, of similar significance, besides Lenin and the Bolshevik tradition, were Karl Liebknecht and Rosa Luxemburg, and their political activities and assassination in January 1919.[10] The interwar communist movement, analogously to the pre-1914 social democrats, also adopted a tradition of past revolutionary struggles, starting with the Spartacus revolt. For example, the German radical socialist group founded in 1916, which later merged with the Communist Party of Germany (KPD), took the name *Spartakisten*, and in the 1920s, the communist movement called its mass sport rallies *Spartakiada*.[11]

Like all revolutionary movements, the Bolsheviks aimed to purge areas of memory understood to be reactionary, primarily from religious and monarchist traditions. In April 1918, the Council of People's Commissars in the Soviet Union decreed the removal of all tsarist monuments before the first anniversary of the revolution.[12] In an attempt to synchronize with the European revolutionary movement, the Western calendar was adopted; in contrast to the French Revolution, no attempt was made to create a new calendar and year numbering. The most radical step taken was the abolition of Christmas in 1928, which was revised under Stalin (a fir tree and Father Frost appeared again in Soviet propaganda from 1935 on)[13] and never again abolished in the countries where communists came to power after 1945.

Political regimes that arise from revolutions generally build on them through legitimizing narratives. The Russian Revolution of 1917, called at first the October Coup (*Oktyabrsky perevorot'*), later the October Revolution (*Oktyabrskaya revolyutsiya*) and finally the Great October Socialist Revolution (*Velikaya Oktyabrskaya sotsialističeskaya revolyutsiya*), was no exception. The revolution commemoration soon became the state holiday; it was praised in numerous publications, museums, movies, etc. One aspect of its commemoration—i.e., the collecting of memoires by rank-and-file revolutionaries—is discussed in this volume by **Oksana Klymenko**. What clearly distinguished it from the old Marxist tradition was the cult created around Lenin, which began when he was still alive and culminated after his death. The intensity and extent of Lenin's cult represented something totally distinct from pre-1914 Western socialist traditions. We can only speculate whether it was due to the exceptional role of Lenin in the event, to some older traditions such as the cult of Marx in the nineteenth-century socialist movement or to Russian national traditions. The Russian communists' decision to commemorate Lenin beginning in 1924 was an undertaking of vast scope. It was in fact decided to 1) change the name of Petrograd to Leningrad, 2) make the day of Lenin's death the annual day of national mourning, 3) erect Lenin's monuments in important Soviet cities, 4) publish his collected works, 5) embalm his body and 6) construct his mausoleum in front of the Moscow Kremlin wall.[14] The avant-garde artists in the Communist Party of the Soviet Union (CPSU) opposed this, claiming that figurative memorials were incompatible with the principles of the new order. On the other side, Stalin and most party members were attracted to this form of commemoration.[15] The fashion of erecting statues of Lenin as central communist symbols expanded after 1945 in the countries of the so-called Eastern Bloc and even underwent a renaissance during the Leonid Brezhnev era, as **Stanislav Holubec** demonstrates in his chapter.

According to Graeme Gilles, the Soviet Union had to create several "modes of legitimation" or "myths," the first of which was the idea of birth through revolution narrated as having been fought for by the people and led by a genial leader. The subsequent construction of socialism constituted the second myth, which interpreted the post-revolutionary period as oriented toward a glorious achievement, toward the construction of communism. The third myth involved the concept of leadership and stressed the crucial role of political leaders either as charismatic personalities (Lenin, and later Stalin), or in the form of the collective charisma of the party. The fourth myth, which concerned an internal and external opposition, told the story of enemies inside and outside the country intent on destroying the revolution from the beginning. In the course of time, only one new myth was added—i.e., the myth of the preponderant role of the Soviet Union in the victory over fascism, which was established after 1945. Within all five legitimating myths, there were of course shifts in interpretation and importance, but they generally remained unchallenged until the 1980s. They not only had an effect on the interpretation of Bolshevik and Soviet history but also on that of older historical traditions.[16]

In the interwar period, European communist parties did not develop their own historical narratives rooted in their national cultures but rather adopted the politics of history formulated by the Bolsheviks and the Comintern. For example, the Czechoslovak communists of the 1920s commemorated Marx, Engels, Lenin, the October Revolution, the Paris Commune and the assassination of Liebknecht and Luxemburg, but tended to neglect their own national traditions. The identity of Czechoslovak communists from the 1920s, built around historical referents, can be better understood when we consider the proposal made in the Czechoslovak National Assembly in 1925 by one of the communist members of Parliament. He suggested replacing October 28—the commemoration of the birth of the Republic in 1918—with October 14, the date when social democrats organized the first big rally "for the socialist republic" in the same year. Second, he proposed commemorating the death of Lenin, Liebknecht and Luxemburg; the birth of Marx; the "Russian proletarian revolution"; and the "Paris Commune." His most radical idea was to abolish Christmas and Easter as state holidays in imitation of Bolshevik Russia.[17] The Hussite movement, which became one of the most important communist *lieux de mémoire* in 1950s Czechoslovakia, was not attractive for Czech communists until 1935 when the Comintern prescribed the turn to national traditions in keeping with its new Popular Front policy and the common struggle against fascism.

The first important turning point in the historical narrative of the Soviet state and the international communist movement was the advent of Stalinism. Two aspects were particularly interesting: the cult of Lenin, which was created mostly after his death and in 1929 turned into a double cult of Lenin-Stalin, and the post-1933 cult of Stalin, which overshadowed that of Lenin. In the late 1930s, Stalin decided, for example, to cancel the project of the tallest statue of Lenin on the roof of the planned Palace of Soviets.[18] Second, the threat posed by internal enemies—i.e., Leon Trotsky and other "traitors," took on special significance and served as a mobilizing factor. Third, Stalinism initiated a turn to important figures in Russian history who began to be perceived as its *spiritus agens* instead of the masses.[19] Interestingly, the cult of personality was created around those who in the first years after the revolution were considered reactionary. The cult of Ivan the Terrible, initiated in 1933, or later on that of Alexander Nevsky are the most striking examples,[20] but also notable are those of Peter the Great or of artists previously condemned by the Soviet avant-garde, such as Alexander Pushkin, Mikhail Glinka and Nikolai Rimsky-Korsakov.[21] State propaganda began to laud "socialist patriotism," and several international traditions were replaced by national ones: In 1941, the Paris Commune, which was the socialist movement's most celebrated event before 1914, disappeared from the list of national days.[22] Negative images of the Tsarist Empire were downplayed and the turn to Russian nationalism in history was accompanied by the cult of peasants and folklore traditions, which to some extent displaced the cult of the urban proletariat. Modernist architecture was replaced by monumental "socialist realist architecture." A similar shift occurred in the international communist movement: Alongside the Popular Front strategies adopted by the Comintern at its Seventh World Congress in 1935, communist parties throughout Europe were encouraged by Comintern chair Georgi Dimitrov to use national progressive traditions whose previous underestimation he criticized.[23]

A crucial turning point in the communist historical narratives became the Great Patriotic War (*Velikaya Otechestvennaya Voyna*) in the Soviet Union (1941–1945) and communist resistance movements in Nazi-occupied Europe. They overshadowed the memory of the Russian Revolution and the victory of Bolsheviks in the Civil War of 1917–1922. The Great Patriotic War was turned into a new legitimation myth of the USSR and the communist movement. Its cult further strengthened tendencies to celebrate Russian patriotic traditions, such as the war against Napoleon in 1812, personified in the names of national heroes Alexander Suvorov and Mikhail Kutuzov or Alexander Nevsky and his battle against the Teutonic Knights in 1242.

Within historical narratives constructed by postwar Eastern European states, too, the figure of communist anti-Nazi resistance and Soviet liberation in 1945 played a significant role.[24] It prepared the ground for the concept of eternal friendship between the newly established socialist countries and the Soviet Union, as well as of the brotherhood of nations within the existing federations. An example of the second is the large-scale Czechoslovak archaeological exploration in the 1950s of the early medieval state of Great Moravia, which resulted in the major exhibition of 1963 that interpreted Great Moravia as the "first common state of Czechs and Slovaks," and downplayed Christian traditions connected to it, such as the mission of Cyril and Methodius.[25] The new socialist countries also used old national narratives of Slavs fighting against Germans or feudal lords (for example, the Czech narratives of the Hussites or the Poles's projection of the Battle of Grunwald in 1410), but purified of religious motives. For example, the Czech Hussites were presented not as a religious but as a social and patriotic movement.[26] The Stalinist cult of leaders was superimposed on the past—for example, on Jan Žižka, the Hussite military leader. On the other hand, the space occupied by general European history in school curricula was reduced and the idea of mutual relations between Central and Western Europeans suppressed. A positive effect of the West on Central Europe was rejected as demonstrated in this volume by **Darina Volf**'s article on post-1948 Czechoslovak public discourse that characterized the role of the US in the pre-war period and in the 1945 liberalization as "imperialist." The recent past, particularly the pre-war regimes, has been described "as a period of darkness replete with inequality and without freedom or justice."[27] Enemies were called "representatives of the past," while communists were described as those who embodied the present and the future. In the shadow of victory in the Second World War, all uncomfortable and inexplicable facts—such as the Molotov-Ribbentrop Pact of August 23, 1939, the Soviet-Finnish War of 1939–1940, the Katyn massacre of 1940 and the 1940 absorption of the Baltic states into the USSR—were hidden or interpreted in favor of the Soviet Union. The perspective of Soviet victory in 1945 also covered up military defeats of the Red Army in the first months after the Nazi attack on June 22, 1941, as well as numerous Soviet deficiencies in conflict with the image of the Soviet Union as a developed and modern country. Furthermore, any memory of Russians or Ukrainians fighting arm in arm with the Nazis had to disappear, as it did not fit the picture of all Soviet peoples involved in the anti-fascist struggle.

Western communist parties made participation in the anti-Nazi and anti-fascist resistance movement a key element of their historical narratives as well. They presented themselves both as martyrs and courageous fighters, maintaining silence about their passivity between 1939 and 1941. The French Communist Party called itself the "party of the shot" (*le parti des fusillés*).[28] Those commemorations clearly overshadowed the heroic narratives about pre-war communist actions, such as strikes, uprisings and demonstrations. The anti-fascist memory remained central for the identity of Greek or Italian communists until the 1990s, while for French communists, it lost its attractiveness already in the 1960s. Significant in this context was the 1970s affair when the French communist leader Georges Marchais was exposed as having lied about his own wartime past: It happened that he had voluntarily joined the program for Frenchmen working in Germany. In several European countries, not only was the role of communists in the resistance movement exalted but also their part in postwar reconstruction and democratization.[29]

The end of Stalinism meant another turning point in the pattern of communist historical narratives. Everything connected with Stalin was erased, and his cult was replaced by that of Lenin and the party.[30] As demonstrated in this volume by **Agnieszka Mrozik**'s chapter on the post-1956 memoirs of Polish communist women, the memory of the October Revolution was renewed and used to purify the idea of communism, to return to its roots. Stalinist language was abandoned, and the history of the Soviet Union began to be narrated in a less exalted and Manichean manner. However, post-Stalinist narratives on history were revised only to some extent: Although many European Communist Party leaders murdered by Stalin in the course of the 1930s were rehabilitated, free discussion of Stalin's crimes was not allowed until the 1980s for fear of being taxed with revisionism. The Stalinist suppressions of "party deviations" were still understood as correct, and interpretations of Soviet foreign policy from the years 1939–1941 remained untouched. It did, however, then become possible to express different views through art that dealt with the recent past. The best-known examples of this "thaw" were Aleksandr Solzhenitsyn's *One Day in the Life of Ivan Denisovich* (published in 1962) and Milan Kundera's *The Joke* (1968). In some cases, critical writing on the recent past was quite liberally allowed from the 1960s on (in Hungary and Poland); while in others, it was suppressed after several liberal years (in the Soviet Union, Czechoslovakia and Romania).

Nikita Khrushchev's condemnation of Stalin's crimes, which coincided with the Soviet invasion of Hungary in October 1956, opened a space for Western communist parties to start slowly developing their own historical narratives, whose tone was often critical of the Soviet Union. Their existence in liberal democracies forced them to produce narratives reliable enough to sustain the social support they had gotten after 1945. When creating official party history, they had to take into account the critical voices of both party members and non-communist political and academic circles. Facing strong anti-communist tendencies, they also had to persuade public opinion that they were rooted in national traditions and free from foreign influences (in other words, that they were not "tools of Moscow").[31] Some decided to build their identity on the critique of Stalinism, but many remained reluctant. For example, the French Communist Party continued adhering to rather orthodox historical narratives uncritical of the Soviet Union, while the Italian Communist Party adopted a more critical stance; however, the Italian party did not terminate its support for the Soviet Union until 1968, and it supported it even in the 1980s when it backed the Soviet invasion of Afghanistan.[32] Not only political events but also historiographical publications damaged the image of communism in Western societies. Starting in the mid-1960s, books by French historians who broke with the party were published (for example, those of Annie Kriegel and Jacques Fauvet),[33] but truly groundbreaking were the translations of Solzhenitsyn's *Gulag Archipelago*, first published in 1973. The result of these testimonies to Stalin's victims was severe critique of communism as such and often also defection from the communist movement.

De-Stalinization opened more space for local variants of historical narratives in Eastern Bloc countries. They differed in the extent to which they used nationalist and liberal democratic traditions. In terms of nationalism, the most striking example, described in this volume by **Monica Ciobanu**, was Gheorghe Gheorghiu-Dej's and especially Nicolae Ceaușescu's Romania, which from the 1970s propagated a romantic belief known as *protochronism*, which presented the culture of the mythicized Dacians during antiquity as in many respects superior to Rome. Moreover, later Romanian achievements were seen as anticipating Western European phenomena (for example, the 1784 Romanian peasant uprising was interpreted as the precursor of the French Revolution).[34] The German Democratic Republic (GDR), which renounced any national unification project, chose to invent local traditions to strengthen the "East German" national identity. This was accomplished by references to the figures living on the territory of the future GDR such as King Frederick the Great and Martin Luther, a key figure in the Protestant Reformation, accompanied by that of Thomas Müntzer, a theologian and preacher of the early Reformation, who by the 1950s was popularized as a true revolutionary.[35] In Czechoslovakia, the cult of Tomáš Masaryk, first president of the country before World War II, was renewed in 1968 and then abandoned and replaced by the Marxist-Leninist cult of Klement Gottwald, party leader and first communist president. Since the 1960s, the turn to national traditions was also accompanied by the increased sensitivity of socialist states to their architectural heritage, including churches and monasteries. For example, in Czechoslovakia, a new law on heritage preservation was adopted, certain cities were declared "protected historical areas" and objects of particular importance became "national cultural memorials." In the Soviet Union, too, the closing of churches was moderated after 1965, and the All-Russian Society for the Preservation of Historical and Cultural Monuments was established in 1966. In Czechoslovakia, heritage preservation was primarily oriented toward older traditions associated with independent Czech statehood (Gothic and Renaissance architecture), while the baroque tradition associated with reactionary Catholicism and Habsburg rule was neglected.

Another change in the historical narrative of Eastern European socialist countries during the Khrushchev era was sparked by the launch of Sputnik and Yuri Gagarin's 1961 flight. For a short period, their celebrations overshadowed those of the October Revolution and the Second World War, and were smoothly integrated into the narrative of building the future. Several new memorials were dedicated to the exploration of the universe, the best known being the Monument to the Conquerors of Space unveiled in Moscow in 1964. A certain cult was created around the cosmonauts: They were usually present on tribunes during state festivities together with party leaders and heroes of the Great Patriotic War. Although there had been a cult of aviators under Stalin (with, for example, Valery Chkalov and Alexey Maresyev), a new cult of space exploration overshadowed their deeds, as it did anniversaries of other important technical projects, such as the building of dams, canals or the Moscow metro. In subsequent years, as a result of American success in space exploration, the myth of cosmonautics was downplayed. However, in other countries of the socialist bloc, cults of local cosmonaut heroes were developed in the course of early spaceflights in the late 1970s and early 1980s.[36]

In the 1960s, the new politics of history was developed around anti-colonial struggles and revolutionary movements in the so-called Third World. Assassinated revolutionary leaders were its key figures. Briefly after his murder, Patrice Lumumba, the first democratically elected prime minister of Congo, became a cult personality in the socialist bloc countries: Peoples' Friendship University in Moscow was so named in 1961, numerous streets were named after Lumumba and several monuments erected to him. The reception of Chilean president Salvador Allende and Ernesto "Che" Guevara, one of the key figures of the Cuban Revolution in the 1950s, was similar, although the "Che" cult was much weaker in Soviet propaganda than among the Western radical left. The latter also admired Ho Chi Minh, prime minister and president of the Democratic Republic of Vietnam, and Mao Zedong, the founding father of the People's Republic of China, who like "Che" became Western pop culture icons.[37] In those countries where the revolutionary socialist movement took power, cults of local rulers were developed already during their lifetimes, ranging from quasi-religious worship (as with North Korean leader Kim Il-sung or Ho Chi Minh) to a restrained cult, probably owing to reaction against the Stalinist model (Fidel Castro, leader of the Cuban Revolution and the country's long-ruling president, prohibited any manifestation of personality cult). In contrast to what happened in the post-Stalinist Soviet Union, all of these countries more or less retained the cult of the leaders after their death. Even in China, the party's Central Committee declared in 1981 that Mao was 70 percent correct and only 30 percent wrong.[38] This statement materialized in public space through the gesture of removing some of his statues, while other images, including his huge portrait in Tiananmen Square, were allowed to remain.

The 1970s brought a neo-Stalinist turn in the politics of history in several Eastern Bloc countries, such as the Soviet Union, Czechoslovakia and Romania. Lenin's cult was again reinforced, and Khrushchev's condemnation of Stalin's crimes was replaced by speaking of his "mistakes." Stalin's ninetieth and hundredth anniversaries were commemorated by the CPSU's central organ *Pravda* [Truth].[39] In 1970, Stalin's bust appeared on his grave at the Wall of the Kremlin where he had been buried after laying in the mausoleum between 1953 and 1961; however, no further steps were taken. A stronger emphasis was placed on celebrating historical anniversaries. The October Revolution, Lenin and the Great Patriotic War were brought back to the center of public discourse. In 1965, the Victory Day of May 9 was declared a public holiday in the USSR.[40] Numerous war memorials were erected, with the best known being in Volgograd (Stalingrad) in 1967.

There was also a shift in the narratives of socialist construction. In the first postwar decades, modernization and future-oriented narratives appear to have prevailed, while starting in the 1970s, emphasis was placed on the good life and high living standards in the present without much attention to the future. This was reflected in shifts in commemoration: The Brezhnev era gave birth to the culture of numerous, pompous celebrations, particularly of May Day and the October Revolution, perceived by most of the public as highly ritualized events. In the course of the 1960s and 1970s, socialist memorial landscapes described in this volume by **Aleksandra Kuczyńska-Zonik** and by **Stanislav Holubec** became so enormous and extensive that their destruction after 1989 may be compared in European history only to the removal of Roman memorials by Christian zealots in late antiquity. The formalization and ritualization also appeared in historical narratives and textbooks. For example, contemporary Czechoslovak history textbooks presented the postwar decades simply as a series of five-year plans and party congresses deprived of appeal and charisma. As Czech historian Kamil Činátl put it, "History represented in this way loses its linear (narratively graspable) character and turns into a cyclic structure of constantly repeating 'non-events.' Nothing happens in history; it is hard to narrate anything."[41] In this approach, there was no space for conflicts within socialism, as the society was organized according to the "scientific worldview" and heading toward the horizon of communism.

In the countries where anti-communist uprisings or reform movements were crushed by pro-Soviet forces (Hungary 1956, Czechoslovakia 1968, Poland 1980), specific regimes of memory had to be developed afterward. They generally proffered a story of "forces of destruction"—that is fascist, pro-Western, hooligans, etc.—that pushed socialist countries toward civil war and a renewal of capitalism—a trend that could only be stopped by the "healthy forces." An example in the 1980s is the official narrative of the suppression of the "Solidarity" (*Solidarność*) movement in Poland discussed in this volume by **Jakub Szumski**.

In 1987, Mikhail Gorbachev declared his willingness to overcome all "blank pages" in Soviet history.[42] Similarly to Khrushchev and Brezhnev, he also proclaimed a return to Lenin, but interpreted by him as a reform communist. In the words of the Italian communist intellectual, Lucio Magri, "[Gorbachev] spoke of a return to Lenin, but as if all Lenin had done was invent the New Economic Policy in 1921."[43] In his speeches up to 1989, Gorbachev remained faithful to the Stalinist narrative of the need to defeat party "deviations" and the positive evaluation of the 1930s collectivization; however, he returned to Khrushchev's condemnation of the thesis of the aggravation of class struggle and the creation of the "administrative-command system." In 1988, he went even further than Khrushchev and rehabilitated party leaders annihilated during the Great Purge: Grigory Zinoviev, Lev Kamenev and Nikolai Bukharin, but not Trotsky. He also avoided discussing the "blank areas in history" such as the Katyn massacre, the Soviet annexation of the Baltic countries in 1940 or the invasion of Hungary in 1956 and Czechoslovakia in 1968.

The liberal party wing around Boris Yeltsin went further than Gorbachev and started to consider not only Stalinism but also Lenin's politics and the October Revolution as great mistakes, and prepared themselves psychologically to abandon these two central pillars of Soviet state socialism fully. The much weaker Stalinist wing formed around the rank-and-file party member Nina Andreyeva, who interpreted perestroika as an attempt to negate the glorious socialist past and called for rehabilitation of Stalin in her famous 1988 essay.[44] In June 1990, the CPSU approved a new program titled "Towards a Humane, Democratic Socialism," and Gorbachev ceased to mention Lenin in his speeches.[45] In the same year, the leader of Italian communists, Achille Occhetto, said at the party congress that the Italian Communist Party "feels itself to be the child of the French Revolution . . . and not, as is always said, the heir of the October Revolution."[46] The most symbolic break with the Soviet past was the gesture of renaming Leningrad in September 1991 after the failed coup d'état in Moscow. However, Lenin remained a respected public person even in democratic Russia under Yeltsin; his body remained in the mausoleum, and his monuments remained untouched in contrast to other post-socialist countries. As **Ekaterina V. Klimenko** demonstrates in this volume, the Soviet past is seen more positively in Russian public opinion than the communist past in most Eastern European societies.

After its historical collapse in 1989–1991, the communist movement or, better, those parts of it which decided to preserve communist identity, developed what Wolfgang Schivelbusch called the "culture of defeat."[47] It included a discussion of the reasons for the "historical defeat" and of how to reinterpret one's own past in order to overcome strong anti-communism and to develop a new legitimizing narrative. Most communist parties in Eastern and Western Europe condemned the crimes of Stalinism and formulated apologies.[48] Those communist parties that were transformed into social democratic parties did not pay much attention to the politics of history, attempting instead to present themselves as new political forces starting from the scratch. In this volume, **Csilla Kiss** describes this phenomenon with the example of the Hungarian Socialist Party. Those who decided to remain communists or positioned themselves to the left of social democracy (as was the case with the German Party of Democratic Socialism) had to come to terms with their own history. Some positioned themselves as bearers of the anti-Stalinist left tradition of "democratic socialism," "Luxemburgism,"[49] while more conservative parts of the movement concentrated on the achievements of the Soviet Union and remained silent about the difficult aspects of its history. This difference, illustrated by the Russian and German examples, is described in this volume by **Thorsten Holzhauser** and **Antony Kalashnikov**.

The historical narrative defending the past offers in essence the following explanation: The whole socialist movement and Bolshevik revolution resulted from disastrous capitalism, and its crucial ideas were constructed by "humanist thinkers," Marx and Engels. The communists modernized the Soviet Union, defeated fascism and improved education, health care and living standards. This narrative often rejects the crimes of Stalinism, declares affiliation with the democratic socialist tendencies in the history of communism and sees the causes of the 1989 defeat in the system's inability to adopt democratic standards. It emphasizes, however, that the crimes committed "in the name of communism" were also due to the pressure from capitalist countries and that bureaucratic socialism was replaced by the "restoration of capitalism." The main proponents of this narrative are Germany's DIE LINKE and Greece's Syriza.[50] The pro-Stalin (or in their language "Marxist-Leninist") groups see the cause of defeat in the revisionist turn of 1956, and Gorbachev's policy is interpreted as betrayal resulting in "counterrevolution." This narrative is mainly represented by the Portuguese and Greek communist parties, and by the Workers' Party of Belgium. For the nationalistically oriented Communist Party of the Russian Federation Stalin is even a more important source of identity than the "cosmopolitan" Lenin.[51]

The collapse of state socialism was confronted by anti-communist historical narratives, which became dominant in societies of the former Eastern Bloc. Anti-communists could claim that their view of communism as a non-functioning criminal system was confirmed by history. At the same time, the anti-communist narrative failed to demonstrate the alleged totalitarian nature of communism since the reform impulse came from the party itself, and socialist regimes abolished themselves almost voluntarily.

Anti-communism was strong immediately after the collapse of state socialism, particularly in the countries where this occurred via revolution. However, it soon lost its appeal, as the 1990s post-socialist societies preferred to identify with hopes for a better future than with the politics of history. Popular anti-communism experienced a renaissance in Central and Eastern Europe in the early twenty-first century. It was manifested primarily in legislation—for example, in laws condemning state socialism—and in prohibiting the provision of public services to persons involved in the former regimes, as well as in establishing anti-communist research institutions (for example, the Institutes of National Remembrance in Poland and Romania), museums (for example, the House of Terror in Budapest) and school curricula. The principal cause of this rise of anti-communism appears to be the failure of the dominant transformation narratives—such as the "catch up with the West" and the "building of democracy"—and the disappointment of Eastern European societies, especially Polish, Hungarian or Romanian, with their elites perceived as reincarnations of communism. In the case of Czechs and Slovaks, anti-communism can be explained as an expression of frustration by the middle classes or elites dissatisfied with the lower classes and older generation who allegedly do not appreciate democracy, capitalism and a pro-Western orientation, and are supposed to have pro-communist sympathies.

Anti-communism also proved to be a useful tool in ethnic conflicts. This occurred, for example, in the 1990s Yugoslav War when Serbs were called "Serbo-communists" by Croats, and Croats were called "fascists" by Serbs; to some extent this also characterizes Czechoslovakia's breakup, in which Slovaks were depicted by Czechs as nostalgic for state socialism,[52] and the 2013 Maidan events in Ukraine. The most visible deeds of Ukrainian anti-communism were the destruction of Lenin's memorials and the banning of the Communist Party of Ukraine and of other communist symbols. By contrast, the Eastern Ukrainian rebels opposing the Kiev government have adopted nostalgic Soviet rhetoric and symbols (for example, the Luhansk People's Republic has been using a red-star seal, which resembles the Soviet symbol).

Communism was seen as something that divided Europe, but anti-communism had the same effect: While Eastern European countries aim to make it part of their state ideologies, the Western European countries that set the tone for the European Union (EU) are not willing to integrate anti-communism into their foundations. The Western reluctance to adopt anti-communism was visible in the mixed reactions to *Le livre noir du communism* [The Black Book of Communism],[53] which was published in France in 1997 during the *gauche plurielle* [plural left] government under Lionel Jospin formed by socialists, communists and greens. Adopting anti-communism as a founding myth of European integration seems impossible because the Holocaust and the Gulag are incommensurable both in their basic ideas and in the numbers of casualties. To pose the crimes of Stalinism as being on the same scale as those of Nazism, the center of which was the Holocaust and condemnation of which was a central founding myth of Europe,[54] would be perceived as relativizing the extermination of European Jews by Nazis. The other reason why it is so improbable that anti-communism could be made into a foundation myth of European integration is that the Western communist parties either lost their significance after the war or were transformed into political forces that easily became part of parliamentary democracy. The politics of history practiced by contemporary European left socialist and communist parties is discussed in this volume by **Walter Baier**. In contrast to radical right-wing political violence during the 1990s,[55] the leftist terrorism of the 1960s and 1970s ceased to exist. Organizations such as the Red Army Fraction or the Red Brigades, which in any case had only loose ties to Western communist parties, ceased their activities during the 1980s. In several countries of Western Europe, communists or former communists (most notably Italian) were in leading executive positions. Members of the 1968 generation who in their youth were Maoists, Trotskyists or had other radical left affiliations became respected social democrats or greens.[56] Therefore, the EU cannot accept the central anticommunist claim that communism is equal to Nazism and as such deserves to be condemned, as was proposed by new EU members, particularly the Baltic states, after 2004. The memory of communism is therefore still dividing Europe along the lines of the former Iron Curtain.

***

This book is concerned with the historical memory of the communist movement and of state socialism in Eastern Europe before and after 1989. We decided to follow the retrospective logic, which can be called "archaeology of the memory," from the most recent upper strata to older and deeper ones. The first section analyzes the post-1989 memory of communism and the self-identity of the left in the former West (mostly France and Italy, but also Austria, Greece, Spain and Portugal) and East (Hungary, East Germany and Russia). The second section is devoted to analyses of socialist and post-socialist memorial landscapes in former GDR, Czechoslovakia/Czech Republic, Poland, Lithuania, Ukraine and Russia. The final part concentrates on the narratives the movement established, when in power, about its own past, with the examples of the Soviet Union, Poland, Romania and Czechoslovakia, also addressing the unwanted past during the regime crisis with the example of Poland.

We have standardized terminology and adopted the term "communism" to designate the movements, parties and programs that themselves used the term and identified with it. We sometimes use the term "communism" interchangeably with "labor movement" or "radical" or "revolutionary left." In view of the Marxist definition of "communism" as a practice moving toward a classless society, we have decided to use the terms "state socialism" or "real or actually existing socialism" to describe the social and economic situation of post-World War II Eastern European countries, designated here as "Eastern Bloc countries" or "socialist block countries." In so doing, our aim is to mark our distance from the belief widespread in current public debate in Eastern Europe that the Soviet Union exercised unlimited control over the so-called people's republics. Both the authors and the editors have tried to demonstrate that particular socialist states struggled to build their own policies of history and memory in various historical periods, even if this effort was inevitably linked to events and conditions in the USSR.[57]

Notes

1 Filip Blažek, "Plakáty, které změnily náš život," *SANQUIS* 71 (2009): 20, www.sanquis.cz/index2.php?linkID=art2563, accessed May 1, 2017.
2 See, for example, Michal Kopeček, ed., *Past in the Making: Historical Revisionism in Central Europe After 1989* (Budapest: Central European University Press, 2008); Corina Dobos and Marius Stan, eds., *History of Communism in*

Europe, vol. 1: *Politics of Memory in Post-Communist Europe* (Bucharest: Institute for the Investigation of the Communist Crimes and for the Memory of the Romanian Exile, 2010); Maria Todorova, Augusta Dimou and Stefan Troebst, eds., *Remembering Communism: Private and Public Recollections of Lived Experience in Southeast Europe* (Budapest and New York: Central European University Press, 2014); Maria Todorova and Zsuzsa Gill, eds., *Post-Communist Nostalgia* (New York: Berghahn Books, 2010); Georges Mink and Laure Neumayer, eds., *History, Memory and Politics in Central and Eastern Europe: Memory Games* (Basingstoke: Palgrave Macmillan, 2013); Michael Bernhard and Jan Kubik, eds., *Twenty Years After Communism: The Politics of Memory and Commemoration* (Oxford and New York: Oxford University Press, 2014); David J. Clark, "Communism and Memory Politics in the European Union," *Central Europe* 12.1 (2014): 99–114.

3 See, for example, Ron Eyerman, "Social Movements and Memory," in *Routledge International Handbook of Memory Studies*, eds. Anna Lisa Tota and Trever Hagen (London: Routledge, 2015), 79–83.

4 See Alvin W. Gouldner, *The Two Marxisms: Contradiction and Anomalies in the Development of Theory* (London: Palgrave Macmillan, 1980), 48.

5 Robert Tombs, *The Paris Commune* (London: Routledge, 1999), 191–206.

6 Jürgen Herres, *Das Karl-Marx Haus in Trier, 1727—heute* (Trier: Neu GmbH, 1993), 47–49.

7 Tristram Hunt, *Marx's General: The Revolutionary Life of Friedrich Engels* (New York: Picador, 2009), 351.

8 It is only in the US that a different day is celebrated: the first Monday in September. This day was proposed by some unions in the early 1880s, but was declared a national holiday by the government in 1887, at a time when the governments of Europe were reluctant to introduce the First of May as a public holiday. The decision by the US administration was a response to the mass Pullman Strike of 1894 to deflect any heated confrontation and as a progovernmental alternative to the May Day celebrated by radicals. See more Emil Brix and Hannes Stekl, eds., *Der Kampf um das Gedächtnis: Öffentliche Gedenktage in Mitteleuropa* (Wien and Köln and Weimar: Böhlau, 1997).

9 See more Siegfried Scholze, *Der Internationale Frauentag einst und heute: geschichtlicher Abriß und weltweite Tradition vom Entstehen bis zur Gegenwart* (Berlin: Trafo, 2001); Cho Chatterjee, *Celebrating Women: Gender, Festival Culture and Bolshevik Ideology, 1910–1939* (Pittsburgh: University of Pittsburgh Press, 2002).

10 Eric D. Weitz, *Creating German Communism, 1890–1990: From Popular Protests to Socialist State* (Princeton: Princeton University Press, 1996), 179–185. The Liebknecht-Luxemburg cult maintained its importance in the GDR, but it had a certain subversive potential since Luxemburg had opposed Lenin's neglect of democracy. Barbara Könczöl, "Reinventing a Socialist Heroine: Commemorating Rosa Luxemburg After Unification," in *Remembering the German Democratic Republic: Divided Memory in a United Germany*, eds. David Clarke and Ute Wölfel (New York: Palgrave Macmillan, 2011), 80.

11 See, for example, Petr Roubal, *Československé spartakiády* (Praha: Academia, 2016).

12 Zeynep Aygen, *International Heritage and Historic Building Conservation: Saving the World's Past* (New York: Routledge, 2013), 70.

13 Richard Stites, *Revolutionary Dreams: Utopian Vision and Experimental Life in the Russian Revolution* (Oxford: Oxford University Press, 1989), 230–231.

14 Christopher A. P. Binns, "The Changing Face of Power: Revolution and Accommodation in the Development of the Soviet Ceremonial System: Part 1," *Man: The Journal of the Royal Anthropological Institute* 14.4 (1979): 599–600.

15 Sergiusz Michalski, *Public Monuments: Art in Political Bondage, 1870–1997* (London: Reaktion Books, 1998), 114.
16 Graeme Gill, *Symbols and Legitimacy in Soviet Politics* (Cambridge: Cambridge University Press, 2011), 264.
17 *Dokumenty českého a slovenského parlamentu*, Společná česko-slovenská digitální parlamentní knihovna, www.psp.cz/eknih/1920ns/ps/stenprot/336schuz/s336008.htm, accessed May 17, 2017.
18 Michalski, *Public Monuments*, 114.
19 Gill, *Symbols and Legitimacy in Soviet Politics*, 122.
20 Maureen Perrie, *The Cult of Ivan the Terrible in Stalin's Russia* (New York: Palgrave Macmillan, 2001).
21 Gill, *Symbols and Legitimacy in Soviet Politics*, 122.
22 Binns, "The Changing Face of Power," 605.
23 Jan Randák, *V záři Rudého kalicha: Politika dějin a husitská tradice v Československu 1948–1956* (Praha: NLN, 2016), 78.
24 Christoph Links, *Revolution der Erinnerung: Der Zweite Weltkrieg in der Geschichtskultur des spätsozialistischen Polen* (Berlin: Ch. Links Veralg, 2016).
25 *Velká Morava: výstava o prvním společném státě českého a slovenského národa, pořádaná u příležitosti 1100: výročí příchodu byzantské misie do našich zemí a počátků slovanského písemnictví* (Brno: Dům umění, 1963).
26 For example, references to God recorded by the contemporary chronicler were removed from the closing speech of Jan Hus in the film by Jan Vávra (*Jan Hus*, 1954), with him referring only to the "people" and "the truth." See Petr Čornej, "Husitská trilogie a její dobový ohlas," in *Film a dějiny*, eds. Petr Kopal and Petr Blažek (Praha: NLN, 2005), 84–98.
27 Dejan Jović, "Communist Yugoslavia and Its Others," in *Ideologies and National Identities: The Case of Twentieth-Century Southeastern Europe*, eds. John Lampe and Mark Mazower (Budapest: Central European University Press, 2006), 277–302.
28 Gérard Vincent, Perine Simon-Hahum, Rémi Leveau and Dominiques Schapper, "Cultural Diversity in France," in *History of Private Life*, vol. V: *Riddles of Identity in Modern Times*, eds. Antoine Prost and Gérard Vincent (Cambridge, MA: Harvard University Press, 1991), 318.
29 Walter Baier, *Das kurze Jahrhundert: Kommunismus in Österreich: KPÖ 1918 bis 2008* (Wien: Edition Steinbauer, 2009).
30 See Pavel Kolář, "The Party as a New Utopia: Reshaping Communist Identity After Stalinism," *Social History* 37.4 (2012): 402–424.
31 Cyrille Guiat, *The French and Italian Communist Parties: Comrades and Culture* (London: Frank Cass, 2003), 9.
32 Guiat, *The French and Italian Communist Parties*, 11.
33 Gilbert Merilo, "Der Kommunismus in der Geschichtskultur Frankreichs," in *Kommunismusforschung und Erinnerungskulturen in Ostmittel- und Westeuropa*, ed. Volkhard Knigge (Köln: Böhlau, 2013), 96.
34 See more Katherine Verdery, *National Ideology Under Socialism: Identity and Cultural Politics in Ceaușescu's Romania* (Berkley: University of California Press, 1991), 167–214.
35 Alexander Fleischauer, *Die Enkel fechten's besser aus: Thomas Müntzer und die Frühbürgerliche Revolution—Geschichtspolitik und Erinnerungskultur in der DDR* (Münster: Aschendorff Verlag, 2010).
36 See, for example, Marcin Zaremba, *Komunizm, legitymizacja, nacjonalizm, Nacjonalistyczna legitymizacja władzy komunistycznej w Polsce* (Warszawa: TRIO, 2001), 380–382.
37 Richard L. Harris, *Che Guevara: A Biography* (Santa Barbara: Greenwood, 2011), 198.

38 Rebecca E. Karl, *Mao Zedong and China in the Twentieth-Century World: A Concise History* (Durham and London: Duke University Press, 2010), 166.
39 "K 90-letiiu so dnia rozhdeniia I. V. Stalina" and "K 100-letiiu so dnia rozhdeniia I. V. Stalina," *Pravda*, December 21, 1969, and December 21, 1979. On the very same day, Stalin was commemorated by the article in the Czechoslovak Communist Party organ *Rudé právo*: Vladimír Gerloch, "Sto let od narození J. V. Stalina," *Rudé právo*, December 21, 1979, 6.
40 Gill, *Symbols and Legitimacy in Soviet Politics*, 199.
41 Kamil Činátl, "Jazyk normalizační moci," in *Tesilová kavalérie, Popkulturní obrazy normalizace*, eds. Petr A. Bílek and Blanka Činátlová (Příbram: Pistorius a Olšanská, 2010), 30–31.
42 Gill, *Symbols and Legitimacy in Soviet Politics*, 226.
43 Lucio Magri, *The Tailor of Ulm: Communism in the Twentieth Century* (London and New York: Verso, 2011), 365.
44 Nina Andreyeva, "Ne mogu postupatsia printsipami," *Sovetskaia Rossiia*, March 13, 1988, 2, https://archive.org/stream/ICannotGiveUpMyPrinciples/MicrosoftWord-Document2_djvu.txt, accessed May 31, 2017.
45 Gill, *Symbols and Legitimacy in Soviet Politics*, 259.
46 Lucio Magri, *The Tailor of Ulm*, 369–370.
47 Wolfgang Schivelbusch, *Culture of Defeat: On National Trauma, Mourning, and Recovery*, trans. Jefferson Chase (New York: Metropolitan Books, 2004).
48 See also Hélène Le Dantec Lowry and Ambre Ivol, eds., *Generations of Social Movements: The Left and Historical Memory in the USA and France* (New York: Routledge, 2016).
49 Michael Schumann, *Wir brechen unwiderruflich mit dem Stalinismus als System*, December 8–9 and 16–17, 1989, http://archiv2007.sozialisten.de/partei/parteitag/sonderparteitag1989/view_html/n3/bs1/zid24832, accessed May 19, 2017.
50 On the identity of Germany's DIE LINKE see Kate Hudson, *New European Left: A Socialism for the Twenty-First Century?* (Basingstoke: Palgrave Macmillan, 2012). On Syriza see Kevin Ovenden, *Syriza: Inside the Labyrinth* (London: Pluto Press, 2015).
51 As an example of the Stalinist narrative of history, see Ludo Martens, *Un autre regard sur Staline* (Anvers: EPO, 1994).
52 Stanislav Holubec, "Post-Socialist Society and Its Enemies: Perception of Russians, Slovaks and Germans in the Czech Weeklies," in *Popular Culture and Subcultures of Czech Post-Socialism: Listening to the Wind of Change*, eds. Ondřej Daniel, Tomáš Kavka and Jakub Machek (Newcastle upon Tyne: Cambridge Scholars Publishing, 2016), 79.
53 Stéphane Courtois et al., *Le livre noir du communisme: Crimes, terreur, répression* (Paris: Robert Laffont, 1997).
54 Claus Leggewie, *Der Kampf im die europäische Erinnerung: Ein Schalchtfeld wird besichtigt* (München: C. H. Beck, 2011).
55 For a comparison of right-wing and left-wing extremism in Europe, see Jan Oskar Engene, *Terrorism in Western Europe: Explaining the Trends Since 1950* (Cheltenham and Northampton: Edward Elgar, 2004).
56 See, for example, Andreas Kühn, *Stalins Enkel, Maos Söhne: Die Lebenswelt der K-Gruppen in der Bundesrepublik der 70er Jahre* (Frankfurt and New York: Campus Verlag, 2005), 278–300.
57 In order to follow contemporary research on the concept of "communism" and its discursive uses, see, for example, Katarzyna Chmielewska and Grzegorz Wołowiec, eds., *Opowiedzieć PRL* (Warszawa: Wydawnictwo IBL PAN, 2011).

Part I
Memory of the Left in Post-Socialist Europe

1 "Of the Past Let Us Make a Clean Slate"

The Lack of a Left-Wing Narrative and the Failure of the Hungarian Left

Csilla Kiss

Introduction

In Hungary, the left is in a comatose state; there is no left-wing party in Hungary today that is sufficiently strong to play a role in political life. Although post-communist Hungary was not without left-wing successes, by 2010, the left seemed to have lost its footing and suffered a devastating defeat that was only slightly better than the results of the Polish left—which had lost all of its seats in the Polish Parliament—while the right-wing Fidesz scored an overwhelming victory. Despite significant efforts, the opposition did no better in the 2014 elections. There are many reasons for this, and it is important to consider them because, as the history of post-communist Hungary suggests, the left was not doomed to failure and was still capable of regeneration and resurrection.

Hungary's main left force is the Hungarian Socialist Party (HSP), which can and has been regarded by many as a so-called successor party, as it was created from the Hungarian Socialist Workers' Party (HSWP), the ruling party during Hungary's period of "real socialism." The HSWP was reformed in 1989 and changed its name to HSP. On the one hand, the name change was necessary because when regime change was already on the agenda, among other "historical" parties the Hungarian Social Democratic Party (HSDP) was also re-founded (the party had disappeared in 1948 when the social democrats united, or were forced to unite, with the Hungarian Communist Party to create the Party of Hungarian Workers). The newly recreated HSDP also participated in the Opposition Round Table with other newly formed opposition parties. Although they did not gain parliamentary seats in the 1990 elections, their existence prevented the HSWP from calling itself social democratic. On the other hand, the word "socialist" reflects an ideological and historical debate within the party, because while certain of the party's groups, or "platforms" as they were called, embraced social democracy and democratic capitalism, other groups hoped that the party could stay to the left of social democracy and not unequivocally embrace the regime change: They rejected market economy and hoped for a version of democratic socialism. A coalition with the Alliance of Free Democrats,

Hungary's liberal party in 1994, as well as economic troubles and perhaps the force of foreign examples, such as the changes in the British Labor Party under Tony Blair, caused the party to move toward what, under the prime ministership of Ferenc Gyurcsány (2004–2009), became truly Third Way rhetoric and policies.[1] Moreover, coalition government with the liberals, which always occurred from 1994 on, led the socialists to describe themselves as "left liberal," further cementing the Third Way image and impeding a truly leftist stance.

As Tony Judt points out in his *Ill Fares the Land*, the end of any kind of social democracy is imminent when instead of ideological debates we only talk about calculations and data, and discussions about the economy become depoliticized.[2] Furthermore, the Eastern European left can necessarily only have a very limited vision, since after the regime change, it has been taken for granted that capitalism is the only possible economic system, and, moreover, among the many forms of capitalism, it was Anglo-Saxon-type neoliberalism that prevailed. In Eastern Europe, it has become a ruling paradigm that economic crises and hardships can only be cured through more hardships, with austerity being seen as unavoidable and beneficial in the long run. Complaints or the idea of a different possible solution are usually countered by blaming the current woes on the previous socialist system and its lingering vestiges, on the one hand, and sternly warning against harboring illusions about an alternative economic system, on the other, by pointing to examples of the history of real socialism (or "communist history," which is the shorthand used by many political scientists and by the right wing in the political arena to convey how terrible that system was). Thus the 2008 crisis did not help the left, and, using anti-communism in 2010, Fidesz won a landslide victory, while the HSP, in the absence of an attractive vision for the future and burdened by numerous scandals during its two terms in government (2002–10), was reduced to a handful of representatives in Parliament—a situation it has found difficult to break out of ever since.

Although an opposition party like the HSP has to react continuously to political events in the country, the time spent in opposition would also be useful for regrouping and clarifying the party's political line as well as its ideological outlook and location within the country's history. This appears to me to be one of the most important problems: The HSP seems to have no coherent politics of history. This, on the one hand, was not surprising because the party had been continuously attacked on account of its past, and it tried to avoid historical issues. On the other hand, history and memory are clearly very important in Hungarian society and politics, and so it would seem imperative that the HSP formulate its relationship to the country's history as well as to the history of the left, especially in the twentieth century.

It is all the more important because one of the main features of postcommunist, especially post-2010, Hungary is that the left allowed the political right to frame the country's politics of history, which made the left defenseless in key debates that served as the ideological foundations for numerous political decisions.

The Hungarian political right was eager from the beginning to employ a politics of history and establish a narrative it wanted to enshrine as the decisive memory of the whole country: In 2011, Fidesz did not even hesitate to include it in the Constitution.[3] The most notable attempt at the institutionalization of memory politics by the first Fidesz government was the opening of the House of Terror Museum in 2002. While playing a significant part in the electoral campaign of the party that year, the museum also presents Fidesz's view of history, which it hoped to make the official view accepted by the whole nation. In 2014, as a sort of extension of the exhibition and the historical emphasis projected by the House of Terror, the Fidesz government also erected a monument commemorating the German occupation on Szabadság Square next to the Soviet liberation memorial, as if to suggest the existence of two occupations in contemporary Hungarian history, exonerating Hungary and Hungarians from responsibility for subsequent acts, including the deportation and murder of Jewish citizens, since these would then have to be regarded as the responsibility of the occupying power. As Viktor Orbán said at the opening of the House of Terror, neither the Nazi nor the Soviet dictatorship could have been introduced and maintained without foreign troops.[4]

Although Fidesz lost the elections in 2002 despite its fierce campaign, it gained a supermajority in 2010, which allowed the party to ratify a new Constitution, or Fundamental Law as they have called it, claiming that the Constitution in effect up to then was a communist (Stalinist) heritage.[5] The new Fundamental Law enshrined certain principles concerning the history of the country both in the "Preamble" and the basic text itself, declaring the incompatibility of the communist and the successor regimes; it calls the Communist Party a criminal organization, whose leaders

> shall have responsibility without statute of limitations for [. . .] thwarting with Soviet military assistance the democratic attempt built on a multi-party system in the years after World War II.

It names the HSP as the successor to the criminalized Communist Party and "as beneficiaries of their unlawfully accumulated assets."[6] This and other acts of the right, including the rehabilitation of certain fascist politicians, means, according to Iván Harsányi, that the political right with Fidesz as its representative is trying to reevaluate the basic ideological and political pillars of the anti-fascist coalition/consensus and thus revise the whole historical configuration that existed after the victory of the anti-Hitler coalition. This, he argues, is part of the right-wing project everywhere in Eastern Europe, and the left finds it difficult to oppose it effectively.[7]

The Politics of History in Contemporary Hungary

While the political right has been and remains very active in framing the politics of history and memory, the left allows it to do so, looking on meekly as the right takes over these important issues. If anything, what we can discern is either continuous penance performed by the socialists—they have kept apologizing for their past, that is for the real socialist era in general and for the repression during and after the 1956 uprising in particular—or they have at best tried to keep silent about their past.[8] One of the major goals of the right is to force the left in general and the socialists in particular to regard the crimes of the Kádár regime as an inheritance they cannot shake off.[9] But the socialists' contrition is only in part due to the continuous attacks.

While the feeling of guilt and responsibility on the one hand, and the desire not to be forced to continuously defend the party on the other, may account for the lack of a left politics of history, it is also possible that the political left does not find anything in Hungary's left-wing past that it would like to tout, either because none of it appears attractive enough for them, or because Hungary's left tradition is very thin. In fact, it can be argued that the political left suffers from both the burden of the so-called communist period and the lack of left-wing traditions during the twentieth century as a whole, with the exception of the Hungarian Soviet Republic of 1919, which, however, does not provide a proud memory, as we will see. At the same time, the left has no coherent narrative regarding whatever left-wing traditions the country actually has, and, what is worse, it is unable to give a left answer to the political right's approach to national history. Thus if we see memory politics as a field of struggle, then the picture is very lopsided in Hungary.

In what follows, I will show how the Hungarian left, despite some weak attempts, has not managed to create its own narrative that could counter that of the right. In this respect, it is first of all necessary to clarify what we mean by left in Hungary. I will concentrate on political parties, especially the HSP, not because there are no significant civil-society actors or participants of social movements playing important political roles and classifiable as left, but because I consider political parties to be the main actors of political life and the most important mediating institutions between the citizenry and the state, even though other social actors also participate in decision-making, for instance trade unions, interest groups, lobbies and other civil-society organizations or movements. For the present, without political parties "a modern representative democracy is not conceivable," as "they articulate and integrate different interests, visions and opinions." "They are also the main source for the recruitment of political elites" and thus they deserve to be prioritized in analyses.[10] I will concentrate on the HSP as the main left-wing actor in Hungarian politics, only then looking briefly at the other left formations.

Hungarian Left-Wing Narratives of History: Key Events

In 2007, the Hungarian left journal *Eszmélet* [Consciousness] asked various thinkers, academics, activists and writers what they saw as the reasons for the malaise of an anti-capitalist left in Central Europe in general and in Hungary in particular.[11] There were numerous answers touching on the post-transformation party structure and socio-economic structures, but several respondents also cited the lack of a left narrative that a Hungarian left could call its own. Two principal problems are comingled here: first, the burden of real socialism and the difficulty of overcoming it cast a shadow over any effort to create a true left-wing narrative, and, second, this narrative would be difficult to create in any case because of the dearth of material to base it on, even that being tainted by the propaganda of the postwar era. What is more, the post-transition, right-wing narrative popularized the idea that the history of the Hungarian—and international—left only contains poverty, blood and terror. We need to examine the most significant moments in the history of the left and the associated problems.

A social democratic movement has existed in Hungary since the nineteenth century; it was active toward the end of the Austro-Hungarian Monarchy, first through trade union membership and then in the form of the Social Democratic Party of Hungary founded in 1890. It fought for universal suffrage and improvement in working conditions, among other demands. Its predecessor, the General Workers' Party of Hungary, was founded a decade earlier, and this party became the Social Democratic Party of Hungary upon joining the Second International. Although the social democrats, aside from their political activities, did important work in educating their membership and providing a social life for the members, they had always been in a minority, and even progressive historical figures such as Oszkár Jászi disliked them for their internationalism and anti-Kossuth outlook;[12] opposing the cult of Lajos Kossuth signaled that the party did not support Hungary's independence from the Austro-Hungarian Monarchy.[13] This lack of unconditional support for national independence was seen, for example, in 1905/1906, when the social democrats sided with the Habsburgs rather than with the nationalist Independence Party.[14]

This highlighted a very important problem that accompanied the history of socialist and social democratic movements in the world, including in Hungary: the continuous conflict between nationalism and progress. In the view of many historians and thinkers, this dichotomy has been one of the fundamental problems of Hungarian history, as conservative nationalists rejected social and state reform on behalf of traditions and national independence, since "fear for the community's existence" took precedence over all else.[15] The question of nationalism has worried socialists since the end of the nineteenth century, as nationalist slogans had significant appeal for voters and supporters of mass movements; thus, the question of nationalism became a central debate in the Second International, even though, as Eric Hobsbawm pointed out, Karl Marx had little interest in the theoretical foundations of nations and nation-building.[16] Hungarian philosopher and political activist, Gáspár Miklós Tamás argues that the greatest enemy of the left and of socialism has always been nationalism: the substitute for the lack of a bourgeois social solidarity.[17] During the twentieth century, the Hungarian left continuously struggled with the problem of nationalism in a country in which it has been one of the most important political creeds throughout its history. While after the regime change of 1989 the socialists did everything to avoid appearing "anti-national," they themselves contributed to this charge by accepting the association of the term "national" with the right, not contesting the latter being called the "national side" or the "national forces." This in itself was already self-defeating, and things were made worse by calling Jobbik, the extreme right party, "national radicals" instead of neo-Nazis—a characterization that was adopted only recently.[18] The HSP has continuously struggled with the issue of nationalism, either by repeating its own "commitment to the nation," thus accepting the discourse of the right, or by trying to formulate its own interpretation of "nationalist," tying patriotism to progress.[19]

The most glorious hour of the Hungarian left was the Hungarian Soviet Republic (*Magyarországi Tanácsköztársaság*) of 1919, together with the preceding revolution of 1918, the Aster Revolution (*Őszirózsás forradalom*). These revolutions fit into the contemporary trend of sociopolitical, usually left-wing uprisings, such as the German Revolution, inspired and fueled by the chaos and crisis due to the lost war, on the one hand, and foreign examples, especially the October Revolution in Russia, or the Spanish and Italian strike movements, on the other. Although the Hungarian Soviet Republic that claimed to introduce the dictatorship of the proletariat only lasted 133 days, it became one of the most sensitive issues of Hungarian history. An essay on the Hungarian Soviet Republic by historian Tibor Hajdú begins by pointing out how many times it has been asked whether these 133 days should be considered a part of Hungarian history at all.[20] While asking such a question necessarily contradicts the whole meaning of studying history, that it could be asked at all is of course very telling.

In fact, the reputation of the Soviet Republic fluctuated throughout history, depending on current power relations and ideological predispositions. During the interwar period, when Hungary was ruled by Admiral Miklós Horthy (who played a leading role in crushing the Republic), it was obviously regarded as the low point of Hungarian history, together with the preceding democratic revolution that brought Count Mihály Károlyi first to head the new government (October 31, 1918–January 11, 1919) and then to the provisional presidency of a new People's Republic (January 11, 1919–March 21, 1919).[21] For a while after the Second World War, the Hungarian Communist Party distanced itself from the violence of the Soviet Republic, along with other parts of its past it deemed to be unpopular. Besides obvious political tactics, this also showed that the communists themselves were not always at peace with their own history, and we could argue that this reflects a general problem of the left. However, after the communist takeover of the 1950s, "the glorious 133 days" of the Soviet Republic became the high point of history, contrasted to the "coward" Károlyi and the bourgeois revolution. Official historians, such as Erik Molnár, emphasized the mass movements (strikes and factory and land occupations) that preceded the revolution in order to make them part of an organic process that logically followed from historical developments, blaming failure exclusively on external circumstances, especially on the occupation of the country by the forces of the Entente and Little Entente.[22] While the Soviet Republic doubtless figured as a high point of communist history, during the Stalinist period, it was problematic to commemorate it. Béla Kun, its leader, perished in the Gulags as a victim of Joseph Stalin's purges, and so mentioning this was uncomfortable; by contrast, during the 1950s, Mátyás Rákosi's role was exaggerated beyond his merits. Kun only regained his standing as a "good communist" during the Kádár regime (1956–1989) and received a statue only in 1986. As a concession to the non-communist left and in order to be more inclusive with respect to Hungarian history, the post-1956 Kádár regime became more accommodating toward Károlyi, who even received a statue in 1975 and toward the 1918 revolution itself as the necessary antecedent to 1919. The regime change in 1989 demoted the Soviet Republic to its interwar status as the low point of Hungarian history: The statues and street names celebrating it were removed (Kun's statue was placed in the Memory Park of socialist-era sculpture in the outskirts of Budapest). In 2012, the right-wing government even removed Károlyi's statue from in front of Parliament.

The right logically regards the Soviet Republic as a disastrous event. The last testimony to this was Prime Minister Viktor Orbán's speech on the national holiday of March 15, 2016, in which he stated the right's official view, according to which the tradition of 1919, too, is still with us—though fortunately its pulse is just a faint flicker. Yet at times, it can make quite a noise. But without a host animal, its days are numbered. It is in need of another delivery of aid from abroad in the form of a major intellectual and political infusion; unless it receives this, then after its leaves and branches have withered, its roots will also dry up in the Hungarian motherland's soil, which is hostile to internationalism. And this is all well and good.[23]

While this kind of worrisome talk on the part of the contemporary Hungarian right has become increasingly less surprising, it is at the same time remarkable that the right would want to make such gratuitous references to 1919 and even more that the left is very reticent on the topic, demonstrating its inability to come to terms with one of the most significant left-wing episodes of history. It is even more problematic because although the socialists have tried instead to plant their roots in 1918, the Soviet Republic had in fact at least as much, if not more, of a social democratic presence as it did communist presence, since it came to power by the merger of the social democratic and the communist parties. The Communist Party of Hungary was formed in November 1918, but in 1919, most of its leaders were arrested and only released on March 21 when Károlyi decided that he and the social democrats alone could not overcome the political and military crisis. Thus the two left-wing parties merged (under the name of Socialist Party of Hungary), and they proclaimed the Soviet Republic. Most of the commissars, however, were social democrats. At the same time, the Soviet Republic can be regarded as the most consistent effort to overcome the petrified structures of the pre-war Kingdom of Hungary; therefore, it cannot be separated from the socialist movements and from progress—goals that should also resonate today.[24]

Even more interesting is the fact that the Károlyi government handed power over to Béla Kun because it did not want to accept the memorandum of the Entente with its prescribed demarcation lines in Hungary, and it was hoped that the Soviet Republic would protect the borders of the country; in fact, the Károlyi government received significant support from the population for stepping aside in favor of the Soviet Republic. When it became obvious that the new government could not protect the borders, its base shrank, suggesting that even in the revolutionary atmosphere of the times, there was not a sufficiently strong left workers' movement behind the revolution but only one that supported some degree of nationalism and hoped to defend the country.[25] Despite these genuine efforts, the Horthy regime accused the revolutions and thus the left of failing to preserve the country's territorial integrity, and the public believed its propaganda. The left, at the same time, did nothing to counter these charges and argue that it was in fact trying to protect the country's borders. Neither during Horthy's regime nor after the regime change did the left put forward such an argument, even though this might have countered the accusations of not caring for the nation. In the interwar period, among others, the left was blamed for the 1920 Treaty of Trianon, possibly the biggest trauma of Hungarian history, which resulted in the country losing two-thirds of its historical territory and population. Looking for potential democratic allies against the authoritarian Horthy government in other Eastern European states (which also benefited from Trianon and incorporated former Hungarian territories), the left did not find support or even understanding in the nationalist climate of the country either, and thus it once again found itself in conflict with nationalism, branded as the enemy of the nation. It was also unable to compete with or surpass the nationalism of the counterrevolutionary Horthy government, and thus the contradiction between socialism and nationalism was thrown into the relief again.

While Trianon and the Hungarian minority outside the borders of Hungary were taboo subjects during the postwar socialist era, after the regime change of 1989, the issue returned to the political agenda. In general, it was a topic used by the right, although every political party agreed that the Treaty of Trianon was unjust and placed a large number of Hungarians in a disadvantageous (and under the rule of Romanian dictator Nicolae

Ceaușescu, even precarious) position; the solution was sought in good relationships with the neighboring countries in general; however, the right pursued more assertive policies toward the Hungarian minorities. The general stance of the HSP can be summarized by former minister of education and culture István Hiller who in 2010 called the treaty "one of Hungary's greatest tragedies, if not the greatest," while at the same time suggesting that the solution to the minority problem is Europe and claiming to proudly feel allegiance to both the Hungarian and the European Union (EU) flags.[26] This of course omits those Hungarians who are not citizens of EU member states (for instance, citizens of Serbia and Ukraine). There are also people inside the party who feel uncomfortable that this does not show sufficient national commitment, which was especially problematic in the case of the 2004 referendum on offering Hungarian citizenship to Hungarians outside the borders; Gyurcsány, for example, participated in a debate opposing this kind of dual citizenship.

The interwar period was not very good for the Hungarian left either. The Communist Party was illegal, and its members acted at best clandestinely during the Horthy regime, with the threat of martial law hanging over them the whole time; indeed, many were executed. The illegal party was not particularly numerous, as many communist leaders had immigrated after the defeat of the Soviet Republic to the West, through Vienna, or were imprisoned by the Horthy regime. Later, many were allowed to go to the Soviet Union, where a number of former leaders, such as Béla Kun himself, perished as victims of the Stalinist purges. This of course made the appreciation of the Soviet Republic a delicate matter not only during Hungary's Stalinist period (1948–1953) but also in the second half of the 1930s. Those who survived, such as Mátyás Rákosi or György Lukács, returned to Hungary after the liberation and were regarded by many as Stalin's servants—except for Lukács, the teacher of many who later became acclaimed members of the liberal opposition, and who, as a philosopher, continued to be held in very high repute in important scholarly circles, while Rákosi lived out the end of his life in exile, with a blanket reputation as a Stalinist murderer. (His Jewish origins, such as those of Béla Kun and many of the Soviet Republic's leaders, also furnished a convenient excuse for today's antisemitism.) Several communists also fought for the Republic in the Spanish Civil War, which is another leftist tradition the current socialist party does not embrace, even though the memory of the International Brigades is honored not only in Western Europe but also even in today's Czech Republic where commemorative events have been organized.[27]

Since the communists inside Hungary were occupied with the day-to-day functioning of the illegal party, serious debates could only take place in foreign exile where people discussed the lessons of the Soviet Republic and tried to account for its defeat. The main criticism involved the merger with the social democrats and thus the lack of a truly revolutionary party. The social democrats were also blamed for not supporting the transformation of the working class from a class "in itself" to become a class "for itself" in which every member is aware of his or her own class interest and acts accordingly. Later, as a member of the Comintern, the Communist Party's analysis became increasingly sectarian.[28] Unlike the communists, the liberals and social democrats could legally participate in political life, but the latter were especially defensive during the interwar period, since they always had to stake out positions vis-à-vis Károlyi and Bolshevism, and their political participation depended on serious compromises.[29] Similarly, the postcommunist socialists were equally defensive following the regime change, as they now also had to work out their position regarding the postwar communist period.

Although many of those who took part in the *Eszmélet* exchange in 2007 point out certain important and even positive developments that occurred under the real existing socialist regime, the reaction of the contemporary left consists of nothing but incessant apology. Péter Agárdi reflects on the ahistorical elimination of the real socialist period from national continuity,[30] which exhibits some analogies to the treatment of the Soviet Republic. That the right criminalizes the period is not surprising; in fact, in the new Fundamental Law, Fidesz went so far as to deny any historical continuity, which of course created the piquant situation of regarding Horthy's regime as the last free and organic Hungarian era. However, what is particularly striking is the amnesia and forced compensation exhibited by the "ashamed" left, which denies that the period had any progressive features,[31] thus internalizing the guilt attributed to them by the right.[32] Many of *Eszmélet*'s respondents call for an equal appreciation and accurate evaluation of both the good and bad qualities of the system, especially so that the left might revive and regain confidence, but, as Annamária Artner ruefully pointed out, 1945 is regarded as having moved history from its "normal" course.[33] This is a very important observation, because in 2007, this was precisely the claim of the former socialist prime minister.

While, up to the 1989 regime change, 1945 and the end of the Second World War were clearly seen as "liberation"; this changed after the transition. Not only was April 4 abolished as a national holiday; it was not even replaced by a celebration of May 8 or 9, as in many European countries. There have been serious controversies around this date, and it does not help matters that, as an ally of Germany, Hungary had practically lost the war in 1945. The House of Terror actually talks about a "double occupation" (by Germany in 1944 and by the USSR in 1945). While "occupation" is a widely accepted word on the right, others argue for a compromise solution, claiming that while "liberation" is ideologically loaded and does not show sufficient sensitivity to the victims of the Soviet troops, it should also be recognized that many people were at least "freed" from fascism when the war ended. Only small extra-parliamentary, left-wing parties still celebrate April 4; the HSP prefers the solution of including May 9 among the national holidays, such as "Europe Day." Regarding 1945 as the beginning of dictatorship is also problematic, because although the Fundamental Law canonized this view, others have a more nuanced periodization and distinguish the relatively democratic period of 1945–1947 from the subsequent Stalinist, and then Kádárist, phases.

The other cardinal moment in Hungarian memory, as well as left-wing history, is the 1956 October uprising. Although crushed by Soviet troops in the name of socialism, and branded as a "counterrevolution" by János Kádár and his regime, the uprising was arguably more anti-Stalinist than anti-socialist, and although the 13-day uprising was composed of many trends, its socialist characteristics, such as the spontaneous formation of workers' councils, were significant. It is thus hard to understand why the socialists do not try to make more use of this event and its memory to conceptualize a more acceptable socialist vision and theorize the uprising as a struggle for true socialism. While there is certainly something ironic in the fact that the uprising can today be celebrated thanks to the return of capitalism, what is truly puzzling is why the left allowed the political right to completely appropriate the event. Fidesz leader and Prime Minister Viktor Orbán claimed that in 1956 a "bourgeois revolution" (*1956-os polgári forradalom*)[34] took place, while recently the extreme right party Jobbik went so far as to assert that the uprising was possible thanks to the patriotism of the interwar Horthy regime.[35] This statement ironically confirms Kádár's accusations that the uprising was as an attempt at bringing fascism back to the country, and even here the left has offered no counter-reading.

A Socialist Narrative?

Up to now, only Prime Minister Ferenc Gyurcsány has experimented with situating himself and his party, the HSP, within historical narratives. His predecessor, Péter Medgyessy (2002–2004), despite beating Fidesz in 2002 and thereby leading the socialists to victory, was in no position to offer a convincing narrative, as he was immediately involved in a scandal. Shortly after the elections, the right-wing daily *Magyar Nemzet* [Hungarian Nation] revealed that during the Kádár regime Medgyessy served as a secret agent of Hungarian counterintelligence.[36] Although this was not as bad as being a domestic secret service agent and spying on citizens, the discovery received ample attention in the press and even led to a conflict with the liberal coalition partner. Medgyessy defended his activities, claiming that even in that position he served the Hungarian national interest, trying to hide important policy initiatives from the Soviet Union, such as the country's joining the International Monetary Fund. However, he was in no position to offer a valid reading of the socialist past; if anything, he tried to make conciliatory gestures toward the right, such as a visit to the House of Terror, the emblematic space of the right-wing politics of memory, without any significant results as far as reconciliation is concerned.

On the one hand, Gyurcsány was in a better position than Medgyessy, or before him Gyula Horn (1994–1998), because due to his age, he had little involvement in the previous regime (only having had a post in the Communist Youth Organization). On the other hand, he was at the same time in a very bad position because of his acknowledgment in autumn of 2006 that he had lied about the country's financial situation before the elections. This led to serious unrest stirred up especially by the extreme right, which undermined his government. But the situation was also exploited by Fidesz, which was still smarting from the loss of the 2006 elections. Thus Gyurcsány's long essay entitled *Szembenézés* [Confrontation], published in *Népszabadság* [Liberty of the People] on January 26, 2007,[37] served a double purpose: Besides situating the HSP within Hungarian history and on the ideological and historical map, it also attempted to placate the political right. His attempt failed thanks to the deep divisions within Hungarian society and to Gyurcsány having by then become unacceptable for the right. But, aside from this, the essay was in fact very problematic, amounting to a complete surrender as far as historical narratives are concerned. To begin with, Zoltán Ripp, one of the most important researchers of the HSP and a member of its intellectual "think tank," as well as former member of its social democratic platform, suggests that even without the 2006 disturbances, Gyurcsány had already painted himself into a difficult corner: When coming to power in 2004, he had emphasized his belonging to the new generation that bore no responsibility for the old regime. According to Ripp, this meant that he accepted the political right's thesis that there is a straight lineage, and therefore shared responsibility, connecting the crimes of the communist regime and the post-transition socialists.[38]

Although the essay criticized the right in general, and Fidesz in particular, for impeding the modernization of the country and not respecting parliamentary and representative democracy, its approach to history is very debatable. Faithful to the apologetic tradition on the left, it rejects the communist takeover after the Second World War as a past in no way acceptable for the left, despite those potentially positive social changes and modernizing features mentioned by those who responded to *Eszmélet* at about the same time, and even though modernization is also important in Gyurcsány's vocabulary. He also claims that the communist takeover could only happen because of Russian occupation. On the one hand, with this he seems to have agreed with Viktor Orbán's earlier cited 2002 statement that in Hungary, dictatorships could only arise because of foreign occupation. On the other hand, he fails to mention the general left turn all over Europe and also in Hungary in the immediate postwar era. While without Russia the left-wing ideas and political leanings of the period may not have led to a full-blown Stalinist regime in the 1950s, saying nothing about it means that Gyurcsány missed an opportunity for the socialists to fit Hungary into general European trends and point to a time in history when Hungary was once again more or less in synch with progressive European developments.

Even more striking, however, is that he characterizes the communist takeover as the event that derailed Hungarian history from its "normal course." This raises very serious questions regarding the left's historical narrative, as it suggests, on the one hand, that it was only the Russian and not the German occupation that disrupted Hungary's otherwise normal development, while, on the other hand, it appears to consider the Horthy regime as fitting within the "normal course," even though it was a regime that proudly called itself counterrevolutionary, rejected all the values dear to the left and was anti-democratic and oppressive. Moreover, Hungary, long before Nazi Germany, started introducing laws against its Jewish citizens and then entered a military alliance with Adolf Hitler's Germany during the war.[39] Thus one could argue that it is not only the right and Fidesz that abandoned the anti-fascist consensus with the Fundamental Law, but also, as Gáspár Miklós Tamás writes,[40] with his, to say the least, tolerant attitude toward the interwar regime, Gyurcsány did the same. While he did not desert the anti-fascist consensus that used to be one of the left's main principles, for the sake of reconciliation, he attempted a more tolerant portrayal of the Horthy regime and acquitted it of the crime of joining the axis powers in the war.[41]

With respect to the communist regime itself, Gyurcsány tries to put forward an acceptable tradition from the recent past when he claims that between János Kádár and Imre Nagy, the democratic left must choose the latter: the martyred prime minister of the 1956 uprising. This of course could be regarded as an attempt to embrace the uprising itself as an appropriate tradition, but he offers no interpretation of 1956. This had been missing from the creed of the HSP and thus the right had every opportunity to portray the uprising to fit its politics of history, while the socialists made no attempt to emphasize its socialist features. At the same time, the rejection of Kádár also meant the rejection of the socialist past, which appeared problematic as well, since the former party leader did enjoy remarkable popularity when nostalgia for the security of the old system started to spread as it became clear that the expectations of the new system were not being fulfilled. The emphasis on the Kádár *versus* Nagy dichotomy had the potential of drowning the party in historical battles dictated by the right.[42] Recognizing people's nostalgia, the rejection of Kádár was then modified and accompanied by an understanding for the people who lived under that regime and are nostalgic for the social security and predictable life it offered. Moreover, the simple description of the system as a dictatorship does not leave room for the modernization narrative so important for the socialists, nor for the idea of a welfare state, however distorted it might have been. According to then leader of the HSP parliamentary group, Ildikó Lendvai, the criticism of the Kádár era also met with disapproval from the inner circles of the party, and therefore this section of Gyurcsány's essay had been rewritten, making room for the point of view of the "Kádárist little man."[43] Besides this interpretation of history, the essay is also concerned with the political actors' attitude toward one another—i.e., the left and the right's lack of empathy for each other.

While this is a more or less accurate description of the situation that underpins what some term the "cold civil war" in Hungary, the essay claims that after 1945, the right suffered more and was more disadvantaged than the left—a generous interpretation, to say the least. One would think that mention should be made of the many true leftists, for example, István Angyal who were persecuted and even executed after 1956.[44] The HSP thus missed the opportunity to a) offer a critique that would simultaneously criticize the Kádár regime and recognize its modernizing and egalitarian features and b) emphasize the socialist features and left-wing heroes of 1956 in order to advocate credible and genuine left traditions that could serve as a foundation for the party. The consequences of this lapse were especially serious as there was no left oppositional alternative in Hungary that could have effectively stressed the strong points in the country's left history; instead, those who in the late 1980s belonged to the oppositional faction in the party (for example, László Békessy and Lajos Bokros) all advocated (neo)liberal economics.

The essay and Gyurcsány's call to choose between Kádár and Nagy had already created problems at the party congress in early 2007: Gyula Horn, representing the old guard, went so far as to claim that Kádár himself used to be a social democrat, while the representative of the younger HSP leaders' generation, Tibor Szanyi, suggested that neither Kádár nor Nagy were appropriate models.[45] Despite this disagreement within the party, no theoretical effort comparable to Gyurcsány's was made. The two socialist prime ministers preceding him did not put forward anything like it. Horn came out with an autobiography (Cölöpök [Piles], 1991) in which he wrote at length of the opening of the Iron Curtain and also tried to account for his participation in the anti-uprising law and order brigades in 1956.

Conclusion

Although the HSP has been the focus of this survey, there are also other organizations that are worth mentioning, especially seeing as the left landscape has undergone changes since the big defeat of 2010.

Since the regime change, there has been a Workers' Party, led by Gyula Thürmer, to the left of the HSP. It rejected the transition and remained faithful to Kádárism, or what it interpreted as Kádár's legacy. The party is insignificant in political life, but it has repeatedly played the role of a predator, with the goal of stealing votes from the HSP. After the party decided to adopt a communist profile in 2005, its progressive wing split and established a new party, cooperating with other left-wing radical progressive groups united in the Green Left Party, which for a while had Gáspár Miklós Tamás, the Marxist philosopher and activist, as its president. The party did not win any political representation, but it made headlines when its leader,

Attila Vajnai, wore a red star at a demonstration. Since the red star is prohibited as a "symbol of totalitarianism," Vajnai had to stand trial and was sentenced to pay a fine, but he was acquitted after he won an appeal at the European Court of Human Rights in Strasbourg.[46]

More successful are the two new left-wing parties, Together and Dialogue for Hungary; they both managed to enter Parliament in 2014, although it is not clear how they would perform independently, as their electoral results were in the context of a coalition with the HSP and Democratic Coalition. Since they are relatively new parties that grew out of protest against Fidesz and the Orbán government, it is not yet clear how left their policies would be if they ever came to power. The most important program proposed so far, an unconditional basic income, was presented by Dialogue and introduced by their mayor in one of Budapest's districts.

Another party, Democratic Coalition, was founded by Gyurcsány after he left the HSP. Although it is referred to as "left liberal" in everyday parlance, the party is more accurately described as a liberal organization that has tried to fill the void created by the disappearance of Hungary's liberal party, the Alliance of Free Democrats. After the departure of Gyurcsány and his followers, the HSP necessarily became a little more homogeneous, but it still has divergent platforms and a need to clarify its stance further.

The other opposition party to the left of Fidesz is Politics Can Be Different. It underwent its own crisis as Dialogue for Hungary broke away from it before the 2014 elections because of disagreements concerning opposition cooperation. While Politics Can Be Different is in Parliament in its own right and regularly calls the other opposition parties, including the HSP, "pseudo-leftist," its own stance is not clear; it claims to be ecologist and anti-globalization.

I believe that to clarify their positions, these parties need to more completely come to terms with Hungarian left history, but they also need to position themselves in relation to European left parties, such as the Labor Party under Jeremy Corbyn, or even Podemos. The example of some other post-communist countries is varied but not necessarily promising. For example, initially, the Polish post-communist left's fate appeared to be in synch with that of the Hungarian socialists—or vice versa, as the Hungarian socialists' victory of 1994 followed that of the Polish left in 1993. We can also discern some similarities in the two parties' treatment of the past: In Poland, too, the right tried to use the communist past against the socialists because the latter made some effort to impede the condemnation of Wojciech Jaruzelski for the 1981 martial law. By now, however, the Polish left has disappeared, leaving even less traces than the Hungarian, and the Polish political scene seems to be dominated by a center right and an extreme right party. This might be the future of Hungarian politics; however, in Hungary, the left is holding on to some parliamentary seats, and studying the Polish example might suggest some pitfalls it can avoid. The Czech Republic offers a more promising example, but this might merely be due to the country's more European and less post-communist constellation. The Czech Social Democrats had a long and honorable history, and therefore they were less burdened by the past when they re-founded themselves, while at the same time, the country can boast of an unreconstructed communist party that insufficiently distanced from its past or attempted to whitewash it. Interestingly, the party is relatively successful despite the memory of its pre-1989 authoritarian rule. The current economic hardships, the failure of neoliberal economics and the attendant nostalgia for the economic and social security of the state socialist regime earns it steady support through nostalgia and protest votes.[47] Although its uncritical approach is no model, the reason for the party's significant support is worth studying for political as well as comparative purposes.

The significance of current European trends is all the greater in that the right's politics, at least as far as the ruling ideology and the politics of history are concerned, are derived from and focused on the past, and its ideology is thus far from being in synch with developments in today's European states or the EU, of which Hungary is a member. Consequently, drawing more attention to nationalism and emphasizing the nation-state as opposed to European cooperation cannot be an appropriate strategy for the left, as in this respect, the right will always be more able to stir emotions, and socialists will continuously be put on the defensive and forced to play at their opponents' game. That being the case, espousing the European anti-fascist consensus and criticizing the right's nostalgia for the interwar period's political system and for some of its protagonists, including certain antisemitic historical figures, might be a fruitful way to oppose the right's politics of history, and it would also elicit the support and cooperation of some civil-society organizations. Hungarian left parties agree in their support of anti-fascism, especially in light of the emerging extreme right parties and movements in Europe in general and in Hungary in particular. Of course, this would require drawing certain distinctions such as the difference between the right's anti-communism and fascism on the one hand, and clarifying the relationship between the Horthy regime's nationalism and its connection to fascism on the other. Doing this is a delicate and difficult matter, since in the nationalist narrative on which the Horthy regime was based and which is today put forward by the right, the emphasis placed on the negative things done by communists either during the Soviet Republic or under state socialism, along with the Trianon Treaty as the nation's major historical trauma—with all this contrasted to a preceding and glorious past—is very effective in creating emotional identification,[48] which complicates the criticism of nationalism in general and of the Horthy regime in particular. This is even more important because anti-fascism is often regarded as the key feature that needs to be preserved from the communist legacy, while at the same time the specter of fascism appears as a real danger in today's Hungary.

"Of the Past Let Us Make a Clean Slate" 37

There are many pitfalls to avoid in formulating a suitable politics of history, especially for a post-communist party that feels burdened by its past and is continuously driven to feel guilty. It is not surprising that the HSP prefers to operate with phrases devoid of politics or ideology, as well as history, claiming to represent nonpolitical peace, pragmatism and expertise, rejecting "divisive" and unnecessary ideological conflict.[49] However, not taking the initiative to project appropriate and attractive left traditions, and letting the right create the politics of history and memory for a nation is dangerous; formulating the left's own narrative needs to be paired with the creation of a suitable and truly left program. The one should reinforce the other.

Notes

1 On the success of successor parties in the post-transition era, see, for example, Alison Mahr and John Nagle, "Resurrection of the Successor Parties and Democratization in East-Central Europe," *Communist and Post-Communist Studies* 28.4 (1995): 393–409.
2 Tony Judt, *Ill Fares the Land* (New York: Penguin Press, 2010).
3 I have written about the right-wing's politics of history and memory through the employment of Transitional Justice among others in Csilla Kiss, "We Must Remember Thus: Transitional Justice in Service of Memory in Hungary," *Studia Universitatis Cibiniensis: Series Historica* 9 (2014), supplement (*Transitional Justice and Politics of Memory in Europe*): 71–87.
4 The text of the speech in Hungarian available at www.youtube.com/watch?v=DAQpHYU3m3s, accessed November 8, 2017.
5 While it is true that the Constitution of the Republic of Hungary of 1989 was the legal successor of the document established in 1949, besides the stipulation that Hungary's capital is Budapest, everything had been changed after the transition by the freely elected Parliament. As a result, the Constitution can in no way be called communist and was appropriate for a democratic state governed by the rule of law.
6 "Communist" is used in the original text of The Fundamental Law of Hungary. See: www.kormany.hu/download/e/02/00000/The%20New%20Fundamental%20Law%20of%20Hungary.pdf, accessed November 8, 2017.
7 Agárdi Péter, Artner Annamária, Harsányi Iván, Kállai R. Gábor, Krausz Tamás, Kunfi Frigyes, Mark Pittaway, Szalai Erzsébet, Szerdahelyi István, Tamás Pál and Z. Karvalics László, "Miért beteg a közép- és kelet-európai baloldal?," *Eszmélet* 74.19 (2007), http://eszmelet.hu/szalai_erzsebet-miert-beteg-a-kozep-es-kelet-europai-balold/, accessed February 22, 2016.
8 Zoltán Ripp, "A szocialisták identitásproblémái," *Mozgó Világ*, July 2007, http://epa.oszk.hu/01300/01326/00089/03ripp.htm, accessed November 8, 2017.
9 Zoltán Ripp, "A Horthy-reneszánsz és a mai baloldal," *Mozgó Világ*, August 2012, http://epa.oszk.hu/01300/01326/00142/pdf/EPA01326_mozgo_vilag_2012_08_5759.pdf, accessed November 8, 2017.
10 Wilhelm Hofmeister and Karsten Grabow, *Political Parties: Functions and Organisation in Democratic Societies* (Singapore: Konrad Adenauer Stiftung, 2011), 8.
11 The whole discussion is available in "Miért beteg a közép- és kelet-európai baloldal?," see en. 7.
12 Lajos Kossuth was one of the leaders of the Hungarian revolution and the 1848–1849 struggle for independence of 1848/1849 against the Habsburg Empire.

After the defeat of this effort, he immigrated and forever remained the symbol of Hungary's aspiration for national independence.
13 Faithful to Marx's interpretation, the Social Democratic Party regarded the Compromise of 1867 and the dual monarchy positively, as a construction that would keep both German and Russian imperialisms at bay. See, for example, Tibor Erényi, "A magyar szociáldemokrácia és a szomszédos országok," História, April 1990, www.tankonyvtar.hu/hu/tartalom/historia/90-04/ch04.html, accessed April 28, 2016. In fact, the very name "Social Democratic Party of Hungary," rather than Hungarian Social Democratic Party, signified that the party wanted to represent every nationality within the Kingdom of Hungary, not only Hungarians.
14 This was the first time since the creation of the Austro-Hungarian Monarchy that the Independence Party, hoping for Hungary's secession from the dual monarchy, won the elections. However, the emperor Franz Joseph appointed a minority government that was faithful to the monarchy. In this crisis, the social democrats did not support the independentists-nationalists, who consisted of a feudal, conservative high nobility, but continued their fight for universal suffrage and social reforms and progress.
15 See for example István Bibó, "Eltorzult magyar alkat, zsákutcás magyar történelem," in *Válogatott tanulmányok*, vol. 2, ed. Tibor Huszár (Magvető: Budapest, 1986).
16 Eric J. Hobsbawm, *Nations and Nationalism Since 1780: Programme, Myth, Reality* (Cambridge: Cambridge University Press, 1990), 44.
17 Gáspár Miklós Tamás, "Egyszerű és nagyszerű kapitalizmus," *Eszmélet* 19.75 (2007), http://eszmelet.hu/tamas_gaspar_miklos-egyszeru-es-nagyszeru-kapitalizmus/, accessed March 30, 2016.
18 This, of course, is not a new dilemma. It is interesting to consider what former Spanish communist and writer Jorge Semprún said about being a "red," which was an identity he eventually voluntarily embraced, but it was also almost forced upon him. Initially he found it absurd and distasteful: Why should one call Franco's rebels "nationalists" when they used Moroccan troops, German planes and the Littorio Division. The republicans would be much more rightfully called, if not nationalists, at least patriots. Jorge Semprún, *Le Grand Voyage* (Paris: Gallimard, 1963), 123.
19 Ripp, "A szocialisták identitásproblémái."
20 Tibor Hajdú, "A Tanácsköztársaság mint a közép-európai forradalom része," in *1919: A Magyarországi Tanácsköztársaság és a kelet-európai forradalmak*, eds. Tamás Krausz and Judit Vértes (Budapest: L'Harmattan—ELTE BTK Kelet-Európa Története Tanszék, 2010), 17.
21 Ignác Romsics, "Magyar történeti problémák, 1900–1945," in Ignác Romsics, *Múltról a mának* (Budapest: Osiris, 2004), 320.
22 See, for example, Erik Molnár, "A Magyar Tanácsköztársaság történelmi jelentősége," *Történelmi Szemle* 2.1–2 (1959): 1–7. See also Ignác Romsics, "Magyar történeti problémák, 1900–1945."
23 "Speech by Prime Minister Viktor Orbán on 15 March," www.kormany.hu/en/the-prime-minister/the-prime-minister-s-speeches/speech-by-prime-minister-viktor-orban-on-15-march, accessed March 21, 2016.
24 Attila Pók, "A Tanácsköztársaság helye a magyar történelemben," in *1919: A Magyarországi Tanácsköztársaság és a kelet-európai forradalmak*, 31.
25 György Litván, "'Magyar gondolat—szabad gondolat': Nacionalizmus és progresszió a század eleji Magyarországon," in *Magyar gondolat—szabad gondolat, Válogatott történeti tanulmányok*, ed. György Litván (Budapest: Osiris, 2008), 15–104.

26 Péter Szegő, "Hiller: Európa a gyógyír a trianoni tragédiára," *HVG.hu*, June 4, 2010, http://hvg.hu/itthon/20100604_hiller_istvan_trianon_europa, accessed May 6, 2016.
27 www.international-brigades.org.uk/sites/default/files/IBMT1-16Web.pdf, accessed May 20, 2016.
28 György Borsányi, "A moszkvai emigráció: A magyar kommunista mozgalom tanácsköztársaság-képének alakulása," *História* 6 (1989), www.tankonyvtar.hu/en/tartalom/historia/89-06/ch08.html, accessed May 1, 2016.
29 Their political operation during the interwar period was constrained and limited by the 1921 Bethlen-Peyer Pact between Prime Minister István Bethlen and Social Democratic leader Károly Peyer. It stipulated that the social democrats could return to politics and enjoy limited assembly rights and parliamentary representation in exchange for giving up "radical" republican views, as well as organizing agricultural workers and public employees, and not criticizing the government's foreign policy. While the communist era regarded this as treason on Peyer's part, with the result that no effective weapon was left in the hands of the left, the post-communist right, especially former Prime Minister, Péter Boross, has found the pact exemplary and useful.
30 "Miért beteg a közép- és kelet-európai baloldal?"
31 "Miért beteg a közép- és kelet-európai baloldal?"
32 Ripp, "A szocialisták identitásproblémái."
33 "Miért beteg a közép- és kelet-európai baloldal?"
34 Orbán clearly interpreted the event as an attempt to renew capitalism in Hungary and was therefore sympathetic to it. But it should be noted that his view of 1956 became more radical with time, as Debreczeni emphasizes. In 1997, Orbán said this, but three years earlier, in 1994, he did not use the adjective "bourgeois," but said instead that the goal in 1956 was not to reestablish private property and that the rebellion cannot be seen as the origin of the market economy. By 1997, he was more inclined to employ the past in his own interest. József Debreczeni, *Arcmás* (Budapest: Noran Libro, 2009), 119–120.
35 Vona Gábor, "1956 a Horthy-rendszer utolsó fellobbanása volt," http://mandiner.hu/cikk/20151023_vona_gabor_1956_a_horthy_rendszer_utolso_fellobbanasa_volt, accessed May 2, 2016.
36 "Titkos ügynök a kormány élén," *Magyar Nemzet*, June 18, 2002, http://mno.hu/migr_1834/titkos-ugynok-a-kormany-elen-791262, accessed May 2, 2016.
37 Ferenc Gyurcsány, "Szembenézés," http://nol.hu/archivum/archiv-433050-242100, accessed May 3, 2016.
38 Ripp, "A szocialisták identitásproblémái." On the issue of post-transition lustration that affected the HSP and was also used as potential political blackmail, see, for example, Csilla Kiss, "The Misuses of Manipulation: The Failure of Transitional Justice in Post-Communist Hungary," *Europe—Asia Studies* 58.6 (2006): 925–940.
39 Left-wing historian, Tamás Krausz also criticized this view, among other things, in an open letter. See "Nyílt levél Gyurcsány Ferenc miniszterelnökhöz," http://nol.hu/archivum/archiv-434528-243427, accessed May 4, 2016. Two years later, he left the party itself.
40 Gáspár Miklós Tamás, "Az utolsó tengelyhatalom," *Magyar Narancs*, June 7, 2012, http://magyarnarancs.hu/publicisztika/az-utolso-tengelyhatalom-80383, accessed March 31, 2016.
41 To be fair, it is important to stress that Ferenc Gyurcsány has been and has remained a strong anti-fascist figure in Hungarian politics both in government and in opposition. This is why it is so surprising to read in his essay something that can so easily be taken as breaking with this consensus.

42 Ripp, "A szocialisták identitásproblémái."
43 "Szembenézés: a Kádár-kor értékelése vitát váltott ki az MSZP-ben," http://nol.hu/archivum/archiv-433058-242106, accessed May 3, 2016.
44 István Angyal was one of those communists who fought against Stalinism in 1956 but, strikingly, also flew the red flag on the barricade on November 7 to signal that he and his comrades were the representatives of the true workers' power. On Angyal, see László Eörsi, *Angyal István (1928–1958)* (Budapest: Noran, 2008), or András Lukácsy, *Angyal szállt le Budapestre* (Budapest: C.E.T. Belvárosi Könyvkiadó, 2006).
45 Ripp, "A szocialisták identitásproblémái."
46 "A vöröscsillag-perben felmentették Vajnai Attilát," www.jogiforum.hu/hirek/20094, accessed May 9, 2016.
47 See Stanislav Holubec, "Die Radikale Linke in Tschechien," in *Von Revolution bis Koalition: Linke Parteien in Europa*, eds. Cornelia Hildebrandt, Birgit Daibler and Anna Striethorst (Berlin: Karl Dietz Verlag, 2010), 313–329.
48 Ripp, "A szocialisták identitásproblémái."
49 Gáspár Miklós Tamás, "Ellenforradalmak," *Élet és Irodalom* 46.28 (2002), www.es.hu/tamas_gaspar_miklos;ellenforradalmaink;2003-01-10.html, accessed May 3, 2016 (subscription needed).

2 Communist Successors and Narratives of the Past

Party Factions in the German PDS and the Russian CPRF, 1990–2005

Thorsten Holzhauser and
Antony Kalashnikov

Introduction and Theoretical Context

In the decades following the demise of state socialism in Eastern and Central Europe, transition societies have developed various historical narratives of the state socialist past. Being the main representatives of this legacy in the political arena, (post-)communist successor parties have been faced, more than other actors, with the need to account for the past. Indeed, collective memory of the state socialist experience became a fundamental part of successor parties' political identity and strategy. However, there has been some debate over the factors that influence and shape the identity and strategy of successor parties in former Eastern Bloc states. "Internalist" conceptions focus on the alignment of forces within a party and the key choices of party elites. "Externalist" approaches, by contrast, see institutional and sociopolitical contexts as determining the nature of (post-)communist successor parties.[1] This chapter seeks to clarify the debate between "internalist" and "externalist" approaches by focusing on the memory discourses within Germany's Party of Democratic Socialism (PDS) and the Communist Party of the Russian Federation (CPRF).[2] We arrive at a mixed conclusion: While party leaders and factions determined party identity, nationally specific sociopolitical and institutional contexts were crucial in determining the *parameters* of a party's discourse.

Our methodology stems from discomfort with the way the internalist/externalist debate has taken shape. Most studies of (post-)communist successor parties are limited to single-case investigations. These investigations set out to explain why a party made this or that decision with respect to identity or strategy—i.e., why key actors perceived a given "choice" as advantageous. The most careful studies have noted that these actors differed with regard to the ideological "lens" through which they interpreted favorable and unfavorable outcomes. For instance, many have noted a three-way factional cleavage between orthodox Marxist-Leninists, social democrats and statist nationalists within the CPRF,[3] whereas the PDS has been described as a "pluralist" party polarized between orthodox communists and reformers.[4]

However valuable single-case analyses may be, by focusing on key actors and actions, they inadvertently overemphasize the scope of "free choice," a priori biasing conclusions in favor of "internalism."

By contrast, a handful of comparative studies have shown that sociopolitical and institutional contexts *do matter*, as analogous conditions lead to very similar identities and strategies. Thus John Ishiyama argues that the previous regime type ("patrimonial," "national consensus" and "bureaucratic-authoritarian communism") is a good predictor of both the identity and political fortunes of communist successor parties.[5] Nonetheless, comparative approaches are not without their own flaws, particularly in their dependence on simplified coding. Ishiyama himself admits that his tripartite distinction may "[run] the risk of overgeneralization."[6] Similarly, comparative approaches usually depict successor parties as monolithic entities[7]—a simplification that detailed, single-case studies have problematized. Fundamentally, this distillation of complex political phenomena into simple labels is what allows for broad "externalist" generalizations.

Our methodology rejects both approaches, which, we believe, often predetermine conclusions.[8] Using the example of *collective memory* within the PDS and CPRF (in the period up to 2005), we develop an alternative approach. We analyze and compare memory discourses in both parties, fully appreciating their internal factions and contradictions. The choice of the PDS and CPRF for our comparison is premised on two baseline similarities. Unlike other Central and Eastern European successor parties, they have not transformed into Western-style social democratic formations, but have retained some attachment to their communist heritage (although to a different extent, as the discussion will show).[9] Moreover, both parties share the experience of post-socialist transformation coinciding not only with the fall of the state socialist regime and the planned economy but also with the erasure of the former state. At the same time, as we will demonstrate, these situations had certain specificities, with the result that the two parties operated in very particular sociopolitical contexts.

Our conclusion is hard to place in either the "internalist" or "externalist" camp. First, we find both important similarities and differences between PDS and CPRF memory discourses. This may or may not advantage "externalist" explanations, depending on the degree to which one sees the German and Russian post-socialist circumstances as similar. Second, in line with "internalist" explanations, we affirm the agency of the party (or party elite) in identity fashioning, part of which involved the production of memory discourses. Both pragmatic considerations and the interpretative ideological lenses of party leaders and factions shaped the content of these discourses. Third, and most importantly, we affirm the power of external, nationally specific contexts in determining the *parameters of memory discourse*. While the memory discourses of various factions in either the CPRF or the PDS were significantly different, factional discourses *responded to similar issues* that concerned the whole party. These issues were specific to the particular national context the CPRF and PDS found themselves in, but in certain cases, these conditions were similar to those in other post-socialist societies. Our conclusions support the classic, Halbwachsian notion of memory (and more broadly, political identity) as *dialogical*: engaged with and responding to external (in our case, national) social contexts.[10] That is, collective memory is articulated, reproduced and modified in dialogue with and in response to *external* circumstances (as opposed to self-conscious identity fashioning).

This chapter is organized as follows: After introducing the two successor parties and their internal divisions, we compare the different national contexts and the ways the different CPRF and PDS factions responded to external circumstances and expectations. We will first examine party narratives against the backdrop of prevailing public memory discourses and the expectations that successor parties account for the socialist past. We will then compare the successor parties' response to Western historical narratives and, finally, explore the mobilization of memory by successor parties and their opponents in the context of power politics.

The CPRF and PDS as Successor Parties

Both contemporaries and researchers have described the CPRF and PDS as the main successors to former communist parties, the Communist Party of the Soviet Union (CPSU) and the Socialist Unity Party of Germany (SED), respectively. In both cases, successorship had significant consequences for the parties' attitudes toward their predecessors and for their historical narratives in general. The CPSU and its Russian section (the Communist Party of the Russian Soviet Federative Socialist Republic) were banned following the failed August 1991 coup; the CPRF was reestablished in late 1993 after the Constitutional Court lifted this ban. The CPRF's choice to frame itself as successor to the old Soviet Communist Party is well documented in the scholarship and was based on several strategic considerations. First of all, the party could take advantage of the traditional loyalties of "believers" for whom supporting the Communist Party (regardless of its actual political stance) was a matter of quasi-religious duty.[11] The CPRF could also exploit the political values and discourses already built up in the Soviet period.[12] Third, and most importantly, it allowed the CPRF to capitalize on nostalgia, which was particularly strong given the economic woes and social breakdown of the 1990s.[13] This choice to position itself as a successor party furthered the need for the party to formulate a historical narrative.

Nonetheless, at least throughout its first decade of existence, the CPRF was beset by factionalism, being ideologically divided into orthodox Marxist-Leninist, social democratic and statist nationalist camps, which produced divergent memory discourses. In trying to profit from nostalgia, all factions called for a "return to the past," but the past was conceptualized in different ways.[14] The orthodox Marxist-Leninist faction, led by Teimuraz Avaliani (1932–), Nikolai Bindiukov (1936–), Viktor Iliukhin (1949–2011), Richard

Kosolapov (1930–), Anatolii Luk'ianov (1930–) and Al'bert Makashov (1938–), called for a wholesale restoration of the Soviet system, which was touted as wholly superior to any variant of liberal democracy.[15] In doing so, they supplied endless comparisons of Soviet achievements in the economy, social policy, defense, foreign politics, etc., praising the Stalin period particularly. Joseph Stalin was credited with achieving "the highest growth rates in the world,"[16] building "the best system of government,"[17] cracking down on corruption and indiscipline[18] and strengthening national unity.[19] In these comparisons, the disparity between past and present was assigned to systemic differences between (true) socialism and capitalism (as opposed to the costs of transition, or the mistakes of current leaders). Taken together, the (usually unspoken) conclusion was that "the [new] regime should be like the one under Stalin [. . .] a modern Stalinism is the foundation for overcoming the current crisis."[20]

By contrast, social democrats,[21] led by Valentin Kuptsov (1937–), Iurii Masliukov (1937–2010), Ivan Mel'nikov (1950–), Sergei Potapov (1951–) and Gennadii Seleznev (1947–2015), turned to the past only in terms of the general values and political principles that they felt should inform CPRF identity. They wanted to retain "collectivism, brotherly mutual aid, social security for workers, and democracy."[22] At the same time, they too did not miss the opportunity to compare the Soviet record favorably to current conditions. Unlike orthodox narratives, these measures were drawn almost exclusively from the late Soviet period and centered on social policy: education, health, security, science and culture.[23]

The nationalist faction,[24] which included party leader Gennadii Ziuganov (1944–), Iurii Belov (1938–) and Aleksandr Shabanov (1938–), also appealed to Soviet superiority but situated this in the wider context of "traditional" patterns, which had undergirded the nation's successes in the past and was put forward as the model for the CPRF's program.[25] Allegedly, the Soviet Union encapsulated Russians' natural collectivist outlook and their yearning for social justice.[26] The centralized state was in line with Russian traditions of collectivism, national self-sufficiency, military security and trust in an able leader.[27] Nationalists also supplied comparisons of Soviet achievements (from various periods) with current conditions, but drew primarily from areas highlighting state power and prestige.

Unlike the CPSU and many other communist state parties, the East German SED was not banned or disbanded. Instead, the party was rechristened in the winter 1989/1990 as the Party of Democratic Socialism in order to underline its democratic restart under a new leadership and with a new "anti-Stalinist" platform.[28] By rebranding the party (rather than refounding it), the PDS attempted to retain its membership and, like the CPRF, capitalize on traditional loyalties and nostalgia, particularly among those seeking an emotional "home" during rapid economic and social change.[29] Moreover, the party tried to retain large parts of the SED's economic and organizational assets.[30] Yet, as a result of this decision, the PDS was also confronted with demands to make clear its position on its own past and on its darker aspects in particular. Thus the status of "SED successor party" or even "SED continuation party"—[31]an epithet employed by media and political opponents rather than by the PDS itself—became a heavy burden, as it raised negative associations within large parts of the public, not only in West but also in East Germany.

Like its Russian counterpart, the PDS was not a monolithic block but rather a party with multiple currents and party factions, among which the polarization between *reformers* and *orthodox communists* was the most influential and enduring.[32] The so-called reformers within the PDS were the driving force behind the intra-party democratization and viewed the 1989 revolution as a chance to restart the socialist project. They represented a former SED minority, which was inspired by Mikhail Gorbachev's perestroika and advocated a "Third Way" between socialism and capitalism.[33] They accepted the capitalist-democratic regime of unified Germany but sought to overcome the predominance of the profit motive in society gradually.[34] Thus they believed in social reform, a mixed economy, civil liberties, rule of law and democratic participation.[35] The reformers claimed the party's strategic leadership, set the agenda and dominated among the party's top ranks.[36] For example, all of the party's principal leaders, such as Gregor Gysi (1948–), Lothar Bisky (1941–2013), André Brie (1950–), Roland Claus (1954–) and Gabriele Zimmer (1955–), have been described as representatives of the party's reformist faction.[37] But in terms of historical memory, they were not as homogeneous but rather divided between a minority that identified as "radical-moralist" and a majority that was accused of being somewhat apologetic about the past.[38] The latter were more willing to tolerate the views of a more conservative membership who wished to maintain the SED's communist tradition at least in part.[39]

Thus reformers tolerated an orthodox communist minority within the party, which remained devoted to class struggle and Marxism-Leninism, and opposed to any form of capitalism and bourgeois democracy.[40] They referred positively to the German Democratic Republic (GDR) as a "first actually existing socialism"[41] and viewed its breakdown in 1989/1990 as part of a capitalist restoration or even counterrevolution.[42] As will be seen, their leading representatives—Sahra Wagenknecht (1969–), Ellen Brombacher (1947–) and Michael Benjamin (1932–2000)—disagreed with the reformers in particular over the importance and character of the alleged crimes committed by the SED regime and the responsibilities for its eventual failure.

As we have demonstrated, both the PDS and the CPRF consisted of opposing internal factions, each of which developed their own historical narratives. All of them relied on nostalgia among the party membership and electorate. However, having made this decision, the two parties were forced to respond to several externally imposed, contextual challenges. We argue that both parties had to react to 1) the public's expectation that these parties would account for the historical realities of late socialism, 2) perceived Western hostility and 3) anti-communism in the context of power politics.

Accounting for the Realities of Socialism

We have already noted that the CPRF and the PDS intended to capitalize on nostalgia. On the surface, this strategy had great potential. In Germany, so-called *Ostalgie* [eastern nostalgia] was—although limited to the eastern part of the country—a common phenomenon in the transition and unification process.[43] In Russia, as Neil Munro has demonstrated, positive overall evaluations of the Soviet period had support from over half the population, rising throughout the 1990s to about two-thirds and plateauing since then.[44]

Yet there were at least three important caveats. First, nostalgia could largely be an apolitical phenomenon, a grieving for youth and past times and places, or at most for former values (collectivism, social equality, etc.), rather than institutions or communist leadership.[45] Second, nostalgia could have less to do with positive memories of "really existing socialism" than with a marginally favorable comparison to the status quo of the transition period.[46] Third, even if "a return to the past" was preferred in theory, this did not necessarily translate into active support for restoration, as this could be viewed as impossible.[47]

In order to channel potential nostalgia into political support, the CPRF was forced to provide a historical narrative that would account for the lived experiences of socialism, explaining that the party would not bring back "fixed pricing, shortages, empty shelves, [. . .] queues, ration tickets and cards, [. . .] confiscation and nationalization of private property."[48] After all, by 1991, the Soviet order had squandered what little support it had left, which the failure of the August coup decisively demonstrated. The Communist Party, similarly, had left the political scene beset by internal crisis and at a rock-bottom level of popularity. There was also a wide distrust of individual communist leaders—a legacy that continued to follow CPRF politicians for years.[49] Less directly, the regime was discredited by a series of widely publicized revelations about the dimensions of its past crimes and the system's pervasive dependence on violence, which severely shook the ideological foundations of the communist project.[50] Indeed, Memorial, one of the largest civil-society organizations in Russia throughout the 1990s, was actively committed to preserving the memory of Stalinist crimes and furthering an anti-totalitarian political culture.[51] Not only was the CPRF forced to grapple with the realities of state socialism but also it had to account for its collapse and demonstrate that the socialist model was still viable. After all, credibility was severely undercut when its promises of inevitable communist triumph appeared to be disproved.

Each faction in the CPRF responded to this conundrum in different ways. Nationalists responded to both issues (the crimes and hardships of socialism and the unviability of the Soviet model) through the "two parties" narrative.

Ostensibly, from the very start, individuals who were cosmopolitans, Marxist fanatics and simply traitors and scoundrels contaminated the CPSU. They were responsible for all the trials and tribulations of the Soviet period. Leon Trotsky's vulgar class approach, for instance, resulted in various "cruelties," including anti-Cossack operations, Civil War concentration camps and hostage taking, starvation and anti-religious/class repressions.[52] By listing Lavrentiy Beria, Lazar Kaganovich, Nikita Khrushchev (sometimes Leonid Brezhnev) and Gorbachev as part of this "other party," nationalists absolved the "good," "patriotic" wing of the CPSU of all Soviet crimes. These patriots, the wellspring of all Soviet successes, were now to be found in the cleansed CPRF. The "two parties" narrative also explained the fall of the Soviet Union. Allegedly, as a result of waning spirituality and patriotism, the CPSU leadership was taken over by democratic reformers, "Party renegades [...] foreign agents, dissidents, parts of the de-nationalized intelligentsia," a fifth column of "artists, demagogues, intriguers, careerists, and those refusing to serve the Fatherland."[53] They led the people astray with mock-socialist slogans, stoked nationalism in the republics and engineered the August coup as a pretext for seizing power.[54]

Orthodox Marxists-Leninists, in general, tried to bypass the unpalatable aspects of late socialism (where they did engage with them, they blamed Trotskyist and liberal contamination of the CPSU).[55] However, they did launch a controversial defense of the Stalin period. Repressions were justified as a necessary evil for the sake of the greater good: rapid industrialization and victory in the Great Patriotic War.[56] The number of those repressed was said to be greatly exaggerated,[57] and in any case, the number of Gulag prisoners did not appear particularly large when compared with the per capita prison population in Russia and the US currently.[58] In accounting for the collapse of the Soviet Union, they followed a strategy similar to that of the nationalists, accusing key individuals (Gorbachev, Boris Yeltsin) of treason. Sometimes, a more "Marxist" perspective qualified this; allegedly, the CPSU leadership's actions over the years created a hostile, quasi-bourgeois class[59] and then provided it with an opportunity to take power in a "capitalist-bureaucratic counter-revolution."[60]

Social democrats took a significantly different position on the Soviet experience. Instead of denying, justifying or redirecting blame, they acknowledged Soviet crimes and promised to make a clean break with these practices. They denounced "revolutionary expedience" as the cause of arbitrariness and the precondition for the Red Terror, Stalinist show trials and the hounding of the dissidents.[61] They criticized the Soviets and labor unions as undemocratic, with ultimate power belonging to the nomenclature.[62] Social democrats argued that the Soviet collapse resulted from systemic issues. On the one hand, the planned economy was wholly inadequate and planted a structural time bomb.[63] At the same time, the party remained out of touch with the masses and was fatally mired in dogmatism.[64]

While the CPRF had to account for the past vis-à-vis a nascent anti-totalitarian political culture, the PDS had to deal with a similar situation to an even greater extent[65] because of West Germany's history of anti-totalitarianism.[66] In the unified Germany, an alliance of West German elites and East German former dissidents sought to revive the Federal Republic's "anti-totalitarian consensus" and to expand it to East Germany.[67] Their approach toward historical memory was based on the assumption that a reestablishment of democracy in the former GDR depended on a critical and thorough reckoning with the "totalitarian" past.[68] Moreover, they wanted to avoid the long period of amnesia that initially characterized the historical memory of National Socialism.[69] In this sense, West Germany's culture of *Aufarbeitung* [working through the memory of National Socialism] was used ubiquitously as a model for dealing with the so-called second German dictatorship as well.

On a legal and judicial level, the German institutions implemented a comparatively extensive program of transitional justice and lustration.[70] In the field of historical memory, the Bundestag created a central inquiry commission (*Enquête-Kommission*) on "Dealing with History and Consequences of the SED Dictatorship in Germany," which was supposed to foster a common democratic culture and to create a new "anti-totalitarian consensus" in the unified Germany.[71] In operation from April 1992, the inquiries eventually focused on political institutions, on the repression and persecution of the GDR opposition movement and the fundamental illegitimacy not only of the SED regime but also of the East German state in general.[72] This assessment was based on the majority's conviction that liberal democracy—as realized in the West—was "the only legitimacy a state order can refer to."[73]

From the beginning, those anti-totalitarian narratives put the PDS on the defense. Party factions reacted to this situation in different ways. The reformers tried to initiate a dialogue on historical memory that was supposed to be self-critical and "free from any apologetics [and] embellishment."[74] Like the CPRF's social democratic faction, the PDS reformers acknowledged "Stalinist crimes,"[75] and some of them publicly apologized to victims.[76] Moreover, they attributed the failure of state socialism to dogmatic economic planning and to a systemic lack of democracy within the so-called Stalinist party hierarchy.[77] Their anti-Stalinism was not only directed against Stalin's regime of "mass terror" but also against the "administrative-centralist socialism"[78] of post-Stalinist times (including the 1970s and 1980s). A critical reckoning with the past, reformers believed, was to prevent undemocratic backlashes in the future and help realize a more authentic form of socialism.[79] Yet, at the same time, they rejected any attempts at delegitimizing the GDR in general. Instead, they were willing to defend the "historical" and "moral" legitimacy of the East German state and of its ideological foundations as an attempt at overcoming fascist traditions and at building a just society.[80] While viewing Stalinism as a "degeneration" of socialism,[81] they referred to the alleged anti-Stalinist aspects of the socialist past such as the 1953 uprising in the GDR, the 1956 events in Hungary and the 1968 Prague Spring, which they interpreted as "attempts to correct" and to "renew" socialism on a more democratic basis.[82] Thus only a minority of reformers were willing to accept the anti-totalitarian mainstream consensus.[83] For example, Dietmar Keller (1942–), a former GDR minister and the party's delegate to the first inquiry commission, identified "totalitarian structures" in the GDR and was even open to a controversial comparison of the SED state to Germany's National Socialist experience.[84] Yet he was harshly criticized from within the party as adopting the views of the political enemy.[85]

While the majority of reformers propagated a so-called anti-Stalinist, rather than an "anti-totalitarian," consensus,[86] the orthodox communist faction rejected both of those interpretations.[87] Like their Russian counterparts, some orthodox communists within the PDS were even willing to defend Stalin's (and Walter Ulbricht's) rule against historical revisionism. Sahra Wagenknecht, for instance, blamed so-called opportunists such as Gorbachev (but also Khrushchev and Brezhnev) for the failure of socialism.[88] Not "Stalinism" or Marxism-Leninism, she argued in a controversial 1992 article, but opportunism and revisionism had "proven fatal to the socialist society."[89] In a 1995 treatise, she elaborated this position by considering post-Stalinist revisionism a reaction to the "imperialist" anti-socialism of the West, which eventually succeeded in "bringing down the first socialism" in the Eastern Bloc.[90] In contrast to the reformers, orthodox communists implied that the demise of state socialism had not been systemically caused but had been provoked by individual failure, by Gorbachev's "betrayal" and by Western hostility[91]—a conclusion that was common among the orthodox wings of the German and Russian successor parties.

Perceived Western Hostility

Russian public perceptions of Western hostility were extremely widespread in the 1990s, stemming from a number of factors. First, the loss of the Cold War coincided with the collapse of the economy, the breakup of the multinational union and social breakdown. These associations set the context for a blame game in which the so-called West was a major culprit, perceptions aided by decades of Cold War propaganda "unmasking" the West's imperialist nature. Second, the diminution of Russia's status on the international stage reanimated nationalism (which had been toyed with throughout the Soviet era, but never wholeheartedly embraced) and even revanchism—emotions, which all parties on the political scene were keen to exploit. Third, the West was seen as colluding with the unpopular Yeltsin government—for instance, in contributing economic "advisors" to disastrous reforms and failing to respond to Yeltsin's undemocratic and violent actions against Parliament in 1993.[92] Finally, the 1990s saw an unprecedented cultural opening of Russia, into which Western products, discourses and lifestyles flooded. Unavoidably, this produced a culture shock of sorts, especially among older generations.[93] The rise of nationalist sentiments became apparent as early as the 1993 elections, when the ultra-right Liberal Democratic Party of Russia became the largest party in Parliament with almost 22.9 percent of the popular vote. Taken together, all of these factors produced a situation in which perceptions of a hostile West were widespread; all CPRF factions (and not only, as one might expect, the nationalist faction) had to engage with this in some way.[94]

Accordingly, the CPRF mobilized historical narratives to demonstrate the continuities in Western aggression and to oppose Western historical narratives. Orthodox Marxist-Leninist narratives framed the East-West opposition in terms of the imperialism narrative. The Soviet Union was allegedly a serious challenge to global imperialism, defending the socialist system against foreign interference and counterrevolutionary reaction (for example, in Korea, the GDR, Poland, Cuba, Vietnam and Czechoslovakia), and supporting anti-fascist, anti-colonial and anti-aggression movements elsewhere (for example, anti-colonial movements in Asia, Africa and Latin America).[95] According to this interpretation, the imperialist West fought against its Soviet competitor in a string of aggressive acts or ploys: from the fascist option (Operation Barbarossa), to the Zionist plot (*Protocols of the Elders of Zion*), to involvement in the Chernobyl catastrophe, to forcing an arms race on the USSR.[96] It ultimately succeeded with the help of Gorbachev's and Yeltsin's fifth column, and was now disposing of its colonial spoils.

Nationalist narratives were similar in characterizing Western aggression against Russia and its ultimately successful strategy.[97] However, they differed in framing the conflict with the West as a timeless, civilizational opposition. At times, this was phrased in the mock-scientific language of geopolitical confrontations (Atlanticism *versus* Eurasianism)[98] and at other times as the struggle of Orthodox Russia against a Zionist oligarchy, which had captured the West.[99]

Social democrats constructed the most moderate narrative in this respect. They did not emphasize confrontation with the West but appealed to broader international standards. Thus they saw the October Revolution as a rallying point in the worldwide struggle for political empowerment and social justice. Conversely, the latter were negatively affected by the Soviet collapse.[100] They did not assign blame to the West, but implicitly criticized its record.

Having framed the outlook and role of the West in the aforementioned ways, CPRF narratives responded to perceived Western historical narratives. Both nationalists and orthodox Marxist-Leninists saw these anti-Stalinist and anti-Soviet discourses put forward by the West as crucial to Soviet collapse. Recognizing Soviet strength, the West's principal instrument was a "psychological, informational, and intellectual war" aimed at weakening it from within.[101] Having secured lackeys in the Soviet leadership (that is, Gorbachev and company), they launched the

> large-scale, intentional ideological manipulation of the population in a "democratic spirit" [in order to] rid the disoriented masses of a natural immunity derived from intuitive, healthy conservatism and a self-preservation instinct.[102]

They saw it as natural that the West continued to defame the Soviet past in order to keep its stooges in power, cement the "neoliberal" order in Russia and preserve the relative weakness of the country. The Soros Foundation, which financed and published Russian history textbooks in the 1990s, was the subject of particular ire.[103] It was said to glorify globalization, sideline Russian history and cast it in an entirely negative light (specifically, in minimizing the Soviet contribution to victory in World War II).[104] Iliukhin even went so far as to charge the Soros Foundation with working with the CIA; in the 1980s (sic!), the foundation allegedly fomented sedition, organized the corruption of officials and interfered in the internal politics of Eastern European states.[105] Social democratic input was notably absent on this issue.

In the German context, anti-Western attitudes were equally important, but they were embedded in a rather different context, being part of an intrastate conflict and not primarily directed against foreign powers (although anti-Americanism was also prevalent among German post-communists).[106] Unlike Russia, East Germany not only lost its international status but also its entire statehood. Politically and economically, German unification was supposed to be an expansion of the allegedly successful Western system and its institutions into the east of the country.[107] West Germany, therefore, played a major role in the East German transformation process. This resulted in widespread feelings of inferiority and impotence among many East Germans, who developed a certain *Abgrenzungsmentalität* [mentality of self-demarcation].[108] Historical narratives played a significant part in this development, as many East Germans were dissatisfied with the hegemonic reading of GDR history. While the anti-totalitarian discourse focused on acts of state terror, repression and ideology (rather than everyday life), many Easterners perceived this as an attack on their historical and biographic identity—a nullification of their positive memories and achievements.[109] Moreover, the economic transition failed to satisfy the high expectations of many Easterners and seemed to bring unemployment and deindustrialization rather than the "flourishing landscapes" (*blühende Landschaften*) promised by the Helmut Kohl government during the 1990 electoral campaign. As a result, many people became skeptical about Western-style democracy and market economy, and idealized the GDR's record of full employment and social security.[110] This formed the basis for "*Ostalgie*."[111]

The PDS tried to capitalize on this mélange of anti-Westernism and nostalgia by championing the interpretation of the East German transformation as an act of Western "occupation" and "colonization."[112] Post-communists from all factions actively supported anti-Western sentiments and styled themselves as *the* defenders of East German interests vis-à-vis an overly powerful Western establishment.[113] By doing so, the party gained recognition as an "East German regional protest party."[114] As part of this strategy, the PDS framed the anti-totalitarian reading of the past—which was hegemonic in German mainstream discourse—as a Western dictate.[115] In order to counter the hegemonic binary of a "good" (that is, Western) and a "bad" (that is, Eastern) German state, PDS politicians from all factions pointed at undemocratic developments in the West German past, in particular at Western Cold War anti-communism of the 1950s—a phenomenon that was both ignored by westerners and exaggerated by post-communists.[116] While the orthodox faction, as noted earlier, unequivocally blamed the West for the Cold War, the reformers' narratives were more ambiguous. On the one hand, they were willing to acknowledge positive "achievements" of Western postwar history and of its "social democratic era" in particular, which they believed to be threatened by "neoliberalism."[117] Yet, on the other hand, they also noted the so-called achievements of socialism in the GDR in their push back against perceived "Western arrogance" and "Western occupation policy."[118]

For post-communists of all factions, this strategy served three different functions: First, they were able to both profit from long-standing anti-Western attitudes socialized under the socialist regime and from recent feelings of humiliation and frustration among East Germans.[119] Second, it allowed for the attribution of East Germany's economic and social problems, such as high unemployment and low competitiveness, to the Western transition strategy rather than to the economic legacy of the GDR.[120] And, finally, it also served a self-protective function within the party's own membership and clientele of former SED functionaries, as it facilitated the attribution of their own marginalization in the unified Germany to Western "victor's justice."[121] This interpretation was reinforced by the way post-communists perceived particular acts of transitional justice such as the prosecution of former border patrols and of former members of the SED Politburo.[122] Moreover, the opening of the state security files under the Stasi Records Act of late 1991 led not only to intense scholarly activity but also fueled an already sensationalist media coverage of convicted or alleged Stasi informers.[123] Often, these "Stasi scandals" were directed, rightly or wrongly, against leading PDS politicians from the reformist camp (such as party manager André Brie and party leader Gregor Gysi)[124] and, thus, produced a climate of in-group solidarity, favoring strategies of self-defense and self-victimization. When it came to questions of individual guilt and transitional justice, only a minority of reformers (such as Dietmar Keller) and of nonorthodox radicals supported a stringent prosecution of former GDR officials who were accused of having committed crimes in the past, while the reformist leadership around Gregor Gysi and Lothar Bisky rejected this so-called morally rigorist approach.¹²⁵ Instead, they argued in favor of a so-called tolerant and humanist position,¹²⁶ which meant solidarity with former GDR officials.¹²⁷ A critical reckoning with the past, they argued in accordance with their orthodox colleagues, should not be "the main cause" of the party.¹²⁸

Anti-Communism and Power Politics

Perhaps the key issue that the CPRF and PDS were forced to respond to was the renaissance of anti-communist strategies (which was particularly pronounced in the Yeltsin and Kohl periods). Having been a crucial factor in European politics throughout the twentieth century, the opposition between (alleged or self-declared) communists and anti-communists remained an important issue even after the end of communist rule in Europe—not only, as noted earlier, as part of an anti-totalitarian public discourse but also as a strategic instrument in power politics.

While anti-communism was prevalent in many Central and Eastern European countries, including Germany, as part of the transition process,¹²⁹ Russia even saw violence between communists and the Yeltsin government. As noted previously, Yeltsin had banned the Communist Party by decree in August 1991 and attempted to maintain the ban during the Constitutional Court's trial of the Communist Party. The government also banned the CPRF (briefly) in the aftermath of the October 1992–1993 crisis (the violent standoff between Yeltsin and the Parliament), in large part to interfere with the CPRF's electoral campaigning. In all of this, scholars have noted the regime's heavy dependence on anti-communist rhetoric, particularly during the events of 1993, in the lead-up to the referendum on Yeltsin's super-presidential constitution¹³⁰ and in the 1996 presidential campaign.¹³¹

Not only was the CPRF a strong competitor to the ruling regime but also the very real prospect of CPRF electoral victory terrified oligarchical elites who lent unequivocal support to the government through their central media holdings.¹³² Not only did they deny the CPRF campaign airtime on television but also they kept up an unrelenting barrage of anti-communist rhetoric. As Graeme Gill writes, the media

> reminded readers about the restrictions on foreign travel imposed on people under the Soviet period, the "genocide" and deportation of small national groups under Stalin, suppression of religion, food shortages, the poverty of life on the kolkhoz, the harassment of intellectuals, the role of parapsychologists in the Kremlin under Brezhnev, destruction of the kulaks as a class, and the invasion of Afghanistan, [. . .] food shortages [. . . and] the harassing and repressive actions of the KGB.¹³³

The media predicted a repetition of all of the aforementioned in the event of communist victory. For instance, posters in the lead-up to the 1996 presidential elections declared "the Communist Party hasn't changed its name; it won't change its methods either."[134] This intense media barrage resulted in momentous reversals in public opinion: Despite his single-digit approval rating in January, Yeltsin nonetheless decisively defeated Ziuganov in the second round of the presidential election in July.[135]

The Putin period saw at least a partial abatement of anti-communist rhetoric. However, the regime attempted more than ever to steal the CPRF's monopoly on the Soviet experience. Thus emotive events such as victory in the Great Patriotic War, the space program, etc., were emptied of associations with communism per se and framed as *national* achievements. Whitewashed in this way, they generated legitimacy for the Putin regime, which campaigned on nationalism and statism, undercutting the CPRF's support base.[136]

The regime's actions had two effects. On the one hand, it forced the CPRF to counter with historical narratives of its own, challenging associations with Soviet crimes. The orthodox Marxist-Leninist faction responded in full force. At the same time, the regime's stance (and the failure of the CPRF's electoral bids) eventually led to a reassessment, helping to push the party in the direction of compromise. By the late 1990s, the nationalist and social democratic factions reoriented the strategy of the CPRF: Supporting the government in the Parliament gave the party committee appointments, input into legislation, steady financing and ended harassment from the regime.[137] At the same time, as an ostensibly oppositional and "anti-system" party, the CPRF had to continue to *appear* hostile to the regime, if only through superficial gestures.[138] Thus, like their orthodox counterparts, nationalists and social democrats were also led to push back against the regime's anti-communist narratives.

This was carried out through a number of strategies. First, nationalists and orthodox Marxist-Leninists noted the continuity of the ruling regime with the actors responsible for Soviet collapse. We have already noted that the orthodox Marxist-Leninist and nationalist narratives blamed Gorbachev, Yeltsin and other democratic reformers for collapse and the travails of transition. Not only did this seek to channel popular animus away from communists and onto the government but also CPRF narratives warned of "repeat" betrayal and collapse.[139] Most pressingly, the government's decentralization policies could lead to a breakup of the Russian Federation.[140] Social democrats took a somewhat different approach. Positioning themselves as the champions of a new order that would break with the evils of both the Soviet past and transition, they accused the government of continuity *with the Soviet* regime. Thus they argued that the "old monopolism was replaced by a new one—more aggressive, impatient and corrupt."[141] For instance, the size of the Russian bureaucracy became even larger than in Soviet times and became more corrupt, unaccountable and self-serving, establishing strong connections to the criminal underworld and the oligarchy.[142] Likewise, they noted that homelessness and mortality were worse than in the postwar period,[143] and employment conditions resembled a "prison-camp work regime" akin to the Gulag.[144]

Second, the CPRF (with the exception of the social democratic faction) argued that the anti-communist propaganda currently deployed by the government was also one of the causes of Soviet collapse. In particular, they pointed to the defamation of the Soviet experience in the late 1980s: presenting its history as a series of totalitarian, imperialist regimes, branding collectivist values as mere "herd mentality," courage as fanaticism and state defense structures as repressive apparatuses.[145] Allegedly, this was accompanied by indiscriminately honoring the ostensible "victims" of repression in Soviet period, even Vlasovite (WWII pro-Nazi) traitors.[146] This had important effects: Historical revisionism whipped up nationalism among minorities.[147] It taught youth to disrespect history, to "doubt their fathers."[148] By attacking Vladimir Lenin, it shook the ideological foundations of the regime and created "social disorientation and a paralysis of vigilance" in the Soviet people, facilitating the fall of the regime.[149]

Third, the CPRF members of all factions sought to unmask the ulterior motives of the government's narratives of the Soviet experiences. Most notably, they complained that allusions to the Gulag were used to manipulate public opinion against the CPRF.[150] Memory was also used in political maneuvering and provocation, such as the campaign to remove Lenin from the mausoleum, engineered to discredit a complacent CPRF leadership in the eyes of its supporters, or else to force the party into a radical stance and use radicalism as a pretext for reprisals.[151] The attack on Soviet history, they held, was also used to redirect attention away from the inadequacies of the current regime, including "prostitution and [poverty. . .], the alienation of laborers from property and power, unemployment, wage arrears, and obeisance towards American dictates."[152]

In the context of party politics, the CPRF was forced to use memory in defending its title as *the* successor to the CPSU and against other communist parties vying for this heritage. Indeed, the literature has noted up to a dozen groups claiming the heritage of the banned CPSU in the early 1990s.[153] Admittedly, most of these were outmaneuvered by the CPRF because of its prestige in contesting the ban on the party, the inclusivity of its program and the party's political pragmatism (such as its tolerance of dual party membership).[154] Also important was the CPRF's participation in the 1993 parliamentary elections (from which other communist parties were banned or which they voluntarily boycotted), which gave the CPRF increased visibility and popular acceptance as *the* successor party.[155] Nonetheless, the CPRF had to be wary of straying too far from the Soviet legacy, lest its political space be lost to a party further left (which Richard Sakwa sees as the main restraint preventing the CPRFs social-democratization).[156] After all, a coalition of radical communist parties attained 4.53 percent of the party-list vote in the 1995 parliamentary elections. In memory discourse, these parties were implicitly marginalized as "pretenders" to the CPSU's heritage.

Indeed, only the Russian Communist Workers Party (RKRP) was recognized as being genuinely communist; all others were labeled "sects."[157] The action of CPRF members is telling; at the 1998 Thirtieth CKP-CPSU congress (a federation of post-Soviet communist parties), CPRF delegates voted (unsuccessfully) to *remove* the allusion to the CPSU from the federation's name.[158]

Unlike the CPRF, the PDS did not face significant competitors within the communist or post-communist camp. Instead, the reformist leadership was struggling to overcome the party's image as a "communist" organization and as the "SED successor party," since those attributions raised negative associations (especially in West Germany, where anti-communism had been a crucial feature of the political culture for many decades). Even though there is much evidence that the 1990s saw a renaissance of anti-communism as a strategic factor in German party politics;[159] its exact nature and long-term impact is still to be clarified by historical research. Whereas considerations of transitional justice and of "anti-extremism" led to rather stringent—but not absolute—ostracism in the first years,[160] this national anti-PDS consensus soon gave way to a debate on how to deal with the legacy of state socialism in the unified Germany.

The Social Democratic Party, West Germany's major center-left party, played a key role in these debates, but was divided over how to deal with the new competitors in East Germany. As a reaction to the PDS's electoral success in East Germany in the mid-1990s, social democrats gradually shifted from an exclusionary strategy to one of integration.[161] Starting with Saxony-Anhalt in 1994 and Mecklenburg-West Pomerania in 1998, the PDS was eventually included in several government alliances on a subnational level, and, via Germany's federal chamber (Bundesrat), even cooperated with the center-left "red-green" alliance of Chancellor Gerhard Schröder on a federal level. Thus the Schröder era saw a partial "normalization" of the PDS and a significant decrease of anti-communist rhetoric in German party politics.[162]

However, throughout the 1990s, the PDS faced significant hostility from Germany's conservative camp. Whereas the Kohl government never seriously attempted to ban the PDS (in part due to stringent constitutional requirements), the chancellor's conservative party alliance reacted to PDS electoral success by re-activating anti-communist campaigning strategies, so-called fear campaigns,[163] from West Germany's Cold War period. Those strategies aimed at delegitimizing the PDS in the eyes of its voters and, at the same time, sabotaging potential left-wing alliances between post-communists, social democrats and greens.[164] Most prominently, this was the case in the 1994 *Rote Socken* [red socks] campaign, when conservatives warned against a new "left front."[165] As part of this strategy, historical associations were regularly deployed to link the PDS to alleged communist crimes in the past, such as the division of Germany, the construction of the Berlin Wall, killings on the inner-German border, special (prison) camps but also "the October Revolution" and "the Gulag Archipelago."[166] Among Germany's conservative parties, any post-communist government participation was seen as a "qualitative change"[167] of historical dimensions, which would "shake the very foundations of our democracy."[168] Conservative politicians and journalists even made analogies to Adolf Hitler's *Machtergreifung* [seizure of power], thus evoking associations between post-communists and national socialists.[169]

These anti-communist campaigns had contradictory effects on the PDS's discourse on historical memory. On the surface, they strengthened the party's in-group solidarity and inter-factional cohesion. Whereas the orthodox communists considered anti-communism a capitalist strategy in the class struggle and felt affirmed in their anti-capitalist views,[170] most reformers were also committed to defending so-called democratic communist positions against anti-communist attacks from outside.[171] They considered communism an important historical "liberation ideology"[172] and turned to the commemoration of early communists such as Rosa Luxemburg and Karl Liebknecht, both representing the traditions of communism and of "democratic socialism."[173] Gysi interpreted contemporary campaigns against his party as a continuation of the Cold War and its "almost totalitarian anti-communism" on the Western side of the wall.[174] Moreover, as a response to criticism from social democrats, PDS reformers repeatedly reminded them of their own "historical errors" such as their alleged betrayal of the revolutionary cause in the interwar period.[175]

At the same time, however, orthodox communists and reformers both tried to make use of anti-communism as an argument in their intra-party power struggle. The reformers accused leading orthodox communists not only of pursuing a "primitive" and "inhuman" ideology[176] but also of facilitating conservatives' attempts to delegitimize or even ban the PDS.[177] When, in 2002/2003, reformers, for a short time, seemed to be losing some of their power in the party to more dogmatic elements, long-time reformist leader Gregor Gysi even publicly attacked the "dogmatic left" on the grounds of misusing intra-party tolerance and "pluralism" for an undemocratic cause and seeking to establish a dictatorship.[178] The orthodox communists, in turn, accused reformers of furthering the anti-communist campaigns of their opponents by condemning Stalinism and by appeasing the capitalist class.[179]

These mutual accusations were mostly motivated by incompatible ideological convictions but also linked to different strategic aspirations. Like CPRF social democrats and nationalists, the reformist PDS leadership reoriented the party's strategy during the 1990s from fundamental opposition to cooperation with non-communist forces. In Germany's federal democracy, this meant opening up to parliamentary cooperation and government participation (at first, on the subnational level). Whereas the orthodox communists opposed this strategy and rejected any cooperation with "capitalist" parties,[180] the reformist party leaders were highly interested in overcoming their isolation on the party system level.[181] Memory politics played a significant role in those aspirations, as the party's potential allies such as social democrats and greens linked the possibility of government alliances with post-communists to the latter's willingness to adopt the historical interpretation of anti-totalitarianism and to show that they had "learned from the past."

Moreover, the reformist leadership aspired to expand the party's activities to West Germany, believing that a national presence was the only guarantee of lasting survival. Therefore, they had to attract Western voters who were open to leftist politics but critical of the PDS's communist image and its attitudes toward the past.[182] In order to create "lasting public awareness for the party's critical attitude towards real socialism,"[183] the PDS reformers made concessions to the hegemonic "anti-totalitarian" reading of the state socialist past.[184] In the 2001 Berlin election campaign, for example, reformist leaders conceded that the formation of the SED in 1946 involved "deception, constraints, and repression," and that an apology was owed to the "people of the GDR."[185] At the same time, they considered the construction of the Berlin Wall in 1961 an unjustifiable act and evidence for the inferiority of Stalinism compared to Western capitalism.[186] They expressed regret for the "inhumane border regime," the deaths, injuries, imprisonments and the "injustice," which the SED had been responsible for.[187]

This strategy seemingly helped the party to counter anti-communist campaigns from the conservative camp,[188] to raise support outside its core electorate and to secure its first government participation in the capital in January 2002. In its subsequent coalition agreement with social democrats—negotiated on the PDS side by leading reformist politicians[189]—the PDS even called the Berlin Wall a "symbol of totalitarianism and contempt for mankind," and explicitly accepted the blame for persecuting, imprisoning and killing the SED's opponents; suppressing the 1953 uprising; and other human rights violations,[190] thus accepting the focus of memory politics on communist crimes and communist guilt.[191] Instead of deploying an anti-Western rhetoric, the document called for "reconciliation and inner unity," and accepted the Federal Republic's historical affiliation with the "Western value community."[192] Those positions put forward by the reformist faction differed significantly from previous statements by the party's official "historical commission," a group of renowned Marxist researchers, who, for example, referred to the Berlin Wall's negative effects but also to its stabilizing functions during the Cold War.[193] Thus the reformist leaders had to defend their strategy before their membership as a necessary compromise to gain political power[194] and to counter "lasting fears and worries about the PDS [. . .] in particular in the Western part of the city."[195] However, the orthodox communists uncompromisingly rejected these positions, accusing reformers of distortion of historical facts and a "demagogic unilateral recrimination of the GDR and state-socialism."[196] In their eyes, the Berlin Wall was justified as a means of protection against Western espionage and capitalist propaganda.[197] Thus to them the reformers' historical narratives represented an opportunistic surrender to the "imperialist and social democratic historical ideology" of the Cold War period rather than an act of historical learning.[198]

Conclusion

Thus, taken together, we see that PDS and CPRF historical narratives in the period under scrutiny can be interpreted as reactions to the specific sociopolitical contexts of the time. Although there are many differences between these national contexts, we also see significant commonalities, which somewhat qualify the common perception of East German and Russian uniqueness.[199] Both the Russian and the East German successor parties were confronted with (different kinds of) anti-communist strategies by their opponents, which highlights the notion of anti-totalitarianism or anti-communism as important features of post-socialist societies.[200] Yet, at the same time, the Russian and German successor parties were able to capitalize on nostalgic feelings among those unconvinced by anti-communist elite discourses. Moreover, in comparison to other post-communist parties such as those in Hungary or in Poland,[201] for instance, both Russian communists and German post-communists continued to serve anti-Western sentiments among their voters. This can, at least to some extent, be attributed to the specific national contexts of both countries, which were characterized by feelings of inferiority, injured pride and perceived Western hostility; while this allowed for the rise of a distinct nationalist faction within the CPRF, the PDS upheld a certain East German regionalist identity.

We see the main differences in the field of party politics and political competition. Whereas the CPRF had to defend the communist successorship against challenges from other parties, the PDS sought to downplay its monopolistic status as "successor party" in order to overcome its political isolation. As a result of anti-communist strategies, both PDS reformers and CPRF social democrats and nationalists aimed to maximize political power by moderating their anti-regime policy.

At the same time, it was only in Germany that the Western-dominated party system and its "anti-totalitarian consensus" led some post-communists to adopt some of the hegemonic anti-totalitarian narratives themselves. Most of all, reformist historical narratives were influenced by the existence of an established and strong Social Democratic Party and the PDS reformers' willingness to establish parliamentary cooperation with other center-left forces and to "arrive" and be part of the new Germany.[202] Moreover, aspirations to expand to West Germany made them moderate their anti-Western rhetoric. In the Russian case, by contrast, the context of the political system and the national discourse pulled the CPRF in the direction of nationalism, as the party aimed to ally itself with the parties on the (radical) right under a program of "national liberation." This led—among other factors—to diverging intrafactional dynamics. Following a party split in 2004, the

CRRF finally settled on a nationalist identity, combined with a conciliatory stance toward the Putin regime. The PDS reformers, by contrast, succeeded in strengthening their hegemony and marginalizing the orthodox party faction.[203] By allying itself with Western trade unionists and leftist social democrats, the PDS eventually expanded to West Germany and transformed itself into a new nationwide Left Party (DIE LINKE) between 2005 and 2007. Today, DIE LINKE has settled on an anti-neoliberal platform focusing on left-wing issues such as social inequality and redistribution rather than questions of historical memory. At the same time, debates over the communist past and the character of the GDR have occasionally reemerged and continue to divide the party between different groups and factions fighting for an intra-party hegemony.[204]

As we have demonstrated, and in contrast to simplistic "externalist" accounts, the different national contexts did not, by themselves, determine successor party strategies and identity. At the end of the day, this was a matter of the internal political choice of concrete actors, and neither the PDS nor the CPRF responded homogeneously. At the same time, we also see that national contexts do matter—not in determining a set historical narrative that a party takes, but in establishing the discursive framework to which different factions within a party respond in various ways.

Notes

1 This debate is outlined in more detail in Ekaterina Levintova, "Being the Opposition in Contemporary Russia: The Communist Party of the Russian Federation (KPRF): Among Social Democratic, Marxist-Leninist and Nationalist-Socialist Discourses," *Party Politics* 18 (2012): 728–729.
2 In line with the established literature, we see the CPRF and PDS as successor parties, given that a) the parties consciously framed themselves as (reformed or unreformed) successors, and b) both their supporters and political opponents saw them as such. We label them (post-)communist because they succeeded parties that were self-avowedly communist (striving to realize communism). At the same time, the really existing society in which they ruled is termed "state socialist," while post-1989 (in the USSR's case, post-1991) societies are understood as "post-socialist."
3 This paradigmatic schema, developed in Urban and Solovei's pioneering study (Joan Barth Urban and Valerii D. Solovei, *Russia's Communists at the Crossroads* (Boulder: Westview Press, 1997)), is sometimes presented under slightly different labels. See Judith Devlin, *Slavophiles and Commissars: Enemies of Democracy in Modern Russia* (London: Macmillan Press, 1999), 161–170; M. R. Kholmskaia, "Kommunisty Rossii: mezhdu ortodoksal'nost'yu i reformizmom," in *Politicheskie partii Rossii: istoriia i sovremennost'*, eds. Aleksandr Izrailevič Zevelev et al. (Moskva: ROSSPEN, 2000), 565–569; Ekaterina Levintova, "Being the Opposition in Contemporary Russia"; Richard Sakwa, "Left or Right? CPRF and the Problem of Democratic Consolidation in Russia," *The Journal of Communist Studies and Transition Politics* 14.1 (1998): 138–142. Luke March has proposed a modification, analytically dividing the party into "moderate" and "radical" camps. See Luke March, "For Victory? The Crises and Dilemmas of the Communist Party of the Russian Federation,"

Europe—*Asia Studies* 53 (2001): 263–290; Luke March, *The Communist Party in Post-Soviet Russia* (Manchester: Manchester University Press, 2002); Luke March, "The Pragmatic Radicalism of Russia's Communists," in *The Left Transformed in Post-Communist Societies: The Cases of East-Central Europe, Russia and Ukraine*, eds. Jane Leftwich Curry and Joan Barth Urban (Lanham: Rowman and Littlefield, 2003), 163–208. However, this classification partially overlaps with the earlier triad (nationalists and social democrats are simply collapsed into the "moderate" faction). It also reflects March's greater emphasis on *strategy* rather than *ideology*, which is less appropriate for the purposes of this chapter.

4 This dual schema has been used by most researchers to account for conflict within the PDS, for example, Franz Oswald, "The Party of Democratic Socialism: Ex-Communists Entrenched as East German Regional Protest Party," *Journal of Communist Studies and Transition Politics* 12.2 (1996): 179; Michael Gerth, *Die PDS und die ostdeutsche Gesellschaft im Transformationsprozess: Wahlerfolg und politisch-kulturelle Kontinuitäten* (Hamburg: Verlag Dr. Kovač, 2003), 186–188; Jürgen Lang, *Ist die PDS eine demokratische Partei? Eine extremismustheoretische Untersuchung* (Baden-Baden: Nomos, 2003); Michael Koß, "Durch die Krise zum Erfolg? Die PDS und ihr langer Weg nach Westen," in *Die Linkspartei: Zeitgemäße Idee oder Bündnis ohne Zukunft?*, eds. Tim Spier, Felix Butzlaff, Matthias Micus and Franz Walter (Wiesbaden: VS Verlag für Sozialwissenschaften, 2007), 128; Christian Lannert, *"Vorwärts und nicht vergessen"? Die Vergangenheitspolitik der Partei DIE LINKE und ihrer Vorgängerin PDS* (Göttingen: Wallstein, 2012), 39–41. Some studies have developed this into a four-fold classification, following the lead of PDS leader Gregor Gysi (Gregor Gysi, "'Ich kandidiere nicht erneut für den Vorsitz': Brief an die Mitglieder des Bundesvorstandes und des Bundesparteirates der PDS, 30. November 1992," in Gregor Gysi, *Das war's. Noch lange nicht!*, 3rd edition (München: Econ Taschenbuch, 2001 [1992]), 309–312). However, not all of those groups showed equal interest in questions concerning the state-socialist past and historical memory. For the comparative purpose of this chapter, therefore, the terms "reformist" and "reformers" will be used both for "reform socialists" and "reform pragmatists." While the reform socialists are considered more ideologically informed and devoted to the socialist perspective, the pragmatists are believed to be more interested in pragmatic politics and in administrating the status quo. See Michael Brie, "Die PDS—Strategiebildung im Spannungsfeld von gesellschaftlichen Konfliktlinien und politischer Identität," in *Die PDS im Parteiensystem*, eds. Michael Brie and Rudolf Woderich (Berlin: Dietz, 2000), 33–34; Eva Sturm, *"Und der Zukunft zugewandt"? Eine Untersuchung der "Politikfähigkeit" der PDS* (Opladen: Leske + Budrich, 2000), 100. The minor party faction of radical fundamentalists will be (mostly) ignored in this chapter; while their oppositional attitudes towards capitalist society resemble those of the orthodox Communists, their positions towards historical memory do not differ significantly from the "radical-moralist" wing of the reformist faction.

5 John Ishiyama, "The Sickle or the Rose? Previous Regime Types and the Evolution of the Ex-Communist Parties in Post-Communist Politics," *Comparative Political Studies* 30 (1997): 299–330; John Ishiyama, "Strange Bedfellows: Explaining Political Cooperation Between Communist-Successor Parties and Nationalists in Eastern Europe," *Nations and Nationalism* 4 (1998): 61–85; John Ishiyama, "The Communist Successor Parties and Party Organizational Development in Post-Communist Politics," *Political Science Research Quarterly* 52 (1999): 87–112; John Ishiyama, "Candidate Recruitment, Party Organisation and the Communist Successor Parties: The Cases of the MSzP, the KPRF

and the LDDP," *Europe—Asia Studies* 52.5 (2000): 875–896; John Ishiyama, "Europeanization and the Communist Successor Parties in Post-Communist Politics," *Politics & Policy* 34.1 (2006): 3–29; John Ishiyama, "Historical Legacies and the Size of the Red—Brown Vote in Post-Communist Politics," *Communist and Post-Communist Studies* 42.4 (2009): 485–504. Organizational structure, Ishiyama argues, is influenced further by presidential and electoral systems. Agreeing with this analysis, Daniel Ziblatt and Nick Biziouras have contended that this also depends on the mode of transition from state socialism. See Daniel Ziblatt and Nick Biziouras, "Doomed to be Radicals? Organization, Ideology, and the Communist Successor Parties in East Central Europe," in *The Communist Successor Parties of Central and Eastern Europe*, eds. András Bozóki and John Ishiyama (Armonk: M. E. Sharpe, 2002), 287–302.

6 Ishiyama, "The Sickle or the Rose?" 300.
7 For instance, Urban (who elsewhere developed the CPRF factional typology cited earlier), nonetheless generalizes that Soviet successor parties remained neo-Leninist, while Central European ones moved in the direction of social democracy. Notably, the PDS is listed as an exception: Joan Barth Urban, "The Post-Communist Left: Divergent Trajectories, Shared Legacies," in *The Left Transformed in Post-Communist Societies: The Cases of East-Central Europe, Russia and Ukraine*, eds. Jane Leftwich Curry and Joan Barth Urban (Lanham: Rowman and Littlefield, 2003), 245.
8 It should be noted that this historiographic description is itself a generalization. Many studies fall somewhere between internalism and externalism, but have less analytical clarity. There are also exceptions, for instance, Anna Grzymala-Busse's detailed comparative study of Central European successor parties, which largely sided with the internalist interpretation. See Anna Grzymala-Busse, *Redeeming the Communist Past: The Regeneration of Communist Parties in East Central Europe* (Cambridge: Cambridge University Press, 2002).
9 Urban, "The Post-Communist Left," 245; Daniel F. Ziblatt, "The Adaptation of Ex-Communist Parties to Post-Communist East Central Europe: A Comparative Study of the East German and Hungarian Ex-Communist Parties," *Communist and Post-Communist Studies* 31.2 (1998): 119–137; March, "The Pragmatic Radicalism of Russia's Communists," 164–169.
10 As Halbwachs writes, "A man must often appeal to others' remembrances to evoke his own past. He goes back to reference points determined by society, hence outside himself." Maurice Halbwachs, *The Collective Memory*, trans. Francis J. Ditter Jr. and Vida Yazdi Ditter (New York: Harper and Row, 1980 [1950]), 51.
11 Jeremy Lester, "Overdosing on Nationalism: Gennadii Zyuganov and the Communist Party of the Russian Federation," *New Left Review* 221 (1997): 36; March, "For Victory?" 265; March, *The Communist Party in Post-Soviet Russia*, 27.
12 Ishiyama, "The Sickle or the Rose?" 307–308; March, *The Communist Party in Post-Soviet Russia*, 169; S. F. Cherniakhovskii, *Protivorechivost' kommunisticheskoi oppozitsii v sovremennoi Rossii* (Moskva: Mezhdunarodnyj Nezavisimyj Ekologo-Politologicheskij Universitet, 2003), 177.
13 March, "The Pragmatic Radicalism of Russia's Communists," 172; Devlin, *Slavophiles and Commissars*, 173; Lester, "Overdosing on Nationalism," 36; Urban, "The Post-Communist Left," 246.
14 Antony Kalashnikov, "Strength in Diversity: Multiple Memories of the Soviet Past in the Russian Communist Party (CPRF), 1993-2004," *Nationalities Papers: The Journal of Nationalism and Ethnicity* 45.3 (2017): 370–392.
15 In line with this maximalist goal, they lobbied the party to pursue a confrontational stance toward the government, both in parliament and on the streets.

Communist Successors and Narratives 63

16 Quoted in Richard Kosolapov, "Uverenno torit' tropu v budushchee: Doklad R. Kosolapova 'O resheniiakh XX i XXII s'ezdov KPSS po voprosu *O kul'te lichnosti i ego posledstviiakh* na Chrezvychainom XXXII s'ezde SKP—KPSS 21 iiulia 2001 g.," *PartArkhiv INDEM* online archive, July 21, 2001; Richard Kosolapov, "Nezagadochnyi Stalin: Doktor filosofskikh nauk, professor Richard Kosolapov v besede s Viktorom Kozhemiako," *Sovetskaia Rossiia*, January 15, 1998.
17 Quoted in Kosolapov, "Uverenno torit' tropu." See also Anatolii Luk'ianov et al., "Tirran kakogo kalibra?" *Tribuna*, March 5, 2003.
18 Viktor Iliukhin, "Korruptsiia vchera i segodnia," *Zavtra*, July 17, 2001.
19 Nikolai Bindiukov, "O pozitsii KPRF po natsional'nomu voprosu (Doklad na IV Plenume TsK KPRF 14 fevralia 1998 goda)," *PartArkhiv INDEM* online archive, February 14, 1998; Richard Kosolapov, *Stalin i Lenin*, Moskva: ZAO "Gazeta Pravda," 2000, 499.
20 Albert Makashov and A. Prosvirin, "Monakh i voin (Beseda generala Al'berta Makashova s igumenom Aleksiem (Prosvirinym)," *Zavtra*, January 19, 1999.
21 The social democrats' flexible programme usually involved support for a mixed economy and strengthening democratic governance.
22 Valentin Kuptsov, *V. A. Kuptsov. Izbrannye vystupleniia (1991–2001)* (Moskva: Parad, 2001), 164–165.
23 Iurii Masliukov, "Smotret' v budushchee (Strategiia promyshlennogo razvitiia strany)," *Zavtra*, September 5, 2000; Ivan Mel'nikov, "Bez bol'shoi nauki u rossii net budushchego: Obrashchenie k uchenym, rabotnikam nauchno-tekhnicheskoi sfery i obrazovaniia Rossii k nauchnym kollektivam, sovetam, soiuzam, obshchestvam i ob'edineniiam, rossiiskim profsoiuzam rabotnikov nauchno-tekhnicheskoi sfery," *Sovetskaia Rossiia*, September 19, 2000; Gennadii Seleznev, "Gennadii Seleznev, predsedatel' Gosudarstvennoi Dumy: Obrazovanie dolzhno stat' prioritetnym," *Uchitel'skaia gazeta*, March 27, 2002.
24 The nationalist faction advocated statism, a mixed economy and collaboration with the government.
25 Gennadii Ziuganov, *Derzhava* (Moskva: Informpechat, 1994), 41; Gennadii Ziuganov, "Kogda Otechestvo v opasnosti: Beseda korrespondenta 'Pravdy' Vladimira Bol'shakova s liderom KPRF i NPSR Gennadiem Ziuganovym," *Pravda*, February 9, 1999.
26 Iurii Belov, "S planety SSSR: Sovetskii chelovek v labirinte istorii," *Sovetskaia Rossiia*, November 16, 2000; Aleksandr Shabanov and Stanislav Terekhov, *Sovremennyi etap istoricheskogo spora o modeli razvitiia obshchestva: K voprosu o roli ideologii gosudarstvennogo patriotizma pri perekhode k novomu urovniu razvitiia obshchestva* (Moskva: Sistema, 1994), 52; Gennadii Ziuganov, *Manifest NPSR: Politichestkii doklad Vtoromu s'ezdu narodno-patrioticheskogo Soiuza Rossii* (Moskva: ZAO "Gazeta Pravda," 1998), 13–14.
27 Iurii Belov, "Russkii putnik (Beseda Aleksandra Prokhanova i sekretaria Leningradskogo obkoma KPRF Iuriia Belova)," *Zavtra*, March 23, 1999; Iurii Belov, "Sim pobedishi (o edinstve sotsializma i patriotizma)," *Sovetskaia Rossiia*, August 19, 1999; Aleksandr Shabanov et al., *Dukhovnaia bor'ba* (Moskva: Izdatel'stvo Moskovskogo Universiteta, 1997), 172–173.
28 Dan Hough, Michael Koß and Jonathan Olsen, *The Left Party in Contemporary German Politics* (Basingstoke: Palgrave Macmillan, 2007), 16.
29 Brie, "Die PDS," 32; Peter Barker, "From the SED to the PDS: Continuity or Renewal?" in *The Party of Democratic Socialism in Germany: Modern Post-Communism or Nostalgic Populism?*, ed. Peter Barker (Amsterdam and Atlanta: Rodopi, 1998), 2.

30 Hough et al., *The Left Party in Contemporary German Politics*, 15; Jonathan Olsen, "Germany's PDS and Varieties of 'Post-Communist' Socialism," *Problems of Post-Communism* 45.6 (1998): 45.
31 Barker, "From the SED to the PDS," 1.
32 Barker, "From the SED to the PDS," 4.
33 Gregor Gysi, quoted in Lothar Hornbogen, Detlef Nakath and Gert-Rüdiger Stephan, eds., *Außerordentlicher Parteitag der SED/PDS. Protokoll der Beratungen am 8./9. und 16./17. Dezember 1989 in Berlin* (Berlin: Karl Dietz Verlag, 1999), 5; André Brie, *Ich tauche nicht ab: Selbstzeugnisse und Reflexionen* (Berlin: Edition Ost, 1996), 126; also see Barker, "From the SED to the PDS," 6–8.
34 Ralph Guentzel, "Modernity Socialism versus Orthodox Marxism: Ideological Strife in the Party of Democratic Socialism (PDS), 1993-1999," *Historian* 74.4 (2012): 714–715.
35 Gregor Gysi, "Was Will Die PDS in Deutschland?," in *Wir brauchen einen dritten Weg: Selbstverständnis und Programm der PDS*, ed. Gregor Gysi (Hamburg: Konkret Literatur Verlag, 1990), 15–19; Brie, *Ich tauche nicht ab*, 124–135; Guentzel, "Modernity Socialism versus Orthodox Marxism," 715–717; Brie, "Die PDS," 33–34.
36 Guentzel, "Modernity Socialism versus Orthodox Marxism," 711; Brie, "Die PDS," 35; Barker, "From the SED to the PDS," 6.
37 David F. Patton, *Out of the East: From PDS to Left Party in Unified Germany* (Albany: State University of New York Press, 2011), 31–35; Brie, "Die PDS," 30.
38 Dietmar Keller, "Zwischen Anspruch und eigener Blockade: Zu einigen Fragen des Verhältnisses der PDS zur Geschichte der SED und der DDR," in *Die PDS: Postkommunistische Kaderorganisation, ostdeutscher Traditionsverein oder linke Volkspartei? Empirische Befunde und kontroverse Analysen*, eds. Michael Brie, Martin Herzig and Thomas Koch (Cologne: PapyRossa, 1995), 131–145.
39 Brie, "Die PDS," 35; Thomas A. Baylis, "Political Adaptation in Germany's Post-Communist Party of Democratic Socialism," in *The Left Transformed in Post-Communist Societies: The Cases of East-Central Europe, Russia and Ukraine*, eds. Jane Leftwich Curry and Joan Barth Urban (Lanham: Rowman and Littlefield, 2003), 151.
40 Guentzel, "Modernity Socialism versus Orthodox Marxism," 716; Brie, "Die PDS," 34.
41 Sahra Wagenknecht, "Marxismus und Opportunismus—Kämpfe in der Sozialistischen Bewegung gestern und heute," *Weißenseer Blätter* 92.4 (1992): 12–26.
42 Ellen Brombacher, "Zum Sonderparteitag vom Dezember 1989," in *Die PDS—Herkunft und Selbstverständnis: Eine politisch-historische Debatte*, eds. Lothar Bisky, Jochen Czerny, Herbert Mayer and Michael Schumann (Berlin: Dietz, 1996), 147; Sebastian Prinz, *Die programmatische Entwicklung der PDS: Kontinuität und Wandel der Politik einer sozialistischen Partei* (Wiesbaden: VS Verlag für Sozialwissenschaften, 2010), 259–260.
43 Thomas Lindenberger, "Experts with a Cause: A Future for GDR History Beyond Memory Governance and Ostalgie in Unified Germany," in *Remembering Communism: Private and Public Recollections of Lived Experience in Southeast Europe*, eds. Maria Todorova, Augusta Dimou and Stefan Troebst (Budapest and New York: CEU Press, 2014), 29–42.
44 Neil Munro, "Russia's Persistent Communist Legacy: Nostalgia, Reaction and Reactionary Expectations," *Studies in Public Policy* 409 (2006): 293; March, *The Communist Party in Post-Soviet Russia*, 109.
45 Svetlana Boym, *The Future of Nostalgia* (New York: Basic Books, 2001), 49–56; Lindenberger, "Experts with a Cause," 39.

46 Joakim Ekman and Jonas Linde, "Communist Nostalgia and the Consolidation of Democracy in Central and Eastern Europe," *Journal of Communist Studies and Transition Politics* 21.3 (2005): 354–374.
47 Munro, "Russia's Persistent Communist Legacy," 292; also see Cherniakhovskii, *Protivorechivost' kommunisticheskoi oppozitsii v sovremennoi Rossii*, 180–181.
48 "'Stsenarii ekonomicheskogo razvitiia narodnogo khoziaistva' predstavil segodnia na press-konferentsii odin iz glavnykh razrabotchikov ekonomicheskoi programmy kommunistov, deputat Dumy Iurii Masliukov, kotoryi byl poslednim predsedatelem Gosplana SSSR," *Vestnik "Politicheskii Kalendar,"* June 27, 1996.
49 For instance, when serving as Minister of Industry, Iurii Masliukov kept facing accusations of trying to restore elements of the Soviet economy, presumably because of his former position as head of Gosplan. Iurii Masliukov, "Zhestkim davleniem—izmenit' kurs," *Zavtra*, January 21, 1997; Iurii Masliukov and E. Rossel, "Predlozheniia E. Rosselia i Iu. Masliukova," *Nezavisimaia Gazeta*, October 2, 1998.
50 R. W. Davies, *Soviet History in the Yeltsin Era* (Basingstoke: Macmillan Press, 1997).
51 Anne White, "The Memorial Society in the Russian Provinces," *Europe—Asia Studies* 47.8 (1995): 1343–1366.
52 Iurii Belov, "Udary po stvolu," *Sovetskaia Rossiia*, March 19, 1997; Gennadii Ziuganov, "Vozrozhdenie Rossii i mezhdunarodnoe polozhenie," *Pravda*, December 10, 1993, 18–19; Gennadii Ziuganov, "Tselilis' v kommunizm—popali v Rossiiu," *Sovetskaia Rossiia*, October 7, 1999.
53 Respectively, Belov, "Russkii putnik"; Belov, "S planet SSSR"; Gennadii Ziuganov, *Rossiia i sovremennyi mir* (Moskva: IIA "Obozrevatel," 1995), 35–36.
54 Iurii Belov, "Razmezhevanie neizbezhno. K X s"ezdu KPRF," *Sovetskaia Rossiia*, February 17, 2004; Gennadii Ziuganov, *Znat' i deistvovat': otvety na voprosy* (Moskva: MP Paleia, 1996), 11; Gennadii Ziuganov, "K piatiletiiu KPRF (vstupitel'noe slovo Predsedatelia TsK KPRF G. A. Ziuganova na Plenume TsK KPRF 14 fevralia 1998 goda)," *PartArkhiv INDEM online archive*, February 14, 1998.
55 Viktor Iliukhin, *Spasti Rossiiu: Stat'i vystupleniia, analitichestie materialy, pis'ma predsedatelia Komiteta Gosudarstvennoi Dumy po bezopasnosti* (Moskva: Unita, 1995), 17–19; Kosolapov, *Stalin i Lenin*; Makashov and Prosvirin, "Monakh i voin."
56 Kosolapov, "Uverenno torit' tropu v budushchee"; Kosolapov, "Nezagadochnyi Stalin."
57 Kosolapov, "Uverenno torit' tropu v budushchee."
58 Viktor Iliukhin, "Press-konferentsiia V. Iliukhina," *Biulleten' Levogo informtsentra* 347.36 (September 1998); Kosolapov, "Uverenno torit' tropu v budushchee."
59 Iliukhin, *Spasti Rossiiu*, 17–19; Richard Kosolapov, *Istina iz Rossii* (Tver': Severnaia Korona, 2004), 441–442; Vasilii Safronchuk, "Oazis sleva: Trekhstoronniaia vstrecha v Tripoli," *Sovetskaia Rossiia*, October 26, 2000.
60 Quoted in T. Avaliani, "Obrashchenie v Prezidium TsK KPRF," *PartArkhiv INDEM* online archive, March 10, 1998; Kosolapov, *Istina iz Rossii*, 20–21, 441–442; Anatolii Luk'ianov, *V vodovorote rossiiskoi smuty (razmyshleniia, dialogi, dokumenty)* (Moskva: Kniga i biznes, 1999), 99–100.
61 Gennadii Seleznev, *Vsia vlast'—zakonu! Zakonodatel'stvo i traditsii ukaznogo prava v Rossii* (Moskva: Gruppa "Segodniia," 1997), 50–52.

62 Kuptsov, V. A. *Kuptsov*, 93–94; Gennadii Seleznev, "Novomu spikeru blizka shvedskaia model," *Nezavisimaia Gazeta*, January 19, 1996.
63 Kuptsov, V. A. *Kuptsov*, 93–95; Iurii Masliukov, "Iurii Masliukov: 'Reformy— eto razvitie.' Dialog Aleksandra Prokhanova s Iuriem Masliukovym," *Zavtra*, August 1, 1996; Gennadii Seleznev et al., *Dvizhenie "Rossiia": vzgliad v budushchee* (Moskva: Graal, 2000).
64 Valentin Kuptsov, "Pakhar' izbiratel'nogo polia: Beseda s pervym zamestitelem predsedatelia Tsentral'nogo Komiteta KPRF V. A. Kuptsovym," *Pravda*, October 14, 1999; Sergei Potapov, "Doklad Potapova S. A.," *PartArkhiv INDEM online archive*, July 19, 2004; Ivan Mel'nikov, "Shtab pobedy (Zamestitel' predsedatelia TsK KPRF Ivan Mel'nikov otvechaet na voprosy Nikolaia Anisina)," *Zavtra*, February 29, 2000.
65 Hilary Appel, "Anti-Communist Justice and Founding the Post-Communist Order: Lustration and Restitution in Central Europe," *East European Politics and Societies* 19.3 (2005): 379–405.
66 Thomas Schaarschmidt, "Auf dem Weg zu einem neuen antitotalitären Grundkonsens? Die Erinnerung an die Diktaturvergangenheit und der Übergang zur Demokratie in Deutschland nach 1945 und 1989," in *Das Ende des Kommunismus: Die Überwindung der Diktaturen in Europa und ihre Folgen*, eds. Thomas Großbölting, Raj Kollmorgen, Sascha Möbius and Rüdiger Schmidt (Essen: Klartext, 2010), 31–32.
67 Andrew H. Beattie, *Playing Politics with History: The Bundestag Inquiries into East Germany* (New York and Oxford: Berghahn Books, 2008); Deutscher Bundestag, "Entschließungsantrag CDU/CSU, SPD, F.D.P., Bündnis 90/Die Grünen zum Bericht der Enquete-Kommission 'Aufarbeitung von Geschichte und Folgen der SED-Diktatur in Deutschland,'" *Drucksache* 12.7983, June 16, 1994, 5.
68 Schaarschmidt, "Auf dem Weg zu einem neuen antitotalitären Grundkonsens?," 35.
69 Lindenberger, "Experts with a Cause," 33.
70 Appel, "Anti-Communist Justice," 384–385; Lindenberger, "Experts with a Cause," 32–33; Jan-Werner Müller, "East Germany: Incorporation, Tainted Truth, and the Double Division," in *The Politics of Memory: Transitional Justice in Democratizing Societies*, eds. Alexandra Barahona De Brito, Carmen Gonzalez Enriquez and Paloma Aguilar (Oxford: University Press, 2001), 248–274; Helga A. Welsh, "Dealing with the Communist Past: Central and East European Experiences After 1990," *Europe—Asia Studies* 48.3 (1996): 418.
71 Deutscher Bundestag, "Entschließungsantrag," 5. See Hermann Weber, "Rewriting the History of the German Democratic Republic: The Work of the Commission of Inquiry," in *Rewriting the German Past: History and Identity in the New Germany*, eds. Reinhard Alter and Peter Monteath (New Jersey: Humanities Press, 1997), 197–207.
72 Beattie, *Playing Politics with History*, 11.
73 Deutscher Bundestag, "Entschließungsantrag," 5. As Social Democratic commissioner Hartmut Soell stated, the inquiry was supposed to "delegitimize the SED and its leadership as the main bearers of responsibility for the left-wing variant of the totalitarian temptation in Germany's most recent history." Deutscher Bundestag, "Stenographischer Bericht: 93. Sitzung," *Plenarprotokoll* 12.93, May 20, 1992.
74 Michael Schumann, quoted in Hornbogen et al., *Außerordentlicher Parteitag der SED/PDS*, 191. See also Klaus Höpcke, "Zur Eröffnung der Konferenz," in *Der Stalinismus der KPD und SED—Wurzeln, Wirkungen, Folgen: Materialien der Konferenz der Historischen Kommission beim Parteivorstand der PDS am*

17./18. November 1990, ed. Historische Kommission beim Parteivorstand der PDS (Berlin: Eigenverlag, 1991 [1990]), 5.
75 Michael Schumann, quoted in Hornbogen, Nakath and Stephan, *Außerordentlicher Parteitag der SED/PDS*, 191.
76 Deutscher Bundestag, "Stenographischer Bericht: 234. Sitzung," *Plenarprotokoll* 12.234, June 17, 1994, 20449.
77 Gregor Gysi, "Was Will Die PDS in Deutschland?," in Gregor Gysi, *Wir brauchen einen dritten Weg*, 13; also see Dan Hough, *The Fall and Rise of the PDS in Eastern Germany* (Birmingham: University Press, 2001), 28.
78 Gregor Gysi, quoted in Hornbogen et al., *Außerordentlicher Parteitag der SED/PDS*, 51; Brie, *Ich tauche nicht ab*, 176–177.
79 André Brie, "Die PDS und die Aufarbeitung deutscher Geschichte," *Neues Deutschland*, March 7/8, 1992; Brie, *Ich tauche nicht ab*, 186–187.
80 Deutscher Bundestag, "Stenographischer Bericht: 234: Sitzung," *Plenarprotokoll* 12.234, June 17, 1994, 20449; Lannert, *"Vorwärts und nicht vergessen"?*, 98–99; Beattie, *Playing Politics with History*, 95; Hough, *The Fall and Rise of the PDS in Eastern Germany*, 156.
81 Michael Schumann, quoted in Hornbogen et al., *Außerordentlicher Parteitag der SED/PDS*, 185.
82 Michael Schumann, quoted in Hornbogen et al., *Außerordentlicher Parteitag der SED/PDS*, 188.
83 Prinz, *Die programmatische Entwicklung der PDS*, 279–286.
84 ADS, BT/12.WP—009: Dietmar Keller, "Anregendes und Streitbares für eine Diskussion zum Thema: Diktaturen in Deutschland/'diktatorische Regierungsformen' in Deutschland. Material für die Fraktionssitzung am Dienstag, 10.11.1992. Bonn," November 5, 1992.
85 ADS, BT/12.WP—007: Festlegungsprotokoll der Fraktionssitzung vom 19.05.1992; Dietmar Keller, *In den Mühlen der Ebene: Unzeitgemäße Erinnerungen* (Berlin: Dietz, 2012), 224–227.
86 Brie, *Ich tauche nicht ab*, 171–178.
87 Ellen Brombacher, Rolf Priemer, Heinz Stehr and Sahra Wagenknecht, *Zu Aspekten des "modernen" Antikommunismus* (Essen: Eigendruck, 1993).
88 Wagenknecht, "Marxismus und Opportunismus."
89 Wagenknecht, "Marxismus und Opportunismus," 22.
90 Sahra Wagenknecht, *Antisozialistische Strategien im Zeitalter der Systemauseinandersetzung: Zwei Taktiken im Kampf gegen die sozialistische Welt* (Bonn: Pahl-Rugenstein, 1995), 7–9; see Sturm, *"Und der Zukunft zugewandt"?*, 123–126.
91 Brombacher, "Zum Sonderparteitag vom Dezember 1989," 148.
92 March, *The Communist Party in Post-Soviet Russia*, 110.
93 For a discussion of the sources of anti-Westernism, see Devlin, *Slavophiles and Commissars*.
94 It also formed the basis of so-called red-brown alliances in the 1990s, where the CPRF (spearheaded by the nationalist faction) formed coalitions with right-wing parties, in the name of national salvation.
95 Nikolai Bindiukov, *Globalizatsiia i Rossiia: paradigm, sotsial'no-politichestkii aspect, strategiia levykh sil* (Moskva: ITRK, 2004), 48–53.
96 Kosolapov, *Istina iz Rossii*, 384–387; Nikolai Bindiukov and Petr Lopata, *Osobaia Tret'ia Sila—novyi politicheskii fenomen* (Moskva: ITRK, 1999), 49, 58; Anatolii Luk'ianov, "Na poroge tret'ego tysiacheletiia," *Obozrevatel'-Observer, Informatsionno-analiticheskii zhurnal* 112.5 (May 1999).
97 Gennadii Ziuganov, *Globalizatsiia i sud'ba chelovechestva* (Moskva: Molodaia gvardiia, 2002), 121–124.

98 Gennadii Ziuganov, *Sovremennaia russkaia ideia i gosudarstvo* (Moskva: RAU-Korporatsiia, 1995); Gennadii Ziuganov, "Russkaia al'ternativa," *Pravda*, December 7, 2001.
99 Shabanov and Terekhov, *Sovremennyi etap istoricheskogo spora o modeli razvitiia obshchestva*; Shabanov et al., *Dukhovnaia bor'ba*.
100 Viktor Kuptsov, "O podgotovke VII s'ezda partii i zadachakh partiinykh organizatsii," *PartArkhiv INDEM* online archive, September 21, 2000; Iurii Mel'nikov, "Vozrozhdenie solidarnosti: Beseda zamestitelia predsedatelia Tsentral'nogo Komiteta KPRF Ivana Mel'nikova i politicheskogo obozrevatelia 'Pravdy Rossii' Viktora Trushkova," *Pravda Rossii: Gazeta Kommunisticheskoi partii Rossiiskoi Federatsii*, January 16, 2002; Sergei Potapov, "Sergei Potapov: nyneshnee rukovodstvo KPRF na obnovlenie nesposobno," *PartArkhiv INDEM* online archive, June 25, 2004.
101 Quoted in Iurii Belov, "Odna Rossiia, nam drugoi ne znat," *Sovetskaia Rossiia*, November 23, 1996; Shabanov et al., *Dukhovnaia bor'ba*, 278; Ziuganov, "Vozrozhdenie Rossii i mezhdunarodnoe polozhenie."
102 Quoted in Gennadii Ziuganov, *Veriu v Rossiiu* (Voronezh: Gennadii Ziuganov, 1995), 50–51; Iurii Belov, "Na rasput'e: Grekhi i mucheniia intelligentsii," *Sovetskaia Rossiia*, November 16, 1999; Kosolapov, *Istina iz Rossii*, 382.
103 Bindiukov and Lopata, *Osobaia Tret'ia Sila*, 87; Luk'ianov, *V vodovorote rossiiskoi smuty*, 268; Ziuganov, *Znat' i deistvovat'*, 36.
104 Iurii Belov, "U perepravy: KPRF, kak i vsia Rossiia, nakanune surovykh ispytanii," *Sovetskaia Rossiia*, June 18, 1998; Iurii Belov, "Na semi vetrakh: Otvet moim kritikam," *Sovetskaia Rossiia*, February 22, 2001; Iurii Belov, "Ispolin: Stalin i russkii vopros," *Sovetskaia Rossiia*, March 4, 2003.
105 Iliukhin, *Spasti Rossiiu*, 72–73. Specific historians were rarely addressed directly; the CPRF preferred to the battle against "general" heresies (although Belov and Makashov derisively mentioned Volkogonov, Radzinskii and Tucker). See Belov, "Na rasput'e"; Makashov and Prosvirin, "Monakh i voin."
106 Ivo Bozic, "Der ferne Westen: Ostdeutsche Heimatliebe und Antiamerikanismus in der PDS," in *Nichts gegen Amerika: Linker Antiamerikanismus und seine lange Geschichte*, ed. Michael Hahn (Hamburg: Konkret Literatur Verlag, 2003), 66–76.
107 Andreas Rödder, *21.0: Eine kurze Geschichte der Gegenwart* (München: C.H. Beck, 2015), 203; Jan-Werner Müller, "East Germany."
108 Hough, *The Fall and Rise of the PDS in Eastern Germany*, 130.
109 Lindenberger, "Experts with a Cause," 83–88.
110 Gero Neugebauer, "The Party of Democratic Socialism in Germany: Post Communists with a New Socialist Identity or as Replacement of Social Democracy?" in *The Crisis of Communism and Party Change: The Evolution of West European Communist and Post-Communist Parties*, eds. Joan Botella and Luís Ramiro (Barcelona: Institut de Ciències Polítiques i Socials, 2003), 183.
111 Lindenberger, "Experts with a Cause," 39.
112 ADS, PDS-PV-140: André Brie, Strategie der PDS zu den Wahlen 1994 (Entwurf), vertraulich. Vorlage für den Parteivorstand der PDS zu einer Wahlstrategie 1994. 10. Dezember 1992; Lannert, *"Vorwärts und nicht vergessen"?*, 138–144.
113 Dietmar Bartsch, ed., *Programm der Partei des Demokratischen Sozialismus: Beschlossen von der 1. Tagung des 3. Parteitages der PDS, 29. bis 31. Januar 1993* (Berlin: PDS, 1998), 5, 11; see Hough, *The Fall and Rise of the PDS in Eastern Germany*.
114 Oswald, "The Party of Democratic Socialism."
115 Beattie, *Playing Politics with History*, 41. While the orthodox Communists highlighted the interests of the Western capitalist class, the reformers underlined the cultural differences between East and West.

116 Beattie, *Playing Politics with History*, 39.
117 Gregor Gysi, *Ingolstädter Manifest: Wir—mitten in Europa: Plädoyer für einen neuen Gesellschaftsvertrag* (Berlin: PDS, 1994), 4; Gregor Gysi, *Zwölf Thesen für eine Politik des modernen Sozialismus: Gerechtigkeit ist modern: Eine notwendige Antwort auf Gerhard Schröder und Tony Blair* (Berlin: Rosa-Luxemburg-Stiftung, 1999), 5.
118 Gregor Gysi, quoted in Lannert, *"Vorwärts und nicht vergessen"?*, 74; ADS, PDS-LV MV, Alt-Sign. 2008-XVII-109: Helmut Holter, Rede auf der Landesbasiskonferenz der PDS Mecklenburg-Vorpommern am 29. February 1992, 10.
119 Neugebauer, "The Party of Democratic Socialism in Germany," 193.
120 Lannert, *"Vorwärts und nicht vergessen"?*, 138–141.
121 Stefan Berger, "Former GDR Historians in the Reunified Germany: An Alternative Historical Culture and Its Attempts to Come to Terms with the GDR Past," *Journal of Contemporary History* 38 (2003): 79.
122 ADS, BT/12.WP-008: Uwe-Jens Heuer, Ekkehard Lieberam, and Michael Schumann, Der Honecker-Prozeß und wir. Bonn, 18.09.1992; ADS, BT/12.WP-008: Festlegungsprotokoll der 21. Sitzung der Abgeordnetengruppe am 22.09.1992; Müller, "East Germany," 260; Lannert, *"Vorwärts und nicht vergessen"?*, 158–162.
123 Beattie, *Playing Politics with History*, 3.
124 While André Brie had to come out as a former Stasi informer in 1992, Gregor Gysi denied the allegations brought against him and, to date, no clear evidence has been found. See Jens König, *Gregor Gysi: Eine Biographie* (Berlin: Rowohlt, 2005), 183–184.
125 Gysi, " 'Ich kandidiere nicht erneut für den Vorsitz,' " 310.
126 Gysi, " 'Ich kandidiere nicht erneut für den Vorsitz' "; ADS, PDS-PV-135: Sachprotokoll der Tagung des Parteivorstandes am 26. Oktober 1992, 9.
127 Hough, *The Fall and Rise of the PDS in Eastern Germany*, 153. For example, the party board declared its solidarity with former Stasi employees "unless they had committed any crimes against humanity" (ADS, PDS-PV-140: Erklärung zum Beschluß des 2. Parteitages der PDS "Zur konsequenten offenen und öffentlichen Auseinandersetzung der PDS mit der Problematik der Staatssicherheit" [undated]).
128 Gysi, " 'Ich kandidiere nicht erneut für den Vorsitz,' " 312.
129 Appel, "Anti-Communist Justice"; Seán Hanley, Brigid Fowler, Tim Haughton and Aleks Szczerbiak, "Sticking Together: Explaining Comparative Centre-Right Party Success in Post-Communist Central and Eastern Europe," *Party Politics* 14.4 (2008): 407–434.
130 Graeme Gill, *Symbolism and Regime Change in Russia* (Cambridge: Cambridge University Press, 2013), 145–146; Davies, *Soviet History in the Yeltsin Era*, 50–61.
131 Kathleen E. Smith, *Mythmaking in the New Russia: Politics and Memory During the Yeltsin Era* (Ithaca: Cornell University Press, 2002), 131–157; Gill, *Symbolism and Regime Change in Russia*, 148–151; March, *The Communist Party in Post-Soviet Russia*, 199; Cherniakhovskii, *Protivorechivost' kommunisticheskoi oppozitsii v sovremennoi Rossii*, 76.
132 Smith, *Mythmaking in the New Russia*, 142. This resulted in the CPRF's dependence on the weaker, regional media and party-controlled press. It was only starting in 1999, when the threat of CPRF victory receded, that the party started exploiting rifts within the elite, for example, in securing support from Gusinkii's media empire "Most" in the 1999 parliamentary elections. Cherniakhovskii, *Protivorechivost' kommunisticheskoi oppozitsii v sovremennoi*, 116.
133 Gill, *Symbolism and Regime Change in Russia*, 147–149.

134 Smith, *Mythmaking in the New Russia*, 132.
135 Urban and Solovei, *Russia's Communists at the Crossroads*, 173.
136 Gill, *Symbolism and Regime Change in Russia*.
137 March, "For Victory?" 273–274; March, "The Pragmatic Radicalism of Russia's Communists," 173; S. Pluzhnikov and D. Shevchenko, *Ziuganov.net: Tainaia istoriia KPRF 1990–2008* (Moskva: Stolitsa-Print, 2008), 81; Sakwa, "Left or Right?" 135–136; A. Verkhovskii et al., *Levye v Rossii: ot umerennykh do ekstremistov* (Moskva: Institut Eksperimentalnoy Sotsiologii, 1997), 162.
138 March, "For Victory?" 274; March, *The Communist Party in Post-Soviet Russia*, 236; Robert C. Otto, "Gennadii Ziuganov: The Reluctant Candidate," *Problems of Post-Communism* 46 (1999): 42.
139 Nikolai Bindiukov, "O pozitsii KPRF po natsional'nomu voprosu (Doklad na IV Plenume TsK KPRF 14 fevralia 1998 goda)," *PartArkhiv INDEM* online archive, February 14, 1998; Viktor Iliukhin, "Vremia trudnikh reshenii," *Pravda*, July 30, 1998; Gennadii Ziuganov, "Smuta: Novye boiare gotovy prinesti interesy Rossii v zhertvu svoim interesam," *Elektronnaia versiia Nezavisimoi Gazety*, October 17, 1996.
140 Anatolii Luk'ianov, "Anatolii Luk'ianov: 'Ot Konstitutsii El'tsinskoi—k Konstitutsiii sovetskoi' (beseda s Aleksandrom Prokhanovym)," *Zavtra*, February 11, 1997; Luk'ianov, "Chto stoit': dom ili tiur'mu?," *Sovetskaia Rossiia*, May 27, 2000; Luk'ianov, "Vlast' vlast': Dlia kogo? (Beseda eks-predsedatelia Verkhovnogo Soveta SSSR, predsedatelia komiteta Gosdumy po zakonodatel'stvu Anatoliia Luk'ianova s zamestitelem glavnogo redaktora 'Zavtra' Nikolaem Anisinym)," *Sovetskaia Rossiia*, June 13, 2000.
141 Ivan Mel'nikov, quoted in "Ne boites' prizrakov," *Pravda Rossii: Gazeta Kommunisticheskoi partii Rossiiskoi Federatsii*, December 16, 1998.
142 Valentin Kuptsov, "Zashchita interesov trudovogo naroda—glavnaia zadacha KPRF: Doklad V. A. Kuptsova XII plenumu TsK partii," *PartArkhiv INDEM* online archive, June 27, 2003.
143 Ivan Mel'nikov, "Problemy obrazovaniia: vchera, segodnia i zavtra," *Pravda Rossii: Gazeta Kommunisticheskoi partii Rossiiskoi Federatsii*, December 10, 1998.
144 Seleznev et al., *Dvizhenie "Rossiia,"* 53–54.
145 Belov, "Odna Rossiia"; Gennadii Ziuganov, *Uroki Zhizni* (Moskva: Gennadii Ziuganov, 1997), 263–264.
146 Richard Kosolapov, "Epokhal'noe nichtozhestvo," in *ludino semia* (Moskva: Richard Kosolapov, 1996), 34–43; Kosolapov, *Stalin i Lenin*, 531.
147 Iliukhin, *Spasti Rossiiu*, 128–129; Ziuganov, *Uroki zhizni*, 263–264.
148 Iurii Belov, "Rossiia dolzhna sosredotochitsia," *Sovetskaia Rossiia*, October 1, 1996; Ziuganov, *Uroki zhizni*, 263–264.
149 Quoted in Richard Kosolapov and I. Khlebnikov, "Kommunisty protiv 'kontsa istorii,'" . . . *Izm* 22.2 (1999); Belov, "Na rasput'e"; Bindiukov, Lopata, *Osobaia Tret'ia Sila*, 152.
150 Bindiukov and Lopata, *Osobaia Tret'ia Sila*, 78; Kosolapov, "Nezagadochnyi Stalin"; Gennadii Ziuganov, "Uveren v pobede: Beseda lidera KPRF i NPSR Gennadiia Ziuganova s glavnymi redaktorami gazety 'Zavtra' Aleksandrom Prokhanovym i gazety 'Sovetskaia Rossiia' Valentinom Chikinym," *Sovetskaia Rossiia*, August 26, 2003.
151 KPRF, "Ziuganov rezko kritikuet Chubaisa za prizyv k zakhoroneniiu tela Lenina," *PartArkhiv INDEM* online archive, December 6, 2000; Gennadii Ziuganov, "Ni odin soldat ne vystupil by protiv pravitel'stva, podderzhannogo narodom," *Nezavisimaia Gazeta—Elektronnaia Versiia*, August 12, 1999.
152 Quoted in Kosolapov, "Nezagadochnyi Stalin"; Kuptsov, *V. A. Kuptsov*, 156.

Communist Successors and Narratives 71

153 Geir Flikke, "Patriotic Left-Centrism: The Zigzags of the Communist Party of the Russian Federation," *Europe—Asia Studies* 51 (1999): 275, 277; March, "The Pragmatic Radicalism of Russia's Communists," 168; Sakwa, "Left or Right?" 131–132; Urban and Solovei, *Russia's Communists at the Crossroads*, 20–32.
154 March, *The Communist Party in Post-Soviet Russia*, 31–39; March, "The Pragmatic Radicalism of Russia's Communists," 168; Urban and Solovei, *Russia's Communists at the Crossroads*, 53, 110–116.
155 Urban and Solovei, *Russia's Communists at the Crossroads*, 53, 110–116; March, *The Communist Party in Post-Soviet Russia*, 37; Cherniakhovskii, *Protivorechivost' kommunisticheskoi oppozitsii v sovremennoi Rossii*, 40.
156 Sakwa, "Left or Right?" 138.
157 "V Moskve prokhodit soveshchanie liderov KPRF s predstaviteliami zarubezhnykh kommunisticheskikh, rabochikh i levykh partii," *PartArkhiv INDEM* online archive, December 4, 2000.
158 KPRF(l), "Obraschenie plenuma Kemerovskogo obkoma KPRF(l) k kommunistam Kemerovskoi oblasti, kommunistam Rossii," *Biulleten' Levogo informtsentra* 331.20 (May 1998).
159 Andrew H. Beattie, "A 1950s Revival: Cold War Culture in Reunified Germany," in *Cold War Cultures: Perspectives on Eastern and Western European Societies*, eds. Annette Vowinckel, Marcus M. Payk and Thomas Lindenberger (New York and Oxford: Berghahn Books, 2012), 299–320.
160 Patton, *Out of the East*, 59–68.
161 Thorsten Holzhauser, "'Niemals mit der PDS'? Zum Umgang der SPD mit der SED-Nachfolgepartei zwischen Ausgrenzung und Integrationsstrategie (1990–1998)," *Vierteljahrshefte für Zeitgeschichte* 62.2 (2014): 285–308.
162 Patton, *Out of the East*, 89–118.
163 ACDP, CDU Berlin, 03-012-144/2: Protokoll der 2. Sitzung der Wahlkampfkommission am 17. August 1990, 3.
164 Hough, *The Fall and Rise of the PDS in Eastern Germany*, 26; Beattie, "A 1950s Revival," 311.
165 CDU-Bundesgeschäftsstelle, ed., *Zukunft statt Linksfront: PDS-Gefahr von links!* (Bonn: CDU, 1994); Beattie, "A 1950s Revival," 64.
166 Helmut Kohl, quoted in ACDP, 08-012-127/2: CDU/CSU-Fraktion im Deutschen Bundestag, 12. Wahlperiode, Protokoll der Sondersitzung der Fraktion am 22. Juli 1994, 14. Also see Patton, *Out of the East*, 63–64.
167 Helmut Kohl, quoted in ACDP, 08-012-127/2: CDU/CSU-Fraktion im Deutschen Bundestag, 12. Wahlperiode, Protokoll der Sondersitzung der Fraktion am 22. Juli 1994. Bonn, July 22, 1994, 18.
168 Michael Glos, quoted in "CDU-Ministerpräsident Seite: Rundumschläge gegen PDS bringen nichts—CSU sieht durch Politik in Magdeburg Demokratie gefährdet," *dpa*, July 23, 1994.
169 Johannes Volmert, "Die 'Alt-Parteien' außer Fassung: Reaktionen und Kampagnen auf die Wahlerfolge der PDS—ein Pressespiegel," in *Die PDS: Postkommunistische Kaderorganisation*, eds. Michael Brie et al., 165.
170 Brombacher et al., eds., *Zu Aspekten des "modernen" Antikommunismus*.
171 PDS, "Sozialismus ist Weg, Methode, Wertorientierung und Ziel: Zu den fünf wichtigsten Diskussionspunkten der gegenwärtigen Debatte in der PDS," *Disput* 3-4.95 (1995): 27. There was, however, also a small group of post-communists who identified as socialist "anti-communists." Prinz, *Die programmatische Entwicklung der PDS*, 130.
172 Prinz, *Die programmatische Entwicklung der PDS*, 138.
173 Barbara Könczöl, "Reinventing a Socialist Heroine: Commemorating Rosa Luxemburg After Unification," in *Remembering the German Democratic*

Republic: Divided Memory in a United Germany, eds. David Clarke and Ute Wölfel (Basingstoke: Palgrave Macmillan, 2011), 77–87.
174 Gregor Gysi, *Ein Blick zurück, ein Schritt nach vorn* (Hamburg: Rowohlt Taschenbuch, 2002), 105.
175 Gregor Gysi, "Haben wir das Recht, historische Chancen ungenutzt zu lassen? Offener Brief des Vorsitzenden der PDS an die SPD in der DDR und BRD," *Zeitschrift für sozialistische Politik & Wirtschaft* 54 (1990): 28; Gabriele Zimmer and Petra Pau, "Vor 55 Jahren: gewollt und verfolgt: Geschichte lässt sich nicht aufrechnen," *PDS Pressedienst*, April 20, 2001. See Holzhauser, "'Niemals mit der PDS'?" 290–291.
176 ADS, PDS-PV-137: André Brie, "Also zurück zu Stalin? Eine Auseinandersetzung mit ideologischen Positionen Sahra Wagenknechts," November 16, 1992, 1.
177 ADS, PDS-PV-138: Auszug aus dem Sachprotokoll zur Sondersitzung des Parteivorstandes am 30. November 1992, 4.
178 Gregor Gysi, *Was nun? Über Deutschlands Zustand und meinen eigenen* (Hamburg: Hoffmann und Campe, 2003), 184–185.
179 Brombacher et al., eds., *Zu Aspekten des "modernen" Antikommunismus*. See Baylis, "Political Adaptation," 154.
180 Guentzel, "Modernity Socialism versus Orthodox Marxism," 714.
181 They therefore successfully campaigned for an ideological moderation which eventually led to coalition governments in the German states of Mecklenburg—West Pomerania, in 1998, and of Berlin, in 2002. See Patton, *Out of the East*, 89–118. At times, the PDS even played a significant role in national politics as a majority provider for Germany's center-left government in the Bundesrat. Patton, *Out of the East*, 99–100.
182 Neugebauer, "The Party of Democratic Socialism in Germany," 206.
183 Carola Freundl and Harald Wolf, "Vor der Kür kommt die Pflicht: Arbeitspapier zu den politischen Aufgaben der PDS-Fraktion bis 2004," January 22, 2001, www.die-linke-berlin.de/politik/positionen/politik_fuer_berlin/rot_rotes_regieren/vor_der_kuer_kommt_die_pflicht/, accessed June 1, 2017.
184 Neugebauer, "The Party of Democratic Socialism in Germany," 198–199.
185 Zimmer and Pau, "Vor 55 Jahren."
186 PDS Parteivorstand, "Auseinandersetzung mit der Geschichte nicht instrumentalisieren," *PDS Pressedienst*, May 11, 2001.
187 PDS Parteivorstand, "Auseinandersetzung mit der Geschichte nicht instrumentalisieren."
188 Majid Sattar, "Lautes Gedenken," *faz.net*, August 12, 2001, www.faz.net/aktuell/politik/mauerbau-lautes-gedenken-128520.html, accessed June 1, 2017.
189 Rolf Reißig, *Mitregieren in Berlin. Die PDS auf dem Prüfstand* (Berlin: Dietz, 2005), 14; Gysi, *Was nun?*, 82–83.
190 *Koalitionsvereinbarung der Sozialdemokratischen Partei Deutschlands (SPD) Landesverband Berlin und der Partei des Demokratischen Sozialismus (PDS) Landesverband Berlin für die Legislaturperiode 2001–2006*, Berlin, January 16, 2002, 4.
191 The reformist Berlin post-communists even accepted the Social Democratic interpretation of the 1946 SED formation as a "forced merger" ("*Zwangsvereinigung*") (*Koalitionsvereinbarung*, 4)—a term which was the subject of much controversy between social democrats and democratic socialists. See Holzhauser, "'Niemals mit der PDS'?," 290.
192 *Koalitionsvereinbarung*, 4–5.
193 Historische Kommission beim Parteivorstand der PDS, "Zum 40. Jahrestag des Baus der Berliner Mauer," *PDS Pressedienst*, July 6, 2001.
194 Gabriele Zimmer, "Wir wollen Gesellschaft verändern: Rede auf der Außerordentlichen Tagung des 8: Landesparteitages der PDS Berlin am 12. Januar 2002," *PDS Pressedienst*, January 17, 2002.

195 Stefan Liebich, "Nicht das Wünschenswerte, aber doch das Bestmögliche für Berlin: Rede des Landesvorsitzenden der PDS Berlin auf der Außerordentlichen Tagung des 8. Parteitages am 12. Januar 2002," *PDS Pressedienst*, January 17, 2002. They sought to "steer a middle course among its more nostalgic members, potential voters, and possible coalition partners" (Baylis, "Political Adaptation," 151.) Thus, they emphasized their plan to erect a monument to KPD founding member Rosa Luxemburg, demonstratively countering accusations of having adopted anti-communist interpretations of the past. Liebich, "Nicht das Wünschenswerte"; SPD/PDS, *Koalitionsvereinbarung*, 81.
196 Heinz Karl, "Historische Wahrheit—ein politischer Selbstbedienungsladen?," *Mitteilungen der Kommunistischen Plattform*, April 2002.
197 Bundeskoordinierungsrat der Kommunistischen Plattform, "Anmerkungen zu einem Delegitimationspapier," *PDS Pressedienst*, July 13, 2001.
198 Karl, "Historische Wahrheit."
199 Welsh, "Dealing with the Communist Past," 423; Maria Todorova, "Introduction: Similar Trajectories Different Memories," in *Remembering Communism*, 16.
200 Welsh, "Dealing with the Communist Past"; Appel, "Anti-Communist Justice"; Todorova, "Introduction," 17; Urban, "The Post-Communist Left," 261–263.
201 Jane Leftwich Curry, "Poland's Ex-Communists: From Pariahs to Establishment Players," in *The Left Transformed in Post-Communist Societies: The Cases of East-Central Europe, Russia and Ukraine*, eds. Jane Leftwich Curry and Joan Barth Urban (Lanham: Rowman and Littlefield, 2003), 40, 52; Diana Morlang, "Hungary: Socialists Building Capitalism," in *The Left Transformed in Post-Communist Societies: The Cases of East-Central Europe, Russia and Ukraine*, eds. Jane Leftwich Curry and Joan Barth Urban (Lanham: Rowman and Littlefield, 2003), 73–75; Urban, "The Post-Communist Left," 252.
202 André Brie, "Ankommen in der Bundesrepublik," *Blätter für deutsche und internationale Politik* 10.96 (1996): 1161–1165.
203 Patrick Moreau and Rita Schorpp-Grabiak, *"Man muß so radikal sein wie die Wirklichkeit"—Die PDS: Eine Bilanz* (Baden-Baden: Nomos, 2002), 193.
204 Klaus Schönhoven, "Gemeinsame Wurzeln und getrennte Wege: Zum historischen Selbstverständnis von SPD und Linkspartei," *Jahrbuch für Historische Kommunismusforschung* (2015): 266–267. For example, following the 2014 state elections in Thuringia, DIE LINKE, the SPD and the Greens agreed to form a coalition government and elect Bodo Ramelow, a leading representative of DIE LINKE's reformist faction, as prime minister. Controversially, as a prerequisite, DIE LINKE had to agree that the GDR had not only been a *"Diktatur"* [dictatorship] but also an *"Unrechtsstaat"* [state of lawlessness, state of injustice]—a term that had been traditionally rejected by all factions within the PDS because of its alleged function of delegitimizing the GDR *in toto*.

3 The Memory and Identity of the Western European Left in the Light of European Integration
View from Inside

Walter Baier

Many observers were surprised that after the period of heavy defeats in the 1990s, the radical left had not disappeared but that a group of parties regarded as the successors to communist movements[1] began to grow in strength again at the end of the twentieth century, mainly in Western and Southern Europe. During the European Parliament elections in May 2014, they garnered the support of 13 million voters (8 percent of the electorate) throughout the then 28 member states of the European Union (EU). This made them the fifth-strongest group in the European Parliament.

Political parties always function as repositories of memory. Past experiences increase the scope of action that political parties can take, whereas conflicts, which are suppressed to ensure that parties can go about their daily business, lead to "repetition compulsion" in which the conflicts constantly resurface. This is particularly the case for the European radical left parties, which strongly felt the validity of Karl Marx's words from 1852 that "the tradition of all the dead generations weighs like a nightmare on the brains of the living." However, according to him, the social revolution "cannot draw its poetry from the past, but only from the future"; it "must let the dead bury their dead."[2]

What happened to the historical memory of the radical left after the collapse of the Eastern Bloc? Serge Wolikow comments on the two flagships of Western European communism: the communist parties of Italy and France: "They emerged in the same period, at the beginning of the 1920s, and today they have both disappeared in their historic form."[3] Other actors have appeared in their place. Parties such as Syriza in Greece or the Spanish alliance composed of Podemos and Izquierda Unida have taken their place in the spectrum of European parties as left challengers of the social democrats—perhaps temporarily or perhaps for a long time to come. But with this a new, radical left has emerged. I am going to discuss in the following paragraphs their relation to their historical precedents, the communist movement and in what way the historic collapse of the latter influenced them.[4]

Of the current approximately 1,000 entries on the website of the Party of the European Left (EL) from 2004 to 2017, the content of less than 3 percent has to do with historical events. Public actions on symbolic occasions take place on the basis of the national initiatives of member parties, if also with the support of the EL. The examples are the annual commemoration of the murder of Karl Liebknecht and Rosa Luxemburg in Berlin, which usually dictates the scheduling of a meeting of the EL directorate and the annual celebrations of Portugal's Carnation Revolution and of the establishment of the International Brigades in 1936, which fought on the side of the Republic in the Spanish Civil War. Public declarations were issued on the seventieth anniversary of the victory over fascism, on the anniversary of the murder of Chile's socialist president Salvador Allende and of the beginning of the Iraq War.[5] Particularly noteworthy is the call issued in May 2017 by the newly elected chair of the EL, Gregor Gysi, to celebrate the two hundredth anniversary of Marx's birth in a major way.[6] There are just as few signs of a new "red thread" of history as there are of an attempt to develop a common narrative of the EL.

Past and present of the radical left are interacting. From the outset, the commemoration of past struggles, and their victims and heroes, represented an aspect of communist culture, which constructed a continuity of militants dating back to the Paris Commune, in which present action appeared to be the fulfillment of a legacy. In the twentieth century, the focus of this culture of commemoration was expanded to include the anti-fascist, anti-colonial, feminist and civil rights movements in which communists participated and to which felt they felt connected. As Italian historian Enzo Traverso correctly noted, the collapse of the communist narrative affected not only the communists but also the entire radical left, including those sectors that had traditionally been critical of it and could see their criticism vindicated. However, the perception of history changed in a still broader sense because of the fact that "entire dimensions of the past—anti-fascism, anti-colonialism, feminism, socialism, and revolution—are buried under the official rhetoric of the 'duty of memory.'"[7] No part of the radical left, so far as they did not withdraw from the arena of political and social confrontation, could blind itself to the realization that "revolution was not a tabula rasa"; it needed "its own vision of the past, as a kind of countermemory opposed to the official interpretations of history."[8]

Three books can be mentioned that typify the endeavor to confront this legacy. One is Harald Neubert's (1932–2009) *Die Hypothek des kommunistischen Erbes* [The Burden of the Communist Legacy].[9] The author was a long-time staff member of the International Department of the Central Committee of the SED (*Sozialistische Einheitspartei Deutschlands,* the GDR's ruling party) and in charge of relations with the Western and Southern European parties. He was involved in the drawing up of the paper published in 1987 by the SED and SPD together, with which Erich Honecker aimed at using the enlarged political space created by Mikhail Gorbachev for more autonomy in German politics. He was for a long time directly involved in questions of Eurocommunism, for which reason he took part in the SED's debates with the leadership of the Italian Communist Party (PCI). Nearly a third of his book is taken up with this. By means of documents, reports on his own experience and the results of his own research Neubert demonstrates

> how the international communist movement and "actually existing" socialism [. . .] after an impressive growth phase [. . .] entered a historic dead end in which it proved incapable of renewal in a traditional way and therefore, finding no way out through continuity, historically collapsed.[10]

The perspective from the opposite side of the table is found in Lucio Magri's (1932–2011) book, *The Tailor of Ulm*.[11] The author, who belonged to the left wing of the PCI from which he was expelled in 1969 and which he rejoined 15 years later, reflects on the roots, rise and end of the distinct tradition of Italian communism in order to reconstruct "a collective enterprise stretching over many decades."[12] He offers a cautious "yes" to the questions

> are there rational, compelling reasons why we should resist the psychological mechanisms of denial and repressed memory? Are there, at least, good grounds and favorable conditions today for reopening the critical debate about Communism, instead of consigning it to the archive?[13]

Finally, Enzo Traverso's (1957–) book *Left-Wing Melancholia: Marxism, History and Memory* is written from the perspective of an intellectual who had always had a critical stance toward the policy of communist parties:

> The collapse of State Socialism aroused a wave of enthusiasm and, for a short moment, great expectations of a possible democratic socialism. Very quickly, however, people realized that it was an entire representation of the twentieth century that had fallen apart. [. . .] Instead of liberating new revolutionary energies, the downfall of State Socialism seemed to have exhausted the historical trajectory of socialism itself. The entire history of communism was reduced to its totalitarian dimension which appeared as a collective, transmissible memory.[14]

A creation of certain leftist "countermemory" seems necessary. In this process, seminars, conferences and books appear to be its most important means. This is the terrain of transform! europe, the research institution connected to the Party of the EL. It deals with historical issues in a more comprehensive and thematically more diverse way[15] than does the EL, though its efforts in this field have not been systematically organized yet. Among its outstanding activities are the annual Nicos Poulantzas Lecture, the Marxist-feminist conferences and the Marx conferences in several countries. The centenary of the October Revolution in 2017 was an occasion on which many transform members organized seminars, although there was no Europe-wide event to commemorate this anniversary organized by transform itself.

Definitions and Ambiguities

According to the Greek political scientist Gerassimos Moschonas,

> the area to the left of social democracy is, today, recast and is very different from the communist left of the earlier period. [. . .] The interweaving of the failure of communism, the failure of liberalism and of social democracy has generated a whole range of "post-communist" organizations and attitudes, a real labyrinth of political and ideological trends.[16]

In political science, it has become common to use the term "radical left parties" to denote these parties, including those from the communist spectrum, that have modernized ideologically and—to some extent—in terms of their organizational form. In contrast, some people have proposed the alternative terms "transformatory parties" or "alternative left."[17] However, all these terms mark the differences between the parties they refer to and social democracy, which, at least since the implementation of Tony Blair's "Third Way," has distanced itself from attempts to overcome capitalism. On the other hand, "transformatory" or "alternative left" emphasizes the intention to bring about social change not essentially through "insurrection" and certainly not through minority rule. This parallels with "democratic socialism," the term used by the social democrats of the 1920s to differentiate themselves from communists.[18] This closeness is intentional, of course, as many of today's radical left parties claim to constitute the positive legacy of traditional social democracy and, in keeping with Antonio Gramsci and Otto Bauer, consider obsolete the once marked dichotomy between reformism and revolution.

The terms at hand here are by no means as distinct as one might expect. Until the 1990s, the term "radical left" was mainly reserved for militant, mostly marginal, groups outside of the communist movement.[19] It was not until this movement disintegrated, after having been dislodged from power in Central and Eastern Europe, that the term took on its new meaning. However, "radical left" is still also a subcultural concept that is broader than the party spectrum it is nowadays used to describe. It includes parts of the trade union movement, social movements, nongovernmental organizations and cultural institutions. Indeed, it was the civil-society movements that emerged at the beginning of the twenty-first century, such as the movement critical of globalization and the World Social Forums,[20] which created spaces where the radical left could reestablish itself after the collapse of so-called real socialism. The same can be said of the protest movements against austerity that developed ten years later in Spain and Greece. Whereas these social movements were viewed as novel developments at the time, from a historical perspective, they can be treated as a return of the left to its starting point in civil society.[21] However, some of these movements have recently decided to ally with parties or to create their own parties in order to join the struggle for political power at the parliamentary level. The most important example of this is the Spanish party Podemos founded in 2014 out of the Movement of the Squares. It received 21 percent of votes in the June 2016 parliamentary elections, as an electoral alliance with Izquierda Unida.

The British political scientist Luke March uses the term "radical left" to describe parties that "reject the underlying socio-economic structure of contemporary capitalism and its values and practices," which identify "economic inequality as the basis of existing political and social arrangements," espouse "collective economic and social rights as their principal agenda" and are "internationalist" in terms of their inclination to "cross-national networking and solidarity."[22] "Radical" in this context should be understood in the sense of Marx's famous definition: "To be radical is to grasp things by the root," which leads to "the categorical imperative to overthrow all relations in which man is a debased, enslaved, contemptible being."[23] Alternatively, Italian political scientist Paolo Chiocchetti in a recently published study proposes defining the radical left as a party family that (a) situates itself in the tradition of the "class left," a historical tradition that aims to reform or overcome capitalism from the standpoint of universally conceived working-class interests, and that (b) identifies itself as a separate tendency from, and to the left of, mainstream social democracy.[24] The important advantage of the latter formulation is that it is based on empirically verifiable fact, the tradition of a working-class-centered anti-capitalism in which parties position themselves and the radical left's claim to political independence in the context of its own parties and international associations. Precisely, these aspects differentiate the radical left from left-wing tendencies within social democratic parties.

Communism: An Ambiguous Concept

During the short twentieth century, this "separate tendency" of anti-capitalism was almost exclusively represented within political parties by *communism*. Ideas that today are commonly regarded as communist are indeed much older. Communist inclinations have even been attributed to ancient slave revolts, primitive Christianity and the sixteenth-century peasant uprising.[25] Karl Marx's systematic theory of emancipation through the transformation of the material (economic) relations of humankind, which itself is associated with the scientific worldview that prevailed in the nineteenth century, forms the characteristic feature of communism based on the modern proletariat. In his *Economic and Philosophical Manuscripts* from 1844, Marx defined communism as "the positive transcendence of private property as human self-estrangement, and therefore as the real appropriation of the human essence by and for man."[26] This point led him to define another aspect that was to characterize communism in *The German Ideology* (written together with Friedrich Engels in 1845–1846) as "the real movement which abolishes the present state of things."[27] It was the idea of a "real movement" to be created that led to the founding of the Communist League, the first international communist organization, in 1847. During the second half of the nineteenth century, the "real movement"—even if it used a different name (social democracy or socialism)—experienced an unprecedented historical expansion. However, very soon a division began to develop between moderate and radical tendencies that later flared up both during and after the First World War, resulting in a split. The radical parties that developed out of this situation were gathered under the banner of the Communist International, controlled by the Soviet Union, and they came to epitomize the meaning of communism in today's commonly used sense of the term.

The difficulty with the terms "communism" and "communist movement" is that they can convey different meanings. Talking about communism can refer to 1) the *ideal* of a society free of exploitation and domination, presented by Karl Marx and Friedrich Engels in *The Communist Manifesto* as a necessary result of the historical process; 2) the political parties that arose as a result of Vladimir Lenin's breaking the revolutionary tendency away from the reformist tendency within the socialist movement at the end of the First World War; 3) the economic, social and political system of the Soviet Union and of the state system it led after the Second World War, whose state ideology was "Marxism-Leninism" as formulated by Joseph Stalin.

The individuals' motives for becoming active in the communist movement were as varied and contradictory as communism itself was—enthusiasm for the emancipatory ideal, disillusionment with social democracy or admiration for the Soviet Union's military achievement in the struggle against Adolf Hitler. Nevertheless, the communist party with its hierarchy and discipline was the instrument that provided unity. Once the contradiction between the ideal and its realization in the Soviet Union was ascertained, it was only possible to belong to a communist party if one also took the negative aspects in one's stride. If one joined a communist party from opportunistic motives, then it was necessary to use the vocabulary of the communist ideal as legitimation, a contradiction that is found even in Stalin's public utterances.[28]

The assertion that Stalinism has nothing "to do with our past" is a convenient simplification of a traumatic experience, even in the case of Italian and French communism. Until 1956, all communist parties, including the French Communist Party (PCF) and PCI, kept to the official line that the term "Stalinism" was coined by anti-communist centers and all accusations related to it were only a matter of slanderous claims. At the very least, those party leaders who had spent long years in Soviet exile knew better.

With the Twentieth Party Congress of the Communist Party of the Soviet Union (CPSU) and Nikita Khrushchev's revelations of the countless crimes committed under Stalin's dictatorship, the former line became untenable. The Western European parties began—hesitatingly—to recognize the tragic truth that the greatest persecution of communists had taken place in the 1937 and 1938 in the Soviet Union under the auspices of an alleged "dictatorship of the proletariat."

The Italian party's leader, Palmiro Togliatti, went further than most: In a 1956 interview, he raised the question of the relationship of the terror with a general degeneration of socialism.[29] However, well-known authors, who were frowned upon in the communist movement, have done theoretical work on Stalinism since the 1930s—and not exclusively with anti-communist arguments, as we can see with Leon Trotsky, Otto Bauer,[30] Isaac Deutscher and Werner Hoffmann, to mention some of the more important names. Even Hannah Arendt emphasized that her concept of "total domination," to which anti-communists unjustifiably appeal, did not apply to the Soviet Union after Stalin's death and in the period of the war against Nazi Germany.[31]

In 1967, Werner Hoffmann (1922–1969), a theoretician in the tradition of the Frankfurt School, defined Stalinism as the excessive power exercised in the Soviet Union that went beyond the functions of an "educational dictatorship."[32] One could ask, of course, recalling a quote of the early Marx, who in the educational dictatorship educates the educators,[33] but beyond this, the obvious weakness in this definition, which was largely accepted within the New Left, was that Hoffmann was not in a position to measure the true extent of the "excesses" when he proposed his definition.

In this context, the efforts undertaken by Leon Trotsky, the revolutionary leader exiled from the Soviet Union in 1928, after Stalin's ascendance to unlimited power, to found a new anti-Stalinist Communist International in 1938 are worth mentioning. The ideological tendency named after him, Trotskyism, although always a minority in the communist movement, still has an effect today within the radical left. It is almost impossible to single out chief works here from Trotsky's decades-long literary production. His autobiography, *My Life: An Attempt at an Autobiography*, is a major document of the twentieth century in which Trotsky appears as one of his contradictory, tragic protagonists. With his *Revolution Betrayed* (1937), he offered a profound critique of the political, sociological and cultural aspects of Stalinism. *Permanent Revolution* (1929) may serve as Trotskyism's foundational programmatic document; it combined a Marxist interpretation of the Russian Revolution with a program of world revolution alternative to Stalinist Marxism-Leninism, which, however, proved politically unsuccessful.

Analyzing the astounding, however transitional, success of communism in the twentieth century as a "secular political faith"[34] requires an understanding of its multifacetedness in which intellectual attractiveness, sharp political demarcations and (contradictory) practical efficacy reinforced each other for an entire epoch, until it came apart in a protracted period of crisis. The fact that this chapter focuses on the Western European radical left cannot ignore the context of Eastern European communism, as throughout their entire history, communism and the radical left in East and West have viewed each other as part of a common movement. Worldwide, internationalism was a crucial element legitimizing the rule of communist parties.[35] Of course, when viewed from a practical angle, internationalism was a means of exercising discipline within the Warsaw Pact states. However, the sister parties in the capitalist world never completely broke with the sympathies toward the Soviet Union, even after they began distancing themselves from its policy during the 1970s.[36] Whether such a break would ever have occurred must, because of the revolutionary changes of 1989–1991, remain a matter of conjecture.

The enlargement of the European Union in 2004, 2007 and 2013, which led 11 states in Eastern and Central Europe that had formerly been communist dominated to join the EU, resulted in the development of a common institutional framework. This also increased the importance of the understanding that traditions and political cultures influence each other. This influence should not be viewed as a one-way street beginning in the West and reaching into the East (in other words, the assimilation of Eastern European political cultures into those of Western Europe), because influence also runs in the opposite direction.[37] As a consequence, questions that have been neglected for decades are now taking on new relevance, such as the tangled national relations in Central and Eastern Europe, the existence of transnational ethnic communities in the region and traditional economic, cultural and personal links, including the common roots of the left in Central Europe that reach as far back as the Social Democratic Workers' Party of Cisleithania,[38] which was founded in 1889.

The History of Western European Communism: An Attempt of the Radical Left Narrative[39]

Despite all tradition-founding myths, after the subsiding of the post-1918 revolutionary wave and the failure of all attempts at uprisings in Western Europe, which were encouraged by the Communist International, the communist movement only represented a minor political factor. Its influence was at the peak only between 1945 and 1949, when the communist movement stood in high regard because of the exceptional role it had played in the resistance to National Socialism. Objectively, the deal reached in Yalta and Potsdam reflected the Soviet Union's strategic security interests; however, it worked against the communist movement as a whole since the partitioning of Europe into spheres of influence, as accepted by Stalin, took no account of the balance of power in the states in question. In Italy and France, the communists had become mass parties as a result of their antifascist resistance. Yet Italy and France fell to the West, and the communists were subsequently ousted from their respective governments. In Greece, British military intervention was needed to bring down the communist-led resistance movement. Conversely, in the Soviet sphere of influence, the communist parties, with the exception of Czechoslovakia and Yugoslavia, were comparably weak forces. Nonetheless, social models patterned after the Soviet Union were installed in all states in the Soviet sphere of influence, often using repressive methods.

With the Marshall Plan, the US attached economic aid for reconstruction to the requirement that the recipient countries subordinate themselves to US hegemony or accept the partition of Europe. With its superior economic position, which had been undamaged by war, the US began financing the successful capitalist reconstruction of its part of Europe—the industrially developed West. In contrast, the Soviet Union was devastated; 27 million Soviet people had been killed during the war, and therefore it could not offer a comparable help to is satellites. This notwithstanding, it let itself become involved in a ruinous arms race, which proved disastrous in the long run.

The partition of Europe during the Cold War traumatized the communist movement, which, divided by the Iron Curtain, now found itself in opposing roles: on one side of the demarcation line, it constituted the governing party which, at the latest by the 1950s, resorted to repressive measures, while, on the other side, it constituted a politically isolated opposition and, struggling under conditions of a democracy that it was at pains to consolidate, it used or raised demands for legal means of political action that were denied to opposition forces, including social democrats, in Eastern Europe.

This not only led to the schizophrenic attitude of Western communism toward liberal democracy, which only began to be overcome after the Twentieth Congress of the CPSU in 1956, but also formed the communist view of Western European economic integration during the early 1950s; alongside the establishment of NATO in 1949, the European Coal and Steel Community, as the precursor to the European Economic Community, was seen as part of US preparations for war against the Soviet Union. As realistic as it was from the perspective of Soviet security interests, this view was unable to account for the long-term effects of economic integration on Western European societies. Here, too, the one-sidedness of this analysis led to a vicious circle of political discord within the radical left that has yet to be overcome.

In 1943, the Communist International was dissolved. Soon after, in 1947, the Communist Information Bureau (Cominform), which consisted of the nine most important European communist parties[40] and was created to replace the Communist International, fell apart at the time of the Stalin-Tito split. This was followed by the military suppression of the oppositional workers' movement in Poland and of the uprising in Hungary—a paradox, considering it occurred in the wake of the de-Stalinization introduced in 1956 by the Twentieth Congress of the CPSU. These events ushered in a series of ideological defeats that eroded the political and intellectual foundations of communist internationalism. At the end of the 1950s, Scandinavian communist parties were the first ones to start gradually distancing themselves from their communist identity.⁴¹

The decline of Western European communism only stalled during a short period in the mid-1970s when the crisis of the contemporary accumulation and regulation regimes made new developments possible. The 1968 movement, which was by no means confined only to the universities, alongside the second wave of feminism and the libertarian turn in popular youth culture, created a friendly climate for the left. In addition, a favorable overall political climate developed as a result of the temporary easing of tensions within East-West relations, which helped end the dictatorships in Portugal (1974), Greece (1974) and Spain (1975/1978). The broad support for the communist-led war of liberation against the USA in Vietnam allowed communist internationalism to revive briefly.

For the PCF, May '68 ushered in a new epoch. While the student revolts, with which a part of the working class represented by the PCF solidarized, alarmed the ruling elites—indeed so much so that the president of the Republic Charles de Gaulle was preparing to declare a state of emergency with the help of the military—the party leadership, in view of this danger and certainly also out of respect for the Cold War frontlines drawn up in Yalta, strove for de-escalation rather than sharpening the conflicts in a revolutionary direction. In so doing, it irreparably damaged its relationship to the politicized vanguard of the student movement, which up to 1968 had moved more or less in the orbit of the PCF. The PCF's break with the intellectuals also proved irreparable. Jean-Paul Sartre, for example, joined a small Maoist party in 1968 and was editor of its newspaper, *La Cause du people* [The Cause of the People]. The theoretical innovations that developed out of the school of the philosopher Louis Althusser (who remained a member of the PCF), such as post-structuralism, for example, in the work of Michel Foucault or Pierre Bourdieu's sociological work, unfolded outside the orbit of the PCF and against it. Some of the intellectuals alienated from the PCF radically transformed their views—for example, André Glucksmann and Stéphane Courtois who became Maoists after May '68 and subsequently adopted decidedly anti-communist positions.

With the founding of the *Ligue communiste* (later *Ligue communiste révolutionnaire*) by prominent members of the Communist Youth (Alain Krivine, Daniel Bensaïd, Catherine Samary et al.), who entered the Trotskyist Fourth International, the PCF lost its monopoly in representing the radical left. A few years later, Europe saw the appearance of a plethora of microparties with Trotskyist, Maoist, anarchist or, generally, undogmatic orientations. None of them became an influential political force. Since they laid claim to the radical left space, they significantly contributed to its disintegration.

Although the 1970s were a time of change, none of the major communist parties in Western Europe proved capable of combining the new impulses with their proletarian and anti-fascist cultures as a means of developing an original left-wing response to the crisis of the accumulation and regulation regimes. At the same time, the Western capitalism proved its capacity to renew its hegemony through an astonishing transformation; it overcame internal conservative resistance to absorb the budding libertarian tendencies and, as far as possible, to commercialize and combine them on the ideological and political level with neoclassical economics—a synthesis that today constitutes hegemonic neoliberalism. Nevertheless, the remarkable intellectual and cultural achievements of capitalism through adapting and transforming the impulses of the youth movement cannot conceal the fact that capitalism's self-transformation took place as a violent class struggle, as shown by the defeat of the year-long miners' strike in the United Kingdom by Margaret Thatcher in the mid-1980s.

Evidently, every social defeat, including those of the communist left, consists of a series of political defeats. At the beginning of the 1970s, after the suppression of the Prague Spring, the major Western European communist parties had shifted the focus of their international attention. The Italian, French and Spanish parties began to coordinate their European politics. Paradoxically, the precise origin of the term "Eurocommunism" is not clear; it would seem to go back to a casual remark made by the PCI's general secretary Enrico Berlinguer (1922–1984) during a press conference in July 1975 after a meeting that month with the general secretary of the Spanish Communist Party, Santiago Carillo (1915–2012). In practice, Eurocommunism turned out to be not much more than the catchword by which these three parties marked their growing distance from the "sister parties" in Eastern Europe, which they started to criticize publicly. However, they never achieved agreement on a substantial political program or strategy enabling them to practice common politics on the European scale that the label "Eurocommunism" suggested.

In asserting its political independence, the PCI could draw on its own intellectual sources, in particular, the memorandum that its historic postwar leader, Palmiro Togliatti drafted in 1964 in Yalta in replying to proposals forwarded by the CPSU to convene an international communist conference for the purpose of expelling the Chinese communists from the community of communist parties. In opposition, Togliatti stressed the necessity of a profound policy change of the international communist movement, including those of the ruling parties, which he called on to "overcome the regime of restrictions and suppression of democratic and personal freedom introduced by Stalin."[42] On the unity of the international movement, he noted that it "must be achieved in the diversity of our concrete political positions, conforming to the situation and degree of development in each country."[43]

The trajectory of the French Communist Party was different, as it was traditionally the closest ally of the Soviet Union in Western Europe and in contrast to its Italian counterpart maintained its loyalty even after the invasion of Czechoslovakia in 1968. In 1973, the French Communist Party established a promising electoral alliance with the socialists, the Left Union. This alliance was seen as a chance to open up the communist ideological discourse in order to strengthen the party's position vis-à-vis its ally, which became its strong and, in the end, prevailing competitor for hegemony in the left. Characteristic of this period was a book by party historian Jean Ellenstein (1927–2002) *Histoire du phénomène stalinien* [History of the Stalinist Phenomenon].[44] The purpose of the book was to prepare the PCF for the looming anti-communist offensive; however, even Ellenstein's cautious and inconsistent critique of Stalinism overstepped the bounds of what the PCF was willing to allow, and in 1981, after the collapse of the electoral alliance with the socialists and the PCF's rapprochement with the Soviet Union, he was expelled from the party.

Historically, the biggest achievement of Eurocommunism has been the legitimacy it bestowed on the struggle of the Spanish Communist Party, which after the decades of Franco's dictatorship fought for its relegalization and Spain's peaceful transition to democracy. In 1977, following the end of the dictatorship, the Communist Party—whose general secretary, Santiago Carillo, constituted a central figure of Eurocommunism—once again became a legal political entity. Carillo's book, *Eurocommunism and the State*,[45] which appeared in the same year, is the most important attempt of a party leader to provide a theoretical foundation for Eurocommunism. However, since, despite all persecution the party suffered under Franco and the great increase in membership after its legalization, the party's electoral results were disappointing, and Carillo was removed as general secretary in 1982. At any rate, in contrast to the PCF, the result was not a revival of the orthodox line.

In the mid-1970s, when the PCI was at the zenith of its electoral strength, the conclusion of a "historic compromise" with the Christian Democrats allowing its participation in the government of this important NATO member seemed to be only a matter of time. Nevertheless, despite the temporary respite in the East-West conflict, participation at the government level by the PCI constituted a clear red line for the US. Consequently, the state department under Henry Kissinger used all of its political and diplomatic leverage to prevent this from happening. By 1976, the PCI's political influence at the ballot box had surpassed its zenith, and with the assassination by alleged left-wing terrorists of Aldo Moro (1916–1978), the leader of the Christian-Democratic Party who had advocated the historic compromise, the possibility of forming a government came to an end.

What the Austrian Social Democrat Bruno Kreisky said in 1976 of Enrico Berlinguer, then leader of the PCI, could also be said of Eurocommunism as such: "If he is serious about this he will stop being a communist."[46] I think Kreisky was wrong. It is more accurate to see Eurocommunism as a projection screen for the crisis of European communism than as a unified political tendency. While, in its left wing, theorists such as Nicos Poulantzas, Lucio Magri, Pietro Ingrao and Luciana Castellina explored the possibility of a social transformation of contemporary capitalism, the party leaders were concerned with optimizing their electoral prospects without, however, realizing the effect of the changes in the Soviet Union on their own parties. It was a traumatic experience, and at the beginning of the 1990s, it led the majority of the PCI's leadership to conclude that the party should be renamed and social-democratized. On the whole, it can be said, Eurocommunism meant a "secularization" of historical communism, and it can be understood as a reaction to the loss of its "utopian space," which put the electoral success and government power to the center of its identity.

The history of Italian radical left also contains significant groups outside the Communist Party. In the hot autumn of 1969, a radical left youth movement formed, which had a base in the universities but also in the industrial plants of northern Italy. From this base, a neo-Marxist theory known as *operaismo* was developed around the journal *Quaderni rossi* [Red Papers]. Its best-known representatives, Ranieri Panziero, Antonio Negri and Mario Tronti, referred, above all, to workers' struggles, which had been regaining their earlier dynamic; they situated them at the center of a strategy for winning hegemony in society.[47] In this, they were in conflict with the PCI's leadership, which was seeking a path to power via the institutions and the government. The politics of the historical compromise, which the PCI leadership—under the effect of the tragic coup against the Allende government in 1973—developed in order to cooperate with the Christian Democrats, met with the opposition of broad sections of the movement. In 1969, communists expelled from the PCI around Luigi Pintor, Luciana Castellina and Rossana Rossanda founded the newspaper *Il Manifesto* [The Manifest], which became a daily in 1971. In 1977, the party Proletarian Democracy (*Democrazia Proletaria*) resulted from the merger of various smaller groups. Although it remained a small party, it had considerable influence on further developments. In contrast to France, this left opposition to the CP involved no anti-communist turns. In 1991, when the PCI majority completed a transformation to become a social democratic party, these tendencies, together with the PCI minority, founded the Communist Refoundation Party (*Partito della Rifondazione Comunista*, PRC). The autonomist culture of Proletarian Democracy, *Il Manifesto* and of *operaismo* not only made PRC into the point of contact for the globalization-critical movements but also accounted for much of the attraction it had for the EL in the first decade of the new century.

With the mass strike in the Lenin Shipyard in the summer of 1980, the founding of the "Solidarity" and the proclamation of martial law in Poland in 1981 the crisis of state socialism entered its final phase. At least as dramatic for Western European communism as the ouster of the Eastern European parties from power in 1989/1990 was the moral defeat that led up to it. Only the most orthodox party ideologues in the Western European communist parties loyal to Moscow (e.g. the Communist Party of Austria and the German Communist Party, DKP) could dismiss movements such as "Solidarity" and Charta 77 as wholesale "counterrevolutionary" or "rightist" from the start. In December 1981, on the occasion of the proclamation of martial law in Poland, the PCI executive declared that the historical phase of the development of socialism opened up by the October Revolution had "exhausted its momentum."[48]

The discourse around the concepts of *perestroika* and *glasnost* initiated by CPSU general secretary Mikhail Gorbachev appeared to refute this thesis and for a short while fueled hopes of a socialist renewal. Only some of the most influential communist parties (for example, in Greece, Portugal and France) were able, albeit with considerable electoral and membership loss, to survive the collapse of Gorbachev's reform project and the disintegration of the Soviet Union. However, none of them could position themselves as a force that could provide a political and ideological orientation for the radical left. A new start was needed, and this could not occur within the framework of the international or European communist movement.

Europe and Radical Left Identity

Faced with this deadlock, the PCI looked to a new arena of political struggle: European integration. Pan-Europeanism consequently became an identity marker of Italian communism. Whereas most communist parties (especially the French) have rejected wholesale the (Western) European institutions that had been created at the beginning of the 1950s, the PCI could draw on its tradition of pan-European anti-fascism epitomized through the famous *Manifesto of Ventotene*, authored by the communist Altiero Spinelli (1907–1986) and the radical Ernesto Rossi (1897–1961) in 1941 during their confinement on the prison island of Ventotene in which they called on the left to abandon its traditional goal of the "conquest of national political power" with the aim of avoiding "involuntarily, play[ing into] the hands of reactionary forces." Instead, they advocated focusing on "the creation of a solid international state [. . .] which will direct popular forces toward this goal, and, having won national power, [to] use it first and foremost as an instrument for achieving international unity."[49]

When the French Communist Party lost ground to its ally, the Socialist Party, in the 1980s, it drew different conclusions from those of its Italian and Spanish counterparts. Its leadership under Georges Marchais (1920–1997) not only initiated rapprochement with the Soviet Union but also with full commitment to the political culture of its own country, began to emphasize more strongly the national level within its policies. The traditional differences between the French and Italian communists, therefore, were also reflected in European policy.

Whereas the Italian communists, alongside their Spanish comrades, advocated expanding the European Community to include Spain, Greece and Portugal, the French and the Portuguese opposed the change. At the same time, the Greek Communist Party was divided between Eurocommunists ("party of the interior") and orthodox communists ("party of the exterior").

In 1979, the first direct elections to the European Parliament resulted in communist and allied parties winning 44 seats of 410. In fact, this group was less a political than a technical alliance, which facilitated the parliamentary operations of its members who put forward conflicting positions when it came to European integration. Consequently, in 1989, it split into the integration-friendly Group for the European United Left (EUL/GUE)—which comprised 28 MEPs from Denmark's Socialist People's Party, the PCI, Spain's United Left (IU) and Greece's Synaspismos—and the Euro-critical coalition "Left Unity," with 14 MEPs from the French, Greek and Portuguese communist parties, as well as the Workers' Party of Ireland. After the collapse of the communist regimes in Eastern Europe, Italy's Communist Party completed its transformation into the Party of the Democratic Left and joined the social democratic fraction in the European Parliament. Meanwhile, in Italy, the newly founded Communist Refoundation Party rapidly grew to 100,000 members, became anchored in Parliament anchoring and, as mentioned earlier, became the role model of a successful radical left party throughout the next decade because of its connection to radical social movements, in particular alter-globalists who rallied against the G-7 summit in Genoa, 2001, but also to the charisma of its general secretary Fausto Bertinotti (1940–). In 1994, the remaining EL MEPs formed the Confederal Group of the United Left (GUE—*Gauche Unitaire Européenne*). In 1995, this group expanded to include MEPs from Finland, Denmark and Sweden (constituting the Nordic Green Left Alliance) and united with the GUE. This resulted in the rather long name Confederal Group of the United European Left/Nordic Green Left (GUE/NGL). In 1999, Germany's Party of Democratic Socialism PDS (which later became DIE LINKE) joined, as did the Czech CP and the Cypriot Progressive Party of Working People in 2003, along with Ireland's Sinn Féin and Portugal's Left Bloc.[50]

If, in addition to its usefulness at the structural level, joining a common parliamentary group in the European Parliament also came with a financial incentive, there was still very little motivation toward increased cooperation at the party level. In 1990, the New European Left Forum was formed in Madrid in order to pick up the pieces at the party level. This loose framework of reformed communist, left-socialist, red-green and democratic left-wing parties decided to establish a party at the European level. In March 2003, the Greek left-wing party Synaspismos invited these groups to Athens.[51] Their decision to establish a European party coincided with the ongoing demonstrations being organized by the "anti-globalization movement," or "alter-globalization movement." This global social movement had begun with resistance against the Multinational Agreement on Investment, the mass demonstration in Seattle (in summer 1999) and the first World Social Forum in Porto Alegre (January 2001), which was organized as an alternative to the World Economic Forum in Davos. In fact, after the collapse of communism, the alter-globalization movement constituted the first sign of a reinvigorated internationalism of the radical left. In 2002, the first European Social Forum was held in Florence, and in 2003, millions of citizens in hundreds of cities throughout the world responded to a call by the World Social Forum to protest against the war that the US administration under George W. Bush was about to launch against Saddam Hussein's Iraq. However, the alter-globalization movement's slogan "Another World is Possible!" demonstrated that many wanted to go beyond the confines of a mere peace movement and were actually striving for the creation of a new anti-capitalist international. Consequently, this movement also provided the space with which to establish a new radical left. Also, Trotskyist or ex-Trotskyist cadres played an important role in organizing the movement. In 2000, several Trotskyist groups founded the European Anti-Capitalist Left, which was intended to unify the left in Europe along the lines of a Trotskyist platform. It was a promising project because, alongside Trotskyist-led parties (such as the New Anti-Capitalist Party in France), influential Trotskyist currents have existed in most radical left-wing parties, and they still do today.[52]

In 2002, at the European Social Forum in Florence, the PRC's secretary general, Fausto Bertinotti, discussed the need to unify the left, but threw open the issue of whether this should be achieved by the Trotskyist initiative to the interpretation of the thousands of attendees.[53] On the initiative of the French organization Espaces Marx, whose directors were alarmed by Bertinotti's ambiguity in Florence, the transform! europe network, of which Espaces Marx had been a founding member two years earlier, invited the chairs of six parties known to favor the formation of a European left-wing party to a workshop in Paris.[54] Over the course of this workshop, they agreed to call publicly for the establishing of the Party of the EL. In May 2004, at a founding congress, 15 parties adopted a common political platform and drew up the party's statute. Fausto Bertinotti, general secretary of the PRC, the host party, was elected chair.

In its statute, the party had a nuanced position on the "communist legacy":

> We defend this legacy of our movement which inspired and contributed to securing the social certainties of millions of people. We keep the memory of these struggles alive including the sacrifices and the sufferings in the course of these struggles. We do this in unreserved disputation with undemocratic, Stalinist practices and crimes, which were in absolute contradiction to socialist and communist ideals.[55]

Although this paragraph is neither exhaustive nor provocative, its adoption did not pass without controversy at the founding congress. As the PRC, the host party would not permit voting on the statute paragraph by paragraph; the Communist Party of Bohemia and Moravia opted to become an observer instead of a full member.

In 2005, the debate was taken up once again in a meeting of the EL's directorate. Responsible for international relations of the Communist Party of Bohemia and Moravia at that time, Hassan Chaffo pointed to "a list of at least 27 European communist parties[56] from Eastern, Central and Western

Europe that were not engaged, not invited to the actions of the European Left Party." In this context, he clearly conveyed the standpoint of his party by demanding that the term "Stalinism" be replaced by the more general formulation "non-democratic." "If we only use the word Stalinist, it will mean that we are not rejecting the practices of Mao, Pol Pot, Ceauşescu, etc." As EL Chair Fausto Bertinotti answered, the explicit

> rejection of Stalinism belongs to our political identity. Without this rejection, many of us would not be in this party. In any case, the rejection of Stalinism has been conceded by any party participating in the founding of the EL and is one of its founding elements. The rejection of Stalinism has nothing to do with our past, but with our future. When referring to our past, when we reject Stalinism, we reject of course all the bad practices, including practices worse than Stalinism. What we radically refuse is the very concept of power which we associate with Stalinism. From there we start to imagine and to have an idea of our future society. Without that refusal, we would not be able to imagine our idea of socialism. That is why this is a very firm point.[57]

The orthodox groups, such as the Greek Communist Party, rejected the EL. In 2013, the Greek Communist Party even established a separate European party, the Initiative of Communist and Workers parties (since 2016: European Communist Initiative),[58] but it has yet to exercise any major influence.

The Contested European Identity

The EL considers itself to be an internationalist party with, however, a focus on European politics. In 2009, the EL adopted its first common platform for the European elections. In the run-up to the elections for the European Parliament in 2014, it nominated Alexis Tsipras, the leader of Syriza, the main opposition party in the Greek Parliament, as its candidate for president of the European Commission. This had a surprising effect: Tsipras appeared in numerous countries and was featured countless times in the media. The televised debate between the top four candidates[59] organized by the European Broadcasting Union reached millions of people. This enabled the EL to present itself to the public as an autonomous political force for the first time.

The direct communication between the electorate and a leftist European leader, who hitherto could only reach the broader public through the national parties, imparted a Europe-wide character to the electoral campaign. The personalized campaign gained momentum through social media such as Facebook and Twitter, and this resulted in new possibilities. In Italy, different left-wing forces united under the name of L'Altra Europa con Tsipras and managed to win back the deputies they had lost in 2009. The Spanish Indignados and their new party Podemos began aligning themselves much more strongly with Greece's Syriza model than with their comrades in Spain's traditional left-wing party, Izquierda Unida. And in Slovenia, a new, successful electoral alliance was established in the presence of Alexis Tsipras.

However, the EL has thus not only explored new tactics; it has also entered new strategic territory. Tsipras's involvement in the public controversy around the president of the commission whose appointment, according to an agreement between the large parties, was to be determined by the parties' electoral results, something that then was questioned by the European Council, was a new kind of move. Although his statement supporting Jean-Claude Juncker, the candidate of the conservatives who won a relative majority in the European Parliament, was a logical consequence of his own candidacy for the office, it nevertheless went beyond the usually cautious statements by the EL on institutional matters and was criticized by some members. This shows the EL's ambiguous stance on European integration. Although European integration can no longer be regarded as an instrument of the Cold War, the Tspipras's statement has aroused skepticism in the radical left because of the decidedly neoliberal foundation it acquired after the Maastricht Treaty and the introduction of the euro.

In addition, the ambiguity of the EL's approach to European integration has been reinforced by the impact of the crisis beginning in 2007. A representative study of the political profiles of the delegates at the EL party congress carried out for transform! europe provides a good example. At the 2016 congress, 223 delegates from 26 parties (78 percent) stressed that they had a European identity, albeit mostly as a supplement to their own national identity. Only 14 percent viewed themselves as merely possessing a national identity, indicating a remarkable increase compared to 2013 (9 percent).[60] Nonetheless, a third (33 percent) believed that EU membership had damaged their country. Regional differences are significant here. Whereas 45 percent of Southern European delegates consider EU membership to have negatively affected their country, only 31 percent of delegates from Eastern Europe and Turkey saw this as the case. A significant part of all delegates (33 percent) favored their country's exit from the EU—by region 28 percent of delegates from Southern European parties and an astonishing 80 percent of those from northern European (Scandinavia) parties.[61] At the very least, these data demonstrate that the crisis and, in particular, the crisis management strategy enforced by Germany, as Europe's hegemonic power, over the European institutions has led to disillusionment about European integration among broad circles of the radical left.

Well-known politicians such as Oskar Lafontaine (DIE LINKE) and Jean-Luc Mélenchon (France Insoumise) seem to privilege national sovereignty (Plan B)[62] over further integration, whereas others, such as Yanis Varoufakis with his DiEM-25 (Democracy in Europe Movement 2025), are calling for the democratization of European institutions. They have articulated their views before well-attended European conferences and gained supporters for their ideas. This may well lead to the development of new transnational structures within the EL that could change the existing architecture of Europe's organizations and institutions. On the other hand, the EL lacks a commonly agreed upon narrative of the EU and subsequently a strategic proposal that could rally the different forces, and thus far it remains unclear whether a consensus can be reached at all. Nevertheless, the virulent crisis of European integration is pushing the party toward taking an explicit position on democracy in Europe.

A Final Comment

Since the collapse of "state socialism" in the Soviet Union and Eastern Europe, the radical left in both parts of the formerly divided Europe has traveled along a path by many contradictions but also several surprising successes. Political actors who once constituted the historically defeated have been able to get a stable position within the European political system. In several countries, those who were once the pariahs of the political arena have now become sought-after coalition partners. Many strategic and tactical issues related to government involvement remain unresolved, but this changes nothing in terms of gaining a new strength in the last two decades.

During this time, radical left parties have been able to achieve considerable success through persistent resistance to austerity, especially in Southern Europe. Moreover, they have strengthened their position with regard to the social democrats. Nevertheless, on the whole, they have failed to meet the high expectations they had raised, particularly during the crisis of 2007. The ongoing weakness of their strategic position seems the result of their failure to target the severe political crisis that Europe is undergoing and their tendency to limit themselves to resisting the economic policies being implemented throughout Europe. This "economistic" one-sidedness, which sometimes gives the impression that they interpret austerity as the only cleavage between the social democratic mainstream and the left-wing opposition, including left-wing parties, has proven to be too narrow an approach.[63]

The conflict that traverses European societies is political and ideological, at least to the same extent as it is economic. The economic policy decisions that are taken on the European level are being made under institutional conditions and political power relations that are highly unfavorable to the left. The Syriza government painfully experienced this in 2015 in its attempts to broker a fair deal with the European institutions. Its failure shattered the credibility of its previous approach to changing the European agenda through electoral success at the national level. This has led Europe to become a controversial issue within the left once again. There is a lot to be said for Gerassimos Moschonas's dry claim that "the European Union structurally, not conjuncturally, undermines the modes of action of historic radicalism." As such, he argues, the structure and workings of the EU raise an enormous issue regarding the effectiveness and practical coherence of the strategic options that have dominated the history of the left (and thus this problem has nothing to do with a conspiracy by the elites or capital). "In the new environment, neither the classical Leninist strategy nor the democratic road to socialism, or that of direct action, appear effective."[64]

As such, the crisis of Europe has raised existential questions about the radical left. As the decline of European social democracy demonstrates, there is no guarantee that great historical movements will continue to exist in the future; instead, their survival depends on ensuring that the right political decisions are made at the crossroads of history. And this also applies to the radical left. However, political decisions are never made on blank pieces of paper. Just as the present gives the past its significance, so the past offers present actors a collection of experiences that enable them to more precisely formulate their expectations. "In other words, past and future interact, related by a symbiotic link. Instead of being two rigorously separated continents, they are connected by a dynamic, creative relationship."[65] The epochal break of 1989 interrupted this dynamic and creative relationship. But it was not eliminated and must be reproduced by a discriminating and critical appropriation. This, however, requires constant intellectual effort, as there always is a danger of it degenerating into the routine business of politics. But what would be the point of a left if it allowed amnesia to lead it to abandon the perspective of a future beyond capitalism?

Notes

1. See, for example, Luke March, *Radical Left Parties in Europe* (London and New York: Routledge, 2011).
2. Karl Marx, "The Eighteenth Brumaire of Louis Bonaparte," in *Collected Works*, vol. 11, eds. Karl Marx and Friedrich Engels (New York: International Publishers, 1979), 99.
3. Serge Wolikow, "Problèmes méthodologiques et perspectives historiographiques de l'histoire comparés du communisme," *Cahier Histoire: Histoires Croisées du Communisme Italien et Français* 112–113 (2010): 21.
4. It is necessary to remark here that Europe's radical left parties are to a very great extent still defined by their national frameworks. A comprehensive history of the radical left has largely been a history of national parties. My contribution here focuses on the attempts made to go beyond these frameworks—i.e., to "transnationalize" politics not only programmatically but also practically, which is required, among other things, by European integration. This too does not occur without presuppositions.
5. Author's own research.
6. Gregor Gysi, "Call for an Honorable Commemoration of Karl Marx," *European Left*, May 5, 2017, www.european-left.org/positions/news-archive/call-honourable-commemoration-karl-marx, accessed June 1, 2017.
7. Enzo Traverso, *Left-Wing Melacholia: Marxism, History and Memory* (New York: Columbia University Press, 2016), 36.
8. Traverso, *Left-Wing Melacholia*, 71.
9. Harald Neubert, *Die Hypothek des kommunistischen Erbes: Erfahrungen, Zeugniss, Konsequenzen* (Hamburg: VSA, 2000).
10. Neubert, *Die Hypothek des kommunistischen Erbes*, 9.

11 Lucio Magri, *The Tailor of Ulm: Communism in the Twentieth Century* (London and New York: Verso, 2011). The name refers to the poem by Berthold Brecht on a sixteenth-century tailor who constructed artificial wings and died during the attempt to fly in front of bishop, who commented that people will never fly.
12 Magri, *The Tailor of Ulm*, 4.
13 Magri, *The Tailor of Ulm*, 4.
14 Traverso, *Left-Wing Melacholia*, 21.
15 See www.transform-network.net/.
16 Gerassimos Moschonas, "The European Union and the Dilemmas of the Radical Left," *Transform: European Journal for Alternative Thinking and Political Dialogue* 9 (2011).
17 Richard Dunphy, *Contesting Capitalism? Left Parties and European Integration* (Manchester: Manchester University Press, 2004), 2; Enrico Calossi, *Anti-Austerity Parties in the European Union Cooperation, Coordination and Integration* (Pisa: Pisa University Press, 2016), 85; Fausto Bertinotti, "15 Thesen für eine alternative europäische Linke," in *Die Europäische Linke*, eds. Michael Brie and Cornelia Hildebrandt (Berlin: Rosa Luxemburg Stiftung, 2003).
18 A concise theoretical presentation of the relationship between democracy and socialism from a democratic socialist point of view is found in Karl Polanyi's 1927 manuscript "On Freedom": There can also be dictatorial justice, and if justice, when it is realized through democracy, really is to mean ethical progress, this is not due to the nature of justice but to that of democracy. "This idea of social freedom is a specifically socialist one." Karl Polanyi, *Chronik der großen Transformation (Artikel und Aufsätze 1920–1945)*, vol. 3 (Marburg: Metropolis Verlag, 2005), 142.
19 In French, *l'extrême gauche*. See Jean-Michel De Waele and Daniel Lois Seiler, *Le partis de la gauche anticapitalisteen Europe* (Paris: Economica, 2012), 2. The delimiting, often pejorative use of the term "radical left"/ "left radicalism" goes back to Lenin's 1920 book *Left-Wing Communism: An Infantile Disorder*. In Vladimir Ilyich Lenin, *Collected Works*, vol. 31 (Moscow: Progress Publishers, 1964).
20 See Ulrich Brand, Bettina Lösch and Stefan Thimme, *ABC der Alternativen* (Hamburg: VSA Verlag, 2007), 250. Among the extensive literature on the alterglobalist movement and on the World Social Forum, see Anita Anand, Arturo Escobar, Jai Sen and Peter Waterman, eds., *World Social Forum: Challenging Empires* (New Delhi: Viveka Foundation, 2004). Francisco Whitaker Ferreira, *Towards a New Politics: What Future for the World Social Forum* (London: Zed Books, 2007).
21 Walter Baier, *Prinzip "EntTäuschung": Von den großen Erzählungen zur neuen Sprache der Politik* (Hamburg: VSA-Verlag, 2007).
22 March, *Radical Left Parties in Europe*, 8, 49. See also Calossi, *Anti-Austerity Left Parties in the European Union: Competition, Coordination and Integration*, 107.
23 Karl Marx, "Contribution to the Critique of Hegel's Philosophy of Law," in *Collected Works*, vol. 3, eds. Karl Marx and Friedrich Engels (New York: International Publishers, 1975), 182. See also March, *Radical Left Parties in Europe*, 8.
24 Paolo Chiocchetti, *The Radical Left Party Family in Western Europe, 1989–2015* (London and New York: Routledge, 2017), 10.
25 See Friedrich Engels, "The Peasant War in Germany," in *Collected Works*, vol. 10, eds. Karl Marx and Friedrich Engels (New York: International Publishers, 1978), 397. On the content and historical limitations of these proto-communist

ideas, see inter alia Leo Kofler, *Zur Geschichte der bürgerlichen Gesellschaft* (Darmstadt: Luchterhand, 1976), 90.
26 Karl Marx, "Economic and Philosophic Manuscripts of 1844," in *Collected Works*, vol. 3, eds. Karl Marx and Friedrich Engels (New York: International Publishers, 1975), 296. Karl Marx, "Ökonomisch-Philosophische Manuskripte," in *Karl Marx Texte zu Methode und Praxis II: Pariser Manuskripe 1844* (Hamburg: Rowohlt, 1966), 75.
27 Karl Marx and Friedrich Engels, "The German Ideology," in *Collected Works*, vol. 5, eds. Karl Marx and Friedrich Engels (New York: International Publishers, 1976), 49.
28 The most striking example for thus doublespeak is the reasoning by Stalin publicly in justifying the new constitution he had instituted in 1936, at the same time as the show trials against Lenin's closest associates took place. See, for example, Isaak Deutscher, *Stalin: A Political Biography* (Berlin: Dietz Verlag Berlin, 1990), 489.
29 Palmiro Togliatti, "Intervista a Nuovi Argomenti," in Palmiro Togliatti, *Opere Scelte* (Roma: Editori Riuniti, 1981), 702–728.
30 Otto Bauer, *Zwischen zwei Weltkriegen? Die Krise der Weltwirtschaft, der Demokratie und des Sozialismus* (Bratislava: Eugen Prager Verlag, 1936), 190.
31 Hanna Arendt, *Elemente und Ursprünge totaler Herrschaft: Antisemitismus, Imperialism, totale Herrschaft* (München: Serie Piper, 1996), 635, 647.
32 Werner Hofmann, *Was ist Stalinismus* (Heilbronn: Distel Verlag, 1984), 84.
33 Karl Marx, *Theses on Feuerbach*, www.marxists.org/archive/marx/works/1845/theses/theses.htm, accessed June 1, 2017.
34 See Thomas Kroll, *Kommunistische Intellektuelle in Westeuropa Frankreich, Österreich, Italien und Großbritannien im Vergleich (1945–1956)* (Köln and Weimar and Wien: Böhlau Verlag, 2007), 9.
35 "Three mighty forces of our time—the world socialist system, the international working class and the national liberation movement—are coming together in the struggle against imperialism." See "Tasks at the Present Stage of the Struggle Against Imperialism and United Action of Communist and Workers Parties and All Anti-Imperialist Forces, Adopted by the International Meeting of Communist and Workers' Parties, Moscow, June 17, 1969," in *International Meeting of the Communist and Workers' Parties, Moscow 1969* (Prag: Verlag für Frieden und Sozialismus, 1969), 12.
36 There were very few exceptions to this: It was only the Danish Socialist People's Party—which, after the defeat of the Hungarian popular uprising, had developed in 1959 through a split of the Communist Party of Denmark—that did not attend the International Meeting of Communist and Workers' Parties in Moscow in 1969. The leaders of almost all other parties, for example, from Sweden, France, Italy and Austria, which had condemned Soviet intervention in Czechoslovakia, attended and expressed their more or less critical view of the intervention. In contrast, during the 1976 Conference of the Communist and Workers' Parties of Europe, the general secretary of the Communist Party of Italy stated that it would be the last consultation in which the Italian communists would be participating. See *Konferenz der Kommunistischen und Arbeiterparteien Europas: Dokumente und Reden Berlin, Juni 1976* (Prag: Verlag für Frieden und Sozialismus, 1976).
37 See the interesting monograph by Ellen Bos and Dieter Segert, *Osteuropäische Demokratien als Trendsetter? Parteien und Parteiensysteme nach dem Übergangsjahrzehnt* (Leverkusen: Verlag Barbara Budrich, 2008).
38 Cisleithania: Austrian part of Austria-Hungary.
39 Chiocchetti, *The Radical Left Party Family in Western Europe*, 38.

40 The Cominform consisted of the ruling parties—the Communist Party of the Soviet Union, the Bulgarian Communist Party, the Socialist Unity Party of Germany (from 1949), the League of Communists of Yugoslavia, the Polish United Workers' Party, the Romanian Workers' Party, the Communist Party of Czechoslovakia, the Hungarian Socialist Workers' Party—and two Western European parties: the French Communist Party and the PCI.
41 In 1959, the Danish Socialist People's Party separated from the Communist Party. In 1961, the wing of Norway's Communist Party, which distanced itself from the Soviet Union united with oppositional social democrats to form the Socialist People's Party. In 1967, Sweden's Communist Party expanded its name to Left Party—the Communists.
42 Palmiro Togliatti, "The Togliatti memorandum," *L'Unità*, September 4, 1964, www.marxists.org/archive/togliatti/1964/memorandum.htm, accessed June 1, 2017.
43 Togliatti, *The Togliatti memorandum*.
44 Jean Ellenstein, *Histoire du phénomène stalinien* (Paris: B. Grasset, 1975).
45 Santiago Carillo, *Eurocommunism and the State* (London: Lawrence and Wishart, 1977).
46 Nikoloas Dörr, *Der italienische Eurokomunismus als sicherheitspolitische Herausforderung für die USA und Westdeutschland 1969–1979* (Köln: Böhlau Verlag, 2017), 176.
47 A summary of the debate within the PCI around this can be found in Magri, *The Tailor of Ulm*, 172, 209.
48 "Was wird aus dem Eurokommunismus?," *Zeit-online*, www.zeit.de/1984/26/was-wird-aus-dem-eurokommunismus/seite-3, accessed June 1, 2017.
49 Altiero Spinelli and Ernesto Rossi, *The Ventotene Manifesto*, 8, www.cvce.eu/content/publication/1997/10/13/316aa96c-e7ff-4b9e-b43a-958e96afbecc/publishable_en.pdf, accessed June 1, 2017.
50 See also: The entry on the web site of the GUE/NGL group in the European Parliament: www.guengl.eu/group/history, accessed June 1, 2017.
51 A more detailed description of the preparation for the founding of the European Left Party can be found in Pedro Marset Campos, *A Short History of the European Left Party* (unpublished manuscript). Marset Campos was a member of the European Parliament for Izquierda Unida between 1994 and 1999 and participated in the preparations that led to founding of the European Left Party.
52 This is the case with the Red-Green Alliance (Denmark), Synaspismos (Greece), Bloco de Izquierda (Portugal) and Communist Refoundation Party (Italy).
53 See Fausto Bertinotti, "15 Thesen für eine alternative europäische Linke. Quintessenz einer Rede Fausto Bertinottis auf dem Europäischen Sozialforum in Florenz im November 2002," 2002, www.kpoe.at/bund/international/EL/bertinotti.pdf, accessed June 1, 2017.
54 The six parties were the KPÖ (Austria), PCF (France), PDS (Germany), Synaspismos (Greece), PRC (Italy) and Izquierda Unida (Spain).
55 Statute of the Party of the European Left, Preamble, see: www.european-left.org/propos-de-la-ge/documents, accessed June 1, 2017.
56 Author's note: among them the Communist Party of the Russian Federation.
57 "Letter of the CP of Bohemia and Moravia," www.european-left.org/positions/statements/letter-cp-bohemia-and-moravia, accessed June 1, 2017.
58 "Founding Declaration of the INITIATIVE of Communist and Workers' Parties to Study and Elaborate European Issues and to Coordinate Their Activity," www.initiative-cwpe.org/en/documents/founding-declaration/, accessed June 1, 2017.

59 The other candidates were Jean Claude Juncker (EPP), Martin Schulz (SPE), Guy Verhofstat (ALDE) Franziska Keller (Greens).
60 *Survey on the Congress of the European Left in 2016* (unpublished manuscript). To analyze these data, it is important to take account of the composition of the delegates: 45 percent of them belonged to the top-level party leaderships (e.g. secretariats, executive boards, etc.), 33 percent to high-level party leaderships (central committees, party boards), 7 percent to middle-level party leaderships and 15 percent characterized themselves as "simple members."
61 *Survey on the Congress of the European Left in 2016*, 60.
62 "A Plan B in Europe," www.euro-planb.eu/?page_id=96&lang=en, accessed June 1, 2017.
63 See Calossi, *Anti-Austerity Parties in the European Union*, 9, 107.
64 Moschonas, *The European Union and the Dilemmas of the Radical Left*.
65 Traverso, *Left-Wing Melacholia*, 25.

Part II
Memorial Landscapes in Central and Eastern Europe

4 Dissonant Heritage
Soviet Monuments in Central and Eastern Europe

Aleksandra Kuczyńska-Zonik

Introduction

Following World War II, huge statues of Joseph Stalin began to appear in all state socialist countries of Central Eastern Europe. Monumental sculptures were a part of a "multi-media propaganda machine," which sought to create a new collective identity.[1] It was meant to counteract and deconstruct national memory in the states of the Eastern Bloc and to replace them by memory of the Bolshevik revolution personified by Vladimir Lenin and extended through the liberation of countries by the Red Army. Polish literary critic Jan Prokop described the process of mythologization of the Soviet heroes as "iconization."[2] Initiated by communist leaders from the Soviet Union together with local activists from other East European states, "monument propaganda" was administrated by the governments at the national, regional and local levels.[3] The initial idea was to educate masses of people. It was not only to overcome the diversity of the different nations' beliefs, opinions and behavior. The concept was universal and total, and was directed to all residents with a view to taking control of the entire public space.[4]

As Serbian anthropologist Ivan Čolović says, any new political system has to be legitimized by new national popular symbols.[5] This is why after the fall of state socialism, beyond political, economic and social transformation, cultural space (in its form, meaning and function) has changed. The process of reorganizing urban space, decoding and giving new meanings to remnants of the former regime, proceeded differently in the individual countries of Central and Eastern Europe. Their "de-Sovietization" in the late twentieth century has meant the ideological "purification" of public space by destroying and removing monuments and plaques, and changing the names of objects and streets. The phenomenon of tearing down monuments was a typical element of the system change in these countries. As a consequence, empty space began to be recreated. New meanings and categories were sought for the existing landscape elements. This process of transforming the functions of the objects and the places where they are exhibited in order to shape national identity and the sense of community has been called "heritagization" by Kevin Walsh.[6]

The heritage methodology and the category of "dissonant" are used here to analyze the contemporary functions and social perception of the Soviet monuments. In this chapter, Soviet monuments include 1) objects commemorating World War II Soviet soldiers and partisans fighting against Nazism, 2) heroes and leaders of the socialist regimes, 3) objects that express gratitude for the Soviet Union and 4) monuments to the brotherhood between the Soviet Union and the socialist states. In some cases, the monuments combine two or more functions—i.e., they commemorate the Red Army while expressing gratitude for the Soviet Union. In political and historical studies, they are usually fundamental indicators of stages in the process of cultural transformation. The principal goal here is to examine the statues' role in constructing the relation between the Soviet monuments and social transition in Central and Eastern Europe. The focus will be on statues in Poland, Lithuania and Ukraine where the controversy and ambiguity of the Soviet heritage are still actual. Our discussion is based on the assumption that heritage is a matter of permanent political and social discourse,[7] seeing Soviet monuments as a dissonant heritage in the context of the ongoing process of de-communization.

A Framework for Analysis

The broad definition of heritage including monuments, groups of buildings and sites which, because of their homogeneity or their place in the landscape, are of outstanding universal value from the point of view of history, art, or science, was formulated by UNESCO during its General Conference on November 16, 1972.[8] The United Nations member states recognized the concept of heritage, which should be protected and preserved for future generations. However, the basic question of how monuments, places and artifacts are transformed into heritage has not been addressed. This problem is essential for Central and Eastern Europe, where the issue of Soviet heritage as a bone of contention seems to prevent the completion of political and social transformation even after 25 years.

Academic definitions offer explanations of heritage that focus on contemporary and selective use of the past,[9] providing social meanings and contexts for historical phenomena by rejecting, redefining or reconstructing objects. A frequently quoted scholar, Gregory J. Ashworth, specializing in the management of cultural heritage, urban tourism and urban planning, defines heritage as a "process when objects, events, places, activities or figures derived from the past can be transformed into the experience of the present."[10] The heritage paradigm, as opposed to protection and maintenance, recognizes buildings, historical sites and monuments as the most visible and clear traces of the past. They are treated as carriers of imagined historicity in an appropriate way to meet contemporary social, political and economic needs. The concept is based on market principles in which through a process of conscious selection, "products" of history considered to be eligible and welcome are selected. "Goods" are produced for contemporary consumption. The meaning of the object is generated during performance and the ignored and disregarded ones become forgotten.

Ashworth's understanding of the term "heritage" is taken to be the most adequate one for the analysis presented in this article. He is also the originator of another term I employ: The term "dissonance" as used in music theory describes the clash between two tones that do not blend harmonically, which results in a feeling of tension. Its first use in cultural theory was by sociologists John E. Tunbridge and Ashworth to describe the situation in which different groups attribute different stories to the same object or landscape.[11] The same object or place can stimulate a positive or negative sensation. Dissonant heritage may be cause for discord: It is simultaneously perceived as pleasant, resulting in satisfaction, or as distorted, with an unpleasant and painful effect.[12] Heritage is a dynamic process of social construction, which has a huge affect on the local, national and global dimension. A flexible approach allows us to see the variation in time and space in which heritage influences other phenomena or is itself influenced. Under certain conditions, heritage can be politicized, which leads to the disappearance of its authenticity and original context. Despite globalization and the socialization and internationalization processes of heritage with the implementation of the Convention Concerning the Protection of the World Cultural and Natural Heritage (UNESCO, 1972),[13] nation-states remain the most serious entities performing or managing heritage. States are responsible for protecting and making decisions that affect the management of heritage in the social environment. The authorities decide heritage roles and functions.[14] They establish how cultural goods are distributed and how social participation in heritage occurs. Strategically, heritage can both unite and divide, because in the process of shaping national identity it can unleash differences and social divisions.[15] Heritage is not only used to promote unity but also legitimates authority. It plays a fundamental role in integrating minority language and religious groups into the dominant nation. Therefore, it is a category that constitutes the homogeneity of the nation and prevents separatist tendencies.

For nation-building purposes, a tangible heritage is usually involved. The central location of the object has a symbolic meaning. Therefore, capitals usually play the most important role in political projects. Certain arrangements of urban space provide architectural, social and ideological harmony, which promotes good relations between the state and its citizens. The analysis and interpretation of changes in urban space may reflect the changes in the identity of the local community, because any change in architecture is a reflection of not only political and economic transformations but also an expression of the strength and direction of the changes occurring in consciousness.[16]

From Rejection to Forgetfulness?

Comparing the states' approaches to the issue of monuments, we can see that after state socialism collapsed in Central and Eastern Europe, the transformation of the memory process in different countries was quite similar. Soviet monuments were demolished or removed to military cemeteries or museums and replaced by statues commemorating national (like the monument to poet Taras Schevchenko in Lviv, Ukraine) and local heroes (as in Bielsko-Biała, Poland—the Monument of the Confederates of Bar, a league of Polish nobles and gentry active between 1768 and 1772 who organized themselves in order to defend Poland's independence from Russia and the privileges of the Roman Catholic Church).[17]

Destruction of Soviet statues has been the most popular way to change the landscape after the collapse of state socialism. Public monuments were the visible coordinates of the regime's power, and each change in regime required new symbols. Iconoclasm involving the destruction of Soviet statues reflected the clash of competing ideas and the evolution of social and political ideas.[18] According to legal scholar Sanford Levinson, the destruction of the monuments was a way of forgetting in order to bring about national purification,[19] as a symbol of moral renewal and the negation of the previous regime and as a symbol of a struggle against corruption and collaboration.[20] Social movements largely inspired the visual change in the architectural space of cities, accompanied by political decisions in the form of legislation that unequivocally condemned the state socialist period.

The process of monument demolition was most intense in the 1990s, but because of complicated administrative procedures, it continued on after this. For example, in Poland, in May 1990, the municipality of Bytom in Silesia decided that on the monument to "Gratitude"[21] only the plaque containing a propagandistic quotation from Stalin would be removed. But then the entire monument was removed two years later, on June 13, 1992. Eight Soviet soldiers were exhumed and reburied in the municipal cemetery three days later. In 1990, the plaque decorated by quotes of Stalin was removed from another monument of "Gratitude" in Bytom and preserved in the Upper Silesia Museum in this city. Currently, the monument is engraved with a new inscription in Polish and Russian: "The soldiers of the Soviet Army and the Soviet captives killed during World War II in Upper Silesia. Honor their memory."[22] Another example is a monument to General Karol Świerczewski, nom de guerre "General Walter" (1897–1947), a commander of the Polish Army in the USSR, designed by Tadeusz Sadowski and erected in 1954 in the City Park in Bytom.[23] On July 18, 1991, it was removed. Moreover, the name "Świerczewski's Park" (*Park Świerczewskiego*) was changed to the more neutral "City Park" (*Park Miejski*).

In the last few years, there have been a few incidents of demolition. A good example is the statue of Ivan Chernyakhovsky (1906–1945) in Pieniężno, Warmińsko-Mazurskie voivodeship, Poland, a Soviet general known for the killings of 8,000 Home Army (*Armia Krajowa*) soldiers and their leaders (for example, colonel Aleksander Krzyżanowski "Wolf" (*Wilk*), 1895–1951) in the Vilnius region. The monument was built in the 1970s. At the beginning of the 1990s, the Soviet hammer-and-sickle symbol was removed from the statue. Moreover, in 2015, former anti-communist activists illegally effaced the inscription commemorating the Soviet commander. The Chernyakhovsky monument survived until September 17, 2015 (the seventy-sixth anniversary of the Soviet invasion of Poland), when the municipality of Pieniężno finally decided to demolish the monument on the basis of its "bad condition." The intention was to transfer the dismantled statue to Kursk oblast, Russia.[24] After the incident, the Russian embassy in Poland was incensed. For Russia, Chernyakhovsky was a Great Patriotic War hero and one of the ablest Soviet commanders. Additionally, according to the 1994 Polish-Russian Agreement, which regulates issues related to the establishment, registration, installation, preservation and proper maintenance of places of memory and grave sites, any attempt to remove commemorating objects or memorials requires the consent of both states. Russia has cited "the obligation to respect international law" and believes that Poland is not fulfilling its obligations, but it has ignored the arguments of its Polish counterparts that the earlier agreement refers not to "symbolic monuments" such as "monuments of gratitude" but only to cemeteries. As a result of the carelessness of the negotiators of both countries, or else deliberate manipulation, the two authentic versions of the agreement differ in their wording. The Russian version is, indeed, imprecise and, if desired, can be interpreted as providing protection for "monuments of gratitude" as well. The Polish version speaks not of "places of memory and grave(s) (sites)" but of "places of *memory and rest*," therefore unambiguously indicating that the agreement refers to cemeteries. The Polish authorities have the right to interpret the agreement based on the Polish version.[25] From the Russian point of view, either the monument's destruction or its removal from its previous surroundings to a less prestigious one would necessarily provoke considerable discontent and protest on Russia's part. This draws Russia and Poland into a sharp dispute and the mutual accusation of falsifying history.[26]

In Lithuania, since the 1990s, a great deal of effort was spent—with several urban competitions organized—to give a new purpose to the sites where Soviet monuments stood, but none of them won sufficient public support. Instead, the monuments have become part of a national metanarrative within which there are two different approaches toward Soviet times. The most important element of this narrative is the memory of World War II. This event is remembered in Western and Central Europe as well as in the Baltics in connection with the Nazi-Soviet Pact of August 23, 1939, and subsequent Soviet occupation of the Baltic States, while in Russia, it is remembered as the Great Patriotic War that began in 1941 when Adolf Hitler invaded the Soviet Union. Thus the years 1939–1941 are not represented in the Soviet (and Russian) memorial landscape. Russia's official interpretation of history is still that Lithuania, Latvia and Estonia voluntarily joined the Soviet Union in 1940 and were liberated from Nazi Germany in 1944.[27] The Soviet monuments in Lithuania, as well in Latvia and Estonia, are deeply linked to historical experience of the war and of the Soviet period as a symbol of heroic victory or occupation, deportation and loss of independence.[28] The symbolic struggle over Soviet monuments is influenced by the local integration problems of Russian-speaking minorities who usually support Russia's interpretation of history.[29]

The discussion over the Soviet monuments in Lithuania has been continuing for years, but the conflict between Russia and Ukraine, which began in 2014, appears to be stirring up the dispute in Lithuania over the Soviet past once again.[30] It should be admitted that a few Soviet monuments are still in Altus (1986–1987, Alytaus voivodeship), Miroslavo (1977, Alytaus voivodeship) and Palanga (1958, Klaipėdos voivodeship). The Soviet memorial stone from Trakai (Vilnius voivodeship) was removed in 2014. However, the older generation of Lithuanians and residents of small towns and villages claim they have become accustomed to the Soviet monuments. They say they have recognized the objects as part of their state history.[31] Some of the Soviet monuments, like the one in Kaišiadorys (1973, Kauno voivodeship), are at military cemeteries, and their protection is supervised by the Russian embassy in Lithuania.[32]

The 1952 Soviet monument on the Green Bridge in Vilnius consisting of four sets of sculptures, each featuring two symbolic figures, is the most recognizable object commemorating the recent past of Lithuania. Each set is related to one state socialist symbol (education, agriculture, industry and the army). In 2005, Lithuanian society appeared to recognize the statues as a cultural site according to the law,[33] but current political and social debate shows the solution has not been so easy. In July 2015, the monument was removed to a conservation workshop for renovation. The discussion seemed to come to a standstill when in 2015 the Lithuanian Immovable Cultural Heritage Assessment Council (LICHAC) confirmed the Soviet-era sculptures were still included in the list of protected cultural monuments,[34] but in January 2016, the Vilnius municipality rejected the idea of reinstallation of the statues on the bridge were their restoration to be completed.[35] In March 2016, LICHAC stated the statues would be removed from the list of protected monuments and their transfer to a museum was recommended. The Lithuanian Ministry of Culture will make the final decision.[36] The solution may eventually lead to even greater polarization of society since the monument on the Green Bridge has become a ritualized place to commemorate the Soviet victory over fascism by Lithuania's Russian-language population. Additionally, the Soviet objects from Green Bridge exemplify legal scholar Igor Martynenko's point that the temporary removal of a statue under the pretext of maintenance or protection is a veiled form of violation of the legal protection of the monument.[37]

In Ukraine, as in most Central and Eastern European states, the process of dismantling Soviet statues started at the beginning of the 1990s. With the Ukrainian population politically, ethnically and socially divided between the pro-Western and Ukrainian-nationalist West and the eastern region, which has strong ties with Russia and has rather positive memories of the Soviet period,[38] the public sphere has been changing more distinctly and peremptorily in the western than in the central and eastern regions. Already in September 1990, Lviv's bronze statue of Lenin was removed. In 1990–1992, the majority of Lenin statues in western areas of Ukraine were demolished. However, following the Euromaidan (Revolution of Dignity) of 2013, a so-called *Leninopad* [Lenin fall] began in central and eastern regions of Ukraine as well. The symbolic date was December 8, 2013, when activists from the Svoboda [Freedom] party demolished the statue of Lenin in the center of Kiev. The demonstrators demanded replacing the monument with the statue of Ukrainian nationalist Stephan Bandera (1909–1959).[39] It should be noted that for years, the process of viewing Nazism as less dangerous than communism in the hierarchy of political and social ideologies of the twentieth century has resulted in an appreciation of fascist traditions in this part of Europe and the rise of extreme right-wing populist parties.[40]

Following the Revolution of Dignity, the Lenin monuments were repeatedly painted in Ukrainian national yellow-blue colors or decorated by Ukrainian flags. Moreover, activists have put a traditional Ukrainian shirt with its typical national ethnic embroidery on a statue of Lenin in Zaporizhya and a statue of Lenin in Odessa, which was converted into the Star Wars character Darth Vader. Painted monuments have become an example of the new Central and Eastern European tradition of using art to express goals of politics of memory. It goes back to 1990 when Czech artist David Černý painted the monument of the Soviet tank in Prague pink. One of the best-known monuments of state socialism in Bulgaria is a huge bas-relief of nine Soviet soldiers located in a park near the center of Sofia. The monument was repeatedly repainted to represent characters from American popular culture, including Ronald McDonald, Superman and the Joker. In August 2013, the forty-fifth anniversary of the Prague Spring (the Soviet-led invasion of Czechoslovakia in 1968), the statue was painted pink once more.[41] In March 2014, it was painted blue and yellow in protest against the Russian Federation's annexation of the Crimea. The Soviet cemetery memorial in Kruopiai, Šiaulių voivodeship, Lithuania, was painted in the same way in September 2014.[42] Even in Krasnoyarsk, Siberia, Russia, in March 2014, in solidarity with Ukraine, the monument of Lenin was signed "Glory to Ukraine" (*Slava Ukrainy*)[43] using red paint, and the star topping a Stalin-era skyscraper in Moscow was painted in blue and yellow Ukrainian colors in August 2014.[44] The artistic motivation can be explained by the euphoria and sense of national revival that accompanied the political transition.

On April 9, 2015, the Ukrainian Parliament passed a law prohibiting communist and Nazi propaganda, which resulted in the removal of monuments commemorating Soviet soldiers. The major problem in implementing the law is in Eastern Ukraine, where most Russian-speaking citizens are nostalgic for the guaranteed employment, social equality and public order that were seen as the most positive features of the old regime.[45] In Ukraine, monuments that were the symbols of the Soviet past were moved to Red Army cemeteries. With their pedestals removed, they became more socially acceptable. The transfer to new, discrete and isolated places suggests that the authorities do not have a solution for the difficult memory problem; as a consequence, the monuments became unnatural, strange and incomprehensible. The bizarre status of the Soviet memorials from Ukraine can be exemplified by the Motherland Monument (*Rodina-mat'*) in Kiev erected in 1981, designed by Vasil Boroday and Eugene V. Vuchetych and dedicated to the victory over Nazi Germany in World War II. In her right hand, the female figure hoists a 50-foot sword into the sky. In her left hand, she holds a massive 13-ton shield decorated with the Soviet Union's seal, which most probably will be removed. However, the huge 334-foot-tall monument commemorating the Soviet victory over Nazi Germany will remain.[46]

Repeated acts of painting Soviet soldier monuments have likewise occurred in Hungary and Poland. They have nothing in common with art, but often no clear-cut distinction between art and vandalism can be established. While the artistic action by Černý was called an act of vandalism by his opponents, the anti-communist slogans, such as "Down with Communism" (*Precz z komunizmem*) or "Red Plague" (*Czerwona zaraza*), that appeared on the monuments in Poland express very literal emotions but not artistic impulses. The Budapest memorial to World War II soldiers of the Soviet Red Army (Statue of Liberty) in Szabadság Square, designed by Zsigmond Kisfaludi Stróbl and erected in 1947—the only remaining monument of its kind in the city—was vandalized and slogans such as "murderers," (*gyilkosok*) "1956" and "traitors" (*áruló*) were daubed on the monument with red paint in February 2010.[47] The Monument of the Soviet Army in Skaryszewski Park in Warsaw has been vandalized many times (for example, in 2011 and 2015).[48] On September 17, 2011, the Warsaw "Brothers in Arms"[49] monument was vandalized as well, and it was removed in the same year and transported to the conservation workshop in Michałowice, near Warsaw,[50] because of construction of the underground line. According to the Warsaw municipality's decision, it was to be reinstalled but moved closer to Saints Cyril and Methodius Street after restoration.[51] However, in 2015, Warsaw authorities refused to reinstall the monument[52] because of the unclear legal status of Soviet monuments; this decision has divided public opinion.

According to a 2013 Polish Regional Court statement, the statues are not under protection because they are not regarded as "monuments." The legal definition of "monuments" includes "objects that commemorate and honor an event or person." Actually, they do not specifically celebrate or favor anything. Instead, according to the court, they are reminders of a tragic falsification of Polish history. Additionally, what is more interesting is the fact that distinguishing between "statues" and "monuments" illustrates the process of categorizing, appreciating or depreciating in the sense established by Pierre Bourdieu. The objects may be valued and protected or at the same time rejected or emptied of meaning. Following Bourdieu, we may say that the approach to Soviet objects of memory in the countries of the former Eastern Bloc may be considered a sign of what he calls "distinction," the purpose of which is to control the values of reemerging nations.[53]

The controversial dissonant nature of Soviet monuments brings them into the spotlight. In Warsaw, there are still four locations where Soviet and Polish soldiers are commemorated; in Szczecin, there are three of them. In Dąbrowa Górnicza, Silesia voivodeship, seven of them remain. The monument of "Freedom" erected in Bytom in 1968 is still standing today.[54] In 1991, the Soviet concrete star on the monument was dismantled and the hammer and sickle was plastered over. However, in 2003, in accordance with the statement signed by the president of Bytom, Krzysztof Wójcik,[55] the monument was restored, and the Soviet symbols reappeared. In 2006, the hammer and sickle were again removed. Members of the Democratic Left Alliance (SLD), a social democratic political party in Poland, continue to celebrate national holidays (May 1, the Labor Day, celebrated in a particularly festive way in the Polish People's Republic; May 3, the Day of the Constitution of May 3, 1791; and November 11, Independence Day. Celebrations of the last two were prohibited in the Polish People's Republic) near the statue and placing flowers there.[56]

A few monuments commemorating Soviet soldiers have continued to exist locally. Their bad condition (some of them have been painted over, are broken or are covered with grass) show that they are no longer used; examples are in Brzeg Dolny, Dolnośląskie voivodeship, erected in 1945 or in Dąbrowa Górnicza-Ząbkowice, Śląskie voivodeship, erected in 1966. In Lubelszczyzna region, there are a few statues of the Polish partisan, Miszka Tatar (Michail Atamanov, 1912–1943). As a Red Army officer, he fought against the Nazis in Poland and died in 1943 in Józefów, Roztocze. His monuments are no longer the object of political debate. Neither residents nor the authorities have been expecting to remove or demolish them. Nor can they agree on restoration. Why are they still there? Are they simply forgotten? Is it for lack of funds for restoration or the unwillingness to practice conservation? Historian Jaś Elsner explains: "The preserved damaged object, in its own material being, signals both its predamaged state—a different past with potentially different cultural, political and social meanings—and its new or altered state."[57] Historian Ewa Ochman adds that those monuments that still exist or have been left as damaged objects in the urban landscape are no longer monuments that possess commemorative value but simply resemble objects from a kind of museum of the Soviet statues.[58]

Here I suggest that those desolate, abandoned monuments have become socially neutral, which is why they do not arouse emotion. Instead, the abandoned status of those objects seems to indicate that the transition has been accomplished, and society is reconciled with the past. Residents do not take care of the objects, thus showing that they are rejecting the past in a more peaceful ("natural") manner. In other words, their attitude toward the objects of memory indicates their attitude toward the past that these objects symbolize. Symbolically, we can compare them to abandoned building complexes in Skrunda, Latvia; in Wünsdorf, East Germany; or in Kłomino, Poland. Soldiers used them during the Soviet period, but after the Red Army's departure, the cities were abandoned and forgotten. They have remained in the same condition for years by now.

Soviet Monuments in Heritage Discourses

The controversial nature of the dissonant heritage represents a challenge for national policy. After state socialism collapsed, national strategies involved demolishing or adapting the Soviet monuments in order to construct national identity. All countries in post-Soviet space had to face this dissonant heritage, although national strategies for heritage management varied. Where social, economic and cultural divisions were great, transformation induced anxiety, suffering, alienation and social exclusion. The initial process of identifying the cultural heritage made state strategy more complex.

The relative anti-communism and of the resistance movements influenced the repressive character of the regime in Poland in the 1970s and 1980s (for example, shooting at workers in December 1970 and introducing martial law on December 13, 1981). Additionally, the nonrevolutionary character of the regime's overthrow made the transformation process more radical. Two narratives represented the post-1989 discourse around Soviet monuments: either discrediting People's Poland completely or legitimizing a few elements of its achievements. There was a rapid process of reconstructing architectural space, the most visible aspect being the change of street names. New names were given to places and the pre-war memorials restored. However, there were still places commemorating Soviet soldiers in the Silesia region, in Wielkopolska, and in Zachodniopomorskie, while the sparsest commemoration is found in Świętokrzyskie and Kujawsko-Pomorskie voivodeships.[59] It is evident that most of the monuments were located in the "recovered territories" (*Ziemie Odzyskane*)—i.e., the territory of the former Free City of Danzig and the pre-war territories (Pomerania, Masuria, Warmia and Upper Silesia) that became part of Poland after World War II. The great majority of the German inhabitants either fled or were expelled from the "recovered territories," while Poles from the former Eastern Poland were resettled here.[60] Soviet monuments were an instrument to influence, ideologically, new immigrants who were relatively empty of local tradition.

According to the "List of Objects of Commemoration of Soldiers and Soviet Partisans in Poland," in 2009, there were 306 Soviet monuments, obelisks, plaques and objects of military equipment (tanks, cannons, etc.) celebrating the Red Army or its individual leaders.[61] Unsurprisingly, this number was almost halved since 1997. The earlier report of "List of Memory Places Commemorating Russian (Soviet) Soldiers Killed in Poland" from 1997 revealed that there had been more than 560 memory places, including 415 monuments. In 2016, the Institute of National Remembrance—Commission for the Prosecution of Crimes against the Polish Nation (IPN) stated there were 229 Soviet monuments still in Poland.[62] This means that the process of destruction and removal of Soviet monuments that started in early 1990s is still ongoing. Recently, after the center-right Law and Justice party (PiS) won the parliamentary elections in October 2015, this confrontation has intensified. But even before the elections, in July 2015, a few members of the municipal council of Legnica, representatives of PiS, initiated the removal of the Monument of Gratitude to the Red Army from the city;[63] nevertheless, up to July 2016, the monument remained in place.

In her "hot-cold" memory concept, art historian Hedvig Turai[64] has defined hot active memory as a living relationship to the past and passive cold memory as closed. She saw the collective memory of the Holocaust in Hungary as still hot, contrary to the memory of the Soviet regime, which she described as cold. In contrast to Turai's concept, my argument here is that the relationship to the Soviet past is "hot" in many post-socialist states. Although the memory of fascism and Nazism is still a sensitive question, we observe that it is the Soviet past that is an emotional issue, and this sparks aggression and mobilizes political forces in Poland, Lithuania or Ukraine.[65] The monograph *Wałęsa. Człowiek z teczki* [Wałęsa. A Man from the File] by Polish historian Sławomir Cenckiewicz,[66] along with information disclosed in February 2016 about Lech Wałęsa, the activist of the anti-communist movement "Solidarity" (*Solidarność*) and former Polish president and Nobel Laureate suspected of having cooperated with the authorities in the 1970s and 1980s,[67] caused excitement and much social commotion, which demonstrates that the collective memory of state socialism in Poland is still alive. The attitude of part of Polish society toward the "unwanted past" was expressed by the Polish Sejm in April 2016 when a so-called de-communization law was adopted prohibiting propaganda in favor of communism or any totalitarian regime by means of the names of buildings, roads, streets, bridges and squares or any public facilities.[58] By law, Polish municipalities have had to remove all symbols of state socialism from public space—for example, the street named after Soviet cosmonaut Yuri Gagarin (1934–1968) in Toruń, Kujawsko-Pomorskie voivodeship; or after Zygmunt Berling (1896–1980), commander of the First Polish Army (part of the Polish Army in the USSR during WWII) in Białystok, Podlaskie voivodeship; or the twenty-fifth anniversary of the Polish People's Republic Park in Gniezno, Wielkopolskie voivodeship.

By contrast, Lithuania seems less restrictive toward memorials of state socialism. It banned Soviet symbols in 2008, but on June 9, 2016, the

Lithuanian Parliament (a majority of whose delegates are from the social democratic party) rejected a draft resolution condemning the former Communist Party of Lithuania, declaring it a criminal organization and responsible for crimes against citizens during the Soviet occupation.[69]

However, this particular analysis points not only to philosophical but also to practical controversies. Should public money be spent to conserve works such as those discussed in the article? How should public monuments currently be designed? But also, are the Soviet monuments symbols of domination by the USSR, or are they just works of art that commemorate the history of a certain state?

Surprisingly, although the permanent presence of the dissonant Soviet heritage in Central and Eastern Europe makes it difficult to integrate or unify the nation, the popularity of "red tourism" or "socialist tourism," where visitors can see and learn about the socialist architecture, sculpture and propaganda posters is growing. The phenomenon of Soviet art museums in post-socialist states in Central and Eastern Europe has various causes. In 1998, Lithuania's Ministry of Culture announced an urban competition to propose a museum for dismantled monumental sculptures from the Soviet period. The preparatory work began in early 1999; the museum was opened in 2001 in Grūtas Park, near the village of Druskininkai, Alytaus voivodeship, in the south of Lithuania.[70] It displays more than 80 Soviet monuments of communist leaders and Lithuanian communist activists such as Vladimir Lenin, Felix Dzerzhynsky, Vincas Mickevičius-Kapsukas (1880–1935—one of the founders of the Communist Party of Lithuania), Jeronimas Uborevičius (1896–1937—Lithuanian commander of the Red Army) and Marytė Melnikaitė (1923–1943—a member of the Communist Youth Organization killed by the Nazis). They are situated in a desolate forested landscape along a 2-kilometer pathway in a countryside resembling Siberia. Imitation watchtowers and remnants of Soviet labor camps are part of the attraction. The monuments that formerly stood in central public places have been neutralized in their current location. They are not on their pedestals and thus are stripped of prestige and authority. The museum exhibits Soviet relics and iconography, and also serves Soviet-era dishes in a nostalgic café to attract tourists. This ironic perspective embodies values diametrically opposed to the communist regime, which the museum is meant to portray. This depreciation of the icons of the Soviet regime (in the form of paintings, statues and fragments of Lenin statues), changed their meaning and made them into commercial goods. It seems to be serving capitalism rather than education. Similar museums are located in Russia (Muzeon in Moscow),[71] Bulgaria (the Museum of Socialist Art in Sophia),[72] Hungary (Memento Park in Budapest),[73] Estonia (Maarjamäe Palace, the Estonian History Museum, in Tallinn)[74] and Poland (Zamoyski Museum in Kozłówka).[75] The next museum is going to be opened in Borne-Sulinowo, Zachodniopomorskie voivodeship, Poland.[76]

By visualizing the official ideology and legitimizing the state's power, memorials constitute collective memory. Their removal from public space is generally a highly political issue and represents an important aspect of "struggles over memory." Research confirms the social acceptance of the Soviet memorials, especially among the older generation,[77] as well as among those who were actively involved in the communist parties or those living in regions with a large Russian-speaking minority, as in Trakai, Lithuania.[78] However, in some cases, for the local Russian-speaking populations, regardless of age, the Soviet monuments do not stand for the communist regime but are recognized as monuments to the peoples from the former Soviet Union who fought against Nazism in Europe. As in Sofia, Bulgaria, the Soviet Army monument itself is a monument to ordinary people: soldiers, women and children.[79] Their "monumental" form allows us to see them as a major landmark of cities, which means the Soviet statues are becoming part of the local environment. Divided attitudes toward the Soviet monuments among post-socialist societies reflect the attitudes toward the state socialist past as a whole. For example, in Romania, the economic situation of recent years has lent more credibility to a positive social perception of state socialism, which was confirmed in opinion polls.[80] On the other hand, in Poland, where society has viewed the system change more positively, the general social attitude toward the socialist state has continued to be as divided as it was in the 1990s.[81] Two-fifths of respondents (40 percent and 44 percent in 1997 and 2014, respectively) admitted to having positive attitudes to the Polish People's Republic period.

Obviously, the monuments discussed in this chapter carry various meanings for different parts of societies as they express alternative points of view about the difficulty of the past. They can be recognized as a platform for communication and reconciliation for societies and their memories, of which we are reminded by historian Pierre Nora who defined as an embodiment of memory certain sites (*lieux de mémoire*) where a sense of historical continuity persists.[82] Ochman, who analyzed Soviet memorials and identities in Poland, argues that the monuments constitute sites for the articulation of new narratives about the country's history, which means their principal effect is more continuity than opposition between past and future.[83] However, those who created the museums of Soviet monuments see the issue differently and clearly intend them to transmit an anti-communist message: For example, according to Polish IPN, the educational park in the Borne-Sulinowo Museum of Soviet Art will help people understand that the "Monuments of Gratitude to the Red Army" are in fact symbols of Soviet violence against Poland.[84]

Nevertheless, today, we are gradually witnessing a changing approach to the future of monuments.[85] The Soviet memorials have been recognized as a social historical heritage and adapted to a new reality with a new appreciation of the monuments as a part of art history. The artistic value of Soviet monuments has usually been neglected in political debate,[86] but the view has been slowly altering in the direction of considering some of the Soviet monuments as prominent examples of a Soviet style of art known as socialist realism.[87] The authors of the vast majority of those monuments were admired sculptors and artists because of the policy pursued by state authorities of legitimizing socialist rule by commissioning famous and celebrated artists known for the quality of their art.[88]

While Central and Eastern European societies interpret socialist realism as a dissonant heritage, the architecture of socialist realism is no longer part of the rejected heritage. Over the past decade, growing interest and appreciation of its legacy have led to giving statutory protection to the most outstanding examples, such as in Poland (the Palace of Culture and Science in 2007, the former Communist Party Headquarters in 2009, the Ministry of Finance in 2012, all in Warsaw), in Croatia (the Petrova Gora Monument in 2004 in Petrovac) and in the Czech Republic (the urban heritage area in Ostrava-Poruba in 2003).[89] By contrast, in Lithuania, the Soviet monument from Green Bridge is going to be excluded from the protected monuments list.[90]

However, the phenomenon of "communist heritage tourism," which involves visits to places associated with the communist past or to sites that represent or commemorate that past, can remind us of what literary theoretician Edward Said described as "orientalism"—that is, the discovery of exotic places, haunting memories and landscapes.[91] As Western visitors, after visiting the exotic "Orient," could once be assured of the rightness of the Western model of civilization, visiting communist monuments in dilapidated states today, collected as they are in museums of communism, placing them in an ironic, demonized or even nostalgic context, leads the visitor to accept the current world order rather than question it.[92]

Conclusions

In the 1990s, social movements initiated the bottom-up process of removing or leaving the Soviet monuments. At that time, the removal seemed to result from a lack of state control over the politics of memory, which in fact caused acts of vandalism in some cases. The most radical acts related to the largest, most distinctive monuments standing in central areas or city squares. Less controversial local monuments remained forgotten. However, both at the local and national levels, there was no consensus about the future of the monuments and historical policy. Currently, this process involving the removal or maintenance of monuments is unfolding as a more orderly and controlled approach to the politics of memory. After a period of chaotic acts aimed against Soviet statues, many states have decided to normalize the monuments' legal status, sanction the former acts and establish strategies and policies to manage the heritage for the future. Central and Eastern European states made the rejection of Soviet symbols into a part of the de-communization process, as in Lithuania in 2008,[93] Georgia in 2011,[94] Ukraine in 2015[95] or Poland in 2016.[96] In some other countries, they are protected as genuine monuments to the anti-fascist struggle or at least in order to maintain good relations with Russia.

The different attitudes of Central and Eastern European societies toward monuments reflect the complexity of the political, economic and social process of transformation. Establishing a homogeneous memory policy is much more difficult in ethnically, politically or socially divided nations. The supporters of right-wing and nationalist parties represent the most radical attitudes. And for the young generation in most Central and Eastern European countries, the Soviet regime still has negative connotations. It represents lack of freedom in general and of expression, opinion, information and of choice in particular, as well as the state of fear and the rationing of food.[97]

The debate around the Soviet monuments is only a part of the broader discussion of the meaning of the state socialist period. This exploration shows that there is no clear and coherent opinion when it comes to these monuments. The differing attitudes are related to the attitudes toward state socialism as a whole, which are shaped by forces and experiences related to different ideological, political, economic and social categories. In other words, these factors influence the bizarre and transitional status of Soviet monuments, as a result of which their perception has been strongly politicized, leading to the disappearance of their original context. The dissonant heritage has been polarizing post-socialist societies as well. These and many others are the still unanswered questions around Central and Eastern European public space.

Acknowledgments

The author would like to thank those who read this chapter in draft form for their suggestions and research support.

Notes

1 Vladimir P. Tolstoy, *Leninskiy plan monumental'noy propagandy v deystvii* (Moskva: Akademiya khudozhestv SSSR, 1961).
2 Jan Prokop, *Wyobraźnia pod nadzorem: Z dziejów literatury i polityki z PRL* (Kraków: Viridis, 1994), 21.
3 Dominika Czarnecka, *"Pomniki Wdzięczności" Armii Czerwonej w Polsce Ludowej i w III Rzeczypospolitej* (Warszawa: Instytut Pamięci Narodowej, 2015), 84–112.
4 Frances W. Harrison, "Reviving Heritage in Post-Soviet Eastern Europe: A Visual Approach to National Identity," *Totem: The University of Western Ontario Journal of Anthropology* 20.1 (2012), http://ir.lib.uwo.ca/totem/vol20/iss1/3, accessed May 13, 2017.
5 Ivan Čolovič, *The Politics of Symbol in Serbia: Essays in Political Anthropology*, trans. from the Serbian Celia Hawkesworth (London: Hurst and Company, 2002); Ivan Čolovič, *Bałkany—terror kultury*, trans. Magdalena Petryńska (Wołowiec: Wydawnictwo Czarne, 2007).

6 Kevin Walsh, *The Representation of the Past: Museums and Heritage in the Postmodern World* (New York: Routledge, 1992).
7 Čolovič, *The Politics of Symbol in Serbia*.
8 UNESCO, "Convention Concerning the Protection of the World Cultural and Natural Heritage," http://whc.unesco.org/en/conventiontext/, accessed December 2, 2016.
9 Brian Graham, Gregory J. Ashworth and John E. Tunbridge, *A Geography of Heritage: Power, Culture, and Economy* (London: Arnold, 2000).
10 Gregory J. Ashworth, "Conservation as Preservation or as Heritage: Two Paradigms and Two Answers," *Built Environment* 23.2 (1997): 92–102.
11 John E. Tunbridge and Gregory J. Ashworth, *Dissonant Heritage: The Management of the Past as a Resource in Conflict* (Chichester and New York: John Wiley, 1996).
12 Gregory J. Ashworth, *Planowanie dziedzictwa*, trans. Marta Duda-Gryc (Kraków: Międzynarodowe Centrum Kultury, 2015).
13 UNESCO, "Convention Concerning the Protection of the World Cultural and Natural Heritage."
14 Elsa Peralta and Marta Anico, eds., *Heritage and Identity: Engagement and Demission in the Contemporary World* (Abingdon: Routledge, 2009), 1–11.
15 Helaine Silverman and D. Fairchild Ruggles, "Cultural Heritage and Human Rights," in *Cultural Heritage and Human Rights*, eds. Helaine Silverman and D. Fairchild Ruggles (New York: Springer, 2007), 3–22.
16 Mariusz Czepczyński, "Krajobraz kulturowy miast po socjalizmie: Tendencje przemian form i znaczeń," in *Przestrzenie miast postsocjalistycznych: Studia społecznych przemian przestrzeni zurbanizowanej*, ed. Mariusz Czepczyński (Gdańsk and Poznań: Bogucki Wydawnictwo Naukowe, 2006), 45–61.
17 Arkadiusz Michał Stasiak, *Patriotyzm w myśli konfederatów barskich* (Lublin: Towarzystwo Naukowe Katolickiego Uniwersytetu Lubelskiego, 2005).
18 Albert Boime, "Perestroika and the Destabilization of the Soviet Monuments," *ARS: Journal of the Institute for History of Art of Slovak Academy of Science* 2.3 (1993): 211–226.
19 Sanford Levinson, *Written in Stone: Public Monuments in Changing Societies* (Durham: Duke University Press Books, 1998), 69.
20 Ewa Ochman, "Municipalities and the Search for the Local Past Fragmented Memory of the Red Army in Upper Silesia," *East European Politics and Societies* 23.3 (2009): 392–420; Ewa Ochman, "Soviet War Memorials and the Re-Construction of National and Local Identities in Post-Communist Poland," *Nationalities Papers: The Journal of Nationalism and Ethnicity* 38.4 (2010): 509–530.
21 The "Monument of Gratitude" built on May 1, 1945, in the city center in front of the Bytom Municipal Office was the first monument erected after the end of World War II. It was dedicated to the Red Army soldiers killed in January 1945 in Bytom. The second "Monument of Gratitude" was erected in the same year in the municipal cemetery at the headquarters of the Soviet soldiers, where more than 6,000 people were buried.
22 Edward Wieczorek, "Powojenne pomniki Bytomia i jego dzielnic," in *Ze spiżu i granitu: Pomniki Bytomia*, ed. Elżbieta Giszter (Bytom: Muzeum Górnośląskie w Bytomiu, 2012), 37–39.
23 Magdalena Nowacka-Goik, "Ciekawa historia fontann Tadeusza Sadowskiego z Bytomia," *Nasze Miasto*, June 28, 2012, http://bytom.naszemiasto.pl/artykul/ciekawa-historia-fontann-tadeusza-sadowskiego-z-bytomia,1459357,artgal,t,id,tm.html, accessed June 2, 2016.
24 "Pieniężno: zbiórka pieniędzy na demontaż pomnika Iwana Czerniachowskiego," *Polskie Radio*, August 4, 2015, www.polskieradio.pl/5/3/Artykul/1484688,

Pieniezno-zbiorka-pieniedzy-na-demontaz-pomnika-Iwana-Czerniachowskiego, accessed June 2, 2016.
25 Łukasz Adamski, "Russia's 'Monumental' Anti-diplomacy," *Intersection*, December 20, 2015, http://intersectionproject.eu/article/russia-europe/russias-monumental-anti-diplomacy, accessed August 4, 2016.
26 "MSZ: w sprawie pomników Rosja uporczywie nie wykazuje woli do dialogu," *Polskie Radio*, December 4, 2015, www.polskieradio.pl/5/3/Artykul/1553530, MSZ-w-sprawie-pomnikow-Rosja-uporczywie-nie-wykazuje-woli-do-dialogu, accessed December 16, 2016.
27 "Kommentariy Departamenta informatsii i pechati MID Rossii v svyazi s vyskazyvaniyami ryada yevropeyskikh politikov otnositel'no 'okkupatsii' stran Baltii Sovetskim Soyuzom i neobkhodimosti osuzhdeniya etogo so storony Rossii," *Ministerstvo Inostrannykh del Rossiyskoy Federatsii*, May 4, 2005, www.mid.ru/evropejskij-souz-es/-/asset_publisher/6OiYovt2s4Yc/content/id/440804/pop_up?_101_INSTANCE_6OiYovt2s4Yc_viewMode=tv&_101_INSTANCE_6OiYovt2s4Yc_qrIndex=0, accessed December 16, 2016.
28 Siobhan Kattago, "Memory, Pluralism and the Agony of Politics," *Journal of Baltic Studies* 41.3 (2010): 383–394.
29 "Issledovaniye: latviyskoye obshchestvo ne speshit osuzhdat' Rossiyu za voyennuyu agressiyu protiv Ukrainy," *Delfi*, June 26, 2016, http://rus.delfi.lv/news/daily/latvia/issledovanie-latvijskoe-obschestvo-ne-speshit-osuzhdat-rossiyu-za-voennuyu-agressiyu-protiv-ukrainy.d?id=47604035, accessed June 13, 2017.
30 Dalva Baronienė, "Kūjus su pjautuvais matysime dar ilgai," *Lietuvos Žinios*, March 2, 2016, http://lzinios.lt/lzinios/Lietuva-be-balvonu/kujus-su-pjautuvais-matysime-dar-ilgai/218912, accessed December 2, 2016.
31 Ida Mažutaitienė, "Okupacinės sovietų armijos karių paminklai—gražiausiose Lietuvosmiestųvietose," *15min*, August 29, 2014, www.15min.lt/naujiena/aktualu/istorija/okupacines-sovietu-armijos-kariu-paminklai-graziausiose-lietuvos-miestu-vietose-582-449380, accessed August 6, 2016.
32 Eglė Samoškaitė, "Raseinių valdžios panosėje balinami paminklai žuvusiems 'už tarybų valdži,'" *Delfi*, December 20, 2010, www.delfi.lt/news/daily/lithuania/raseiniu-valdzios-panoseje-balinami-paminklai-zuvusiems-uz-tarybu-valdzia.d?id=39890347, accessed December 22, 2016.
33 Lietuvos Respublikos kultūros ministro 2005 m. balandžio 29 d. įsakymas Nr. ĮV—190, "Dėl nekilnojamųjų kultūros vertybių pripažinimo saugomomis pakeitimo," *Teisės Aktų Registras*, December 12, 2016, www.e-tar.lt/portal/lt/legalAct/1e3c5f40184211e68eb0b4a9a30fc97f, accessed February 8, 2017.
34 "Soviet Statues Not to Be Removed from Vilnius Green Bridge," *The Baltic Course*, February 10, 2015, www.baltic-course.com/eng/real_estate/?doc=102237, accessed December 8, 2016.
35 "Mer Vil'nyusa: sovetskiye skul'ptury na Zelenyy most ne vernutsya," *Delfi*, January 20, 2016, http://ru.delfi.lt/news/politics/mer-vilnyusa-sovetskie-skulptury-na-zelenyj-most-ne-vernutsya.d?id=70172530, accessed January 17, 2017.
36 "Vieningai balsuota už teisinės apsaugos panaikinimą Žaliajam tiltui su skulptūromis (papildyta)," *Kulturos Paveldo Departamentas Prie Kulturos Ministerijos*, March 1, 2016, www.kpd.lt/index.php?mact=News,cntnt01,detail,0&cntnt01articleid=2217&cntnt01returnid=213, accessed June 2, 2017.
37 Igor' Martynenko, "Snos pamyatnika arkhitektury pod vidom yego restavratsii: ot teorii k ugolovnoy praktike," in *The Soviet Heritage and European Modernism*, eds. Jörg Haspel, Michael Petzet, Anke Zalivako and John Ziesemer (Berlin: Hendrik Bäßler Verlag, 2007), 86–89.
38 Serhy Yekelchyk, *Ukraine: Birth of a Modern Nation* (Oxford: Oxford University Press, 2007), 199.

39 "V Khar'kove predlagayut ustanovit' pamyatnik Bandere vmesto Lenina," *Ria Novosti*, March 21, 2016, http://rian.com.ua/society/20160321/1007042934.html, accessed March 3, 2017.
40 Ruth Wodak and John E. Richardson, eds., *Analysing Fascist Discourse: European Fascism in Talk and Text* (New York: Routledge, 2013).
41 "Bulgarian Red Army Monument Painted Pink in Prague Spring Apology," *Reuters*, August 21, 2013, www.reuters.com/article/us-bulgaria-monument-czech-idUSBRE97K0G520130821, accessed March 3, 2017.
42 "Kruopių miestelyje vandalizmas—sovietų karių kapai išniekinti Ukrainos vėliavos spalvomis," *15min*, September 15, 2014, www.15min.lt/naujiena/aktualu/nusikaltimaiirnelaimes/kruopiu-miestelyje-vandalizmas-tarybiniu-kariu-kapai-isniekinti-ukrainos-veliavos-59–453226, accessed December 2, 2016.
43 "V Krasnoyarske na pamyatnike Leninu napisali 'Slava Ukraine!,'" *Lenta*, March 3, 2014, https://lenta.ru/news/2014/03/03/lenin/, accessed December 2, 2016.
44 Tom Parfitt, "Stalin Skyscraper in Moscow Painted in Ukrainian Colours," *The Telegraph*, August 20, 2014, www.telegraph.co.uk/news/worldnews/europe/russia/11045845/Stalin-skyscraper-in-Moscow-painted-in-Ukrainian-colours.html, accessed January 12, 2017.
45 Stephen White, "Soviet Nostalgia and Russian Politics," *Journal of Eurasian Studies* 1.1 (2010): 1–9; Steve Rosenberg, "The Ukrainians Who Are Nostalgic for Their Soviet Past," *BBC News*, June 8, 2014, www.bbc.com/news/magazine-27743090, accessed July 15, 2016.
46 "Soviet Statue Will Stay but Coat of Arms Removed, Typical Ukraine Junta Mentality," *Novorossia Today*, January 21, 2016, http://novorossia.today/soviet-statue-will-stay-but-coat-of-arms-removed-typical-ukraine-junta-mentality/, accessed July 6, 2016; Sabra Ayres, "Ukraine's Plans to Discard Soviet Symbols Are Seen as Divisive, Ill-timed," *Los Angeles Times*, May 13, 2015, www.latimes.com/world/europe/la-fg-ukraine-decommunization-20150513-story.html, accessed December 2, 2016.
47 "Soviet Monument in Budapest Vandalized," *Politics.hu*, February 16, 2010, www.politics.hu/20100216/soviet-monument-in-budapest-vandalized/; Liberty Statue, *Budapest.com*, www.budapest.com/city_guide/sights/monuments_of_art/liberty_statue.en.html?sid=it73k4nhjflkqtatf0tcq03fn3, accessed August 18, 2016.
48 Lech Marcinczak, "'Precz z komuną' znów na pomniku żołnierzy radzieckich," *TVN24*, September 16, 2015, http://tvnwarszawa.tvn24.pl/informacje,news,precz-z-komuna-znow-na-pomniku-zolnierzy-radzieckich,179296.html, accessed January 16, 2016.
49 The Monument of "Brothers in Arms" designed by Polish and Soviet artists: Stanisław Sikora, Stefan Momot, Józef Trenarowski, Józef Gazy, Bohdan Lachert, Jerzy Jarnuszkiewicz, Grigorij Nenko and A. Korolev, erected in 1945, was the first monument in postwar Warsaw. See Wiesław Głębocki, *Warszawskie pomniki* (Warszawa: Wydawnictwo PTTK "Kraj," 1990), 99–100.
50 Tomasz Urzykowski, "Pomnik czterech śpiących rozpada się z hukiem," *Gazeta Wyborcza*, November 23, 2011, http://warszawa.wyborcza.pl/warszawa/1,34889,10692003,Pomnik_czterech_spiacych_rozpada_sie_z_hukiem.html, accessed January 16, 2016.
51 "Uchwała Rady Miasta Stołecznego Warszawy w sprawie przeniesienia pomnika Polsko-Radzieckiego Braterstwa Broni," no. XVI/300/2011, *Biuletyn Informacji Publicznej m.st. Warszawy*, May 26, 2011, http://bip.warszawa.pl/NR/rdonlyres/83ABFA28-FC17-4662-8327-4B21133BA743/800671/344_druk1.pdf, accessed March 8, 2016.
52 "Pomnik 'czterech śpiących' nie wróci na Pl. Wileński," *Wirtualna Polska*, February 26, 2015, http://wiadomosci.wp.pl/kat,1019393,title,Pomnik-czterech-spiacych-nie-wroci-na-pl-Wilenski,wid,17293364,wiadomosc.html?ticaid=117532, accessed March 7, 2016.

53 Pierre Bourdieu, *Distinction: A Social Critique of the Judgement of Taste*, trans. Richard Nice (Cambridge: Harvard University Press, 1984).
54 This monument may be seen as more neutral despite its Soviet provenance. It commemorates the participants in three Silesian uprisings and the Polish and Soviet World War II soldiers in the Silesia region.
55 He was a member of SLD, a social democratic political party in Poland.
56 Wieczorek, "Powojenne pomniki Bytomia i jego dzielnic."
57 Jaś Elsner, "Iconoclasm and the Preservation of Memory," in *Monuments and Memory, Made and Unmade*, eds. Robert S. Nelson and Margaret Olin (Chicago and London: University of Chicago Press, 2003), 209–321.
58 Ochman, "Soviet War Memorials."
59 Kamilla Staszak, Marta Mizuro, Michał Cyraniewicz, Paweł Majewski and Piotr Litka, "Sowieckie pomniki już nie znikają," *Rzeczpospolita*, May 5, 2014, www.rp.pl/Kraj/305059793-Sowieckie-pomniki-juz-nie-znikaja.html#ap-1, accessed January 16, 2017.
60 Hubert Mordawski, *Ziemie odzyskane 1945–1956* (Brzezia Łąka: Wydawnictwo Poligraf, 2015).
61 Staszak, Mizuro, Cyraniewicz, Majewski and Litka, "Sowieckie pomniki już nie znikają."
62 Agnieszka Sopińska-Jaremczak, "229 sowieckich pomników powinno znaleźć się w skansenie IPN w Bornem-Sulinowie," *Instytut Pamięci Narodowej*, June 28, 2016, http://ipn.gov.pl/pl/dla-mediow/komunikaty/33187,229-sowieckich-pomnikow-powinno-znalezc-sie-w-skansenie-IPN-w-Bornem-Sulinowie.html, accessed January 17, 2017.
63 "Szef rady miejskiej żąda eksmisji pomnika na cmentarz," *lca.pl*, July 31, 2015, http://fakty.lca.pl/legnica,news,54342,Szef_rady_miejskiej_zada_eksmisji_pomnika_na_cmentarz.html, accessed February 2, 2017.
64 Hedvig Turai, "Past Unmastered: Hot and Cold Memory in Hungary," *Third Text* 23.1 (2009): 97–106.
65 Charles S. Maier, "Hot Memory . . . Cold Memory: On the Political Half-Life of Fascist and Communist Memory," *Institut für die Wissenschaften vom Menschen*, www.iwm.at/read-listen-watch/transit-online/hot-memory-cold-memory-on-the-political-half-life-of-fascist-and-communist-memory/, accessed December 16, 2016.
66 Sławomir Cenckiewicz, *Wałęsa: Człowiek z teczki* (Poznań: Wydawnictwo Zyska i S-ka, 2013).
67 "IPN TV: Historia z Piotrem Skwiecińskim: 'Lech Wałęsa,' " *Instytut Pamięci Narodowej*, April 8, 2016, http://pamiec.pl/pa/ipn-notacje-ipn-tv/ipn-tv/15988,IPN-TV-Historia-z-Piotrem-Skwiecinskimquot-Lech-Walesa-Warszawa-8-kwietnia-2016.html, accessed December 16, 2016.
68 "Ustawa z dnia 1 kwietnia 2016 r. o zakazie propagowania komunizmu lub innego ustroju totalitarnego przez nazwy budowli, obiektów i urządzeń użyteczności publicznej," *Internetowy System Aktów Prawnych*, April 1, 2016, http://isap.sejm.gov.pl/DetailsServlet?id=WDU20160000744, accessed July 9, 2016. On June 22, 2017, the overwhelming majority of Polish MPs (95 percent) voted for introducing amendments that made the anti-communist law even more restrictive. According to the amended law, the municipal units such as kindergartens, schools or hospitals have been obliged to change their names if these "glorify communism." The new law also orders local government units to remove from the public space monuments, inscriptions on monuments, obelisks, busts and commemorative plaques that "glorify communism or any other totalitarian regime."
69 "Lithuanian Parliament Rejects Resolution on Listing Communist Party as Criminal Organisation," *The Baltic Times*, June 9, 2016, www.baltictimes.com/lithuanian_parlt_rejects_resolution_on_listing_communist_party_as_criminal_organisation/, accessed July 9, 2016.

70 Amy Berkhout, "A Third Alternative: The Peculiar Case of Grūtas Sculpture Park" (Ph.D. dissertation, Bristol: University of Bristol, 2011), 6.
71 Muzeon, http://park-gorkogo.com/muzeon, accessed July 9, 2016.
72 National Gallery, www.nationalartgallerybg.org/index.php?l=59, accessed July 9, 2016.
73 Memento Park, www.mementopark.hu/, accessed July 9, 2016.
74 Maarjamäe Palace, www.ajaloomuuseum.ee/exhibitions/permanent-exhibitions/noukogude-aegsete-monumentide-valinaitus, accessed July 9, 2016.
75 Muzeum Zamoyskich, http://www.muzeumzamoyskich.pl/92,socialist-art-gallery, accessed July 9, 2016.
76 "229 sowieckich pomników powinno znaleźć się w skansenie IPN w Bornem-Sulinowie."
77 Ivan Dikov, "The Soviet Army Monument in Sofia: Keep It but Explain It!" *Novinite Insider*, January 27, 2011, www.novinite.com/articles/124623/The+Soviet+Army+Monument+in+Sofia%3A+Keep+It+but+Explain+It!#sthash.WuvIQAzE.dpuf, accessed July 9, 2016.
78 Dovilė Jablonskaitė, "Władze w Trokach nie chcą zlikwidować pomnika dla radzieckich 'niszczycieli,'" *Znad Wilii*, August 11, 2014, http://zw.lt/wilno-wilenszczyzna/wladze-w-trokach-nie-chca-zlikwidowac-pomnika-dla-radzieckich-niszczycieli/, accessed July 14, 2016.
79 Dikov, "The Soviet Army Monument in Sofia: Keep It but Explain It!"
80 Ştefan Stanciugelu, Andrei Țăranu and Iulian Rusu, "The Communist Cultural Heritage in the Social Representations of a Post-Communist Generation," *European Journal of Science and Theology* 9.2 (April 2013): 3–21.
81 "Kiedy nam się lepiej żyło—w PRL czy w III Rzeczpospolitej? Bilans zysków i strat," *Centrum Badań Opinii Społecznej (CBOS)*, July 1997, www.cbos.pl/spiskom.pol/1997/k_093_97.pdf, accessed June 20, 2016; Rafał Boguszewski, "PRL—doświadczenia, oceny, skojarzenia," *Centrum Badań Opinii Społecznej (CBOS)*, May 2014, www.cbos.pl/spiskom.pol/2014/k_061_14.pdf, accessed June 20, 2016.
82 Pierre Nora, "Between Memory and History: *Les Lieux de Mémoire*," *Representations* 26, Special Issue: *Memory and Counter-Memory* (1989): 7–24.
83 Ochman, "Soviet War Memorials."
84 "229 sowieckich pomników powinno znaleźć się w skansenie IPN w Bornem-Sulinowie."
85 Sigrid Brandt, Jörg Haspel and John Ziesemer, eds., *Socialist Realism and Socialist Modernism: World Heritage Proposals from Central and Eastern Europe* (Berlin: Bässler, Hedrik Verlag, 2013).
86 Helena Jadwiszczok-Molencka, "Doświadczenie pokoleniowe na przykładzie socjalistycznych form przestrzennych Bytomia," *Pracownia Kultury* 4 (2003), www.laboratoriumkultury.us.edu.pl/?p=25155, accessed June 22, 2016.
87 The artistic phenomenon of socialist realism appeared at the end of the 1920s and beginning of the 1930s in the Soviet Union, and dominated the 1940s and 1950s (from Stalin's to Nikita Khrushchev's declarations on art, architecture and construction) in accordance with the social, political and economic system in the states of the socialist bloc. This artistic method expressed the socialist worldview in the epoch of the struggle to establish and build a socialist society. National forms influenced this artistic perspective of representing objective reality and subordinated to Marxist ideas. See Edward Możejko, *Realizm socjalistyczny: Teoria: Rozwój: Upadek* (Kraków: Universitas, 2001); Nune Chilingaryan and Gagik Gurjyan, "Socialist Realism and Armenian Building Tradition: Steps to Form a Unique Architectural Language," in *Socialist Realism and Socialist Modernism*, 73–79.

88 Kazimierz S. Ożóg, "Rzeźbiarze lubelscy w konfrontacji z władzą ludową," in *Artyści lubelscy i ich galerie w XX wieku*, eds. Lechosław Lameński and Zbigniew Nestorowicz (Lublin: Stowarzyszenie Historyków Sztuki: Katedra Historii Sztuki Nowoczesnej Katolickiego Uniwersytetu Lubelskiego, 2004), 163–173.
89 Brandt, Haspel and Ziesemer, eds., *Socialist Realism and Socialist Modernism*, 12.
90 *Kultūros vertybių registras*, http://kvr.kpd.lt/#/static-heritage-search, accessed August 1, 2016.
91 Edward Said, *Orientalism* (New York: Pantheon Books, 1978), 1–28.
92 Duncan Light, "Gazing on Communism: Heritage Tourism and Post-Communist Identities in Germany, Hungary and Romania," *Tourism Geographies* 2.2 (2000): 157–176.
93 Lietuvos Respublikos administracinių teisės pažeidimų kodeksas 188–18 straipsnis, *Infolex*, July 3, 2008, www.infolex.lt/ta/103787:str188-18, accessed August 4, 2016.
94 "Georgia Passes Law to Destroy Soviet-era Monuments and Street Names," *The Telegraph*, May 31, 2011, www.telegraph.co.uk/news/worldnews/europe/georgia/8549052/Georgia-passes-law-to-destroy-Soviet-era-monuments-and-street-names.html, accessed June 20, 2016.
95 "Zakon Ukrayiny pro uvichnennya peremohy nad natsyzmom u Druhiy svitoviy viyni 1939–1945 rokiv (Vidomosti Verkhovnoyi Rady (VVR), 2015, № 25, st.191)," *Verhovna Rada Ukrainy*, April 9, 2015, http://zakon4.rada.gov.ua/laws/show/315-viii, accessed December 5, 2016.
96 "Ustawa z dnia 1 kwietnia 2016 r. o zakazie propagowania komunizmu lub innego ustroju totalitarnego."
97 Raluca Petre, "Communicating the Past into the Present: Young Voices About Communism and Communists in Romania," *ESSACHESS. Journal for Communication Studies* 5.2 (2012): 269–287.

5 Lenin, Marx and Local Heroes
Socialist and Post-Socialist Memorial Landscapes in Eastern Germany and Czechoslovakia—The Case Study of Jena and Hradec Králové

Stanislav Holubec

Scholars regard the Czechoslovak Socialist Republic (ČSSR) and the German Democratic Republic (GDR) as very similar in terms of the historical conditions for building socialism and their character as communist regimes, which differs from that of the other Eastern Bloc countries (as in Herbert Kitschelt's well-known thesis placing them in the "bureaucratic authoritarian"[1] category in contrast to other communist dictatorships) and also in the way the post-communist transformation took place. A few of the similarities mentioned repeatedly in the literature are as follows: By the late nineteenth century, both Czech lands and Eastern German states attained high levels of industrialization leading to the creation of strong working-class movements and, after 1918, to the foundation of significant communist parties. In both societies, the role of religion was relatively weak by the nineteenth century. Churches, therefore, never become the leading force of opposition during state socialism, in contrast to Poland. In both countries the communist movements played important roles in the anti-fascist resistance. The Czech and East German project of "building socialism" was seen as resulting more from indigenous traditions than from external forces, as, for example, in Hungary or Poland. For the 1970s and 1980s, the rigidity of the Czechoslovak and East German regimes in comparison to Hungary or Poland (for example, the restrictions on travel, publishing and artistic or entrepreneurial activities) has been stressed. The reasons for this rigidity were different in each case: In Czechoslovakia, it was an effect of the defeat of the Prague Spring; in the GDR, it was a reaction to the regime's continuing lack of legitimacy in comparison to the Federal Republic of Germany's successful development. In both countries, we might speculate whether the rigidity also resulted from the historical traditions of communist movements understanding themselves as vanguards more than was the case with the Polish or Hungarian parties, or whether their location on the Eastern Bloc's border with the NATO countries played a role as well.

In the late 1980s, it was in both cases the mass mobilization of the public (which can be called revolutions) led by the political opposition that resulted in the end of the communist regimes, in contrast with the "round-tables" in Poland or Hungary, or the mass mobilization led by significant parts of the ruling elites as in Romania. During the transformation period, both countries went through state disintegration (in one case splitting into two smaller ones and in the other integration into the Federal Republic of Germany). In both countries, the strong anti-communist policies were accompanied by the restoration of historically important social democratic parties and the creation of remarkably stable political landscapes within the context of post-socialist Europe (the same political parties have dominated the East German landscape since 1991; in the Czech case, the same two parties dominated between 1996 and 2013). Also the (post-)communist parties had a similar story: They were marginalized in reaction to their role in the communist regimes, but survived as relatively significant oppositional forces to the left of social democracy, representing those who have been called the "losers of transformation."

Nevertheless, both societies differed in many important respects. First of all, while East Germany is historically a Protestant region, the religious tradition of the Czech area can be called mixed Catholic-Protestant. From the nineteenth century, Eastern Germany was situated within the core of European power, although in terms of economy or culture, its early modern position within German-speaking territory was to be marked by a certain "peripherality" in comparison to the historically more developed west (Rhineland) and south. In contrast to Germans, the Czechs are a small nation, which in the nineteenth century experienced the same process of national awaking that other small European nations underwent, and it won statehood only in 1918. In addition, several other major twentieth-century tendencies occurred only in one of these countries: Germany's move to Nazism in contrast to democracy's survival in interwar Czechoslovak but for its termination owing to outside intervention. The defeat of Germany in 1945, its occupation by allies and subsequent division of the country into zones contrasted with the liberation of Czechoslovakia by the Red Army, where the population enthusiastically welcomed the liberators. The establishment of communist rule in the Soviet zone of Germany is hard to imagine without Soviet occupation, in contrast to the strong support the Czechoslovak public gave to a program of building socialism and an alliance with the Soviet Union, manifested, among other ways, in the last free election in 1946. Perhaps Stalinism took a more radical form in Czechoslovakia than in the GDR, where no big political trials and other repression against the opposition were organized. Communist rule in Czechoslovakia seems also to have been more stable during the 1950s than in the GDR; for example, the protests in 1953 were much weaker in Czechoslovakia. We can mention several telling details illustrating the self-confidence of both communist regimes: The Czechoslovak communists did not consider changing their name after they forced the social democrats to unify with them in 1948; in contrast to the GDR, Czechoslovakia was declared a "socialist state" in 1960 (outside the Soviet Union this happened in Albania, Yugoslavia and Romania); the Czechoslovak communists always had a majority of seats in the Parliament during their rule, while the ruling Socialist Unity Party of Germany (SED) never dared to monopolize power so openly.

In addition, ever since the late 1950s, the "magnetic" effect of West Germany became a significant factor in the GDR, triggering emigration, the adoption of more repressive policies (for example, the Berlin Wall) but also sometimes less repressive ones (for example, the attitude to rock music, the environmental movement and gay and lesbian issues during the 1970s, which was not as liberal as in Hungary, but more relaxed than in Czechoslovakia). Also, the events of 1968 have no parallels in East Germany, and although there were more or less liberal periods in the GDR, nothing like the mass purges in the Czechoslovak party after 1968 were carried out, and it seems that the SED had a higher reform potential in the 1980s than the Communist Party of Czechoslovakia (KSČ). Furthermore, socialism apparently did not lose as much legitimacy in the GDR as in Czechoslovakia, mainly because the horrors of German Nazism are a powerful source of legitimation for the left—for example, the concept of communist totalitarianism was more difficult to believe in Germany than in the Czech Republic during the 1990s, since from the German perspective, it trivializes the crimes of Nazism by putting them on the same level with communism.

The disintegration of the Czechoslovak Republic did not affect peoples' lives as much as the reunification of Germany did, for the latter by and large meant the swallowing up of the GDR by its stronger neighbor. The return of some émigrés to leading positions in the Czech Republic cannot be compared to the West Germans taking over many elite positions in economy, the state apparatus or academia in the new Bundesländer. Furthermore, economic transformation took different forms: on the one hand, the strong decline of East German industry resulting in the explosion of unemployment combined with the expansions of the federal German welfare state and, on the other hand, Czech industry's more successful survival mainly via low wages, without West German financial transfers and with a much weaker welfare state and public sector.

In discussing the differences and similarities between both countries, I decided to adopt a micro-approach in hopes of shedding some new light on the debate by concentrating on the comparison of East German and Czech socialist and post-socialist cultures of memory, a focus, which, as far as I know, has not been previously adopted. My assumption is that the culture of memory provides us with important information about the identities of different societies, particularly in Central and Eastern Europe where, as Rudolf Jaworski argued, there was no possibility of establishing a stably forgotten landscape of memory as in the European West during the twentieth century. For this, Central and Eastern Europe lacked a necessary condition—a quiet and continuous history[2]—and it therefore became a region where memory, with its corresponding symbols and rituals, profoundly changed several times. This, however, makes the question of memory cultures more interesting here than in other parts of Europe. Comparing the whole Czech and East German landscapes of memory would be a topic for a book, not a chapter; I have, therefore, limited the scope of this chapter to the memory cultures of two cities comparable in their sizes, histories, positions in the countries' economies and importance in the cultural landscapes: Jena and Hradec Králové. Both cities, of course, have unique local specifics, but there are also similarities between them and other Czech and East German cities of similar size that allow us to make careful generalizations.

The Histories of Jena and Hradec Králové

In terms of their social and cultural history, both cities have a strong medieval tradition (Jena is first mentioned as a town in 1230 and Hradec in 1225), and their history is an important part of their identity. While Hradec was a natural center of Eastern Bohemia, Jena remained in the shadow of more important cities such as Erfurt and Naumburg, and its importance grew only with the foundation of the university in 1558. Both towns are also characterized by relatively late industrialization: in Hradec because the town was made into a fortress, which existed from 1763 to 1893 and in Jena by its relatively marginal geographic location (its rail connection dates only from 1874, while Hradec's was already established by 1857). Both towns were the supra-regional centers of national cultures and education during the nineteenth century—Jena thanks to its university and Hradec to its famous gymnasium and its clear Czech ethnic majority—in contrast to many other towns in Bohemia at that time. Both cities experienced strong industrial and demographic growth in the late nineteenth century. While the growth of Jena was associated with the Carl Zeiss factory producing highly sophisticated optical instruments, the industrialization of Hradec was more diversified, and its growth depended instead on its suitable geographic location and abolition of the fortress. While the late nineteenth-century and early twentieth-century modernization of Jena is connected with the entrepreneur and social reformer Ernst Abbe (1840–1905), the owner of the Carl Zeiss factory, in Hradec, the analogy is František Ulrich (1859–1939), mayor from 1895 to 1929. Thanks to him, Hradec, where plenty of space was available after the removal of city fortifications, could become a laboratory of urbanism. In Jena, in the late nineteenth and early twentieth centuries, the beautiful hills covered by forests surrounding the town were turned into a special cultural landscape with hiking trails, tourist pubs and numerous memorial stones devoted to different local and national personalities. Something like this could not develop in Hradec, which was surrounded mainly by agricultural countryside. Neither Hradec nor Jena were marked by strong working-class tradition: In both towns, the political left was quite weak in the first half of the twentieth century, and the communist parties got only average results in the last free elections in 1946.

As to their importance after 1945, both cities were considered showcases of socialism. Hradec became the administrative center of Královéhradecký District in 1949 and of the extended East Bohemia District in 1960, a region with more than one million inhabitants, which even included the historical rival of Hradec, the city of Pardubice. Its population grew between 1950 and 1991 from 44,000 to 99,000 inhabitants, while Jena only grew from 80,000 to 100,000. Jena was never a center of regional administration, which was, until 1950, in Weimar, a city considered by some in the nineteenth century as forming a unit with Jena (together they were known as the *Doppelstadt* [twin city]).[3] This did not change in the GDR period: After the administrative reform, Jena was subordinated to Gera, but this did not diminish Jena's importance. Since the 1960s, with the Carl Zeiss factory regarded as the jewel of East German industry, Jena, which became an important object of investments, was called a "technopolis" by historian Rüdiger Stutz,[4] a manifestation of which was the skyscraper finished in 1970 and considered one of the symbols of the GDR, appearing, for example, on school textbook covers.

An important factor in Jena's development was its destruction at the end of World War II through bombing, with 700 victims, 4,500 destroyed apartments and most of the city center and the Zeiss factory in ruins.[5] The city lived in the shadow of this catastrophe over the next two decades, and the ruins of the city center were present until the 1960s. The reconstruction of Jena contrasts sharply with the construction of Hradec after the demolition of the fortress in 1893. There the space left after the fortifications was free for the conceptions of architects, while in Jena, postwar renovation had always presented a dilemma, what with the desire to develop valuable new architecture, the time pressure and the wish to preserve the surviving remnants of the former city, and therefore, Jena could not develop an architectonically coherent model with the high aesthetic qualities characteristic of Hradec.

Socialist Jena was the city dominated by the Carl Zeiss factory, with about 28,000 employees,[6] while Hradec's biggest factory, the machinery ZVÚ, formerly Škoda, had only 5,000 employees in the late 1980s.[7] For Jena, the existence of its university was also of great importance, although the authorities did not permit its expansion. The University of Jena was a crucial factor in the formation of a strong dissident milieu, stronger than in other East German cities of similar size. Hradec had no oppositional movement comparable to that of Jena. Despite several attempts, the city only acquired its university in 2000; however, early faculties existed here since 1945 (branches of Prague's Charles University and the independent Faculty of Education), and in the 1970s and 1980s, the two cities had similar numbers of university students, about 7,000.

In the post-socialist period, too, Jena and Hradec have certain commonalities: They are considered success stories of the transformation, and they are ranked at the top of their countries' quality-of-life scales.[8] Although Hradec lost its position as the administrative center of East Bohemia in

1990, being replaced by the smaller Hradecký Region in 2000, and Jena had to struggle with unemployment (of 45,000 Zeiss employees throughout the whole GDR 17,000 lost their jobs by the end of 1991),[9] in both cities, the universities and hospitals provided new impulses and in Jena also the successful transformation of the Zeiss factory. While Hradec slowly began to lose its inhabitants after 1989 (it declined from 100,000 to 94,000 until 2011), Jena was one of a few East German cities to have experienced a certain population growth (from 101,000 in 1989 to 105,000 in 2011). While the year 1990 brought an expansion of small businesses to Hradec,[10] which were notoriously underdeveloped during state socialism, in Jena, where the existence of certain small businesses was allowed since the 1970s, the transformation was not only marked by the expansion of services but also by the decline of many local businesses because of the competition with West German companies.[11]

As a result of the takeover of the GDR by West Germany and the various economic problems this kind of unification generated, the East German population quickly rediscovered the appeal of the political left, while Czech society retained faith in liberal capitalism for two post-1989 decades.[12] This is clearly visible through the local politics of the two cities. In Jena, the left parties (social democrats, greens and the post-Communist Party of Democratic Socialism, which later became DIE LINKE) received a majority of votes in every municipal election. In Hradec, the left (communists and social democrats) never obtained more than one-third of votes after 1989. Although in the first free municipal elections in 1990, the Communist Party was just as strong in Hradec as the post-communists were in Jena, its support later declined, while the German Party of Democratic Socialism established itself as an important player on the municipal level, becoming the strongest party in the elections of 2004 and 2014. In both cities, minor right-wing liberal parties (Germany's Free Democratic Party and the Czech Republic's Civic Democratic Alliance) had strong electoral results, and their candidates became mayors in the 1990s.[13] Although Hradec and Jena are among the more secular areas of the already very secular East Germany and Czech Republic, in Hradec, the Catholic Church became very influential during the 1990s. This was due not only to the "moral capital" accumulated during the communist persecution but also to the renewal of episcopate, which sought public influence in the city: It established its own lyceum and elementary school, and organized the visit by Pope John Paul II in 1997. The power of episcopate is evident from the fact that the bishop of Hradec was elected archbishop of Prague in 2010.

Comparing Memorial Landscapes

If we compare the memorial landscapes of the two cities before 1945, we can see a longer tradition in Jena where the first secular memorials were already erected in the nineteenth century when Hradec as a fortress was under military regime. The first secular memorial in Jena, dedicated to Goethe, was inaugurated in the Griesbachgarten in 1821 and is commonly regarded as the first German monument to the poet. It is a stone pillar about 3 meters high topped by an eagle. Two other memorials were installed in 1857 near the university to commemorate its famous scholars. They were the first items of the so-called Via Triumphalis, today's series of 16 busts of famous scholars, which runs along the former city wall (the last bust was unveiled in 1987). The city's most important monument in the form of statue was dedicated to Duke Johann Friedrich I, founder of the University; it is located in the main market square and was unveiled in 1858. The city's second-most important monument—dedicated to Ernst Abbe—was built between 1908 and 1911. It took the extraordinary form of a temple such that many passersby do not at all realize that it is a memorial.

In Hradec, there were no secular memorials dedicated before 1918. This is primarily because of the town's military status, only abolished in 1884, and the lack of funds for such purposes before 1914. Czech civil organizations were additionally not economically strong enough to sponsor the monuments. The relatively limited diffusion of Czech national memorials in ethnically Czech cities of Bohemia and Moravia (Hradec was one of them) during the period before 1914 is striking in contrast to the cities with German majorities where various secular memorials were erected before 1914. Even Prague had only two secular monuments of personalities connected with the Czech national movements before 1918 alongside two others devoted to representatives of the Austrian monarchy.[14]

The desire of Czechs to put up their own monuments was largely fulfilled only after the establishment of Czechoslovakia: In Hradec, this was seen in the two memorials to Jan Hus in the early 1920s, a monument to the president of the Republic Tomáš Garrigue Masaryk (1926), one to the local politician Ladislav Pospíšil (1933) and a memorial to the legionnaires (1937). At the same time, only two memorials were erected in Jena—a memorial to the military navigators in 1921 and a monument to the scholar Wilhelm Rein as part of the Via Triumphalis in 1929. Thus the interwar memorial landscape in Hradec was mainly devoted to the nation-building program and less to local tradition, which was represented only by Pospíšil—this in contrast to Jena where memorials had reflected local culture.

The communist regimes aimed actively to change the memorial landscape of both cities but more so in Hradec. The first memorial unveiled here by the communist authorities in 1949 was the Soviet tank on a stone pedestal decorated with the Soviet star located in one of the central squares commemorating the city's liberation by the Red Army in 1945.[15] Jena, a city liberated by the US Army, was obviously not willing to commemorate it. Curiously, one small memorial plaque appeared in Jena in the socialist period on the house where Friedrich Schiller and Johann Wolfgang Goethe once met, with the inscription "destroyed by American terror bombs in 1945."[16] In Hradec, Stalinism brought the destruction of the Masaryk memorial in 1953, which had been installed in his lifetime in 1926, destroyed by the Nazis and restored in 1947.[17] With the campaign against the interwar republic by the communist authorities, the name of Hradec mayor František Ulrich had to disappear; the name of Ulrich Square was changed after 1948, and the mayor was often not mentioned in books on the history of Hradec. According to one testimony, the Stalinist radicals in Hradec even proposed replacing the Baroque Marian column with a statue of the Hussite military leader Jan Žižka,[18] and some party members also proposed building a memorial to Stalin.[19] We have no information on proposals to build a Joseph Stalin memorial in Jena, but it seems improbable. In Hradec, during the 1968 Prague Spring, an initiative to restore the Masaryk memorial was organized and public donations collected for it, but "normalization" thwarted these attempts, and the monument was restored only in 1990.

In Jena, there was no symbol comparable to Masaryk that could become the target of the regime's hatred. The GDR authorities mainly attempted to destroy or change monuments connected to the imperial past or to German militarism. This was the case with the monument to German military navigators erected in 1921 on one hill above Jena, which was "demilitarized", meaning that the German military cross was changed to a normal Christian one and the oak leaves and German helmet removed.[20] The eagle on the 1821 Goethe Memorial was similarly seen as an imperial eagle (*Reichsadel*), and this was a reason, besides its damaged state, for removing it in 1962. However, it was restored in its former shape by 1974 as a result of changes in the party line on heritage preservation.[21] The Ernst Abbe memorial did not have to face the hostility of GDR authorities, although Abbe's role was perceived as controversial in the 1950s.[22] The memory of Abbe, whose contribution to Jena's development was analogous to that of Mayor František Ulrich's in Hradec, was still allowed to continue on in the names of streets, with nobody proposing the monument's destruction. Furthermore, Abbe was given another monument in 1979 when he was finally accepted by the GDR authorities as a progressive social reformer. The second Abbe monument, however, was not a new one; it was actually a remodeling of the 1929 monument to educational theorist Wilhelm Rein from 1929. The Rein monument was recycled because its metal had been removed during the war (to be used for military purposes) and because Rein was in any case not approved of by the communist regime because of his nationalist leanings.[23] In the GDR period, five scholars were added to the Via Triumphalis: Karl Marx (1953), Schiller (1973), Heinrich Luden (1983), Ludwig Feuerbach (1983) and Georg Wilhelm Friedrich Hegel (1987).[24] While the names of scholars whose busts were installed before 1945 are largely forgotten and had only local significance, in the GDR, new busts were installed of figures having Germany-wide importance who were at the same time considered representative of progressive German thinking.

The cult of local anti-fascists promoted by the authorities of both cities after 1945 was quite similar: in Hradec, this involved the personality of communist resistance activist and teacher at the economic lyceum Jiří Purkyně (1898–1942), and in Jena, it included worker and communist resistance activist Magnus Poser (1907–1944). The cult around Poser was stronger, with several schools named after him and a small museum opened in the house where he lived. In both cities, small museums of revolutionary traditions were established in the 1970s: in Hradec in the house where the Communist Party was founded and in Jena in the museum commemorating revolutionary traditions including Karl Liebknecht and Poser.[25] With these, the Nazi dictatorship was remembered in Jena by two monuments: a stone tablet dedicated to the victims of fascism (1972) and a statue of Hans and Sophie Scholl (1968), both somewhat outside the city center, and by several memorial plaques.

The early 1970s saw the noteworthy construction of two new memorials in Hradec as the normalization regime attempted to demonstrate its strength and victory over the Prague Spring reformers in the area of historical policy. Hradec, like many other Czech towns, saw the installation of statues of the two key figures in the neo-Stalinist memory regime: Vladimir Lenin and the leader of Czechoslovak communists and "first workers' president" Klement Gottwald. The statue of Lenin was unveiled in 1970[26] and the statue of Gottwald in 1973. The choice of Gottwald was particularly significant, because his "cult of personality" was very closely connected to Stalin's in the early 1950s, though Stalin's was not revived in the 1970s. Furthermore, the key representative of normalization, general secretary and later president of the Republic Gustáv Husák, was persecuted under Gottwald and spent nine years in jail.[27] Several other small government memorials were erected in Hradec in the early 1970s (for example, a bust of Gottwald in the lobby of the main railroad station and a relief commemorating various workers' demonstrations on the main square, particularly the communist takeover in February 1948). Important institutions were given political names—for example, the Theater of Victorious February and the Plant of Victorious February; various schools, streets and squares were also given new names. Contemporary photographs make it clear that communist symbols had more presence in Hradec than in Jena. Red stars decorated all-important public buildings, and huge letters spelling out "with the Soviet Union forever" were displayed on the roof of the administrative building alongside the tank memorial. The only permanent red star in Jena was installed on the roof of the highest building: The Carl Zeiss factory.

Government propaganda was obviously much more intense in Hradec than in Jena under socialism, particularly during the 1970s, and we can assume that the same comparison can be made between other Czech cities and other cities of the GDR.[28] As far as we know, no one ever considered renaming the Carl Zeiss plant or the municipal theater. The streets of central Jena were less frequently named after communist heroes than were those of Hradec. These names were more typically found in Jena's outskirts. There was no statue of Lenin, Ernst Thälmann or Wilhelm Pieck in Jena. The only pro-communist memorial was already mentioned: the bust of Marx on the Via Triumphialis. Another statue constructed for purposes of government propaganda was the allegory of the "working class and the intelligentsia"— a female student and a male worker holding a child. The allegory graced the main square after 1975 and was meant to symbolize the strong tie between the university and the Zeiss factory.[29] Another example is the 1984 allegorical homage to Salvador Allende in the housing blocks periphery of Lobeda showing stylized human figures defending the revolution and mourning its martyrs.[30] The best-known example of political renaming was Jena's main square, Eichplatz, which was changed to Platz der Kosmonauten after the space flight of the GDR citizen Sigmund Jähn in 1979. In Hradec, the propagandistic fascination with cosmonauts materialized in the construction of a smaller copy (about 10 meters high) of the Moscow Monument to the Conquerors of Space erected in an apartment-block district. Finally, there was the university skyscraper that became the icon and symbol of GDR socialism in Jena. Although there has been no research on how it was perceived by the citizens of Jena, some evidence indicates that it was quite unpopular, as it destroyed a significant part of the historic city center. An indicative example of the less restrictive policy in public space in Jena (and the whole GDR) during the late socialist period is the construction of the Protestant center, the Martin Niemöller Haus, in 1983 in Lobeda, the biggest apartment-block district. This was possible as the result of a national agreement between the government and the Protestant church. Although this was not a church, the building was topped by a several-meters-high cross, something that would have been unimaginable in Hradec.[31]

The 1989 changes in Jena and Hradec were characterized by the great zeal in destroying communist places of memory, changing street names and establishing a new memory culture. In Hradec, none of the three communist memorials survived the change. The Gottwald statue was the most hated symbol and was removed on January 11, 1990, during the organized happening that included the trial and execution of Gottwald, which sent him "to hell with Stalin and Ceauşescu."[32] The demolition was approved by the municipal government and was justified not by the crimes of Gottwald but simply by the fact that the original architect of the square, Josef Gočár, did not plan for any monument and that therefore the statue did not fit his original conception.[33] The statue of Lenin was removed on February 20, this time without any celebration, but also without significant opposition to the decision.[34] The most contested memorial was that of the Red Army, which survived the months after the revolution as the most neutral of the three. The municipal administration decided to remove it in spring 1991, but at that point, a certain amount of opposition occurred. It was the Communist Party that did not want to give up so easily as it did with the first two memorials, and it defended it by using anti-fascist arguments.[35] The petition organized by the party was signed by 3,000 Hradec inhabitants.

But non-communist municipal politicians made the claim in local newspapers that the tank was in fact booty seized from the Red Army at the end of the war by the Wehrmacht and then abandoned in Hradec. (There is no evidence to establish whether or not this is a mere legend.) They also argued that in reality, Hradec was liberated first by the US Army. (In fact, however, it was not the US Army but the US military mission, negotiating with the Wehrmacht commanders in a nearby town, that traveled through Hradec in several jeeps before the arrival of the Red Army and was welcomed by the local population.) Reference was also made to the 1968 Soviet intervention,[36] the low aesthetic quality of the memorial, the anti-militaristic values[37] and, curiously, the possibility of selling the tank to the US for dollars. There was also a proposal to build a wall around it and wait for the decision. The tank was finally removed on June 5, 1991, again without any celebration, and as nobody bought it, it ended in a scrap heap.[38] The only remaining communist symbols in the city are now found in cemeteries on the graves of Red Army soldiers.

In Jena, the bust of Marx became the most contested monument. It began to be discussed only in early 1991. The voices arguing for removal stressed that Marx had never visited Jena and that his teachings had proven to be a failure.[39] The opponents argued that Marx is not responsible for the crimes of the SED, that the university should respect the plurality of its traditions and that he is still a world-famous philosopher who might help the tourist industry in Jena.[40] As in the case of the tank in Hradec, a petition was signed for preserving the monument, in this case by thousands of citizens and 144 university teachers.[41] The bust was nevertheless removed by decision of the university council in March 1992.[42] In succeeding years, the Party of Democratic Socialism struggled repeatedly, but without success, to reinstall the bust.[43] In addition, Marx's famous eleventh thesis on Feuerbach disappeared from the university auditorium,[44] and the allegory of worker and student was transferred from the city square to the garden of the hospital.

In both cities, the red stars and government slogans disappeared from public space and a wave of street renaming followed. Similar to the demonstrations in Hradec demanding the renaming of Gottwald Square, the demonstrations in Jena in November 1989 demanded the renaming of Square of the Cosmonauts. In both cases, a return to the former names was preferred: in Jena Eichplatz[45] and in Hradec Ulrich Square. During the Jena demonstrations, criticism of the university tower was voiced, which one speaker dubbed the "biscuit package" (*Kekserolle*),[46] but its demolition was not seriously considered. In Hradec, no public building was so strongly associated with the communist regime; there the demand was to turn the pompous party headquarters from the 1980s into an institution serving the population. The fashion of street renaming was much stronger in Hradec. The communist names were replaced by names referring to the interwar republic traditions (presidents Tomáš Masaryk and Edvard Beneš), Christian traditions (St.

Wenceslas Square and, after 2005, even John Paul II Square), local personalities (mayor Ulrich) and neutral geographic names (Great and Small Square, Elbe Bridge). Several street names—such as Salvador Allende, Karl Marx or Friedrich Engels—that survived in Jena were renamed in Hradec. In Jena, the population began to be unhappy with the economic transformation early on and to oppose renaming streets by the fall of 1990, while in Hradec, street renaming did not face any significant opposition.[47]

Furthermore, new memorials were built or old ones restored. This issue was again more important in Hradec, where the statue of Masaryk destroyed both during the Nazi occupation and under Stalinism remained strong in the public's memory. Already during the Velvet Revolution, a photograph of the destroyed monument was displayed at its former location, and people lit candles around it. Within weeks of the revolution, the decision was made to restore it. As in the year 1968, public donations (especially by one particular Czech émigré to the US) combined with public funds assured that the copy of the destroyed statue was speedily finished, and the memorial was unveiled by Václav Havel during the national holiday on October 28, 1990.[48] Several other small plaques and busts of Masaryk were restored throughout the city.

The post-1989 decades, however, did not bring many new figural memorials, which are generally very expensive. This genre is to some extent out of fashion, while attempts at creating postmodern statues are often controversial. Nevertheless, two stylized memorial statues of sitting figures appeared in Hradec: the first was of John Paul II, unveiled in the inner court of the Bishop's Palace in 2003, and the second was a monument to Mayor Ulrich erected in 2010 on the bank of the river. The latter immediately came under strong criticism because of its alleged unorthodox shape or low aesthetic qualities, and it was removed within the year.[49] No figurative monument was unveiled in Jena during this period, but there was discussion of constructing a monument to Carl Zeiss, and in 2016, its foundation stone was laid.[50]

At the end of the last century, memorials commemorating the crimes of communist regimes also began to appear in both cities. In Hradec, the most notable of these was the Memorial to the Victims of Communism unveiled in 1998;[51] in Jena, the principal example is the memorial of The Persecuted 1945–1989, unveiled in 2010. In both cases, the memorials are allegorical, with the first being a stone stele in the shape of a gravestone and decorated by a prison bar motif and the second resembling a pile of Stasi files. The memorial in Hradec bears the inscription "to the victims of communism 1948–1989"; the inscription in Jena reads "to all whose human dignity was injured, to the prosecuted who righteously spoke out against communist dictatorship and for democracy and human rights 1945–1989." In 1998, a second memorial to the "victims of the fight for freedom and human rights was built" in Hradec. It is a stone with the names of battlefields in which Czechs fought in the First and Second World Wars, the names of Nazi extermination camps, a list of Nazi crimes in Czech lands and the names of communist work camps. One plaque installed on the court of justice in Hradec after 2000 commemorates the "victims of the national, political, and moral struggle and resistance against German occupation and communist violence." Another plaque was unveiled on former party headquarters commemorating "the victim of communist violence Pavel Wonka" (1953–1988), the local opposition activist who died in jail because of negligent medical care in 1988. A comparable cult of local dissident heroes was also created in Jena, but the plaques commemorating them differ from those in Hradec by their more factual tone and the tendency to omit the term "communism." The plaque at the aula of the University of Jena unveiled in 1992 bears the inscription "to the victims of political suppression 1933–1945/1945–1989." Also, the plaque commemorating Alfred Diener (1927–1953), who was executed after the suppression of the rebellion in June 1953, unveiled in 2002,[52] contains no references to communism, totalitarianism or any other ideology.[53] Another well-known Stasi victim from Jena, Matthias Domaschk (1957–1981), has so far not been given a plaque and only a street and one university lecture hall has been named after him.

Conclusion

We can conclude that in terms of memorial sites, the two cities, and in fact both countries, have differed enormously. In the memorial landscape of its cities, Czechoslovakia in the 1970s and 1980s was more ideologically rigid than GDR, and its post-socialist attempts at eradicating the official memory of communism seem more radical as well. We have several explanations for this. The first has to do with cultural-religious traditions. The Czech lands as part of Catholic Europe have a stronger culture of statues and religious symbols in public space. Crucifixes at crossroads; small chapels; splendid baroque temples; statues of John of Nepomuk, the main patron saint of Bohemia; and memorial columns in the square—all of these were present in the Czech countryside and towns, and absent in the Protestant parts of Germany. Jena had and still has only one figurative monument in the city center (Johann Friedrich, 1858), while Hradec Králové had six such monuments: that of Masaryk (1926), Vice Mayor Jan Ladislav Pospíšil (1933), Hussite leader Jan Žižka (1971) and the writer Božena Němcová (1950), along with the destroyed monuments of Lenin (1970–1990) and Gottwald (1973–1990).

Secular memorial landscapes began to appear later in Czech towns than in Germany, mostly after 1918. The years after the breakup of the Habsburg Empire were marked by the destruction of monuments considered German-Austrian and by a wave of street renaming. This happened in post-1918 Germany to a much lesser extent. And the Nazi seizure of power was basically not accompanied by the destruction of monuments, as Weimar Germany did not have the time and capacity to develop its own memorial landscape.

Similarly, after 1945, there were not many Nazi monuments that had to be removed, since the Third Reich was not very active in building monuments, and many nationalist memorials made from metal were confiscated for military purposes during the war (an example was the Wilhelm Rein monument in Jena).[54] The GDR period was characterized by the destruction or at least demilitarization or denationalization of memorials from imperial times—an example being the navigators' monument in Jena.

Although the state socialist period can be characterized as an era of monuments, this was true to different degrees in each country and in terms of chronology. In the Czech case, its peak was during the post-1968 "normalization." Its ideology was personified in two figures, Lenin and Gottwald, to whom monuments were built in great quantities during the early 1970s. There have been at least 34 statues and memorials of Lenin (the Russian website registering Lenin statues around the world counted 24 in Czech lands, 8 in Slovakia and 2 in Soviet military bases in the country).[55] The first "workers' president" Klement Gottwald was given a number of figurative memorials in Czech lands similar to that of Lenin, but only two in Slovakia because of his Czech origin. Such a strong cult of deceased communist leaders probably has a parallel only in Bulgaria's Georgi Dimitrov cult or perhaps in the cult of Ernst Thälmann in the GDR, who had at least 15 monuments around the country, about 10 museums and 80 memorial stones.[56]

Briefly comparing the spread of Lenin statues in the Eastern Bloc countries can tell us something about the identities and legitimacies of different regimes. In the Soviet Union, more than 5,000 memorials of Lenin have been estimated. In the GDR, there were 20 Lenin memorials in cities and another 19 in Soviet military bases. East German Lenins seem to be less systematic than in Czechoslovakia, and many important cities did not have a Lenin memorial (Leipzig, Karl-Marx-Stadt/Chemnitz or Magdeburg). The statues of Lenin were as numerous in Hungary as in Czechoslovakia, where they were built continuously since the 1956 revolution until the 1980s, with a presence in all important cities. On the other hand, very few statues of Lenin were erected in Poland, where they were mainly present in Soviet military bases. The only statue of Lenin in an important city was in Nowa Huta, in the district of Krakow, the other five being in small Polish towns, with eight in the Soviet military bases.[57] In contrast to other Eastern Bloc capitals, the Polish regime did not dare erect a Lenin monument in Warsaw.

The post-1989 destruction of memorials and the renaming of street names occurred to a lesser extent in the ex-GDR than in countries such as Poland, Hungary or in Czech territory. In GDR, the representatives of democratic socialist traditions were often allowed to remain in public space (Marx, Liebknecht and Rosa Luxemburg) similar to the communist activists of the anti-Nazi resistance and third-world socialists (e.g. Patrice Lumumba and Salvador Allende). It was obviously the West German social democratic tradition and the anti-Nazi consensus that hindered the wave of anti-communism typical of other former Eastern Bloc countries. In contrast to Czechoslovakia, no liberal democratic period existed in Germany in the public memory as strongly as that of the First Czechoslovak Republic. The Weimar Republic was not as positively remembered as the interwar Czechoslovak Republic was, and it was not identified with a widely respected personality in the way that interwar Czechoslovakia was identified with Masaryk. Therefore, there was no need to commemorate the liberal democratic traditions in post-1989 monuments in Eastern Germany. Although Czechoslovakia had significant leftist and socialist traditions, and its communist regime was originally more strongly supported by the public than were the regimes of Poland, Hungary, or the GDR, it was the post-1968 normalization that shifted the Czech public to an anti-communism of similar strength to that of Poland or Hungary and a similar willingness after 1989 to remove the symbols of the past. Since from 1948 to 1989 Slovakia had a rather successful social development, its population has been more reluctant to remove these symbols.

To more closely perceive the difference in the politics of memory between the former GDR and the Czech Republic during the post-1989 years, it is worth comparing the quantity of streets named after various communist heroes: Concerning the two most important communist anti-fascist martyrs in the former GDR and ČSSR, Ernst Thälmann and Julius Fučík, there is a reluctance to rename the Thälmann streets in the former GDR, and there are currently 82 streets and squares still named after him, prevalently in the smaller towns. (All Thälmann streets were renamed in the former Czechoslovakia.) There are 35 streets named after Fučík in the Czech Republic, again prevalently in small towns, 22 streets in Slovakia and 6 streets in the ex-GDR. Similarly, the streets named after Liebknecht or Luxemburg did not survive in the Czech Republic, while they are numerous in the former GDR. Concerning the places named after Karl Marx, there are several hundred streets and squares still named after him in the ex-GDR and also in Western Germany, but only nine in the Czech Republic. Although it is to be expected that Marx as an ethnic German would be more commemorated in the country of his birth, the disappearance of his name from streets in Czechoslovakia clearly indicates the strength of Czech anti-communism.

As the evidence is often missing and our data is incomplete, only systematic comparative research on issues having to do with the public presence of the visual symbols of communism and socialist and post-socialist memorials and street names in the former Eastern Bloc countries would allow us to understand better the relations between the strength of communist propaganda (including the presence of communist symbols in public space) and other characteristics of communist regimes, placing them on an axis indicating the level of political freedom. This would also allow us to compare the strength and practices of post-1989 public anti-communism. The evidence discussed here, however, suggests that in its self-presentation in the 1970s, Czechoslovakia was not only a harder line country than Poland or Hungary but also matched the GDR in this respect. The degree of street renaming and destruction of memorials after 1989 indicates that the public and authorities of the former GDR were comparatively moderate in dealing with the defeated communism. On the other hand, in its anti-communism, the Czech Republic equaled Poland, with Slovakia standing somewhere in the middle. There were definitely some oppressive features that were more elaborated in the former GDR than in the ČSSR (first of all, system of Stasi surveillance or the greater restrictions on traveling abroad),[58] but it seems that in some important aspects of public life, the GDR's rigidity was weaker. Besides more liberal politics of memory, we can cite its greater tolerance toward alternative music, homosexuals and lesbians or religion,[59] as well as the allowing of small business or less ideologization of the social sciences. This all points to the limits of the popular typology of state socialist regimes that groups the GDR and ČSSR under one "bureaucratic-authoritarian" label.[60] A further complication is that in the post-communist period, there are some signs of a more aggressive approach to the communist past in the former GDR (first of all, lustrations and the pushing out of representatives of the former regime from important positions), but at the same time, post-1989 Eastern German society exhibited a greater acceptance of socialism and the GDR heritage than the societies of Czechoslovakia or Poland did with their socialist heritage. Still, only more detailed comparative research covering wider aspects of East German and Czechoslovak society would allow a more accurate assessment.

Notes

1 Herbert Kitschelt, "Formation of Party Cleavages in Post-Communist Democracies," *Party Politics* 1.4 (1995): 447–450, 453.
2 Rudolf Jaworski, "Denkmalstreit und Denkmalsturz im östlichen Europa—Eine Problemskizze," in *Die Besetzung des öffentlichen Raumes: Politische Plätze, Denkmäler und Straßennamen im europäischen Vergleich*, eds. Rudolf Jaworski and Peter Stachel (Berlin: Fran und Timme, 2007), 186.
3 Katja Deinhard, *Stapelstadt des Wissens, Jena als Universitätsstadt zwischen 1770 und 1830* (Weimar: Böhlau, 2007), 15.
4 Rüdiger Stutz, "Technopolis, Jena als Modellstadt der späten Ulbricht-Ära," in *Sozialistische Städte zwischen Herrschaft und Selbstbehandlung: Kommunalpolitik, Stadtplanung und Altag in der DDR*, eds. Christoph Bernhardt and Heinz Reif (Stuttgart: Franz Steiner Verlag, 2009), 163–187.
5 Jörg Valtin, "Umbruchsituationen in der Jenaer Stadtgeschichte von 1945 bis 1990," in *Jenaer stadtgeschichtliche Beiträge*, ed. Jürgen John (Jena: Academica and studentica jenensia,1993), 237.
6 Mario Schiek and Rüdiger Stutz, "Zur Geschichte der Stadt Jena nach 1930," in *Jenaer stadtgeschichtliche Beiträge*, ed. Jürgen John (Jena: Academica and studentica jenensia,1993), 93.
7 Jaroslav Lněnička, "Kováci se nebojí," *Hradecký kurýr*, July 17, 1990, 1.
8 Tereza Holanová, "Kde se v Česku nejlíp žije," http://zpravy.aktualne.cz/ekonomika/kde-se-v-cesku-nejlip-zije-velke-porovnani-krajskych-mest/r~efd9ff484a4a11e494d7002590604f2e/, accessed June 1, 2017, and Wolfgang Suckert, "Jena ist lebenswerteste Ost-Stadt," http://www.thueringer-allgemeine.de/web/zgt/leben/detail/-/specific/Jena-ist-lebenswerteste-Ost-Stadt-819385667, accessed November 6, 2017.
9 Hans-Werner Kreidner, *Wendezeiten Jena* (Erfurt: Sutton, 2009), 10.

10 In Hradec Králové, there were 24 restaurants in 1981. An Internet search reveals 103 in 2015. Similarly, the number of cafés expanded from 6 to 30 and hotels from 7 to 35. The only declining public facilities were cinemas—from 10 to 3. Jena experienced a similar development, though not as strong. See *Hradec Králové: plán města* (Praha: Geodetický a kartografický podnik v Praze, 1988), and *Jena, Stadtplan* (Berlin and Leipzig: VEB Tourist Verlag, 1988).
11 Kreidner, *Wendezeiten Jena*, 95.
12 Between 1990 and 2013, the former left parties in the GDR (social democrats and post-communists) always received a majority of votes with one exception in 1990. In the Czech Republic during the same period, the left parties received a majority in national elections only once: in 2002.
13 In Jena, the party system established in 1990 has survived to the present day, while in Hradec, just as at the national level, the political-party system partly collapsed as a result of different scandals around 2010 and was partly replaced by new forces, which now are differentiated on the local and national levels. While municipal politics in Jena is still dominated by nation-wide political parties, in Hradec, there are several "independent" voter groups dominating city politics since 2014. See http://de.wikipedia.org/wiki/Jena#Stadtrat, accessed June 1, 2017, and https://www.volby.cz, accessed June 1, 2017.
14 The representatives of the Czech national movement represented in monuments before 1914 were Josef Jungmann (memorial constructed in 1878) and František Palacký (1911). The memorials regarded as "Austrian" were of Franz I (1850) and Marshal Václav Radetzky (1858). The memorial of Czech King Karel IV (1848) was considered politically neutral.
15 Jan Brunclík and Jaroslava Pospíšilová, *Na počest hrdinů* (Hradec Králové: Český svaz bojovníků za svobodu, Okresní výbor Hradec Králové, 2007), 92. In August 1968, the citizens added the date August 21, 1968 to May 9, 1945, carved in the stone.
16 Marco Schrul, "Jenseits der 'via triumphalis': Der Wandel der lokalen Erinnerungskultur in Jena seit 1989," in *Jena. Ein nationaler Erinnerungsort?*, eds. Jürgen John and Justus H. Ulbricht (Köln: Böhlau, 2007), 340, 517–549.
17 See Petra Jeníková, *Oslavy TGM v Hradci Králové, několik ohlédnutí za léty 1918–1935* (Ph.D. diss., Brno: Masaryk University, 2015), http://is.muni.cz/th/361635/ff_m/MGR_TGM.pdf, accessed June 1, 2017.
18 "Dostali jsme Váš dopis," *Puls: časopis města Hradce Králové*, 5.2 (1991): 2.
19 Josef Potoček et al., eds., *Návrat k odkazu svobody, demokracie a mravnosti, znovuobnovení sochy T. G. Masaryka v Hradci Králové* (Hradec Králové: Městský národní výbor, 1990), 26.
20 It was restored in 2009 adopting features that represented a compromise. Immanuel Voigt, "Das Blinkerdenkmal der Feldsignaltrupps des Ersten Weltkrieges in Jena. Erbe und Erinnerungskultur im Dissens," *Zeitschrift für Thüringische Geschichte*, 68.1 (2014): 297–312.
21 Günther Steiger, "Das Jenaer Goethe-Denkmal des Jahres 1821," *Wissenschaftliche Zeitschrift der Friedrich-Schiller-Universität Jena. Gesellschaftswissenschaftliche Reihe* 34.5–6 (1985): 667–682, 682.
22 See Monika Gibas, "Das Abbe-Bild in der DDR. Deutungskonkurrenzen und Deutungsvarianten in einer reglementierten Geschichtskultur," in *Jena. Ein nationaler Erinnerungsort?*, eds. Jürgen John and Justus H. Ulbricht (Köln: Böhlau, 2007), 517–549.
23 www.uni-jena.de/Universit%C3%A4t/Einrichtungen/Stabsstelle+Kommunikation/Uni_Journal+Jena/Archiv/13jour01/Kultur-p-350244.html, accessed June 1, 2017.
24 Brigitte Hellemann and Doris Weilandt, *Jena musarum salanarum sedes: 450 Jahre Universitätstadt Jena* (Jena: Vopelius, 2008), 57.

25 *Jena und Umgebung* (Berlin: Tourist Verlag, 1985), 97.
26 Its aim was "to express a strong internationalist stance and commitment to Marxism-Leninism." "Leninovy myšlenky sjednocují pracující celého světa," *Nové Hradecko*, April 22, 1970, 1. "Long live the friendship between the Czechoslovak and Soviet people as clear as Czechoslovak crystal and strong as Ural steel." "V duchu dlouholetých tradic," *Nové Hradecko*, April 22, 1970, 2.
27 As far as I can discover he was never present at the unveilings of Gottwald's statues. See "Odkaz vítězného února splníme," *Pochodeň*, February 24 and 25, 1973, 1, and "Hold vítěznému únoru," *Pochodeň*, February 27, 1973, 1.
28 However, as various Czech sources point out, normalization was considered more rigorous in Hradec than elsewhere, probably with the exception of the industrial city of Ostrava. See Petr Zimmermann et al., eds., *Radnice v Hradci Králové—její reprezentanti a jejich činnost v letech 1850–1998* (Hradec Králové: Nadace Historica, 1998), 83.
29 Dietmar Ebert, "Kultur an der Friedrich Schiller Universität im Spannungsfeld von Vielfalt, Lebendigkeit und politischer Kontrolle: Von der Eröffnung des Rossenkellers bis zur Aufführung des Revolutionsspektakels 'Sommernachtstraum' 1989," in *Hochschule im Sozialismus, Studien zu Geschichte der Friedrich Schiller Universität Jena, (1945–1990)*, vol. 1, eds. Uwe Hoßfeld, Tobias Kaiser and Heinz Mestrup (Köln: Böhlau, 2007), 1092.
30 Horst Hölzel, "Die neuen Denkmäler der Friedrich Schiller Universität Jena," *Wissenschaftliche Zeitschrift der Friedrich-Schiller-Universität Jena: Gesellschaftswissenschaftliche Reihe* 34.5-6 (1985): 780–794, 783–784.
31 Brigit Stephan and Doris Weilandt, *Neulobeda, Stadtteilchronik 1966–2006* (Jena: Komme e.V., 2007), 32.
32 Jindřich Vedlich, *Sametová revoluce v Hradci Králové* (Hradec Králové: Garamnon, 2009), 194. "K.G. Dolů," *Nové Hradecko*, January 16, 1990, 2. The petition for the removal of Gottwald was initiated on 2 December 1989. "Mítink na Masarykově náměstí," *Nové Hradecko*, January 3, 1990, 1.
33 "Konec jedné modly," *Východočeský večerník*, January 15, 1990, 2.
34 Aleš Franc, "Mít či nemít sochu Lenina," *Nové Hradecko*, February 20, 1990, 2.
35 "Causa tank," *Hradecký kurýr*, February 26, 1991, 3.
36 Martin Dvořák, "Ještě jednou o tanku, Najít správný výklad," *Hradecký kurýr*, March 12, 1991, 3.
37 *Východočeský večerník*, May 27, 1991, 1.
38 Martin Dvořák, "Primátor o tanku," *Hradecký kurýr*, February 19, 1991, 2; Ludmila Hovorková, "Památník nepamátník," *Východočeský večerník*, June 10, 1991, 1.
39 Tobias Kaiser, "'Die Universität Jena kann Karl Marx als einen der ihrigen bezeichnen': Eine Ikone der Arbeiterbewegung in der Erinnerungskultur der Salana nach 1945," in *Jena: Ein nationaler Erinnerungsort*, eds. Jürgen John and Justus H. Ulbricht (Köln: Böhlau, 2007), 337.
40 *Dokumente zur Erinnerung an den Jeaner Denkmalsturz 1991/92 anlässlich des 175: Geburgstages von Karl Marx am 5. Mai 1993* (Jena: Jenaer Forum für Bildung und Wissenschaft e.V., 1993).
41 Hellmann and Weilandt, *Jena musarum salanarum sedes*, 58–59.
42 Hellmann and Weilandt, *Jena musarum salanarum sedes*, 59.
43 Tobias Kaiser, "'Die Universität Jena kann Karl Marx. . . ,'" 338. The last initiative of the PDS, now renamed DIE LINKE, occurred in 2008. See "Wiederaufstellung der Karl-Marx-Büste—eine Beschlussvorlage der Fraktion DIE LINKE im Jenaer Stadtrat," www.also-zeitung-jena.de/stadt/8021stadt.htm, accessed June 1, 2017.
44 Tobias Kaiser, "'Die Universität Jena kann Karl Marx. . . ,'" 318.

45 Johanna Sänger, *Heldenkult und Heimatliebe: Strassen- und Ehrennamen im offiziellen Gedächtnis der DDR* (Berlin: Christoph Links, 2006), 207.
46 Other nicknames were Penis Jenensis and Uhaha (abreviation Universitätshochhaus/ university skyscraper). Kreidner, *Wendezeiten Jena* (Erfurt: Sutton, 2009), 13.
47 Sänger, *Heldenkult und Heimatliebe*, 208.
48 Peace Square (*Mírové náměstí*), where the statue once stood, was renamed *Masarykovo náměstí*, and the idea of restoring the Masaryk monument was already announced during the Velvet Revolution in November 1989. See "Mítink na Masarykově náměstí," *Nové Hradecko*, January 3, 1990, 1. A picture of Masaryk was placed on the square, and people began to light candles around it. Articles about its destruction appeared. The local newspaper wrote, "We have been contacted by citizens who know the names of those who participated in the destruction of the statue. [. . .] Our editorial board has these names and we are prepared to give them to an investigating organ or commission. Some of these people still live in Hradec Králové." "Hradecké hovory o TGM (2)," *Nové Hradecko*, January 9, 1990, 2.
49 Jan Pruška, "Z hradeckého náměstí zmizela socha Ulricha," https://hradecky.denik.cz/zpravy_region/z-hradeckeho-namesti-zmizela-socha-ulricha20110719.html, accessed June 1, 2017.
50 On September 11, 2016. See http://www.zeiss-denkmal.de/aktuelles.html, accessed June 1, 2017.
51 The mayor of the city Martin Dvořák warned against the "malignancy of communist ideology" and against its impact on the youth. *Almanach: okres Hradec Králové 1989–1999* (Hradec Králové: Konfederace politických vězňů, 1999), 45.
52 Anna Kaminski, ed., *Orte des Erinnerns, Gedenkzeichen, Gedenkstätten und Museen zur Diktatur in SBZ und DDR* (Berlin: Christoph Links, 2007), 475.
53 It reads, "On 17 June 1953 20,000 people rose up to demand a change in their society. The uprising was put down. Alfred Diener (26 years old) was shot as the alleged ringleader under martial law."
54 See Hans-Ulrich Thamer, "Von der Monumentalisierung zur Verdrängung der Geschichte. Nationalsozialistische Denkmalpolitik und die Entnazifizierung von Denkmälern nach 1945," in *Denkmalsturz: zur Konfliktgeschichte der politischen Symbolik*, ed. Winfried Speitkamp (Göttingen: Vandenhoeck and Ruprecht, 1997), 109–136.
55 http://leninstatues.ru/place/chehoslovakiya, accessed June 1, 2017.
56 Annette Leo, "Liturgie statt Erinnerung: Die Schaffung eines Heldenbildes am Beispiel Ernst Thälmanns," in *Ernst Thälmann, Mensch und Mythos*, ed. Peter Monteath (Amsterdam: Rodopi, 2000), 26. Peter Moneath counted 331 places of memory devoted to him. See Peter Moneath, "Ein Denkmal für Thälmann," in *Ernst Thälmann, Mensch und Mythos*, ed. Peter Monteath (Amsterdam: Rodopi, 2000), 180.
57 http://leninstatues.ru/, accessed June 1, 2017.
58 The best introduction to the GDR is by Steffan Wolle, *Die heile Welt der Diktatur: Alltag und Herrschaft in der DDR, 1971–1989* (Berlin: Christoph Links Verlag, 1998).
59 For a comparative approach see Stanislav Holubec, "Homosexualität in der tschechoslowakischen Gesellschaft 1948–1989: Gesetzgebung, Subkultur, Diskurs, filmische und literarische Verarbeitungen," in *Ordnung und Sicherheit, Devianz und Kriminalität im Staatssozialismus Tschechoslowakei und DDR 1948/49–1989*, eds. Volker Zimmermann and Michal Pullmann (Göttingen: Vandenhoeck and Ruprecht, 2014), 437–463.
60 Kitschelt, "Formation of Party Cleavages in Post-Communist Democracies," *Party Politics* 1.4 (1995): 453.

6 The Politics of Oblivion and the Practices of Remembrance

Repression, Collective Memory and Nation-Building in Post-Soviet Russia[1]

Ekaterina V. Klimenko

The collapse of the Soviet Union, resulting in the establishment of a number of independent (national) states, intensified the process of building nations and constituting national identities. This presupposed inventing national histories and creating collective memories. Emphasis was often put on the memory of repression suffered under Soviet rule. The historical narrative of a nation as a victim of persecution became the means for forging the nation as such.

Russia—along with the other post-socialist countries—was, and still is, exploiting history (or, to be more precise, the specific historical narrative) as the material for nation-building. Narrating the history of repression is the significant part of this process. The situation in Russia is, however, quite specific.

First of all, Russia has an image as the USSR's primary legatee and, therefore, is often regarded as the only national entity blamable for the crimes committed in its name and on its territory. Moreover, the ethnic, religious, cultural and linguistic diversity of Russian society results in the diversity of historical narratives and heterogeneity of the collective memory. But, most importantly, in the case of Russia, the distinction between the victims and the victimizers—as well as between the descendants of the former and of the latter—is far from being clear-cut and sometimes does not exist. It is, in fact, possible to constitute a national identity and to build a nation based on a narrative of it as either persecutor or persecuted; examples are well known.[2] But it is no easy task to narrate a history of a nation's "auto-genocide"—which is precisely what happened in Russia—as well as to constitute a national identity and to build a nation on the basis of such a narrative.

These circumstances made it nearly impossible to develop a coherent narrative of the repression or the one strategy of their conceptualization that would consolidate the majority—if not all—of Russian society. Hence various strategies have been employed in post-Soviet Russia over the last 30 years: "acknowledgment of the responsibility," "self-victimization," "rationalization" and "oblivion." During this period, Russia drifted from remembering repression toward attempts at suppressing this memory (and rationalizing what could not be forgotten).

This chapter examines the evolution of the strategies of conceptualization of past repression employed by both the state and civil society in post-Soviet Russia. The emphasis is on how the narrative of repression has been exploited in the process of nation-building and constituting national identity.

The current research is based on an understanding of social reality as inalienable from the (type of) knowledge concerning it.[3] The social world exists for the actors that operate in it mediated by the knowledge these actors possess about this world. At the same time, it is knowledge of the social reality that becomes the basis for constructing this reality: (re)producing it in the course of social practice. Subjective meanings that social actors give to the social world are institutionalized and thus become objective social structures; these social structures, in turn, reconfigure the systems of meanings that social actors use and hence predetermine their behavior.

Nation is understood here as an "imagined community."[4] Nations and nationalisms are considered to be cultural artifacts that were socially constructed quite recently but nevertheless have become universal political values. A nation emerges owing to a specific type of imagination that allows its members to envision it as an exclusive and sovereign community, worthy of sacrifice, including that of an individual's life. Building a nation involves constituting national identity perceived as the sense of belonging to a community defined in national terms and deemed internally homogenous and distinct from other communities of the kind.

To build a nation, construction material is required; history—or, to be more precise, collective memory of a common history—is this material. Collective memory is understood as the process of selective recollection of past events thought to be important.[5] Forging a national community is considered to be the process of inventing its uniqueness.[6] Inasmuch as the experience of the repression endured during the Soviet period (and the memory of this experience) allows for the invention of such a uniqueness, it becomes a valuable resource for constituting national identity (and building a nation)—for all the USSR successor states, including the Russian Federation.

Conceptualizing the Repression in the Early 1990s: Victims, Persecutors and the Nation Born Anew

During the period of perestroika, and at the beginning of the 1990s, Russia experienced a growing public interest in what is usually called "difficult questions of history"—that is, the tragic and traumatic experiences of the Soviet past. Among the objects of this interest were the victims as well as the persecutors. A great many academic and popular books about Soviet-era repression were published, movies made, institutions founded to commemorate the victims of repression, cultural practices of remembrance developed and monuments and museums created. The most important step taken during this period was the rehabilitation of the victims.

In fact, the rehabilitation began in 1953, right after the death of Joseph Stalin, and went on until 1965.[7] It took place swiftly and quietly in the form of commutation of sentences and liberation from the sites of imprisonment, exile or deportation. When the rehabilitation process began again in 1985, it was accompanied by heated public debates. On January 16, 1989, the Decree of the Presidium of the Supreme Council of the USSR "On Additional Measures for Restoration of Justice Regarding Victims of the Repression Occurring in the 1930s and 1940s and the Beginning of the 1950s" was enacted.[8] On November 14, 1989, the Declaration of the Supreme Council of the USSR "On Ruling Illegal and Criminal the Repressive Acts Against Nationalities Subjected to Forced Relocation and Enforcement of their Rights" was passed.[9] Finally, on August 13, 1990, the Decree of the President of the USSR "On the Restoration of the Rights of all Victims of Political Repression of the 1920s through the 1950s" was signed by Mikhail Gorbachev.[10] On April 26, 1991, the Law of the RSFSR No. 1107–1 "On Rehabilitation of the Repressed Nationalities" was introduced by the chairman of the Supreme Council of the RSFSR Boris Yeltsin.[11] All of this legislation was focused only on Stalinist repression; the circle of those considered to be the victims of repression according to these laws was thus narrowed; those who suffered during collectivization, the famine of the 1920s or were given prison sentences or committed to psychiatric hospitals for political reasons in the 1960s, 1970s and 1980s were excluded. Stalin and his inner circle were proclaimed (the only ones) responsible for the repression.

The post-Soviet phase of rehabilitation began in 1991 when, on October 18, Law No. 1761–1 "On Rehabilitation of the Victims of Political Repression" was signed.[12] It introduced a number of important changes. First of all, the concept of "political repression" was widened; it now included "different means of compulsion employed by the state for political motives": imprisonment, involuntary commitment to medical and psychiatric institutions, deportation, deprivation of citizenship, involuntary resettlement, exile, forced labor. Second, the understanding of the notion "victims of political repression" was broadened to include children, husbands, wives and parents of those who were executed or died in the places of their imprisonment and were rehabilitated postmortem; the children who were imprisoned or exiled together with their parents; and children who lost one or both of their parents to political repression. The right to familiarize oneself with the documents and other materials of criminal and administrative cases, and to copy them, was accorded to the rehabilitated and their relatives. The right of the rehabilitated to reinstatement and compensations was acknowledged. Finally, the law made possible legal prosecution of those responsible— i.e., members of the law enforcement bodies, such as the All-Russian Emergency Commission for Combating Counter-Revolution and Sabotage

(*Vserossiyskaya Chrezvychaynaya Komissiya po Bor'bye s Kontrrevolyutsiyei i Sabotazhem,* VChK), the State Political Directorate (*Gosudarstvennoye Politicheskoye Upravleniye,* GPU), the Joint State Political Directorate (*Obyedinyonnoye Gosudarstvennoye Politicheskoye Upravleniye,* OGPU), Directorate of the People's Commissariat for Internal Affairs (*Upravleniye Narodnogo Komissariata Vnutrennikh Del,* UNKVD), People's Commissariat for Internal Affairs (*Narodnyi Komissariat Vnutrennikh Del,* NKVD) and Ministry of State Security of the USSR (*Ministerstvo Gosudarstvennoy Bezopasnosti SSSR,* MGB), found guilty of "crimes against justice."

Whether the rehabilitation process that took place in the early 1990s can be said to be successful remains unclear: Millions of people were rehabilitated during this period; nevertheless, the compensations they received were insignificant and sometimes ridiculously small. Even more importantly, none of the persecutors was made responsible for their crimes.

The introduction into the Russian calendar of the Memorial Day for the Victims of Political Repression[13] was another important event of the early 1990s. Celebrated for the first time on October 30, 1991, it has since become annual. The date was chosen for a reason: It was on October 30, 1974, that political prisoners incarcerated in the territory of Mordovia (USSR) initiated a hunger strike in protest at the inhumane conditions of Soviet prisons and camps.

Finally, during the first half of the 1990s, many documents concerning the history of the repression were made public. On June 23, 1992, President Yeltsin signed decree no. 658[14] removing the secrecy labels from the documents that became basis for mass political repression: legislation, decisions of governmental and party agencies and bodies, protocols of the proceedings of nonjudicial organs, information on the number of repressed and other materials were declassified.

The early 1990s were the years when acknowledging responsibility for repression was the strategy of conceptualizing it employed by both Russian civil society and the government of the Russian Federation. It was then that accepting blame for the atrocities committed during Soviet rule—including those against Soviet citizens and foreigners—became a significant part of the policy of memory in Russia. The Katyn case should be mentioned as the most important example.

On April 13, 1990, a report was published by the TASS information agency[15] stating that Lavrentiy Beria and Vsevolod Merkulov (the functionaries of the Stalin administration) were directly responsible for the crimes committed in the Katyn forest; "deep regret" for these crimes was expressed in the report. On the very same day, Mikhail Gorbachev passed the lists of the Polish officers imprisoned in the NKVD camps in 1939–1940 to the president of Poland Wojciech Jaruzelski. The most important documents concerning the Katyn tragedy, however, remained classified. The situation changed more than two years later, when, on October 14, 1992, President Boris Yeltsin handed the so-called Classified File No. 1 containing the regulation of the Politburo of the CK VKPb to execute 14,700 Polish prisoners of war and 11,000 Polish prisoners to the president of Poland Lech Wałęsa. Uttering the words "forgive us" during his official visit to Poland in 1993, Yeltsin laid a wreath at the monument to the victims of Katyn in Warsaw.

The first half of the 1990s was the time when Russian society—as well as the Russian state—attempted not only to acknowledge responsibility for Soviet-era repression but also to employ the strategy of "self-victimization" to conceptualize them. Attempts were made to develop the narrative of the Russian nation as the victim of the criminal government. The demolition of the monument to Felix Dzerzhinsky—the first head of VChK and then GPU, personally and directly responsible for thousands of deaths—may be seen as a metaphor of these attempts. The monument, which had been located on Lubyanskaya Square in Moscow, opposite the headquarters of VChK-GPU-NKVD-KGB, was pulled down on the night of August 22–23, 1991; hundreds of ordinary Muscovites took active part in the process. The establishment of June 12—the day when the first Congress of People's Deputies of the Russian Soviet Federative Socialist Republic (*Rossiyskaya Sovetskaya Federativnaya Sotsialisticheskaya Respublika, RSFSR*) voted for the Declaration of State Sovereignty[16]—as the Independence Day of the Russian Federation became another meaningful event of the period. The Declaration was passed in 1991; a year later, on June 12, 1991, the first presidential elections took place in the Russian Federation and Boris Yeltsin became Russia's first president; since 1991, June 12 has been a national holiday.

The two aforementioned events of the early 1990s—the demolition of the Dzerzhinsky monument and the introduction of Independence Day—embodied the endeavor to rupture with the Soviet past. It was this rupture that became fundamental not only for the strategy for conceptualizing the repression but also—and even more importantly—for the strategy of nation-building developed during this period. Recognizing oneself as responsible for the crimes committed during the Soviet rule—and at the same time as the victims of those crimes—contributed to creating the collective memory of Russian society. The narrative of the "newly born" civic nation of Russians was developed to provide the basis for constituting its specific national identity.

Russian society of the early 1990s was looking for its founding events—and its founding fathers—in 1991. By the beginning of the 2000s, this society's "time horizon" started to change: It was "lengthened" to include the Soviet past. The growing interest in this past reflected (and was embedded in) the urge to invent the nation's founding myth. The latter was no longer related to the events of 1991, but referred to the Soviet period. It was this Soviet period (or the myth of it) that became fundamental for both constituting the new version of identity of the Russian nation and justifying the very existence of the nation as such.

The narrative of the Great Patriotic War (to be more precise, of victory in it) constituted the key element of the Soviet myth. Interestingly enough, the price of this victory did not become part of the newly invented (or reinvented) mythology. Whenever discussed, this price was employed for "privatizing" the victory, for interpreting it as achieved not by the Allies (and not even by the Soviets) but by the Russians. The reasons for such a high price were never debated. "Heroizing" turned into the only admissible style and the only permissible way of narrating the history of the war. A little less, but still, important for (re)inventing the Soviet myth were the achievements of the second half of the Soviet era—from Gagarin's flight to Leonid Brezhnev's "stability." It was by this stability on the one hand and heroism on the other that the image of the Soviet past was now configured.

This "shift" in the "time horizon" followed by—and at the same time following—the change in the nation's understanding of its founding event, and of the events that substantiate its continuing existence, shaped Russia's perception of its own past. To explain what followed, the concept of "return" ("retour") as one of the "forms of oblivion"[17] is useful: The previously "lost"—and long gone—past is rediscovered; the recent past is forgotten; the memory of the "complex" past is suppressed in favor of the memory of the "simple" past. As a result, the connection between the present and the long gone past is established and a sense of continuity created. From the beginning of the 2000s, the Soviet period has become for Russian society the lost and rediscovered "long gone past," while the period of the early 1990s has turned into the forgotten "recent past." Identity implies continuity; the continuity Russian society began to look for was that with the Soviet past—the rupture with it was thus never accomplished.

We can point to various reasons behind this dramatic transformation. First, the need to (re)constitute a somewhat positive national identity predetermined the search for a historical narrative this identity could be based on. The attempt to develop such a narrative around the victory in the Great Patriotic War resulted not only in the aforementioned heroizing of this victory (and of the war in general) but also in an idealization of the historical period the war was "nested" within and the historical context it was related to. Second, the newly adopted strategy of conceptualizing the repression may be considered a response to the attempts to "ethnicize"[18] it occurring in many of the post-Soviet (and post-Socialist) countries.

More "down-to-earth" motives that underlie the change in the conceptual strategy should also be mentioned. The consistent acknowledgment of responsibility for repression would inevitably result in the necessity to identify—and punish—those responsible as well as to compensate the victims. Since the circle of the latter would include not only individuals but also groups and states, the consequences of acknowledging responsibility were unclear and—more significantly—undesired by Russia's political establishment. What also mattered was the fact that some members of this establishment had been personally affiliated with the KGB, the organization related to (and to a certain extent the inheritor of) the agency directly responsible for carrying out the repression. Making this memory an important part of the historical narrative upon which the nation's identity is based would not simply harm the reputation of many members of the new political elite; it would also cause serious damage to—if not the destruction of—its legitimacy.

Toward Rationalization: The Memory of the Repression in the Early 2000s

As we have said, the endeavor to establish continuity with the Soviet past—which replaced the attempts to break with it—led to profound reconceptualization of (the memory of) repression. This reconceptualization involved three dimensions: discursive rationalization of the repression, intensified use of the discourse of "reconciliation" and monopolization of historical knowledge and development of the one and only historical narrative.

The rationalization of Soviet-era repression consisted of interpreting it as a necessary—if not inevitable—instrument of intensified modernization; the key metaphor expressing this rationalization is that of Stalin as an "efficient manager."

The battle around the rationalization of repression was waged in the arena of public education: The key issues in this battle were how the history of the Soviet period should be taught in school and—even more importantly—what the content of the school history textbooks should be. On November 27, 2003, Vladimir Putin held a meeting with historians in the Russian State Library. It was there that he first expressed the ideas he repeatedly cited afterward:

> Until recently, historians have emphasized negative factors since there was a wish to demolish the previous system. Now we have another, constructive, aim. At the same time, it is necessary to remove all the incrustations that have accrued over these years.[19]

Speaking about the content of the school history textbooks Putin claimed, "It is necessary to recount the historical facts, eliciting in the youth a sense of pride in their country."[20]

Later in 2003, the label "Recommended by the Ministry of Education of the Russian Federation" was removed[21] from the school history textbook for the tenth and eleventh grades by Igor Doluckij.[22] This text was famous for its innovative approach to studying history: Its core principle was that of providing students with facts and documents, offering them the opportunity to analyze these facts and documents critically, and develop their own understanding (and evaluation) of various historical events. The same approach—based on asking questions rather than giving answers—was employed by Doluckij when he dealt with the history of repression. While announcing the Ministry's decision, the deputy minister, Victor Bolotov, claimed that for 1994—when the textbook was written—it was "warrantable and appropriate"; by 2003, however, the textbook became "incongruous" since it was "over-politicized." Nearly repeating the president's claims, Bolotov stated, "Today we work not for the opposition and confrontation of opinions, whether left or right, but for the elaboration of mutual understanding within society."[23]

Following these events, a contest was announced by the Ministry of Education of the Russian Federation aimed at creating a new school textbook on Russian history; the competition was won by the team of authors headed by Nikita Zagladin.[24] It was in this text that a specific explanation—if not a justification—for Soviet-era repression was developed. The latter was—for the first time—interpreted as a necessary and inevitable tool for the industrialization and modernization of the country. This then very typical interpretation of the repression was further developed in the works of a group of historians headed by Alexander Filippov and Alexander Danilov. Established in 2006, the group succeeded in creating a number of school textbooks: *History of Russia: 1945–2006: Teacher's Aid*,[25] *History of Russia: 1945–2008*,[26] *Concept of the Teaching Course "History of Russia 1900–1945,"*[27] *History of Russia: 1900–1945*.[28] In every one of these textbooks, the repression was interpreted as a management method adapted to the epoch in which it was employed, collectivization treated as an instrument serving the needs of industrialization, organized famine of the 1930s as if it never existed, the Great Terror of the 1930s as Stalin's reaction to the resistance he faced when trying to modernize the country, occupation of Poland in 1939 as a liberation campaign and the Katyn execution as the response to the deaths of thousands of Red Army prisoners of war in Poland in 1920.

The textbook by Nikita Zagladin, as well as those by Alexander Filippov and Alexander Danilov, became the subject of heated public debates. The most criticized history textbook of the period, however, was written by Alexander Vdovin and Alexander Barsenkov. Their *History of Russia: 1917–2009* for university students—which contained a number of xenophobic and antisemitic remarks—offered the following description of Stalin: "Stalin from the point of view of statehood was a great hero, from the point of view of human rights an assassin and evildoer."[29] The opposition that the textbook provoked[30] ended in the drafting of the Non-Regulatory Motion of the Commission for Relations Between Nationalities and Freedom of Conscience of the Civic Chamber of the Russian Federation: The view the members of the commission took of the textbook was extremely negative.[31] As a consequence, in 2010, the decision was made by the Academic Board of the Department of History of Moscow State University to cease using the textbook;[32] later that year, it was acknowledged by the board that its use had been "inexpedient."[33]

Although it would be an exaggeration to say that the attempts to rationalize the repression were a complete failure, it has to be noted that they were fiercely opposed—and to a certain extent successfully—by some members of Russian civil society as well as by government officials. Among the latter was Dmitry Medvedev, at that time president of the Russian Federation. Addressing the nation in his video blog on October 30, 2009, he stated,

> I am certain that it is as important to remember national tragedies as it is to remember victories [. . .] I am positive that no development of the country, no success, and no goals can be achieved at the price of human sorrow and loss. Nothing can be valued higher than the life of a human being. And there is no justification for repression.[34]

However, this recording in Medvedev's video blog remains up to now the only address to the nation made by the president of the Russian Federation on the official Memorial Day for the Victims of Political Repression. Unlike Medvedev, President Putin has never spoken to the nation specifically on how he views the repression. He did, however, express ideas similar to those voiced in Medvedev's video blog more than once. On October 30, 2007, when visiting the memorial to the victims of political repression in Butovo together with Patriarch Alexey, Putin addressed the reporters:

> Such tragedies have been repeated in the history of humankind more than once; and they always occurred when ideals—initially attractive at but in fact shallow—were valued more highly than human life, above human rights and freedom. In our country, it has been a particular tragedy because its scale is colossal [. . .] And of course, we have been feeling this tragedy for years, until today. And a lot needs to be done so that it is never forgotten, so that we always remember this tragedy.[35]

On April 7, 2010, during the Russian-Polish memorial ceremony in Katyn, Putin—speaking about the repression—stated, "There can be no justification for these crimes. In our country a clear political, legal, moral assessment of the atrocities of the totalitarian regime has been issued: this assessment cannot be revised."[36]

The Presidential Council for Civil Society and Human Rights[37] played an important role in counteracting the attempts to rationalize (and justify) the repression. Since 2011, a Standing Committee for Historical Memory headed by Sergei Karaganov has been working within the council. On February 1, 2011, members of the committee presented a project of the Program for Perpetuating the Memory of Victims of the Totalitarian Regime and on National Reconciliation[38] to Dmitry Medvedev (at the time president of the Russian Federation). The project's key issue was that of national cohesion: The path toward this cohesion was represented as the need to acknowledge that repression actually took place and to commemorate their victims. The "full recognition of the Russian catastrophe of the twentieth century, of the victims and consequences of the totalitarian regime that reigned on the territory of the USSR during the greater part of this century" was called "one of the most important ways of overcoming the mutual alienation of the people and the elite."[39] The aims of the program included the following: " modernization of the consciousness of Russian society through acknowledgment of the tragedy of the people"; "termination of the civil war initiated in 1917"; "the enforcement of the unifying tendencies in the territory of the former USSR and, possibly, in post-socialist space."[40] At the same time, it was directly stated in the project that the program should be focused not on accusing "those of our predecessors who committed the genocide, and the destruction of faith and morale" but on "honoring and perpetuating the memory of the victims of the regime."[41]

The project was debated and rejected. On August 15, 2015, however, the Concept of the State Policy to Perpetuate the Memory of Victims of Political Repression was approved by the Russian Government.[42] It is expected to result in the "enforcement of the unity of cultural space as the prerequisite for the preservation of Russia's state integrity."[43] The concept states that the following measures are to be taken toward this end: facilitating access to archives; establishing the "infrastructure related to the perpetuation of the memory of the victims of political repression," using it "as a development resource for territories"; elaborating and implementing educational programs and performing scientific research; identifying sites of mass graves of the victims of political repression; creating databases and a multimedia book of remembrance. At the same time, neither compensating the victims for harm and loss nor prosecuting those responsible is mentioned among these measures. According to the concept, no political or legal assessment of the repression is to take place.

On September 22, 2015, 40 days after the concept was signed, a member of the Federation Council from the Arkhangelsk Region Konstantin Dobrynin (famous for his criticism of many of the restrictive laws recently passed in Russia) introduced a draft law "On Counteracting the De-stigmatization of the Crimes of Stalin's Totalitarian Regime (Stalinism)."[44] In the draft, destigmatization is defined as

> a positive assessment, and (or) justification, of the need for political repression; the recognition of the practice of mass unjustified persecution of citizens as being just and worthy of support and approval; disavowal of the crimes of Stalin's totalitarian regime—complete or partial refutation of the existence of the practice of mass unjustified persecution of citizens exercised during the period of existence of Stalin totalitarian regime.

An important detail: All of this is only valid in relation to the deeds officially admitted and condemned in the existing legislation on the rehabilitation of the victims of political repression and rehabilitation of the repressed nationalities.

Not only does this draft law not discuss prosecuting the perpetrators and/or compensating the victims but also the repressive measures, whose destigmatization is to be prohibited, are defined as those of "Stalin's totalitarian regime." The draft, thus, does not aim at counteracting the attempts at destigmatizing the repression of the pre-Stalin and the post-Stalin periods. Despite this limited scope of the proposed law and its rather rhetorical character, it was returned to the authors for revising on October 22, 2015, one month after it had been presented. According to the official response of the legal department of the State Duma of the Russian Federation,[45] the legislative draft was rejected because of to it not having indicated how its measures would be funded. On November 6, 2015, the draft was reintroduced to the State Duma of the Russian Federation by Dmitry Gudkov, a member of the party *Spravedlivaja Rossija* [A Just Russia]; Gudkov specified the financial bases of the law stating that its enforcement—were the law to pass—would not require any additional financing.[46] Nevertheless, on December 14, 2015, the draft was rejected again for lack of a judgment issued by the government of the Russian Federation on its compliance with the requirements of the Constitution of the Russian Federation and the State Duma Regulations.[47]

Interestingly enough, the rhetoric of "reconciliation" was (and still is) employed to both justify the rationalization of the repression and counteract such a rationalization. What the adherents of rationalizing Soviet-era repression in fact claim is that national cohesion is only possible through the memory of common victories. The memory of common defeats—to say nothing of common crimes—is self-deprecating, if not self-humiliating, and impedes the development of such cohesion. "Enough of self-criticism" is their stance. For their opponents, it is a lack of the memory of common tragedies that impedes national cohesion. Their aim is not only to honor the memory of the people's suffering but also to achieve reconciliation—with the help of, and at the same time within, this memory.

Reconciling the nation and promoting its integrity thus becomes one of the main goals of the policy of memory, regardless of how the essence of this policy is understood by those endeavoring to shape it. For the nation to be united in the present, it is to be united with its past. The search for this unity now determines the strategy for conceptualizing the repression.

In Search of "National Unity": Remembering and Forgetting the Repression

How can national unity be achieved if not through forgetting the tragedies of the past? A forgetting that becomes more complete the more it is implicit.

One of the first steps toward what was called "national unity" was taken in the early 2000s when the national flag, emblem and anthem were established. The flag as well as the emblem are based on Russia's imperial past and refer to the pre-Soviet period of Russian history. The anthem on the contrary—being a replica of the Soviet one, with music by Alexander

Alexandrov and new lyrics by its original lyricist Sergei Mikhalkov—clearly is a part of the Soviet heritage.

The forging of national unity continued with the establishment of a new national holiday. The Day of People's Unity—celebrated annually on November 4—commemorates the anniversary of the expulsion of the Polish troops from Moscow in 1612; November 4 is also the Day of the Icon of Our Lady of Kazan, important for members of the Orthodox Church. The Day of People's Unity has a rather peculiar history. The "Day of Reconciliation and Cohesion" was introduced in 1996 by President Yeltsin's decree no. 1537 as a substitute for the most important holiday of the Soviet epoch, November 7, the Anniversary of the Great Socialist Revolution;[48] the intent to "prevent confrontation in the future" and the pursuit of "unity and consolidation of Russian society" was the explanation given. Nine years later, in 2005, the date of the holiday was moved from November 7 to November 4, its new historical justification—referring to the liberation from the Polish intervention in 1612—was invented, and the very name of the holiday was changed. The Day of People's Unity thus came into being. Paradoxically enough, despite its name, its connotation ever since 2005 has been one of divisiveness, as it is best known in today's Russia as the day when the Russian Marches—demonstrations by Russian right-wing nationalists—take place in Moscow, Saint Petersburg and other big cities.

Establishing national unity required monopolizing historical knowledge and developing an unambiguous historic narrative. These became (the most) important components of memory policy in Russia from the beginning of the 2000s. The instruments deployed toward these ends were the establishment of institutions aimed at identifying "historical truth" and its promotion on the national as well as on the international "markets," and reestablishing control over the content of school history textbooks.

The battle for historical truth began in 2001. On June 22, the day of the outbreak of the Great Patriotic War, which is the core issue of this battle, Vladimir Putin claimed, "We will vindicate the truth about this war and fight any attempts to twist and distort this truth, to humiliate and insult the memory of the fallen."[49] On May 7, 2009, Dmitry Medvedev (then president of the Russian Federation) published an address to the nation in his video blog. It was entitled "On the Great Patriotic War, Historical Truth and our Memory." In it, he said,

> We began to face more often what today is called historical falsifications. In addition—and perhaps many of you have noticed this—these attempts have been becoming cruder, more malicious and aggressive [. . .] And we in fact find ourselves in a situation in which we have to demonstrate the historical truth and even re-establish the facts that recently had seemed to be absolutely obvious.[50]

By the end of the 2000s, defending historical truth became an institutionalized activity: In 2009, the Presidential Commission of the Russian Federation to Counter Attempts to Falsify History to the Detriment of Russia's Interest[51] was established. Among the stated aims of the commission—headed by Sergei Naryshkin, then the chief of the Presidential Administration—were summarizing and analyzing the information on falsification of historical facts and events for the purpose of disparaging the international prestige of the Russian Federation (although never explicitly specified, it was quite clear that the historical facts and events whose falsification the commission was to counteract were primarily those related to the period of World War II and the Soviet period of Russian history in general), preparing reports to the president and developing a strategy to counteract attempts at falsifying historical facts and events for the purpose of damaging Russia's interests.

Although the commission ceased to exist in 2012,[52] the crusade for historical truth continued. Two institutions for counteracting the falsification of historical truth were established: the Russian Historical Society[53] and the Russian Military-Historical Society.[54] The former is headed by Sergei Naryshkin (then chairman of the State Duma of Russian Federation, today director of the Foreign Intelligence Service of the Russian Federation) and the latter by Minister of Culture of the Russian Federation Vladimir Medinsky. For both of these institutions, counteracting attempts to "distort" Russian history plays the key role.

As counteracting attempts at falsifying history was the aim of the historical crusade initiated by decision makers, school history textbooks naturally became its key battlefield. The debates around the textbooks—whose tenor was political rather than scholarly—began again in 2010. First, Irina Yarovaja, the deputy of the State Duma of the Russian Federation and chair of the State-Patriotic Club *Yedinaya Rossiya* [United Russia] declared the need to develop a "single school history textbook." Three years later, in 2013, Vladimir Putin confirmed this need: School history textbooks should not contain "inconsistencies and dittologies"[55] he said. He later assigned the development of the concept for a single school history textbook to the Ministry of Education and Science of the Russian Federation, the Russian Academy of Sciences, the Russian Historical Society and the Russian Military-Historical Society.[56]

As a consequence of severe public criticism, the very idea of introducing a single school history textbook was rejected and substituted with the concept of a "historical-cultural standard." This document outlines the events of Russian history that are to be included in school textbooks and defines the principles that teaching history at public schools should be based upon. When, following the heated public debates that surrounded the publication of the first draft of the standard[57] its final version appeared in October 2013,[58] it became evident that the authors had taken into account comments made and criticisms expressed. The resulting document is not only schematic but also vague: It seems that Russian history may be narrated in very different ways yet in full accordance with the standard. The account of the repression that the standard provides is not detailed but nevertheless accurate. However, the tragedy of the repression in the text of the standard is "outweighed" by the triumphs of the Soviet era, with the victory in the Great Patriotic War being the most important, but not the only, achievement.

The battle for "historical truth" in which Russia is involved was (and still is) a part of what can be called "wars over history"—waged between different interpretations of the socialist past—that are specific to post-socialist Eastern Europe. The annexation of Crimea (or the integration of Crimea into the Russian Federation) unleashed a new round in these wars. On November 5, 2014, during the meeting with young historians held in the Museum of Modern History of Russia in Moscow, Vladimir Putin explicitly declared history to be "the first line of the ideological front."[59] Historians, he added, should "persuade the majority of the country's citizens of the justness and objectivity of our approaches," "win people's minds and induce them to take an active position on the basis of the knowledge you [historians—E.K.] present as objective."[60]

Rediscovering the Forgotten: Civil Society and the Fight for Memory

In the intensifying struggle over historical truth, Russian civil society seems to have adopted a standpoint in opposition to that of the Russian state. Inasmuch as the efforts of the state are aimed at suppressing memory of the repression, civil society takes responsibility for preserving it.

While the state's policy on the history of repression is in reality a policy of oblivion, the memory of repression is due to the cultural practices initiated by civil society. These practices include discovering the sites of mass murders and graves, creating memorials and monuments that honor the victims of repression, collecting libraries and archives, supporting scholarly research, holding conferences and exhibitions and establishing museums.

Among the nongovernmental organizations (NGOs) that work in the field of the politics of memory, the most important is doubt Memorial.[61] Founded in January 1989, it is today an international organization that unites dozens of branches all over Russia and abroad. Today Memorial is an archive, a museum, a library and a research center. Discovering sites of mass murders and mass graves, as well as instituting memorials and monuments, on these sites holds a very important place in its work.

Another important organization is the Andrei Sakharov Center.[62] Founded in 1990, the center has created electronic databases on victims of repression, monuments and memorials dedicated to them and victims' memoires. The museum of the center contains collections of documents and photographs related to the repression and works of art and craftsmanship produced by the victims during imprisonment. In 2003–2012, the center held an annual competition for teachers of history, social science and literature called the History of Political Repression and the Struggle for Freedom in the USSR.

The Yeltsin Center[63] has been holding an Annual International Scientific Conference, The History of Stalinism, since 2008. The Committee of Civil Initiatives[64] founded in 2012 by ex-minister of finance Alexey Kudrin established a Free Historical Society, which was designed as an alternative to the aforementioned Russian Historical Society and Russian Military-Historical Society.

There are numerous websites and web platforms commemorating the repression and honoring its victims. They contain documents, books and texts on its history; video and audio testimonials of the survivors; and databases of the sites of mass murders and mass graves, and of monuments and memorials dedicated to the repression and its victims. Among the most important are "Lessons of History,"[65] "Historical Memory. XX Century,"[66] "Virtual Museum of Gulag"[67] and Topography of Terror."[68] Two more projects for preserving memory of the repression have been initiated recently: "Immortal Barrack"[69] is a web platform that is to contain family histories written and published by descendants of the victims of repression; the mission of "The Last Address"[70] is to place memorial plaques on the buildings people were taken from (and never came back to) during the repression.

Museums dedicated to the repression are not great in number; nevertheless, at least two are worth mentioning. Perm-36[71] is the only museum in Russia that was founded on the site of a camp where political prisoners were incarcerated. The camp itself—whose unofficial name in the Soviet penitentiary system was "Perm-36"—functioned until 1988 and was the last of the camps on the territory of the RSFSR to be shut down. The State Museum of the History of Gulag[72] is situated in Moscow. Founded in 2001 and opened in 2004, it started operating in a new (larger and better-equipped) building on October 30, 2015. The most important among the memorials related to the repression are Butovo,[73] Kommunarka[74] and Mednoje.[75] There are over 700 monuments, memorial plaques, crosses and stones dedicated to the victims of repression found in Russia. The most famous of them are beyond any doubt the two "Solovetzki" stones (brought from the island of Solovki where the first and one of the most brutal Gulag camps were located) installed in 1990 in Moscow and in 2002 in Saint Petersburg; Mikhail Shemyakin's "Sphinxes" installed in 1995 across the Neva River from *Kresti* [Crosses], the sinister prison of Saint Petersburg; and "Masque of Sorrow" created by Ernst Neizvestny near Sopka Krutaya mountain in Magadan Oblast' in the Russian Far East. The "official" monument to the victims of the repression, however, was created only recently: In September 2015, President Putin made the decision to establish the monument in Moscow.⁷⁶ The monument—the commission for whose design was awarded to Georgi Frangulyan—is named "The Wall of Sorrow" and is located at the corner of Sadovoje Koltzo and Sakharov Prospect, in the center of the Russian capital.

With these two exceptions—the State Museum of the History of GULAG and the Wall of Sorrow—the initiatives for preserving the memory of the repression are driven by civil society: The majority of them are planned, launched, developed and managed by civil activists and NGOs with little or no participation from the state.

It would, however, be a mistake to say that Russian civil society is united in its determination to commemorate the repression and honor the victims. While some civil activists are working to establish memorials to the victims of the repression, others—usually led by, or in some way related to, the Communist Party—advocate the construction of monuments to Stalin (in 2015 alone, such monuments appeared in Lipetsk, in the Pskov region, in the small town of Shelanger in the Republic of Marij El, in the Tver Region). While thousands of people participate in the annual commemoration ceremony "The Return of the Names,"⁷⁷ hundreds come to lay flowers at Stalin's monuments on March 5, the day of his death. In the never-ending debates around the monument to Felix Dzerzhinsky (pulled down more than 20 years ago), the number of those in favor of its reconstruction has been constantly growing and in 2015 reached 37 percent.⁷⁸

The public perception of Stalin has changed over the years: From moderately negative in the 2000s, it became neutral or mildly positive in the 2010s. In 2015, 39 percent of respondents expressed somewhat positive feelings ("admiration"—2 percent, "sympathy"—7 percent, "respect"—30 percent) and 20 percent strongly negative feelings ("dislike, irritation"—9 percent, "fear"—6 percent, "disgust, hate"—5 percent) toward Stalin; 30 percent—claimed to be indifferent.⁷⁹ For 24 percent of respondents, Stalin's death is associated with "the loss of the great leader and teacher," while for 46 percent, it is associated with "the end of terror and mass repression and the liberation from prison of millions of innocent people"; 27 percent were not able to provide an answer for this question.⁸⁰ While 7 percent of respondents stated that the sacrifices of the Soviet people are "definitely" justified by "the great goals achieved in the shortest time," and 38 percent felt that these sacrifices are "justified to a certain extent," 41 percent claimed that "there is nothing that can justify them."⁸¹

It would be a gross exaggeration to say that the majority of Russians (or even a half of them) justifies the repression or supports Stalin's style and methods of "management." A more accurate picture of Russian society would involve three groups: inconsiderable but enthusiastic admirers of Stalin, the equally small in number and no less passionate accusers of him, and the indifferent majority which—being fully supported by the state—retreats to oblivion.

Conclusion

It appears that memory of the repression has become one of the key sources of conflict between Russian civil society and the Russian state. Yet it is still more complicated. Russian society is far from sharing a common memory of this history. At the same time, the state's efforts to conceptualize this memory have always been self-contradictory.[82] This chapter is an attempt to put together a consistent account of highly inconsistent material, and this has inevitably necessitated a certain degree of simplification. Nevertheless, it is possible to formulate some conclusions.

The path Russian society followed from the beginning of the 1990s went from a commitment to commemorate the repression to more or less successful attempts at forgetting it. The destination point Russia has reached is oblivion. Oblivion, however, is far from being an unambiguous concept; it may exist in many forms and on different levels. The oblivion that Russian society faces today is not a "repressive erasure" but a "prescriptive forgetting"—that is, publicly approved forgetting and forgiving in the name of political reconciliation and national cohesion.[83] Being superficially ritualized, the memory of repression in Russia has not been completely erased; it is, however, expelled from public discourse and deprived of the possibility of being articulated.[84]

The "memory project" of today's Russia is aimed at developing a "grand narrative"—which is the narrative of building a great nation (and a great state). Belonging to the era of modernity and being essentially "modernist," this narrative is based on neglecting the local and ignoring the global: It disregards "small" stories of "little people" and is at the same time focused on Russia's "special historical path." It is not surprising, therefore, that the history (and memory) of repression finds no place within this specific narrative which, being focused on the heroic rather than the tragic, recounts victories but not miseries.

Russian society did not decide to break with the Soviet past but is searching for continuity with it: Victory in the Great Patriotic War became this society's founding event and the collapse of the Soviet Union its most important collective trauma.[85] It is in this Soviet past that modern Russia is trying to find its roots. Paradoxically, it is not the memory but the forgetting of this past that becomes fundamental for the current identity of the Russian nation. Would it be possible to constitute such an identity (and build the nation itself) grounded in remembering rather than forgetting? This is the question to which Russian society one day will have to find an answer.

Notes

1 I would like to thank Professor Amir Weiner and the Reading Group for Russian and East European Studies of Stanford University, whose stimulating discussions and thoughtful comments were of invaluable assistance during the preparation of this chapter for publication.

2 For the post-Holocaust collective memories of Jews and Germans see, for instance, Aleida Assmann, *Shadows of Trauma: Memory and the Politics of Postwar Identity*, trans. Sara Clift (New York: Fordham University Press, 2016).
 3 Peter L. Berger and Thomas Luckmann, *The Social Construction of Reality: A Treatise in the Sociology of Knowledge* (Harmondsworth: Penguin Books, 1966).
 4 Benedict Anderson, *Imagined Communities: Reflections on the Origins and Spread of Nationalism* (London and New York: Verso, 1991).
 5 Maurice Halbwachs, *On Collective Memory*, trans., ed. and introduction Lewis A. Coser (Chicago: University of Chicago Press, 1992).
 6 Stuart Hall, "Introduction: Who Needs 'Identity'?", in *Questions of Cultural Identity*, eds. Stuart Hall and Paul Du Gay (London: Sage, 1996), 1–17.
 7 On the history of the rehabilitation process see Elena G. Putilova, *Istorija gosudarstvennoj reabilitacionnoj politiki i obshhestvennogo dvizhenija za uvekovechenie pamjati zhertv politicheskih repressij v Rossii (1953—nachalo 2000-h gg.)* (Ufa: Infiniti, 2012).
 8 "Ukaz Prezidiuma Verhovnogo Soveta SSSR 'O dopolnitel'nyh merah po vosstanovleniju spravedlivosti v otnoshenii zhertv repressij, imevshih mesto v period 30-h—40-h i nachala 50-h godov,'" January 16, 1989, http://base.consultant.ru/cons/cgi/online.cgi?req=doc;base=ESU;n=1714, accessed June 1, 2017.
 9 "Deklaracija Verhovnogo Soveta SSSR 'O priznanii nezakonnymi i prestupnymi repressivnyh aktov protiv narodov, podvergshihsja nasil'stvennomu pereseleniju, i obespechenii ih prav,'" November 14, 1989, http://base.consultant.ru/cons/cgi/online.cgi?req=doc;base=ESU;n=1687, accessed June 1, 2017.
10 "Ukaz prezidenta SSSR 'O vosstanovlenii prav vseh zhertv politicheskih repressij 20-50-h godov,'" No. 556, August 13, 1990, http://base.consultant.ru/cons/cgi/online.cgi?req=doc;base=ESU;n=3475, accessed June 1, 2017.
11 "Zakon RSFSR 'O reabilitacii repressirovannyh narodov,'" No. 1107–1, April 26, 1991, http://base.consultant.ru/cons/cgi/online.cgi?req=doc;base=LAW;n=4434, accessed June 1, 2017.
12 "Zakon 'O reabilitacii zhertv politicheskih repressij,'" No. 1761–1, October 18, 1991, http://base.consultant.ru/cons/cgi/online.cgi?req=doc;base=LAW;n=194954, accessed June 1, 2017.
13 "Postanovlenie Verhovnogo Soveta RSFSR 'Ob ustanovlenii dnja pamjati zhertv politicheskih repressij,'" No. 1763/1–1, October 18, 1991, http://base.consultant.ru/cons/cgi/online.cgi?req=doc;base=LAW;n=119358, accessed June 1, 2017.
14 "Ukaz Prezidenta Rossijskoj Federacii 'O snjatii ogranichitel'nyh grifov s zakonodatel'nyh i inyh aktov, sluzhivshih osnovaniem dlja massovyh repressij i pocjagatel'stv na prava cheloveka,'" No. 658, June 23, 1992, http://base.consultant.ru/cons/cgi/online.cgi?req=doc;base=EXP;n=223368, accessed June 1, 2017.
15 "Zajavlenie TASS," *Izvestija* 104, April 14, 1990, 4.
16 "Deklaracija S'ezda Narodnyh Deputatov RSFSR 'O gosudarstvennom suverenitete Rossijskoj Sovetskoj Federativnoj Socialisticheskoj Respubliki,'" No. 22–1, June 12, 1990, http://base.consultant.ru/cons/cgi/online.cgi?req=doc;base=LAW;n=39472;dst=0;rnd=189271.9247940215282142;SRDSMODE=QSP_GENERAL;SEARCHPLUS=%E4%E5%EA%EB%E0%F0%E0%F6%E8%FF%20%F1%F3%E2%E5%F0%E5%ED%E8%F2%E5%F2%20%F0%F1%F4%F1%F0;EXCL=PBUN%2CQSBO%2CKRBO%2, accessed June 1, 2017.
17 Marc Augé, *Les Formes de l'oubli* (Paris: Éditions Payot and Rivages, 2001), 76–78.
18 By "ethnicization" of the repression I mean their interpretation as ethnically motivated and, thus, performed by ethnic Russians against non-Russians of the

Soviet Union. It should be pointed out that the tendency toward "ethnicizing" and "culturalizing" various economic, social and political issues, which consists in interpreting these issues in terms of ethnicity and culture, is prominent in post-Soviet space. This tendency forms part, and is an inheritance, of the entrenched intellectual tradition of understanding the term "nation" as an ethnolinguistic or ethnocultural substance, "essentializing" the phenomena of nation and ethnicity, regarding nations and ethnic groups as immanently connected with certain cultures. This intellectual tradition—stemming from Soviet academic, political and public discourses—underlies the inclination to perceive "the dominance of the Soviet Union in East European countries, and of the Russians in the Soviet Union" in "not only political but also ethnic terms." Anantoly M. Khazanov, "Ethnic Nationalism in the Russian Federation," *Daedalus*, 126.3 (1997): 128. It is this perception that results in viewing ethnic Russians as the only ones responsible for the repression.

19 "Putin: shkol'nye uchebniki—ne ploshhadka dlja politicheskoj bor'by. Reportazh," *NEWSRU.COM*, November 27, 2003, www.newsru.com/russia/27nov2003/pres.html, accessed June 1, 2017.
20 "Prezident Vladimir Putin v hode vstrechi s uchenymi-istorikami v Rossijskoj gosudarstvennoj biblioteke," *Kremlin Official Website*, November 27, 2003, http://kremlin.ru/events/president/news/29821, accessed June 1, 2017.
21 "Minobrazovanija rekomendovalo shkolam bol'she ne ispol'zovat' uchebnik istorii s kritikoj Putina," *NEWSRU.COM*, November 28, 2003, www.newsru.com/russia/28nov2003/history.html, accessed November 10, 2017.
22 Igor' I. Doluckij, *Otechestvennaja istorija: XX vek: Uchebnik dlja 10–11 klassov obshheobrazovatel'nyh uchrezhdenij* (Moskva: Mnemozina, 2000).
23 "Ministr obrazovanija zapretil . . ."
24 Nikita V. Zagladin, Jury A. Petrov and Sergey I. Kozlenko, *Istorija Otechestva: XX vek: Uchebnik dlja 9 klassa obshheobrazovatel'nyh uchrezhdenij* (Moskva: Russkoe slovo, 2012).
25 Alexandr V. Filippov, *Novejshaja istorija Rossii: 1945–2006 gg: Kniga dlja uchitelja* (Moskva: Prosveshhenie, 2007).
26 Alexandr A. Danilov, Anatoly I. Utkin and Alexandr V. Filippov, eds., *Istorija Rossii: 1945–2008 gg. 11 klass* (Moskva: Prosveshhenie, 2009).
27 Alexandr A. Danilov, ed., *Koncepcija kursa Istorija Rossii: 1900–1945 gg.*, www.prosv.ru/umk/ist-obsh/info.aspx?ob_no=15378, accessed June 1, 2017.
28 Alexandr A. Danilov and Alexandr V. Filippov, eds., *Istorija Rossii: 1900–1945 gg. 11 klass* (Moskva: Prosveshhenie, 2012).
29 Alexandr S. Barsenkov and Alexandr I. Vdovin, *Istorija Rossii: 1917–2009* (Moskva: Aspekt Press, 2010).
30 See for instance: Nikita Sokolov and Anatoly Golubovskij, "Chemu uchat uchitelej istorii," *Iskusstvo kino*, April 2010, http://kinoart.ru/archive/2010/04/n4-article5, accessed June 1, 2017; Zoya Svetova, "Specificheskaja istorija," *New Times*, June 21, 2010, http://newtimes.ru/articles/detail/23445/, accessed June 1, 2017.
31 "Predlozhenija rekomendatel'nogo haraktera po rezul'tatam zasedanija Komissii Obshhestvennoj Palaty RF po mezhnacional'nym otnoshenijam i svobode sovesti, posvjashhennogo obsuzhdeniju soderzhanija uchebnogo posobija A.S. Barsenkova i A.I. Vdovina 'Istorija Rossii. 1917–2009,'" September 6, 2010, www.oprf.ru/documents/497/1548/, accessed June 1, 2017.
32 "Reshenie Uchenogo Soveta istoricheskogo fakul'teta MGU im: M.V. Lomonosova: Protocol No 5," September 15, 2010, www.hist.msu.ru/News/150910.pdf, accessed June 1, 2017.
33 "Vypiska iz Protokola zasedanija Uchenogo Soveta istoricheskogo fakul'teta MGU im. M.V. Lomonosova No 7," November 22, 2010, www.hist.msu.ru/Science/DISKUS/2010/221110.pdf, accessed June 1, 2017.

34 "Pamjat' o nacional'nyh tragedijah tak zhe svjashhenna, kak pamjat' o pobedah," *Kremlin Official Website*, October 30, 2009, http://kremlin.ru/events/president/news/5862, accessed June 1, 2017.
35 "V Den' pamjati zhertv politicheskih repressij Vladimir Putin posetil Butovskij memorial'nyj kompleks," *Kremlin Official Website*, October 30, 2007, http://kremlin.ru/events/president/news/43147, accessed June 1, 2017.
36 "Vystuplenie prem'er-ministra Rossii Vladimira Putina 7 aprelja 2010 goda na memorial'nom komplekse zhertv politicheskih repressij 'Katyn,'" *Prava cheloveka v Rossii*, April 8, 2010, www.hro.org/node/7908, accessed June 1, 2017. It is probably worth mentioning that none of the highest-ranking government officials has ever made any statements explicitly justifying the repression. This remains the appanage of some members of the left-wing part of the so-called *sistemnaja oppozicija* ["opposition within the system"—the most important members and leaders of the Communist Party of the Russian Federation), far-left radicals and pro-communist public figures.
37 Official Website, http://president-sovet.ru, accessed June 1, 2017.
38 "Predlozhenija ob uchrezhdenii obshhenacional'noj gosudarstvenno-obshhestvennoj programmy 'Ob uvekovechenii pamjati zhertv totalitarnogo rezhima i nacional'nom primirenii,'" *Rossijskaja Gazeta*, April 7, 2011, http://rg.ru/2011/04/07/totalitarizm-site.html, accessed June 1, 2017.
39 "Predlozhenija ob uchrezhdenii . . ."
40 "Predlozhenija ob uchrezhdenii . . ."
41 "Predlozhenija ob uchrezhdenii . . ."
42 "Ruling of the Government of the Russian Federation No. 1561—r," August 15, 2015, http://government.ru/media/files/AR59E5d7yB9LddoPH2RSlhQpSCQDERdP.pdf, accessed June 1, 2017.
43 "Ruling of the Government . . ."
44 "Zakonoproekt No 885220–6 'O protivodejstvii reabilitacii prestuplenij stalinskogo totalitarnogo rezhima (stalinizma),'" September 22, 2015, http://asozd.duma.gov.ru/main.nsf/(Spravka)?OpenAgent&RN=885220-6, accessed June 1, 2017.
45 "Otvet Pravovogo upravlenija na sootvetstvije trrebovanijam statji 104 Konstituzii RF," October 7, 2015, http://asozd.duma.gov.ru/main.nsf/(Spravka)?OpenAgent&RN=885220-6, accessed June 1, 2017.
46 "Zakonoproekt No 923007–6 'O protivodejstvii reabilitacii prestuplenij stalinskogo totalitarnogo rezhima (stalinizma),'" November 6, 2015, http://asozd2.duma.gov.ru/main.nsf/(Spravka)?OpenAgent&RN=923007-6, accessed June 1, 2017.
47 "Otvet Pravovogo upravlenija na sootvetstvije trrebovanijam statji 104 Konstituzii RF," November 17, 2015, http://asozd2.duma.gov.ru/main.nsf/(Spravka)?OpenAgent&RN=923007-6, accessed June 1, 2017.
48 "Ukaz Prezidenta Rossijskoj Federacii 'O dne soglasija i primirenija,'" No. 1537, November 7, 1996, www.kremlin.ru/acts/bank/10231, accessed June 1, 2017.
49 "Obrashhenie v svjazi s 60-letiem Velikoj Otechestvennoj Vojny," *Kremlin Official Website*, June 22, 2001, http://kremlin.ru/events/president/transcripts/21271, accessed June 1, 2017.
50 *President Dmitry Medvedev Video Blog*, May 7, 2009, http://blog.da-medvedev.ru/post/11/transcript, accessed June 1, 2017.
51 "Ukaz Prezidenta Rossijskoj Federacii 'O Komissii pri Prezidente Rossijskoj Federacii po protivodejstviju popytkam fal'sifikacii istorii v ushherb interesam Rossii,'" No. 549, May 15, 2009, www.rg.ru/2009/05/20/komissia-dok.html, accessed June 1, 2017.
52 In accordance with the president's decree No. 183, February 14, 2012, http://kremlin.ru/acts/bank/34810, accessed June 1, 2017.

53 Official Website, http://rushistory.org, accessed June 1, 2017.
54 Official Website, http://histrf.ru/ru/rvio, accessed June 1, 2017.
55 "Zasedanie soveta po mezhnacional'nym otnoshenijam," *Kremlin Official Website*, February 19, 2013, http://kremlin.ru/events/president/news/17536, accessed June 1, 2017.
56 "Perechen' poruchenij po itogam zasedanija Soveta po mezhnacional'nym otnoshenijam. Pr—541, p. 5: Srok ispolnenija—1 nojabrja 2013 goda," *Kremlin Official Website*, March 17, 2013, http://kremlin.ru/acts/assignments/orders/17889, accessed June 1, 2017.
57 The draft was first published on July 1, 2013. "Proekt istoriko-kul'turnogo standarta. Uchebno-metodicheskij kompleks po otechestvennoj istorii," http://минобрнауки.рф/документы/3483/файл/2325/13.07.01-Проект_Историко-культурного_стандарта.pdf, accessed June 1, 2017. For the discussion around this document see: http://xn—80abucjiibhv9a.xn—p1ai/документы/3483, accessed June 1, 2017.
58 "Koncepzija novogo uchebno-metodicheskogo kompleksa po Otechestvennoj istorii," August 13, 2015, http://rushistory.org/proekty/kontseptsiya-novogo-uchebno-metodicheskogo-kompleksa-po-otechestvennoj-istorii.html, accessed June 1, 2017.
59 Vladimir Gelaev and Nikolaj Gorodeckij, "Prezident poobshhalsja s molodymi istorikami i odobril napisanie istorii Kryma," *Gazeta.Ru*, November 5, 2014, www.gazeta.ru/science/2014/11/05_a_6289705.shtml, accessed June 1, 2017.
60 "Vstrecha s molodymi uchenymi i prepodavateljami istorii," *Kremlin Official Website*, November 5, 2014, http://kremlin.ru/events/president/news/46951, accessed June 1, 2017.
61 Official Website, www.memo.ru/, accessed June 1, 2017.
62 Official Website, www.sakharov-center.ru, accessed June 1, 2017.
63 Official Website, http://yeltsin.ru, accessed June 1, 2017.
64 Official Website, https://komitetgi.ru, accessed June 1, 2017.
65 Official Website, http://urokiistorii.ru/, accessed June 1, 2017.
66 Official Website, http://istpamyat.ru/, accessed June 1, 2017.
67 Official Website, www.gulagmuseum.org/showObject.do?object=310744, accessed June 1, 2017.
68 Official Website, http://topos.memo.ru/#13/55.7610/37.6283/main-deti-deti_M, accessed June 1, 2017.
69 Official Website, http://bessmertnybarak.ru, accessed June 1, 2017.
70 Official Website, www.poslednyadres.ru, accessed June 1, 2017.
71 It is worth mentioning that in 2014, the control of the museum was turned over from the civil activists who had created it to the state.
72 Official Website, www.gmig.ru, accessed June 1, 2017.
73 Butovo Firing Ground, located near Moscow, was the site of mass executions; between August 8, 1937 and October 19, 1938, over 20,000 people were shot and buried here. Official Website, http://butovo37.ru/index.html, accessed June 1, 2017.
74 Like Butovo, Kommunarka is located not far from Moscow. It is believed that over 6,000 people were shot and over 14,000 buried here. Official Website, http://hram-poligon-kommunarka.ru/index.php, accessed June 1, 2017.
75 Mednoje is situated near the city of Tver, between Moscow and Saint Petersburg. In Mednoje, over 5,000 Soviet citizens, victims of the Great Terror of 1937–1938, and over 6,000 Polish citizens shot in 1940, lie buried. Official Website, www.mk-mednoe.ru, accessed June 1, 2017.
76 "Ukaz Prezidenta Rossijskoj Federacii 'O vozvedenii memoriala zhertvam politicheskih repressij,'" No. 487, September 30, 2015, http://publication.pravo.gov.ru/Document/View/0001201509300028, accessed June 1, 2017. The Wall of

Sorrow was inaugurated in Moscow on October 30, 2017. Vladimir Putin, along with Patriarch Kirill, were present at the inauguration ceremony. See: "Otkrytie memoriala pamjati zhertv politicheskih repressij 'Stena skorbi'," *Kremlin Official Website*, October 30, 2017, http://kremlin.ru/events/president/news/55948, accessed February 7, 2018.
77 The ceremony is organized by Memorial and is held annually on October 29 in many cities of the Russian Federation. It consists in reading out the names, professions and dates of birth and execution of those arrested as "enemies of the people" and shot during the repression. Anyone can take part in the ceremony. Official Website, www.october29.ru, accessed June 1, 2017.
78 "Kak nam obustroit' Lubjanskuju ploshhad'? Press-vypusk No 2891," *WCIOM*, July 29, 2015, http://wciom.ru/index.php?id=236&uid=115333, accessed June 1, 2017.
79 "Stalin i ego rol' v istorii strany," *Levada—Center*, March 31, 2015, www.levada.ru/2015/03/31/stalin-i-ego-rol-v-istorii-strany/, accessed June 1, 2017.
80 "Stalin i ego rol' v istorii strany."
81 "Stalin i ego rol' v istorii strany."
82 The fact that Memorial received a 3 million ruble grant from the president of the Russian Federation ("Tretij konkurs 2015 goda v sootvetstvii s Rasporjazheniem Prezidenta RF No 79—rp ot 01.04.2015," *Official Website of the Competition for State Support for NGOs*, December 7, 2015, https://grants.oprf.ru/grants2015-3/winners/, accessed June 1, 2017) in December 2015, a little over a year after the Ministry of Justice of the Russian Federation filed a plea to the Supreme Court of the Russian Federation thus initiating the legal procedure for the liquidation of the organization ("Minjust: isk o likvidacii 'Memoriala' podan posle dvuh preduprezhdenij v adres organizacii," *TASS*, October 13, 2014, http://tass.ru/politika/1505252, accessed June 1, 2017) vividly illustrates these contradictions. Worth noting is the fact that the Ministry of Justice's plea to liquidate Memorial was rejected by the Supreme Court. "Verkhovnyj sud RF otklonil isk o likvidacii 'Memoriala,'" *Interfax*, January 28, 2015, www.interfax.ru/russia/420565, accessed June 1, 2017.
83 Paul Connerton, "Seven Types of Forgetting," *Memory Studies* 1 (2008): 59–71.
84 See Marian Golka, *Pamięć społeczna i jej implant* (Warszawa: Wydawnictwo Naukowe SCHOLAR, 2009).
85 This idea was expressed by Vladimir Putin who, addressing the Federal Assembly in 2005, stated that the collapse of the Soviet Union was "the greatest geopolitical catastrophe of the twentieth century." Vladimir V. Putin, "Poslanije Federal'nomy Sobraniju Rossijskoj Federazii," *Kremlin Official Website*, April 25, 2005, http://kremlin.ru/events/president/transcripts/22931, accessed June 1, 2017.

Part III
Communist Politics of Memory Before 1989

7 What Happened in 1980?
Memory Forging and the Official Story of Martial Law in the Polish United Workers' Party

Jakub Szumski

Introduction

During the 16 months between August 1980 and December 1981, the Polish People's Republic was the scene of dramatic and critical events. The wave of strikes, the establishment of the independent self-governing trade union "Solidarity" (*Solidarność*), its activity and its eventual destruction reshaped the personal and official memories of people and institutions. From the very start, what happened in Poland in 1980 and 1981 was called a revolution— for example, by one of the leaders of the political opposition Jacek Kuroń (1934–2004).[1] In 1983, Timothy Garton Ash published *The Polish Revolution*, an early and still historically relevant first-hand account.[2] Most Polish historians and scholars agree that the combination of radical transformations in social consciousness, the activism of the masses and changes in the political system justify the term "revolution."[3]

Against the background of a broader sociopolitical conflict, the revolutionary changes also had an unexpected and deep effect on the Polish United Workers' Party (PUWP), the ruling force until 1989. When its leadership's power was weakened, many PUWP members started to act independently of its wishes and orders. The party was losing members. A large group of them belonged at the same time to "Solidarity," an organization clearly in competition with the party. The PUWP started to reckon with its former leaders— for example, Edward Gierek (1913–2001), first secretary between 1970 and 1980—who were accused of corruption and abuse of office. Moreover, the most active party men and women formed nonstatutory factions within the organization. As a whole, these represented significant disobedience within a hierarchical and strictly regulated institution. The scale of all this was by no means huge, but socially influential groups were involved, such as intellectuals, scholars, journalists and even some apparatchiks and party secretaries from important factories throughout the country.

The introduction of martial law (or the state of war) in Poland on December 13, 1981, not only established an unconstitutional military rule, abolished "Solidarity," violated human rights and cost several dozen human lives but also put an end to any sort of independent activity within the

PUWP and prevented a potential reoccurrence of such attempts. After December 13, 1981, any discussion of the party's internal procedures and its role in the state, which occurred after the legal registration of "Solidarity" and which questioned the party's autocratic conduct, ceased to exist. The PUWP became a party ruled through a military discipline decreed by General Wojciech Jaruzelski (1923–2014), PUWP first secretary during martial law, along with his fellow high-ranking officers from the Polish People's Army.[4]

This sudden turn of events called for some explanation. How should PUWP members understand the recent events? How should they perceive their efforts to reform the party from within during the period of "Solidarity"? Why were some 300 of their fellow comrades being imprisoned and their grassroots initiatives banned? Why should they submit to the military administration? From the very beginning, the PUWP leadership under Jaruzelski started to present its clear-cut version of what happened, justifying martial law as necessary and inevitable. The official publications addressed what took place within the party between August 1980 and December 1981, and commented on the events' political and moral meaning. But conveying the official party story in this tumultuous period was part of a bigger offensive in historical narrative performed by the communist regime in its last decade.

"We are still involved in a sharp struggle. It is not taking place in the streets and generally not on the visible surface of life, but primarily in its depths, in the sphere of social consciousness,"[5] declared Wojciech Jaruzelski on December 15, 1983. The goal of the present study is to explore how after the introduction of martial law the PUWP leadership presented to its members what happened inside the party during the "Solidarity Revolution." The analysis is preceded first by an explanation of the theoretical issues involved in story narrative and memory forging after dramatic events, and second by an outline of the most important episodes inside the PUWP during the "Solidarity" period—episodes that were then addressed by the official narrative after December 13.

Forging the Party's Memory?

In a model situation, dramatic and critical historical events—such as Poland's "Solidarity Revolution" and the introduction of martial law mentioned at the beginning of this chapter—are usually succeeded by remembrance and a narrative record. The recalling of a critical event is a complicated process. Present circumstances influence what kinds of events are remembered as significant and how they are remembered. What is being celebrated and positively judged in the public sphere shapes the general understanding of the past.[6]

Governments, and not only undemocratic ones, seek by various means to influence the modes of retrospection. Some scholars call it collective or historical "memory forging." British historian Keith Wilson argues that memory forging consists of granting access to source material for selected historians, promoting a "patriotic" and favorable vision of the past and thus strongly influencing the collective historical imagination.[7] American historian Gary B. Nash adds that memory forging is "calculated, organized memory-making." History is then understood as a way to influence the present and the future, and form a politically useful vision of the recent past. It serves "ideological, cultural and politically informed agendas," Nash argues.[8]

A dramatic event, a "surprising breach," which substantially changes the previous circumstances and is as such recognized by its contemporaries,[9] also generates a universal demand for a story, for an explanation in the form of a narrative. Historian Paul A. Cohen argues,

> The stories [. . .] form a vital part of the community's cultural endowment—what historians often refer to as its "collective" or "popular memory"—as distinguished from its history in a more formal academic sense, and as such they often do more to shape the community's sense of what happened in the past than historians' careful reconstructive efforts.[10]

Cohen finds such "event-story" junctures in various cultures around the globe: the stories of the Battle of Kosovo and the Siege of Masada in, respectively, Serbian and Jewish memory, the story of Joan of Arc for the French, King Goujian of Yue[11] for the Chinese and Alexander Nevsky for the memory of the wartime Soviet Union. These common stories, located between history and myth, cannot be described as merely fabricated. Cohen argues that, although "modified, mythologized, distorted, and misrepresented," they serve pedagogical, explanatory and integration purposes, and therefore contribute to the creation of collective memory.[12]

Did this process, in which a dramatic event is succeeded by a memory-shaping story narrative, also occur in the environment of East European communist parties? When it comes to this region of the world, most scholarly projects focus on the general collective memory after 1989, trying to answer how and why the former system is being remembered.[13] In answering the question whether and how the party leadership influenced the recent memory of its members and what the effect of this effort has been, one might first examine the party leadership's official policy and then undertake detailed and methodologically challenging research into collective consciousness and memory, the horizons of cognition and the values of the party functionaries and members. Actually, there were some attempts in Polish academe to explore the latter phenomena.

Historian Tadeusz Kisielewski, in his 2011 book *Partii portret własny. Polityka i świadomość w PZPR—studium upadku* [The Party's Self-Portrait. Politics and Consciousness in the PZPR—The Study of the Fall], describes the PUWP's last year, as seen from the perspective of the consciousness of its active members and functionaries. What did they know then? How did they think? What was their horizon of understanding and expectation? In his book, Kisielewski attempted "not only an impression but also a detailed reconstruction of the historical picture, a kind of photograph of the party."[14] In order to fulfill this objective, Kisielewski used PUWP internal documents: reports, surveys and analyses sent to the Politburo from the regional structures and the minutes of its meetings.

Sociologist Krzysztof Dąbek, in his similarly titled book *PZPR— retrospektywny portret własny* [PZPR—A Retrospective Self-Portrait], proposes another approach to the topic. Between 1999 and 2001, Dąbek conducted interviews with 33 PUWP professional functionaries—for example, secretaries and heads of departments in the central and regional committees, who remain anonymous in the book—asking them about their motivations, the course of their careers and their everyday lives. Thanks to his method, the interviewees revealed many insights into informal groups, methods of gathering information within the party and hidden impulses that influenced the change of the emotional climate.[15] Historian Krzysztof Kosiński, who analyzes the party members' attitudes toward religion, prefers to speak about their collective "consciousness."[16] Kosiński employs a broad range of primary and secondary sources, with a particular focus on archival party documents and memoirs. In conclusion, the attempt to recreate the "inner life" of the party (of which memory is a part) requires the use of sophisticated theoretical approaches and combing various primary and secondary sources. A full array of archival documents and stenographic records of party proceedings need to be complemented with letters, memoirs, other personal documents, oral history interviews, press analyses, sociological surveys from the period and rich pre-existing secondary literature.

But when we look at the communist parties during the Cold War from the perspective of the official memory-makers, we also come across immediate event-story associations in Paul A. Cohen's sense. In the examples mentioned next, the memory was very recent; it almost blended with the present consciousness. "Normalizations" in Hungary and Czechoslovakia after the Soviet interventions were followed by attempts to control the memory and retell the story of the dramatic events.

After November 1956 in Hungary, when the Hungarian rebellion against Soviet domination was met with military intervention,[17] the János Kádár regime did not employ elaborate methods to convince and explain the meaning of the recent events to the party members. The Hungarian Working People's Party was dissolved, and a new Hungarian Socialist Workers' Party (HSWP) was established. At first, only about 10 percent of its one million members joined the new organization.[18] On December 5, 1956, the Provisional Central Committee of the newly formed HSWP issued a resolution in which the October events (the social protests, the street battles and the Soviet invasion) were blamed on the former Stalinist leadership, irresponsible decisions of the revolutionary leader Imre Nagy and the plotting of "counterrevolutionary" and "imperialist" forces. This interpretation was not broadly discussed and survived as an official story of the 1956 Hungarian Uprising until 1989.[19]

In Czechoslovakia after April 1969, when the neo-Stalinist Gustáv Husák group completely took over the leadership of the party, the Central Committee's Ideological Commission performed screenings and held disciplinary talks. Members of the party were asked whether they agreed or disagreed that the Soviet invasion was a necessary act of international and "fraternal" assistance. As a result, about 28 percent of its members were expelled. When it came to politics on the national level, the authorities generally preferred not to talk about the invasion. Historian Paulina Bren writes, "To re-create a nation as a blank slate without a history or memory [. . .] was a Herculean task that the normalization regime could not hope to accomplish." The dramatic events demanded a story and could not be left alone. The party initiated a retelling of the events, which would serve as the "official collective memory of 1968 as well as an ideological launching pad for normalization." The man in charge was Vasil Bil'ak, member of the Central Committee of the Communist Party of Czechoslovakia, who, in his report finally issued in 1971, blamed the dramatic events on the nation's weak ties to communist ideology and the Soviet leadership, especially on the part of intellectuals. Last but not least, the official report pointed to the influence of Western agents and to direct espionage.[20]

Let us look at another critical juncture in history. From the perspective of Beijing, the end of the Cold War and the Tiananmen Square protests posed challenges to the previous political and ideological state of affairs. In 1990, to properly enter the new era, general secretary of the Communist Party of China Jiang Zemin launched a "national ideological re-education," as historian Zheng Wang writes.[21] The main identity of the party members was to be changed from a Maoist-international to a Chinese-patriotic orientation. Jiang Zemin "used historical memory to construct the rules and norms of the ruling party. In fact, history and memory have provided a complete set of theories to redefine the identity of the Chinese Communist Party," writes Wang.[22] Clear changes in the party program and in its core values were made, underlining China's national interest, providing a new narrative for China's history and setting offensive goals for its foreign policy. In conclusion, it is not very unusual for the political authority of a centralized communist party to forge memory for political ends and create stories around dramatic events. However, this should not be understood as unique to state socialism, as it is used by governments throughout the world, almost regardless of the kind of political system.

Operations designed to create an official story of dramatic events, which would later serve the interest of the ruling elite, were definitely carried out in the Polish People's Republic during the so-called Polish months, especially of June and October 1956, March 1968, December 1970 and, finally,

August 1980 and December 1981.²³ The scale and intensity of the efforts varied, but there was a recurrent pattern. When the social protests led to a change at the highest political levels, the new ruling group was more willing to discuss the nature of the recent upheavals and give their official and elaborate narrative interpretation.²⁴ After 1956 and 1970, when the turmoil led directly to the fall of the incumbent leadership, the PUWP's Central Committee commissions were set in motion to work on reports and assessments of the tragic events. The content of the reports was not made available to the general public but later constituted a base for the narrative addressed to the party members.²⁵ The student protests, the antisemitic campaign and the purges within the administration during the events of March 1968, which were not a direct cause of the leadership change, were by contrast addressed very briefly. The first historical account of the March 1968 events, written from the PUWP perspective, surfaced in 1981, 13 years after they took place.²⁶

After December 1981, the PUWP launched a propaganda campaign to justify martial law and the costs of all those efforts rebounded upon the party's budget.²⁷ The PUWP influenced its members through pamphlets, booklets, reading and training materials, official speeches, addresses and proclamations—in most cases those of General Wojciech Jaruzelski himself, whose every word was widely distributed in the media. Therefore, those materials constitute the main body of evidence for recreating the content of the intended official story.

Moreover, the period after martial law witnessed an accumulation of significant historical events and celebrations of important anniversaries. The bigger picture is that from 1981 to 1986 the communist government attempted to reestablish its rule after the 16-month turbulence of the "Solidarity Revolution." National history, understood not only as the records of the PUWP's activity, played an important role in the process. Historian Tomasz Leszkowicz even argues that between 1981 and 1986, the PUWP conducted its "last offensive on the historical front."²⁸

The process of creating a narrative and forging memory was especially accelerated and reinforced by two important historical occasions. The year 1982 marked the hundredth anniversary of the first Polish socialist political party—the International Social Revolutionary Party "Proletariat," formed by Ludwik Waryński (1856–1889), Polish revolutionary and Marxist theoretician.²⁹ Waryński was an important figure in the regime's politics of memory, and in the 1960s and 1970s, he was honored in many ways. Monuments were erected and streets and factories were named after him. In 1975, Waryński appeared on a 100-zloty banknote.³⁰ The invocation of a national freedom fighter from the period of the Partitions of Poland was meant to demonstrate continuity and traditional legitimacy for Jaruzelski's regime. Two years later, in 1984, People's Poland celebrated its fortieth birthday. Its founding date was established as July 22, 1944, when the Polish Committee of National Liberation was proclaimed as a Polish provisional government under the auspices of Joseph Stalin.³¹ Official teaching materials stated that in the perspective of these two important anniversaries, the PUWP faced a "historical test," which required discipline and consolidation.³²

There were also other occurrences that caused the party to look back to its history and legacy. September 1, 1982, witnessed the death of Władysław Gomułka (1905–1982), who was a leading figure of Polish communism from the interwar period to 1948 and then the PUWP's first secretary between 1956 and 1970. Identified with the period of de-Stalinization in Poland, Gomułka was also responsible for the massacre in December 1970. In the end of December 1970, more than 50 people were killed when the police and military units opened fire against protesting workers in the cities of Northeastern Poland.³³ During the 1970s, Gomułka did not face a tough settling of accounts or any charges for his decision to use force against the striking workers, but his name was absent from public discourse. Beginning with Gomułka's state funeral, Wojciech Jaruzelski rehabilitated the former leader. Press articles and books presented the former PUWP's first secretary as an advocate of national sovereignty. In 1989, a banknote with an image of Gomułka was projected, but it was not to be realized.³⁴

In 1983, the report of the Kubiak Commission was issued. The goal of the body, led by historian, sociologist and party reformer Hieronim Kubiak (1934–), was to look into the sources of Poland's sociopolitical postwar crises and recommend political reforms. The scholars and politicians working in the commission prepared an honest document, stressing that the main causes of recurring crises were not individual mistakes triggered by the successive administrations, but rather the structural failings of the political and economic system of state socialism.³⁵ This intense activity in the field of history left behind it a wave of new publications: monographs on post-1945 history, school and academic textbooks and increased discussion in which the PUWP was omnipresent as a topic. These monographs on Polish history issued after the introduction of martial law also serve as sources for the present study.³⁶

The PUWP During the "Solidarity Revolution": The Party's Four Problems

During the hot summer of 1980, after yet another food price increase, strikes broke out in almost a thousand factories throughout Poland. From August 14, the center of the strikes moved to Gdańsk Lenin Shipyard, which also protested in the name of other state enterprises. Dramatic events, which drew the attention of global public opinion, finally led to a compromise between the state and the rebellious society. On August 31, 1980, Deputy Prime Minister Mieczysław Jagielski (1924–1997) and, in the name of the Interfactory Strike Committee, Lech Wałęsa (1943–) signed the Gdańsk Accords.³⁷ This meant that in accordance with the main demand of the strikers, the authorities accepted and bound themselves to register the independent self-governing trade union "Solidarity" legally, which supplemented the old ineffective and state-controlled trade unions. It was run without interference by the state, with its own statute and executive and regional bodies and units—totally separate from the communist structures of power. "Solidarity," which formally was a trade union, combined national, freedom-oriented and egalitarian economic political ideas. It thus represented a new type of social movement whose independent potential and capacity for mass mobilization posed a threat to the Soviet-backed communist monopoly in Poland. The conflict between the state and "Solidarity" was the most important constant in the events of the early 1980s.

Changes and challenges for the PUWP followed suit. The PUWP faced four main problems. First, the frequent leadership changes; second, the fluctuation in its membership; third, the reckoning with its former leader Edward Gierek; and fourth, the existence and functioning of ideological factions within the party. On September 6, 1980, Edward Gierek, first secretary since December 1970, was forced to resign. The new leader was Stanisław Kania (1927–), a professional PUWP functionary from his early youth. He began his career, like many in his generation, in the Union of Polish Youth, a communist youth organization established in 1948 and dissolved in 1957, and later held many posts in the PUWP's administration, in particular in the Central Committee's Administration Department, among other things responsible for the supervision of the police, the secret services and the judicial system. Under Edward Gierek, in 1975, he was promoted to become a member of the Politburo.[38] Kania lacked charisma and decisiveness, but had a reasonable and sober approach to the challenges presented by the establishment of "Solidarity." With a group of compromise-oriented advisors, he sought an accord with the new trade union. His idea of "socialist renewal" was principally based on enabling discussion among party members. The Kania administration also had a very critical approach to the party's political conduct in the 1970s. Above all, he was determined at all costs to exclude the use of force in resolving the crisis in Poland.[39]

Disappointment among the Central Committee's members with Kania's seemingly "soft" policies led to another personnel change at the highest level. On October 18, 1981, the PUWP's Central Committee elected General Wojciech Jaruzelski as its first secretary. Jaruzelski had served as minister of defense since 1968 and had become Poland's prime minister in February 1981. He brought more discipline and stabilization to the PUWP's otherwise unstructured activity. Army officers started to engage openly in the party's day-to-day activity. General Tadeusz Dziekan (1925–1984) became head of the key Central Committee Personnel Department. Other generals—Minister of Interior Czesław Kiszczak (1925–2015), Chief of Military Propaganda Józef Baryła (1924–) and Chief of the Office of the Council of Ministers Michał Janiszewski (1926–2016)—began to participate regularly in the Politburo's proceedings.[40]

Simultaneously, both Kania and Jaruzelski were pressured by the Soviet party and military leadership to halt "Solidarity's" activity definitively by all possible means. Both leaders were called to Moscow for consultations, during which Leonid Brezhnev and the Soviet marshals demanded radical action against the independent trade union. The Soviet ambassador in Warsaw, Boris Aristov, frequently visited the PUWP Central Committee's headquarters with similar demands. In order to resolve the crisis situation, the plans to introduce the martial law, in preparation since summer 1980, were being finalized.[41]

The second kind of evidence of a structural crisis was the behavior of the PUWP members. American economist Albert O. Hirschman classifies the reactions to crises in organizations in two categories: "exit" and "voice." The "exit" strategy occurs when one withdraws support and leaves the institution. In reaction to crisis, one may also "voice" one's criticism, exhibiting and verbalizing discontent, and trying at the same time to repair the structure from within.[42] Both of these processes took place in the PUWP in 1980 and 1981: The party membership was shrinking, and at the same time, those who remained were criticizing the party and trying to reform it. The extraordinary situation brought yet another attitude, which could be called "dual membership"—that is, simultaneous affiliation to both the PUWP and the "Solidarity" trade union, which meant combining internal criticism with a declaration of support for an alternative institution.

The "exit" strategy was the most visible in the quantitative data. From June 1980—the all-time peak in PUWP membership—to December 1981, the PUWP lost 458,000 of its comrades (Table 7.1).

In November 1980, 699,792 party members were simultaneously members of the "Solidarity" trade union. There was no apparent line or any instructions as to how they should behave in relation to the union. Organizing strikes and applying pressure on local authorities, they struggled between loyalty to the party and to colleagues at the workplace.[44]

The problem of "dual membership" was noticeable at the PUWP's Ninth Extraordinary Congress in July 1981. The delegates to the congress were elected during regional conferences, which were held in every voivodship. Under pressure from discontented members, the election procedure was significantly reformed. In addition to the candidates selected by the election commission, which consisted mostly of representatives of the then leadership, the rank-and-file members were allowed to nominate alternative

Table 7.1 PUWP Membership 1980–1981 (in thousands)[43]

June 1980	September 1980	March 1981	September 1981	November 1981	December 1981
3,150	3,088	2,942	2,770	2,734	2,692

contenders. Every candidate for the congress was obliged to be a member of the conference in which he sought nomination—i.e., to have some background in the region—and exceptions to this rule were allowed only through a special vote. The candidates were also expected to openly state their views and program proposals, which were then the subject of discussion. The new rules enabled many people to participate in the party's most important gathering for the first time.[45] Twenty-one percent of the delegates to the congress simultaneously belonged to "Solidarity." Eighty-seven percent of the Central Committee appointed at the July congress consisted of new people.[46]

Third, after the fall of Edward Gierek, the party entered a bitter internal conflict over the attitude toward political corruption and abuse of offices in its ranks. As in other socialist countries, after years of extensive investments and growth in the 1970s, the Polish economy collapsed from the inability to export its products to the West and repay its foreign credits.[47] In the autumn of 1980, during the gatherings of the PUWP's factory and regional committees, the rank-and-file members began to ask who was responsible for driving the economy into crisis and running up the national debt in foreign currencies. To make things worse, allegations—often in the form of gossip and press exposés—started to surface that in the 1970s corruption and abuse of official power were overwhelmingly common and systematic. Poland's nomenclature was attacked for hording scarce goods, illegally constructing villas and summer dachas, and fraudulently obtaining car coupons. The most important people in the Gierek regime, among them Gierek himself and the deputy prime ministers and members of the Politburo Tadeusz Wrzaszczyk (1932–2002) and Jan Szydlak (1925–1997), as well as radio and television chief Maciej Szczepański (1928–2015), were under investigation by the Supreme Chamber of Control and the General Prosecutor's Office for abuse of power for personal gain.[48]

The official press, especially the regional PUWP daily newspapers, launched an anti-corruption campaign against the former Gierek administration. Press articles gave examples of corruption and abuse of office by local and central party functionaries—mostly involving illegal housing construction—and the high standard of living they enjoyed. On April 29, 1981, the Silesian *Trybuna Robotnicza* [Workers' Voice], an official newspaper of the Katowice Provincial PUWP Committee, published reports accusing Edward Gierek of receiving unpaid services from state enterprises, which were involved in building his private residence. The wave of articles describing the wrongdoings of the 1970s was enabled by the new Stanisław Kania leadership, which wanted to lay the blame for the economic problems—which in daily life took the form, among other things, of market shortages—exclusively on the former party and state administration, and present itself as righteous and open to discussion of past failures. On April 29, 1981, the Central Committee established the Grabski Commission to investigate charges against the former leaders, named after its chair and Politburo member in 1980 and 1981, Tadeusz Grabski (1929–1998).[49]

In an atmosphere of accusations, many attacks were ungrounded and based purely on rumor, although there were also genuine cases of fraud. The stories of the luxury enjoyed by the former elite were exaggerated. Nonetheless, an image of overwhelming corruption entered the minds of rank-and-file PUWP members. This was still noticeable during the proceeding of the Ninth PUWP Congress in July 1981. One of the delegates' proposals was to elect only candidates who had not held administrative posts during the 1970s. The delegates advocated a tough approach to corruption and the introduction of asset declarations for party officials and special taxes for luxury items. The congress almost unanimously expelled seven key political figures of the Gierek administration from the PUWP: First Secretary Edward Gierek, Prime Minister Edward Babiuch (1927–) and members of the Politburo: Jerzy Łukaszewicz (1931–1983), Tadeusz Pyka (1930–2009), Jan Szydlak, Zdzisław Żandarowski (1929–1994) and Zdzisław Grudzień (1924–1982). Through December 1981, 181 people holding executive posts (in regional and central party and state executive administration, PUWP regional first secretaries, ministers and deputy ministers, directors of administrative departments and economic centers and unions, PUWP regional secretaries and voivodes) were also expelled from the party. The anti-corruption campaign and the reckoning with Edward Gierek decreased trust in the party elites, which was noted by many contemporary commentators.[50]

Finally, in times of uncertainty, determined and proactive members emerged who sought opportunities to modify the system according to their points of view. Their solutions to Poland's problems were of two contrasting kinds: either tough measures to suppress any form of social autonomy and to bring Poland into closer cooperation with the Soviet Union, or attempts at radical democratic reforms in the PUWP structures and the search for a compromise between "Solidarity" and the state.[51] In most cases, the factions did not develop any programs for consistent political change and merely responded to the ever-changing situation.

The first conservative or dogmatist faction—in Polish also known as *beton* [concrete]—worked under the political patronage of selected members of the Politburo, such as Tadeusz Grabski along with Stefan Olszowski (1931–), Albin Siwak (1933–) and Andrzej Żabiński (1938–1988). The most industrious of these activists were Bohdan Poręba (1934–2014), Ryszard Gontarz (1930–2017), Henryk Tycner (1924–1990) and Wsiewołod Wołczew (1929–1993). The conservative sympathizers analyzed the crisis of the state based on simplified Marxist-Leninist categories. They perceived "Solidarity" and other spontaneous movements as counterrevolutionary. Among their main values were hard work, modesty and, above all, loyalty to the Soviet Union. Historian Jan de Weydenthal describes them as "loose associations of conservative party members who professed to being appalled by what they regarded as the growing disarray in the party and the political system, [. . .] and argued for the reimposition of discipline and rigor."[52]

The conservative activists employed various methods in their public activity. In many cities in the spring of 1981 discussion clubs and open forums surfaced in which it was possible to openly criticize Stanisław Kania, Wojciech Jaruzelski and the party establishment as a whole. The proponents of the political clubs saw them as a tool to put pressure on the incumbent leaders. The most notable were *Katowickie Forum Partyjne* [Katowice Party Forum], with local mutations in other big cities, *Zjednoczenie Patriotyczne "Grunwald"* ["Grunwald" Patriotic Union] and the *Stowarzyszenie Klubów Wiedzy Społeczno-Politycznej "Rzeczywistość"* [Union of Social-Political Clubs "Reality"]. The dogmatists published the weekly magazines *Rzeczywistość* [Reality] and *Płomienie* [Flames] and cultivated their contacts among Security Service and Armed Forces officers.[53]

The Soviet, East German and Czechoslovak regimes financially supported their activity. The dogmatists often visited the embassies and other diplomatic outposts of neighboring countries, where they discussed the situation of the PUWP. They also clandestinely dialogued with foreign intelligence officers, to whom they divulged information about talks that had taken place in the PUWP behind closed doors. In Moscow, East Berlin and Prague, some of the conservative faction leaders—especially Grabski and Olszowski—were seen as possible candidates for Stanisław Kania's and Wojciech Jaruzelski's replacements.[54]

The second wing of the party was far weaker but intellectually more diverse. The reform movement (also known as the liberals) was politically supported by party secretaries, such as Hieronim Kubiak, Mieczysław Rakowski (1926–2008) and Andrzej Werblan (1924–). While conservatives were tough and hardline, liberals generally preferred dialogue and discussion. Many of the liberal faction enthusiasts were members of both the PUWP and "Solidarity." One of the reformers, chief of the Polish Journalist Union Stefan Bratkowski, summed up their positions in five points: religious tolerance, inclusion of non-communist leftism in the PUWP, acceptance of independent trade unions and other institutions of civil society, private property in farming and the general rule of law. One of the reform groups was the *Stowarzyszenie "Kuźnica"* ["Forge" Society] from Krakow, established in 1975, whose most important figures were Andrzej Kurz (1931–) and Tadeusz Hołuj (1916–1985). The association, which in the late 1970s focused on organizing cultural events, after August 1980 become more of a political discussion club. Distinctly important, among other aspects, were the "horizontal structures," officially called Consultative Commissions of Primary Party Organizations, which emerged in October 1980. They appeared, among other places, in Toruń (where the key personalities were Roman Bäcker (1955–), Zbigniew Iwanów (1948–1987) and Lech Witkowski (1951–)), Poznań (Józef Cegła (1946–1998), Jerzy Mikosz (1942–)) and Warsaw (Wojciech Lamentowicz (1946–)).

The horizontal structures advocated the idea of direct cooperation between party cells, which would eventually lead to forging common programs and policies. From the point of view of Marxist-Leninist party theory, such activity was forbidden and frowned upon. According to the official thesis of democratic centralism, the party was meant to be managed vertically—from the Central Committee all the way down to the smallest unit. The most important place for these new experiments was Toruń in Northwestern Poland with an authentic popular leader of social protest within the party, Zbigniew Iwanów. In September 1980, Iwanów, economist and state-run factory manager in Toruń's Towimor marine engineering plant and member of the party since 1970, became the first secretary of the PUWP Factory Committee in his enterprise. The Committee at Towimor had grown into a local center of intra-party protest and held discussions and political rallies.[55]

The high point of liberal activity was the national conference of horizontal structures from all over the country, held in Toruń on April 15, 1981. The goal of the assembly was to exchange information and opinions and forge common policies for the Ninth Extraordinary PUWP Congress. The conference gathered 750 people from 12 horizontal structures from around the country, party representatives from approximately 100 cities and "Solidarity" delegates. The activists held a press conference and issued declarations and documents, but the actions did not have any significant consequence for countrywide politics.[56] The liberals had some influence in various regional and central newspapers, especially in the Warsaw daily *Życie Warszawy* [Life of Warsaw] and in the prestigious *Polityka* [Politics] weekly magazine. Articles on reformist efforts were often reported by foreign journalists—for example, by the Warsaw correspondent for *The New York Times* John Darnton.[57]

In conclusion, the party lived through times of chaos and uncertainty, which can be summarized in four aspects: frequent leadership changes, membership loss, competition from the "Solidarity" trade union and painful reckonings with the former leaders. Finally, the factional politics brought even more internal conflicts, dividing party members into ideological camps.[58]

The Introduction of Martial Law

Seeking to resolve the crisis in Poland swiftly with the use of force, General Jaruzelski introduced martial law at about midnight on December 13, 1981. Supreme power was assumed by the Military Council of National Salvation, a body consisting of 23 generals and colonels, with a name carrying national and patriotic connotations. The country was in fact under the control of Jaruzelski himself, who from then on ruled People's Poland with a group of officers. For most of the population, martial law meant seeing soldiers with tanks and heavy artillery on the streets, blocked telephone communication and television programming or a 10:00 p.m. curfew. For politically active people, especially "Solidarity" and political opposition activists, there were internments (incarcerations without a court order), repression and lost opportunities. The spirit and technicalities of the martial law, which prohibited almost every form of social or political activity, was also noticeable in the PUWP's ranks.

After all, its essence was a military coup d'état executed without any consultation or consent from the PUWP's statutory bodies, including the Politburo, whose members were not informed about the date and time of the introduction of the martial law. The chief of General Staff of the Soviet Armed Forces marshal Viktor Kulikov was informed in detail only on December 11.[59] Purges in public administration, the judicial system and among journalists were complemented with expulsions within the party.[60] PUWP members perceived as "questionable" were forced to declare loyalty to the martial law administration. Three hundred sixty-five primary PUWP organizations were dissolved and more than 2,000 PUWP functionaries cast out. Three hundred eighteen party members throughout the country were incarcerated without a court sentence and confined to internment camps. Most of them engaged in the reformist factions or were simultaneously "Solidarity" members.[61] February 1982 brought an official ban on any intra-party group activity. On December 16, 1982, the Politburo suspended the dogmatic *"Rzeczywitość"* and liberal *"Kuźnica"* political clubs. The hard-liners and conservatives suffered fewer noticeable losses, but the most outspoken conservative critics of the current administration were put under surveillance by Jaruzelski's secret police.[62] The wave of state and intra-party repression led to further membership loss. From 1982, members continually left (Table 7.2).

The party was ceding its former special status to the military and the central government administration. Special rules on the party's internal conduct introduced during martial law resulted in more centralization. Whatever remained of the autonomy granted to the PUWP's regional committees during the "Solidarity" period was rescinded.[64] In those regions where the influence of "Solidarity" was most significant (Gdańsk, Szczecin, Krakow, Legnica, Wrocław), reaction to the martial law was reported as negative. The reports of the Central Committee's Organization Department gave information on the voices of protest in those parts of the country, where, moreover, the number of PUWP membership resignations was also higher than average. In regions without such apparent "Solidarity" influence, among small rural voivodships of East-Central

Table 7.2 PUWP Membership 1982–1985 (in thousands)[63]

October 1982	December 1982	December 1983	August 1984	December 1984	June 1985	December 1985
2,400	2,372	2,186	2,159	2,130	2,112	2,115

Poland (Siedlce, Ciechanów, Sieradz, Płock), the decision to abolish the free trade union was in many instances even welcomed as something that would put an end to the unstable situation.[65]

PUWP reports of that time indicate that the most common reactions among party members were idleness and uncertainty. People were hoping to wait the situation out, not knowing how to behave during this time of crisis. In the PUWP analyses, attitudes described as "lack of mobilization and offensiveness" were named as key problems among party cadres and members, meaning that what to think and how to behave was not self-evident.[66] In the Provincial PUWP Committee in Radom, central Poland, the functionaries noted "uncertainty and anxiety about spontaneously speaking [one's] mind." Among such party members who before December 13 belonged to "Solidarity," one could also observe "a feeling of shame, embarrassment and even fear."[67] "Why was it necessary to take such a dramatic decision? Against what and whom are the severe rules of state of war aimed? Finally, what can and what should be expected from this extraordinary situation?" asked Jerzy Bąbol and Mieczysław Krajewski, authors of a 1981 PUWP propaganda brochure, very accurately capturing the dilemma of the rank-and-file members.[68]

The Official Story

The answers to all these questions started to appear almost immediately. From 6:00 a.m. on December 13, the proclamation of martial law was regularly broadcast on radio and television. Its content already suggested how General Jaruzelski would come to justify the use of force and what kind of narrative he would construct around it. Jaruzelski largely spoke of two attitudes current in the period of "Solidarity": one that could be called "reasonable" (*rozsądni*) and the other "extremist" (*ekstremiści*). Those with a "reasonable" attitude generally trusted the government and refrained from political and strike activity in order to avoid unpredictable consequences. The "extremists," also present among PUWP members, were driven by emotions and engaged in unconsidered and misguided endeavors. It was unjustified and unnecessary that they sought, on their own, to find solutions for problems present in Poland. "Distressing lines of division run through every workplace and through many Polish homes; the atmosphere of interminable conflict, controversy and hatred is sowing mental devastation and mutilating the traditions of tolerance" continued Jaruzelski in his December 13 proclamation. Discords led to anarchy—i.e., "the negation of democracy." If the party, despite "all the errors and bitter setbacks, still wanted to play a significant role in political life," there was only one way it could. Jaruzelski described the kind of organization desired from now on, consisting of "high-minded, modest, courageous people; people who in every community will be recognized as champions of social justice, for the good of the country."[69]

The official story of the martial law was propagated immediately after December 13, 1981. Its motives needed to be developed and specified. At the first plenary session of the PUWP's Central Committee in February 1982, Jaruzelski proclaimed, "We expect, we even demand, from our historians, sociologists, and journalists an in-depth, well documented analysis of the phenomena and events of the previous period." Moreover, directly after the imposition of martial law, the Central Committee's Organizational Department stated,

> In our society, and to a large degree also among party members, there is a lack of acceptance of the causes that forced the authorities to declare martial law. The view of our official propaganda—that our fundamental national and state interest required the martial law—is not accepted.[70]

The first secretary was thus very aware of how dire a need there was for a convincing narrative. Various didactic materials announced an upcoming "ideological offensive" in which knowledge about the party, its program, history (including its recent history) and legacy will be deepened and developed.[71]

Even in 1984, freelance journalist Ludwik Krasucki wrote that the dramatic events of 1980 and 1981 "are not yet a closed chapter in our history. Quite the opposite, in the party, in the working class and the society as a whole, the emotional memories of these events are still alive." The sources of emotional memories were described by Krasucki as follows: "The dilemmas of a gradual turn in our policy, of personal feuds, the drama of reassessments and reckoning, the pressure of emotions" and, finally, the "splinter activity through extra-statutory structures."[72]

In early 1982, General Jaruzelski ascribed the outflow of party members and their involvement in "Solidarity" to emotional, irrational behavior. He believed that some of the irrational and dangerous people needed to be isolated from their communities, which explained why more than 300 party members were interned on December 13, 1981. Moreover, Jaruzelski declared that not only irredeemable enemies of the state were incarcerated:

> There are also among them persons whose reason has gone astray, who have been engrossed in such activity, not fully conscious of what they were doing. They must think over their errors and recover a sense of responsibility and political reason.[73]

According to PUWP propaganda instructors Edward Modzelewski and Wojciech Wiśniewski, cooperation with "Solidarity" was not possible. Party members had been eliminated from "Solidarity," and the union unjustifiably attacked the PUWP and its leading role in the state, argued the authors.[74] Władysław Góra, historian and author of a 1986 monograph on the history of People's Poland's, concluded that one of the reasons why martial law was inevitable was the destructive activity of some of the members of the party who did not foresee the dramatic consequences of their actions. Engaging in a far-reaching dialogue with "Solidarity," questioning the established rules of the party, they weakened its ability to react to crisis and thus contributed to chaos and danger.[75] Those who in the crisis period did not follow the party's directions "compromised their biographies and contributed to serious social damage." This is how Jaruzelski in February 1982 summed up the activity of party members who were involved in the "Solidarity" movement.[76]

The authors of the party-licensed publications referred to here had difficulty explaining and assessing if and how the anti-corruption campaign and reckoning with Gierek-era politicians led to martial law. For then, on the one hand, the spontaneous attempts to get rid of corrupt leaders was an aspect of the anarchic, uncontrollable burst of emotions on the part of the members of the PUWP, so negatively assessed by Jaruzelski after December 13, 1981. The official 1982 party-training textbook described the "ideological disorientation among party members [whose] entire energy [was] focused on the past."[77] Other authors claimed that the prominence of emotional, anti-corruption arguments during the times of "Solidarity" were clear signs of low political culture and thus no cause for pride and positive memories.[78] The attacks on the Gierek administration for abuse of power raised the social temperature and gave ammunition to outspoken enemies of the PUWP, went the argument. Jerzy Bielecki, PUWP propagandist, concluded, "Just demands for a reckoning with those responsible for leading the country into crisis were dishonestly spun off into a general attack on the party and the state."[79]

At the same time, members of the PUWP who during the "Solidarity Revolution" gave information in cases of corruption and profiting from public office could feel some satisfaction. The official reckonings with the former leaders continued until 1984. On December 13, 1981, 36 former party and state officials, including Edward Gierek, prime ministers Piotr Jaroszewicz (1909–1992) and Edward Babiuch and members of the Politbuto Szydlak, Łukaszewicz, Pyka, Żandarowski, Grudzień and a dozen or so regional functionaries who, according to the Jaruzelski regime, "bear personal responsibility for leading the country into the severe crisis of the 1970s, or who abused their official positions for personal advantage," were placed in an internment camp.[80] In the first weeks of the martial law, the anti-corruption campaign was relaunched, and the authorities appealed to the egalitarian sensibilities of an impoverished society. In 1982, the Parliament altered the Constitution and created the State Tribunal, a special court, for the purpose of bringing the former leaders to justice.[81]

General Jaruzelski claimed that the PUWP "has undertaken a thorough, self-critical evaluation of the past. However, one cannot wear sackcloth and ashes forever."[82] According to Tadeusz Walichnowski, a general of the

Citizens Militia, professor of history and political commentator, corruption and fraud were almost one of the main reasons for the 1980 strikes and the fall of Edward Gierek. Walichnowski wrote as follows:

> The party could not effectively withstand the overwhelming corruption and excessive bureaucracy of some parts of the administrative, economic, and state apparatus. It caused the working people to protest due to their falling standards of living.[83]

The reckonings were generally described in balanced terms and seen as a positive action to purify the party from within.[84]

The settlements and the battle against corruption were presented as opportunities to continue the grassroots initiatives of "socialist renewal" without coming into conflict with the current PUWP leadership.[85] Jaruzelski played with the egalitarian and anti-establishment emotions of the population and, in contrast to Edward Gierek, presented himself as a champion of austerity and personal integrity. The lack of an apparent negative assessment of the process of reckonings meant that it was probably seen as the only aspect of the troublesome 1980–1981 heritage worth cherishing and continuing.

The most important and omnipresent issue in post-martial law publications was that of the extra-statutory factions within the party. Many authors cited in the present chapter claimed that the conflicts and disorientation they created brought the PUWP to the brink of a split. The way they were described and judged in PUWP publications left little doubt that also in this respect there could be no return to "pre-December times." When speaking about the situation in the party, Jaruzelski often invoked the metaphor of "fratricidal combat" or even "the abyss of fratricidal warfare."[86] On February 24, 1982, he said,

> It is time to put an end to dividing the party into wings. We must maintain one common goal, and although we could and should discuss how to achieve this, we must not, and we shall not, relax the rules of iron discipline in implementing our decisions.[87]

Calling for unity, Jaruzelski presented himself almost as a father and authority figure who had the right, and was obliged, to restore order.

PUWP training materials for new members announced that the party was waging a "two-front war: with revisionism and opportunism and with dogmatism and sectarianism."[88] The activists were constantly reminded of the "Leninist norms of party life," which allowed some discussion but unconditionally banned any unsupervised actions. Marxist historian and party ideologue Adolf Dobieszewski summarized it as "freedom of discussion and unity of action" and warned that every form of factional politics, even exercised in good will, leads to demagogy.[89]

In February 1982, Jaruzelski said, "The party is not a sect, nor a discussion club."⁹⁰ Attacks were thus directed against both minority groups: dogmatists and liberals. However, the liberally oriented groups were clearly put under much greater pressure. PUWP historian Władysław Góra accused the liberal faction, though without pointing to any specific persons or groups, of "surrendering to the class opponents." According to Góra, their reform demands would lead to the end of democratic centralism and would limit the party's role to the sphere of ideological and moral activity—this he perceived as a "particular danger." The liberals engaged in "cooperation with extreme, in fact anti-socialist, forces in 'Solidarity,'" which forever condemned them to playing the role of villain in the PUWP's official story.⁹¹ Scholars such as Tadeusz Walichnowski, coming from the Ministry of Internal Affairs, who professionally dealt with unveiling enemy plots and schemes, even suggested that the intra-party movements were directly instigated by undercover agents of the political opposition and were deceptive.⁹²

The complex role of the hard-liners was not that present in historical accounts of the 1980–1981 events. If crushing "Solidarity" was presented as reasonable and justified, it was not so easy to criticize the conservative and dogmatist activists who proposed it from the very beginning, and so their programs could not be directly condemned. Władysław Góra portrayed the dogmatists as people focused on state repression and police activity as ways to resolve the social conflict. They did not draw any conclusions from the summer 1980 strikes—namely, the need to change the old methods of rule, argued Góra.⁹³ Moreover, the resolution commemorating the hundred years of the Polish workers' movement blamed the conservative faction for introducing a self-contained style of politics and "sectarian" and "dogmatic" approach to social life. They did not understand that "Marxism is a guiding orientation, not a dogma," which is how it was put in the official pronouncement.⁹⁴

The events of 1980–1981 as a whole were often described as anarchy, an almost Hobbesian state of nature in which the "war of all against all" prevailed. Tadeusz Walichnowski wrote, "The uncertainty of tomorrow was felt by everybody. The country was struck by waves of violence and terror. Organized economic crime prospered, robberies and delinquency rates rose."⁹⁵ The party was a scene of personal feuds, hostility and internal conflicts: "Many regional party organizations demanded more determined action to stop the anarchy." This is how the situation was described by Jerzy Bielecki in a PUWP booklet entitled *Co wydarzyło się w Polsce od sierpnia 1980 roku?* [What Happened in Poland from August 1980?].⁹⁶

This narrative was maintained in the PUWP's official historiography to the very end of the party's existence. In his 1988 book, which was the last attempt to summarize the party's history before the end of the Cold War, historian and deputy director of the PUWP Central Archive Norbert Kołomejczyk recalled the familiar themes. The martial law was seen as a restoration of order, which "barred the road to counterrevolution." The grassroots initiatives were leading to anarchy. Its animators were at best confused, disoriented or naïve. At worst, they were consciously acting against state socialism and the Polish national interest. The situation after December 13, 1981, meant getting back to normal in contrast to the "Solidarity" period's abominations.[97]

The upshot of this narrative was to propose serenity, discipline, moderation and internal unity as antidotes to the accumulated problems. The conclusions were quite simple: If the PUWP wanted to continue its existence, the events unfolding between August 1980 and December 1981 must never be allowed to recur. Even in a resolution celebrating the hundred years of the Polish workers' movement (1982), one could read that there was still some hope, but that the party members should conform to the will of their leaders and not act out on their own initiative.[98] A "rebirth" or "renaissance" of the party might be possible but only through the "restoration of law and order."[99]

In 1988, Prime Minister Mieczysław Rakowski explained to Mikhail Gorbachev that in the past, "Poles always conspired against the government, not realizing, that without a strong government there is no strong state."[100] From 1982 on, in its public discourse, the Jaruzelski regime increasingly deployed historical examples, bringing up the time of the Partitions of Poland, when the Polish-Lithuanian state fell because of the excess of freedoms enjoyed by its noble citizens. The critique of the anarchy of 1980–1981 was thus connected with the old stereotype of "Polish anarchy," an almost natural inability to establish effective rule.[101]

The dominant motifs and notions used by the PUWP literature allowed the party to derive an official set of values in the new situation. The combat against anarchy led to recognition of the state as a fundamental political value. This legitimation strategy had been used before, but after martial law, it became almost the only strategy. As historian Marcin Zaremba argues, the argumentation combined conservative authoritarianism with nationalism. Jaruzelski, in his speeches at state celebrations or addressing the Polish Parliament, often spoke of homeland, state, reason, national accord, patriotism or national interest. Leftist or revolutionary rhetoric almost disappeared.[102] As the military rose to prominence in the public sphere, so did respect for the armed forces as presented in PUWP publications. Military vocabulary, always very popular in state socialist propaganda, enjoyed wider recognition. The party was conducting "offensives," opening up "fronts," awaiting "consolidation" and "introducing order"—and, finally, "tightening its grip" and "crushing enemy forces," sometimes sadly even in its own camp.[103]

Conclusions

The official story of the events of 1980–1981 inside the PUWP can be summed up as follows: Emotion and lack of reason originating in disappointment with the former leadership and discontent with the political and economic crisis led to unsupervised social and political activity. Weak links within the party resulted in some leaving it or joining the "Solidarity" trade union, a competitor organization. In the free flow of ideas and perceptions, party members intermingled with outspoken critics of the state. Justified critical points of view were displaced by demagogy. The lines between what was acceptable and what was not were blurred. The diversity of chaotic grassroots initiatives caused conflict and discord. Party members began to split into ideological factions. In effect, a state of anarchy prevailed, which needed to be halted through the use of force.

The story told by the party leadership about the events of 1980–1981 obviously simplified the complicated historical experience. Moreover, from the perspective of the official narrative, certain political views and activities were presented as wrong, potentially dangerous and even based on bad intentions. Thus the aim of constructing a specific version of the events was to point out where foes and friends lay, and what kind of values were most important. The official story of the PUWP was, as historian John Harold Plumb puts it, a "confirmatory history" aimed at securing the *status quo*, justifying present authority and preventing potential opposition.[104]

This story thus perfectly fulfilled the narrative's functions of crisis resolution as described by Paul A. Cohen. Jaruzelski's narrative invoked basic values and themes, touched upon national and universal mythology and thus was very effective.[105] The story played on existing sentiments and fears. "Yes, we demanded [martial law]," said one of the PUWP functionaries, interviewed by Krzysztof Dąbek. "What happened with the local party on the local level was unbelievable. [. . .] Back then we didn't call it martial law, but we simply wanted to get things straight."[106] The story proposed reason over madness, moral purity against corruption, unity in contrast to factional warfare and, finally, choosing law and order over anarchy. Polish public opinion was and is still divided in the assessment of the martial law.[107] The Jaruzelski story constituted a powerful memory-forging narrative, which enabled the PUWP leadership to take control of the party and secure their rule over the country—which, as history was to show, would only be for a short time.

Notes

1 On December 1, 1980, during a rally in the Ursus Factory in Warsaw, Jacek Kuroń said, "I believe that what we are right now carrying out is no doubt a revolution. We should nonetheless try to limit these revolutionary features. Do not try to solve everything with one giant leap." Andrzej Friszke, *Rewolucja Solidarności: 1980–1981* (Kraków: Znak Horyzont, 2014), 233.

2 Timothy Garton Ash, *The Polish Revolution: Solidarity, 1980–82* (London: J. Cape, 1983).

3 Andrzej Friszke, "Rewolucja to nie karnawał," in *Lekcje historii PRL w rozmowach*, ed. Andrzej Brzeziecki (Warszawa: W.A.B, 2009), 221–248; Andrzej

Paczkowski, *Revolution and Counterrevolution in Poland, 1980–1989: Solidarity, Martial Law, and the End of Communism in Europe*, trans. Christina Manetti (Rochester: University of Rochester Press, 2015); Jadwiga Staniszkis, *Poland's Self-Limiting Revolution*, ed. and trans. Jan Tomasz Gross (Princeton: Princeton University Press, 1984); Marcin Zaremba, "Od wojny domowej do solidarnościowej rewolucji, czyli społeczeństwo nieprzedstawione dekady lat siedemdziesiątych," *Res Publica Nowa* 8 (2000): 46–54.

4 George Sanford, *Military Rule in Poland: The Rebuilding of Communist Power, 1981–1983* (London: Croom Helm, 1986).

5 Wojciech Jaruzelski, "Statement at the Conclusion of the PUWP Central Committee's 13th Plenary Meeting, October 15, 1983," in *Jaruzelski, Prime Minister of Poland: Selected Speeches*, ed. Robert Maxwell (Oxford and New York: Pergamon Press, 1985).

6 James W. Pennebaker and Becky L. Banasik, "On the Creation and Maintenance of Collective Memories: History as Social Psychology," in *Collective Memory of Political Events: Social Psychological Perspectives*, eds. James W. Pennebaker, Darío Páez and Bernard Rimé (Mahwah: Lawrence Erlbaum Associates, 1997), 3–6.

7 Keith M. Wilson, "Introduction: Governments, Historians and 'Historical Engineering,'" in *Forging the Collective Memory: Government and International Historians Through Two World Wars*, ed. Keith M. Wilson (Providence: Berghahn Books, 1996), 2, 14–15, 21–23.

8 Gary B. Nash, *First City: Philadelphia and the Forging of Historical Memory* (Philadelphia: University of Pennsylvania Press, 2002), 1–13.

9 William H. Sewell, "Historical Events as Transformations of Structures: Inventing Revolution at the Bastille," *Theory and Society* 25.6 (1996): 843–844.

10 Paul A. Cohen, *History and Popular Memory: The Power of Story in Moments of Crisis* (New York: Columbia University Press, 2014), 193–194.

11 King Goujian of Yue (reigned 496–465 BC), after being severely defeated by rival north Chinese King Fuchai of Wu, was forced to personally serve on the latter's court. Goujian suffered three years of humiliating captivity, during which he was sentenced to tend the rival's horses. In an act of generosity, the victor released Goujian and allowed him to return to his kingdom. Ten years after returning to his homeland, Goujian took brutal revenge on the Wu Kingdom, killing the members of the royal family, including the people who helped him and showed him mercy during his captivity. In the Chinese historical imagination, the story serves as an example of perseverance and a lesson that every humiliation ought on principle to be avenged. Paul A. Cohen, *Speaking to History: The Story of King Goujian in Twentieth-Century China* (Berkeley: University of California Press, 2009), 1–30.

12 Cohen, *History and Popular Memory*, 193–207.

13 Michael H. Bernhard and Jan Kubik, eds., *Twenty Years After Communism: The Politics of Memory and Commemoration* (Oxford and New York: Oxford University Press, 2014).

14 Tadeusz Kisielewski, *Partii portret własny: polityka i świadomość w PZPR: Studium upadku* (Warszawa: Neriton, 2011), 8.

15 Krzysztof Dąbek, *PZPR—retrospektywny portret własny* (Warszawa: TRIO, 2006).

16 Krzysztof Kosiński, "'Religianctwo': Napięcie między ideologią a religią w świadomości członków i działaczy PZPR," *Polska 1944/45–1989: Studia i Materiały* 12 (2014).

17 Terry Cox, "Reconsidering the Hungarian Revolution of 1956," in *Hungary 1956—Forty Years On*, ed. Terry Cox (London and Portland: F. Cass, 1997), 2–6.

What Happened in 1980? 187

18 T. Iván Berend, "Contemporary Hungary 1956–1984," in *A History of Hungary*, eds. Peter F. Sugar, Péter Hanák and Tibor Frank (Bloomington: Indiana University Press, 1990), 384–386.
19 Csaba Békés, Malcolm Byrne and M. János Rainer, eds., "Document No. 104: Resolution of the Provisional Central Committee of the Hungarian Socialist Workers' Party, December 5, 1956. (Excerpts)," in *The 1956 Hungarian Revolution: A History in Documents* (Budapest and New York: Central European University Press, 2002), 460–463. I would like to thank András Domány for pointing me to this document.
20 Quoted from: Paulina Bren, *The Greengrocer and His TV: The Culture of Communism After the 1968 Prague Spring* (Ithaca: Cornell University Press, 2010), 62, 63–70.
21 Quoted from: Zheng Wang, *Never Forget National Humiliation: Historical Memory in Chinese Politics and Foreign Relations* (New York: Columbia University Press, 2012), 119–144.
22 Wang, *Never Forget National Humiliation*.
23 The term "Polish months" denotes these kinds of periods in the history of the Polish People's Republic, with recurring crises of the system and contentious social resistance. In this historical conceptualization, the Polish People's Republic was regularly shaken by social protests, which in the end resulted in the fall of communist rule in 1989. The "Polish months" include June/October 1956 (the workers revolt in Poznań and nationwide political protests, which led to de-Stalinization), March 1968 (governmental antisemitic campaign, students strikes and the economy-driven protests of the youngest generation), December 1970 and June 1976 (workers' strikes and street battles after the drastic food price increases), August 1980 (the biggest wave of strikes in Polish history and the establishment of the "Solidarity" Trade Union) and December 1981 (the introduction of martial law). Jerzy Eisler, *"Polskie miesiące," czyli kryzys(y) w PRL* (Warszawa: Instytut Pamięci Narodowej, 2008); Krystyna Kersten, "The Mass Protests in People's Poland—A Continuous Process or Single Events?," trans. Janina Dorosz, *Acta Poloniae Historica* 83 (2001): 165–192.
24 Jerzy Eisler, "'Polskie miesiące'—działania propagandowe w okresie przesileń politycznych w PRL," in *Propaganda PRL: wybrane problemy*, ed. Piotr Semków (Gdańsk: Instytut Pamięci Narodowej, 2004), 36.
25 Andrzej Friszke, *Polska Gierka* (Warszawa: Wydawnictwa Szkolne i Pedagogiczne, 1995), 19; Janusz Rolicki, *Edward Gierek: życie i narodziny legendy* (Warszawa: Iskry, 2002), 92–93.
26 Jerzy Eisler, *Marzec 1968: geneza, przebieg, konsekwencje* (Warszawa: Państwowe Wydawnictwo Naukowe, 1991), 10, 425.
27 Dariusz Stola, "Finanse PZPR w jej ostatnich latach," *Więź* 3 (2000): 140.
28 Tomasz Leszkowicz, "Ostatnia ofensywa na froncie historycznym? Polityka pamięci historycznej Polskiej Zjednoczonej Partii Robotniczej w latach 1981–1986," *Dzieje Najnowsze* 46.2 (2014): 103–120.
29 Anita Prażmowska, *Poland: A Modern History* (London and New York: I. B. Tauris, 2010), 43–45; Norman M. Naimark, *The History of the "Proletariat": The Emergence of Marxism in the Kingdom of Poland, 1870–1887* (Boulder: East European Quarterly, 1979), 108–109; Lucjan Blit, *The Origins of Polish Socialism: The History and Ideas of the First Polish Socialist Party, 1878–1886* (Cambridge: Cambridge University Press, 1971), 51–81.
30 Rafał Habielski, "Przeszłość i pamięć historyczna w życiu kulturalnym PRL: Kilka uwag wstępnych," in *Polityka czy propaganda: PRL wobec historii*, eds. Paweł Skibiński and Tomasz Wiścicki (Warszawa: Muzeum Historii Polski,

2009), 97, 108; Paweł Niziołek, "Propagandowa funkcja pieniądza w PRL," *Pamięć.pl. Biuletyn Instytutu Pamięci Narodowej* 7 (2012): 43.

31 The Polish Committee of National Liberation (The Lublin Committee) was established on July 22, 1944, as a provisional coalition government for the territories liberated from the German occupation by the Red Army. Consisting of politicians active in and subordinated to the Soviet Union, it served as a method of seizing power in the country during the last year of the war. The establishment of the Committee led in effect to the withdrawal of Allied support for the Polish government-in-exile in London and to domination of the government by the communist party. Prażmowska, *Poland*, 151–152; Anthony Kemp-Welch, *Poland Under Communism: A Cold War History* (Cambridge: Cambridge University Press, 2008), 4–5.

32 The National Library of Poland (BN), Documents of Social Life (DŻS), I2a, *W stulecie polskiego ruchu robotniczego* (Warszawa: Książka i Wiedza, 1983), 5, 37.

33 On December 14, 1970, after the authorities introduced drastic food price increases, protest broke out in the Gdańsk Lenin Shipyard. After failed negotiations with the company's management, a throng of 2,000 workers marched to the center of the city towards the headquarters of the Provincial PUWP Committee. Along the way, the large crowd was joined by young people and other inhabitants of Gdańsk and later attacked by police forces. Stun and gas grenades were thrown at the marching crowd, which retaliated with stones and bricks. Street fighting ensued the following morning, and three public buildings were set on fire, including the Gdańsk PUWP headquarters. Alarmed by the police and military reports, First Secretary Władysław Gomułka authorized the use of firearms against the crowd. The militia started shooting, and the army was dispatched to the streets of Gdańsk with machine guns and heavy equipment at the ready. On December 15, at least seven people died, and a few hundred were injured. During the next days, protests and street riots spread to other industrial cities of the Baltic coast—to Gdynia, Szczecin, Słupsk and Elbląg in northeast Poland. Most fatalities were reported on December 17 in Gdynia where eighteen people were shot. All around the country, the military started to regroup and was put on emergency alert. Altogether, the authorities used 9,000 police functionaries as well as military forces: 27,000 troops, 550 tanks, 2,100 other vehicles and 108 aircraft and helicopters. According to official data, 45 died as a result of the December 1970 protests. The bloodshed was finally stopped on December 20, 1970, as the result of a cabinet coup d'état. Gomułka was forced to step down from his post, and Edward Gierek stepped in. Andrzej Paczkowski, *The Spring Will Be Ours: Poland and the Poles from Occupation to Freedom*, trans. Jane Cave (University Park: Pennsylvania State University Press, 2003), 346–351.

34 Anita Prażmowska, *Władysław Gomułka: A Biography* (London: Tauris, 2016), 274–275; Niziołek, "Propagandowa funkcja pieniądza w PRL," 44; Andrzej Paczkowski, *Od sfałszowanego zwycięstwa do prawdziwej klęski: szkice do portretu PRL* (Kraków: Wydawnictwo Literackie, 1999), 200–203.

35 Ray Taras, "Marxist Critiques of Political Crises in Poland," in *The Road to Disillusion: From Critical Marxism to Postcommunism in Eastern Europe*, ed. Ray Taras (Armonk: M. E. Sharpe, 1992).

36 Andrzej Paczkowski argues that in official academic works of the 1980s, even in purely propagandistic publications, one can find genuinely valuable contributions to the topics of contemporary Polish history. For details, see Paczkowski, *Od sfałszowanego zwycięstwa do prawdziwej klęski*, 200–203.

37 The Gdańsk Accords of August 31, 1980, among social demands and pay raises, included the establishment of a new structure of trade unions, independent of

the government and the PUWP, the legal right to strike, the limitation of press and publication censorship, the release of political prisoners and the call for self-governing-oriented economic reforms. Friszke, *Rewolucja Solidarności*, 69–73; Paczkowski, *The Spring Will Be Ours*, 405–410.
38 Tadeusz Mołdawa, *Ludzie władzy, 1944–1991: władze państwowe i polityczne Polski według stanu na dzień 28 II 1991* (Warszawa: Wydawnictwo Naukowe PWN, 1991), 369.
39 Andrzej Friszke, *Polska: losy państwa i narodu 1939–1989* (Warszawa: Iskry, 2003), 381–382; Kemp-Welch, *Poland under Communism*, 272.
40 Andrzej Sowa, *Historia polityczna Polski 1944–1991* (Kraków: Wydawnictwo Literackie, 2011), 492.
41 Andrzej Paczkowski, *Droga do "mniejszego zła": strategia i taktyka obozu władzy, lipiec 1980—styczeń 1982* (Kraków: Wydawnictwo Literackie, 2002), 218–225; Sowa, *Historia polityczna Polski 1944–1991*, 492.
42 Albert O. Hirschman, *Exit, Voice, and Loyalty: Responses to Decline in Firms, Organizations, and States* (Cambridge: Harvard University Press, 1970).
43 Jan B. De Weydenthal, "Appendix 1: Party in Figures," in Jan B. De Weydenthal, *The Communists of Poland: An Historical Outline* (Stanford: Hoover Institution Press, Stanford University, 1986), 229–230.
44 Włodzimierz Janowski, "Członkowie Polskiej Zjednoczonej Partii Robotniczej wobec wprowadzenia stanu wojennego," in *Kościół i społeczeństwo wobec stanu wojennego*, ed. Wiesław Jan Wysocki (Warszawa: Rytm, 2004), 451; Jakub Szumski, "The Party, Solidarity or Both? Transformation of Political Identities in 1980–1981 Poland," in *Post-1945 Poland: Modernities, Transformations and Evolving Identities* (Oxford: St. Antony's College, 2016), 160–172, www.sant.ox.ac.uk/sites/default/files/related-documents/post-1945_poland_working_papers_pomp_2016.pdf, accessed August 26, 2017.
45 Werner G. Hahn, *Democracy in a Communist Party: Poland's Experience Since 1980* (New York: Columbia University Press, 1987), 47–49, 60.
46 Norbert Kołomejczyk, *Polska Zjednoczona Partia Robotnicza 1948–1986* (Warszawa: Książka i Wiedza, 1988), 263–265.
47 Matthew J. Ouimet, *The Rise and Fall of the Brezhnev Doctrine in Soviet Foreign Policy* (Chapel Hill: University of North Carolina Press, 2003), 81–82; Ben Slay, *Polish Economy: Crisis, Reform, and Transformation* (Princeton: Princeton University Press, 2014), 48.
48 Jakub Szumski, "Rozliczenia z ekipą Edwarda Gierka: Przyczynek do zrozumienia zjawiska," in *Zimowa Szkoła Historii Najnowszej 2014: Referaty*, eds. Łukasz Kamiński and Marek Hańderek (Warszawa: Instytut Pamięci Narodowej, 2015), 51–61.
49 Szumski, "Rozliczenia z ekipą Edwarda Gierka."
50 Szumski, "Rozliczenia z ekipą Edwarda Gierka."
51 De Weydenthal, *The Communists of Poland*, 186–187.
52 De Weydenthal, *The Communists of Poland*, 196.
53 Przemysław Gasztold-Seń, "'Lewica' PZPR: Działalność Stowarzyszenia Klubów Wiedzy Społeczno-Politycznej 'Rzeczywistość' w latach 1981–1983," in *Letnia Szkoła Historii Najnowszej 2009: Referaty*, eds. Łukasz Kamiński and Tomasz Kozłowski (Warszawa: Instytut Pamięci Narodowej, 2010), 77–92.
54 Przemysław Gasztold-Seń, "Partia zjednoczona czy podzielona? Różne nurty PZPR w ostatniej dekadzie PRL," *Annales Universitatis Paedagogicae Cracoviensis: Studia Politologica* 10 (2013): 178–183.
55 Jakub Szumski, "Zanim wyrosły 'poziomki': Zbigniew Iwanów do września 1980 r.," in *Letnia Szkoła Historii Najnowszej 2014: Referaty*, eds. Jakub Szumski and Łukasz Kamiński (Warszawa: Instytut Pamięci Narodowej, 2015), 178–188.

56 Roman Bäcker, *Struktury poziome w Toruniu (1980–1981)* (Warszawa: Uniwersytet Warszawski, Instytut Socjologii, 1990), 72–78; Garton Ash, *The Polish Revolution*, 172.
57 Szumski, "The Party, Solidarity or Both?"
58 Dąbek, *PZPR—retrospektywny portret własny*, 262–269.
59 Paczkowski, *Droga do "mniejszego zła,"* 259–260; Andrzej Paczkowski, *Wojna polsko-jaruzelska: stan wojenny w Polsce 13 XII 1981–22 VII 1983* (Warszawa: Prószyński i S-ka, 2007), 32–33.
60 Friszke, *Polska*, 404, 406.
61 Archive of Modern Records (AAN), Central Committee of the Polish United Workers' Party (KC PZPR), IX/102, Dane statystyczne CKKP o internowanych członkach partii, 4 March 1982, LI/39; Notatka Wydziału Administracyjnego KC PZPR dotycząca internowanych członków PZPR, February 27, 1982.
62 Friszke, *Polska*, 411; Gasztold-Seń, "Partia zjednoczona czy podzielona?," 183–186; Gasztold-Seń, "'Lewica' PZPR," 87–92.
63 De Weydenthal, "Appendix 1: Party in Figures," 230.
64 De Weydenthal, *The Communists of Poland*, 209.
65 Janowski, "Członkowie Polskiej Zjednoczonej Partii Robotniczej wobec wprowadzenia stanu wojennego," 462–474.
66 AAN, KC PZPR, XII/3616, Wydział Organizacyjny KC PZPR. Sytuacja w kraju i w partii. Tezy, XII/3466, Informacja o problemach pracy partyjnej w woj. częstochowskim, January 15, 1982, Informacja o niektórych zjawiskach i sytuacji w województwie gorzowskim.
67 Quoted from: AAN, KC PZPR, XII/3607, Ocena aktualnej sytuacji społeczno-politycznej w woj. radomskim.
68 BN, DŻS, I2a, Jerzy Bąbol and Mieczysław Krajewski, *Stan wojenny: próba odpowiedzi na pytania podstawowe* (Łódź: Wydział Propagandy, Agitacji i Kultury KŁ PZPR, 1982).
69 Wojciech Jaruzelski, "Proclamation over the National Radio and TV Network, December 13, 1981," in *Jaruzelski, Prime Minister of Poland: Selected Speeches*, ed. Robert Maxwell (Oxford and New York: Pergamon Press, 1985), 28, 29, 30, 32.
70 AAN, KC PZPR, XII/3616, Aktualna sytuacja w partii i wynikające z niej zadania polityczno-organizacyjne dla komitetów i organizacji partyjnych.
71 BN, DŻS and I2a, "Pytania i odpowiedzi na temat aktualnych problemów ideologicznych," *Biblioteka Lektora i Wykładowcy* 17 (1984): 7.
72 Quoted from: BN, DŻS, I2a and Ludwik Krasucki, "Czyny potwierdzają słowa," *Zagadnienia i materiały* 33 (1984): 3.
73 Wojciech Jaruzelski, "Speech Delivered Before the Sejm of the Polish People's Republic, January 25, 1982," in *Jaruzelski, Prime Minister of Poland: Selected Speeches*, ed. Robert Maxwell (Oxford and New York: Pergamon Press, 1985), 38.
74 BN, DŻS, I2a, Edward Modzelewski and Wojciech Wiśniewski, "Walka ideologiczna we współczesnym świecie a sytuacja polityczna w Polsce: Materiał pomocniczy na zebranie ideologiczne POP PZPR," *Biblioteka Lektora i Wykładowcy* 1 (1983): 28–29.
75 Władysław Góra, *Polska Ludowa 1944–1984: Zarys dziejów politycznych* (Lublin: Wydawnictwo Lubelskie, 1986), 630.
76 AAN, KC PZPR, III/142, Stenogram VII Plenarnego Posiedzenia KC PZPR, February 24–25, 1982, 17–18.
77 BN, DŻS and I2a, *Podstawy wiedzy o partii: program szkolenia kandydatów PZPR: Wydział Ideologiczny KC PZPR* (Warszawa: Książka i Wiedza, 1982), 23.
78 Modzelewski and Wiśniewski, "Walka ideologiczna we współczesnym świecie," 25.

79 BN, DŻS, I2a and Jerzy Bielecki, *Co wydarzyło się w Polsce od sierpnia 1980 roku?* (Warszawa: Książka i Wiedza, 1982), 10.
80 Jaruzelski, "Proclamation over the National Radio and TV Network, December 13, 1981," 29.
81 Szumski, "Rozliczenia z ekipą Edwarda Gierka."
82 Wojciech Jaruzelski, "Speech Delivered Before the Sejm of the Polish People's Republic, October 9, 1982," in *Jaruzelski, Prime Minister of Poland: Selected Speeches*, ed. Robert Maxwell (Oxford and New York: Pergamon Press, 1985), 45.
83 Henryk Dominiczak, Ryszard Halaba and Tadeusz Walichnowski, *Z dziejów politycznych Polski 1944–1984* (Warszawa: Książka i Wiedza, 1984), 306.
84 Góra, *Polska Ludowa 1944–1984*, 618.
85 Władysław Ważniewski, *Zarys historii Polski Ludowej (1944–1983)* (Warszawa: ANS, 1985), 202.
86 Jaruzelski, "Speech Delivered Before the Sejm of the Polish People's Republic, January 25, 1982," 35.
87 Cited in: De Weydenthal, *The Communists of Poland*, 210.
88 *Podstawy wiedzy o partii: program szkolenia kandydatów PZPR*, 25.
89 Adolf Dobieszewski, *Leninowskie zasady życia partyjnego* (Warszawa: Polska Zjednoczona Partia Robotnicza, Komitet Dzielnicowy Ochota, 1981).
90 AAN, KC PZPR, III/142, Stenogram VII Plenarnego Posiedzenia KC PZPR, February 24–25, 1982, 36.
91 Góra, *Polska Ludowa 1944–1984*, 612–613.
92 Dominiczak, Halaba and Walichnowski, *Z dziejów politycznych Polski 1944–1984*, 313–314.
93 Góra, *Polska Ludowa 1944–1984*, 612.
94 *W stulecie polskiego ruchu robotniczego*, 24.
95 Dominiczak, Halaba and Walichnowski, *Z dziejów politycznych Polski 1944–1984*, 364.
96 Bielecki, *Co wydarzyło się w Polsce od sierpnia 1980 roku?*, 14.
97 Kołomejczyk, *Polska Zjednoczona Partia Robotnicza 1948–1986*, 249, 251–252.
98 *W stulecie polskiego ruchu robotniczego*, 16, 18.
99 Góra, *Polska Ludowa 1944–1984*, 636–637.
100 Antoni Dudek, ed., "Nr 42. 1988 październik 21, Moskwa—Zapis rozmowy Sekretarza Generalnego KC KPZR Michaiła Gorbaczowa z Premierem Mieczysławem F. Rakowskim," in *Zmierzch dyktatury: Polska lat 1986–1989 w świetle dokumentów* (Warszawa: Instytut Pamięci Narodowej, 2009), 338.
101 Jerzy Lukowski and Hubert Zawadzki, *A Concise History of Poland* (Cambridge: Cambridge University Press, 2006), 88.
102 Marcin Zaremba, *Im Nationalen Gewande: Strategien Kommunistischer Herrschaftslegitimation in Polen 1944–1980*, trans. Andreas R. Hofmann (Osnabrück: Fibre, 2011), 391–403.
103 Góra, *Polska Ludowa 1944–1984*, 637–638.
104 John Harold Plumb, *The Death of the Past* (London: Macmillan, 1969), 44.
105 Cohen, *History and Popular Memory*, 204.
106 Dąbek, *PZPR—retrospektywny portret własny*, 268.
107 Piotr Tadeusz Kwiatkowski and Jonathan Weber, "Martial Law in the Collective Polish Memory Following the Collapse of Communism," trans. Jonathan Weber, *International Journal of Sociology* 36.4 (2006): 45–66; Barbara Szacka, " 'Solidarity' and the Martial Law in the Collective Memory of Polish History," *Polish Sociological Review* 153.1 (2006): 75–89.

8 "We Must Reconstruct Our Own Past"

1960s Polish Communist Women's Memoirs—Constructing the (Gender) History of the Polish Left

Agnieszka Mrozik

"We Will Turn Every Job into a Battle Post"[1]

In the 1960s, a veritable boom of life writing took place in Poland. The publishing market was flooded with autobiographies, diaries and memoirs by members of social groups that had acquired agency following World War II, such as peasants, blue-collar workers, the working intelligentsia and women of various milieus. A Polish sociologist of culture, Bronisław Gołębiewski, noted that a considerable segment of the life writing of those times was represented by (auto)biographies of women and men involved in communist activity since before the war.[2] Many of them, who belonged to the power-wielding elites of postwar Poland, found themselves in political retirement following October 1956, when Władysław Gomułka (1905–1982) took the helm of the Polish United Workers' Party (PUWP) and of the entire country in the wake of workers' protests and launched a process of de-Stalinization. Their banishment to the margins of political life formed part of a broad-scale process of purification of the party's ranks of its Stalinist cadres.

It is important to stress the gender of the female life writers, which became loaded with significance in the period of de-Stalinization, whose slogan was Gomułka's postulate of "the Polish road toward socialism." Women and Jews in structures of authority became symbols of the "times of errors and distortions," as the period immediately following the war was dubbed in reference to Soviet leader Nikita Khrushchev's (1894–1971) famous speech delivered in February 1956 at the Twentieth Party Congress of the Communist Party of the Soviet Union (CPSU) in which he denounced Stalin's crimes. And so, if postwar times, especially Stalinism, functioned in the collective Polish imagination as the world of a disturbed order, gender and ethnic roles turned upside down and inside out, the purging of Party ranks of "undesirable elements" during "the thaw" was seen as a condition for Gomułka's milieu to gain social legitimization and thus a condition for maintaining the system's integrity.[3] To paraphrase the words of anthropologist Mary Douglas, we could say that dirt and impurities had to be expelled if order was to be maintained.[4]

"We Must Reconstruct Our Own Past" 193

This chapter is dedicated to the analysis of an intense process of (auto)biographication, which in Poland occurred in parallel to de-Stalinization; it involves the telling of the stories of their own lives by female ex-dignitaries of the Communist Party and state who were pushed to the margins of public life.[5] However, the general state of research on this phenomenon shows that it is not only specific to Poland: The private memoirs of female communist activists were published starting in the latter half of the 1950s in many countries of Central and Eastern Europe,[6] but also in Italy[7] and in Spain.[8] These works, simultaneously created by the authors in a gesture of narrating their own lives, shed light on the history of the communist movement in various countries and regions, but also on the history of communism as an inter- and transnational phenomenon, as well as on specific gender issues these authors struggled with.

The protagonists of my chapter are communist women, members or collaborators of the team of Gomułka's predecessor, Bolesław Bierut (1892–1956), who governed in Poland between 1944 and 1956. Many of them—for example, Maria Kamińska (1897–1983), Janina Broniewska (1904–1981), Edwarda Orłowska (1906–1977), Romana Granas (1906–1987), Jadwiga Sabina Ludwińska (1907–1998 or 1999) or Anna Jędrychowska (1910–1989)—up to 1939, were involved in radical left and illegal activities in the structures of the Social Democracy of the Kingdom of Poland and Lithuania (SDKPL; 1893–1918) and/or of the Communist Party of Poland (CPP; 1918–1938), were persecuted, including imprisonment, in tsarist times and/or in independent Poland, and after the war broke out, they found themselves in the USSR. (Of all the women I discuss, only Halina Krahelska (1886–1945) and Wanda Duraj (1902–1994) spent the war years in the territory of Poland. Krahelska did not live to see the end of the war; she died at Ravensbrück concentration camp in April 1945.) Others, such as Marcjanna Fornalska (1870–1963), Zofia Dzerzhinskaya (1882–1968), Helena Bobińska (1887–1968), Zofia Marchlewska (1898–1983) and Jadwiga Siekierska (1903–1984), had already been in the USSR since the time of the October Revolution, and there they dealt with so-called Polish issues, mainly in the area of culture. (Both Bobińska and Siekierska, victims of Stalinist purges of the 1930s, were held in Soviet prisons and labor camps from 1937. Bobińska was released on the petition of the Union of Polish Patriots in 1943 and Siekierska in 1945. They returned to Poland after the war ended.) In the Soviet Union, these two groups participated in the organization of Polish political and military structures. Wanda Wasilewska (1905–1964), whose case I omit in this chapter,[9] was chair of the Union of Polish Patriots; Janina Broniewska was a war correspondent with the Polish First "Tadeusz Kościuszko" Infantry Division; Romana Granas and Edwarda Orłowska were political officers in the Polish Army; Zofia Dzierzhinskaya directed the editorial office of the "Tadeusz Kościuszko" radio station in Saratowo; Jadwiga Sabina Ludwińska was sent to Poland in 1942 to build the party structures there. Their careers in high-level posts and important public functions just after the war[10] became so inconvenient in the Gomułka period that it cost them their careers and condemned them to political marginalization. Their stories were recovered and made available in these memoirs.

In the present chapter, I make references to the memoirs of 13 Polish communist women, although the complete research sample is much broader. One of the criteria of text selection is type. I am interested in works that have been published as separate, longer books. Thus I omit commissioned memoir articles and those forming parts of collective volumes, as well as memoirs sent to the press, memoirs that are transcriptions of interviews conducted after 1956 by party historians with male and female communist politicians and, finally, memoirs that never appeared in print and are still held in archives. In total, then, I make reference to 15 publications (Janina Broniewska was the author of three volumes of memoirs). A second selection criterion is the time of publication.[11] I focus on works published during the secretaryship of Władysław Gomułka—that is, in the years 1956–1970—as well as on those that, though written in this period (a fact communicated by the authors themselves in the prefaces or afterwords), were not printed until the first period of rule of the next PUWP's secretary, Edward Gierek (1913–2001), who held this office from 1970 to 1980. Thus I omit works published in the late 1970s, in the 1980s and after the 1989 transformation. In adopting this time frame, I am guided by the biographical situation of the authors as well as by the specific ideological and communicational situation of the period in which their memoirs were written and made public. Most of my heroines who had performed responsible and often prestigious functions in ministries, at universities and in institutions of culture after the war were banished to "political retirement" with Gomułka's rise to power. Despite good health and willingness to remain active, they were forced to retire, take disability pensions, as in the case of Kamińska, or as a last resort, they were moved to work in less significant positions: Granas kept working until 1963 as deputy editor in chief of *Polityka* [Politics] magazine and Broniewska was a literary editor of the *Kraj Rad* [Land of the Soviets] magazine until 1964. In this way, the new governing group removed from visible space and deprived of influence and significance those female public functionaries who were associated with Stalinist times, or who functioned as a kind of "hallmark" of that period.

This period of forced idleness, however, was not lost time for those in "political retirement," as attested by the memoirs written precisely in this time, whose authors, besides setting the personal records straight, included material more or less openly contesting the policies pursued by their political successors. They were a form of assessment of the political message of the new authorities and, at the same time, a kind of running commentary on the violent social changes—i.e., changes in private lifestyles and in models of public activity, which were rolling through the country in the 1960s.[12] And so, by way of making references to their own experiences, by recalling events from recent history in which they participated and which they coproduced, the authors depicted attitudes and value systems to which they ascribed the role of a signpost for the young generation in the dynamically changing reality:

> What I would fear most for Poland is instilling passivity and indifference in the minds of the youth toward matters of collective life, toward social afflictions, toward the direction in which social transformations are taking shape [. . .] This is one, possibly the chief, reason for which I am publishing this diary.[13]

The memoirs of communist dignitaries of the postwar and Stalinist period are interesting to me not only because they are a specific—personal, subjective—type of historical source, allowing us a glimpse into the history of the Polish radical left, fused with the history of Poland and Europe from the close of the nineteenth century to the end of World War II, told by its active participants and creators. They are interesting also because the authors attempted a critical intervention into contemporary reality at the moment they wrote these memoirs. The authors recalled the common history of Polish communists, which was traced back to pre-war times, and in certain cases, even to before World War I, or, better, they *made it* into a common history by referring to generational events, such as the Revolution in the Kingdom of Poland (1905–1907), the October Revolution, the battle against "white terror" in the interwar period, or the Spanish Civil War in which communists defended the Republic. In doing so, the authors (re)constructed the heroic past of the communist movement but also undertook to judge how faithful the authorities of the post-Stalinist period remained to communist ideals and values, such as internationalism or equal treatment of all people regardless of gender, religion or ethnic origin.

Therefore, the function of these tales about the past was, on the one hand, a nostalgic, therapeutic one, serving as a "binding agent" of the old and current identities of those telling the tales and of the circles they mention[14] and, on the other hand, an interventionist one meant to settle accounts with the politics of the authorities after 1956. Using British language philosopher John L. Austin's term, one could say that these memoirs were a type of "speech act,"[15] a deed, a continuation of the battle waged by the authors when they were still in power. And so these communist activists who had primarily worked with words in their politically active lifetimes—as writers, journalists, agitators, instructors, editors and teachers—seemed to understand writing memoirs as yet another political and educational task on the path toward the overarching political goal—i.e., the building of the communist system. When writing, they were no longer political retirees or ex-soldiers. As spinners of revolutionary reality—revolutionary, not banal, as women's writing is often perceived[16]—they signaled that they were still in the game, still counted in the battle.[17]

"We Must Reconstruct Our Own Past"[18]

The specific "production" of memoirs by communist activists fit right into the atmosphere of Gomułka's times; it corresponded with the interests of the authorities and with the party mission. The memoirs' role was to (re)construct the Polish workers' movement and leftist traditions as both an element of the history and tradition of global left-wing politics, and as part of the history of the Polish nation. Between 1957 and 1968, the Institute of Party History was operating under the aegis of the Central Committee of the PUWP. Its task was, among others, to draft and publish materials on party history, to conduct interviews with communist politicians and to publish commissioned memoirs containing accounts by activists of the workers' movement or the party, or by war veterans.

The Institute of Party History focused on the popularization of the history of the Polish Workers' Party (PWP) (1942–1948) and of the PUWP (established in December 1948 as a result of the merger of the PWP and the Polish Socialist Party), of the "allies" from the Polish Socialist Party and from the People's Party, as well as of participants in "joint battles" against the Germans: soldiers from the People's Army, People's Guard, Peasants' Battalions, Home Army and Socialist Militias.[19] Much less space was devoted to the history of the pre-war CPP or to military formations that emerged during the war with the USSR, such as the Union of Polish Patriots and the First and Second Polish Army. As historian Jerzy Eisler has pointed out, some of the most prominent politicians were personally interested in the commemoration of the youngest Polish parties—i.e., the PWP and the PUWP.[20] These were—namely, Władysław Gomułka, first secretary of the Central Committee of the PWP (1943–1946) and of the Central Committee of the Polish United Workers' Party (1956–1970), and Mieczysław Moczar (1913–1983), who had been commander-in-chief of the People's Guard and of the People's Army during WWII, and in the years 1956–68 served first as deputy minister and then as Minister of Internal Affairs. He was responsible for the antisemitic witch hunt of March 1968, which was a part of the factional wars within the PUWP.[21] According to historian Marcin Zaremba, this interest in the commemoration of the PWP and the PUWP reflected the principle of legitimization, which, in the conception of Poland's liberation from the Nazi occupation, valued the role of "national" factions over the role of the Union of Polish Patriots—a Polish communist organization overtly commended by Stalin.[22]

At this point, we come to the "eruption" of life writing by communist women who marched on the "Soviet road to socialism" in Poland. The first upsurge of these memoirs took place in the late 1950s and early 1960s. They usually dealt with the topic of the October Revolution and the participation in it of communists of various nationalities, including Poles. At that time, Celina Bobrowska's *Wspomnienia rewolucjonistki 1894–1917* [Memoirs of a Revolutionary Woman 1894–1917] was published (1959); Halina Krahelska's *Wspomnienia rewolucjonistki* [Memoirs of a Revolutionary Woman], originally published before the war, was reprinted (1957); and Marcjanna Fornalska's *Pamiętnik matki* [Diary of a Mother] appeared (1960); as well as Jadwiga Siekierska's *Kartki z przeszłości* [Cards of the Past, 1960], Maria Kamińska's *Ścieżkami wspomnień* [Paths of Memories, 1960] and Helena Bobińska's *Pamiętnik tamtych lat* [Diary of Those Years, 1963]. The second upsurge occurred in the late 1960s, with such publications as Zofia Marchlewska's *Piórem i pędzlem* [With Quill and Brush, 1967] and Zofia Dzerzhinskaya's *Lata wielkich bojów* [Years of Great Battles], which was translated from Russian (Soviet Union 1964, Poland 1969). Their authors attested to having participated in the great revolutionary effort (usually on the fronts of propaganda, education and culture) hand in hand with their husbands, fathers and sons.[23] The enthusiastic praise of the bravery, activity and commitment of the participants in the revolution that radiates from the pages of those publications remains striking to this day. Stirring descriptions call up images of a Petersburg and Moscow in ferment where everyone—Poles, Russians and representatives of other nationalities—was a soldier in the service of one cause: the victory of socialism.

The stories told by these authors presented a picture of revolutionary and post-revolutionary Russia as a country saturated with the spirit of the "fraternity of nations," of zealous internationalism:

> Those were times of great love and great hatred. I cannot find any other words for this heated atmosphere in which we lived. The Victorious Revolution put fire in our hearts. The awareness that we were creating a new, heretofore unknown world order (and at the time we were only thinking in terms of a global revolution)—gave us wings. There were no small things,

wrote Bobińska.[24] Siekierska presented internationalism not as a foreign idea, instilled in Polish activists on Soviet soil, but rather as something with time-honored traditions: a project, ethos and attitude hammered out in the course of heated disputes in the international forums in which Poles animatedly participated and which found its embodiment in the October Revolution. Internationalism was an element of the upbringing especially of communists coming from the intelligentsia, a part of the culture in which they grew up, of the atmosphere they breathed at the turn of the nineteenth and twentieth centuries. It was, finally, an ingredient of the lives of those who functioned in the multinational political and cultural circles of Europe and who, owing to the views they propagated, were undesired in various places in the continent, as they were considered dangerous to the imperial *status quo*. They had no home to call their own before they found themselves in a Moscow overcome by revolutionary fever—"the Communist Tower of Babel."[25]

However, the memoirs gave no indication that faithfulness to the internationalist ethos excluded attachment to Poland or pride in Polish participation in the communist momentum: "We were proud of the fact that Polish communists contributed to the victory of the October Revolution."[26] The authors often brought up the Polish origins of the revolutionaries: They painted portraits of people "from the Polish soil," who were a part of the "long tradition" of Poland's class- and independence struggles. In the latter half of the 1960s, this emphasizing of the connections with Poland—of "polonizing" the biographies of revolutionaries—became more intense, as, for example, in the memoirs of Marchlewska and Dzerzhinskaya. This may be a reflection of the personal concern of these authors for the (accurate) remembrance of their loved ones, or of the institutional tweaks of editors and publishers, undertaken in response to the animated party and media discussions about the roots and identity of the revolutionary movement in Poland.[27] Marchlewska's memoirs thus provided an image of Julian Marchlewski as primarily a Polish patriot, a connoisseur and avid enthusiast of native literature and a publisher of Polish works concerned with the Polish education of his daughter. The very same text completely passed over his role in the Provisional Polish Revolutionary Committee, an institution created in 1920 that proclaimed the establishment of the Polish Soviet Republic. Dzerzhinskaya, in turn, put great emphasis on her husband's affiliations with the CPP; she highlighted his concern for the situation in Poland, and she recalled his political message for the Polish revolutionary movement. These devices were to project Felix Dzerzhinsky as a "son of the Polish nation," a "fighter for 'your freedom and ours,'" "who became a symbol of the fraternity of the Polish and Russian nations."[28]

This maneuvering of the Polish memory of the October Revolution and the "tinkering" with biographies of Poles who participated in it may have been an attempt at appeasing Polish society's antipathy toward the USSR, something that recurred after 1956. It may have been an attempt at redirecting this antipathy toward tsarism, an attempt at reminding Poles that the tsar was the shared enemy of the Poles, Russians and other Slavic nations, the inhabitants of the old empire of the House of Romanov, and that this hegemony had been overthrown by the joint efforts of the "proletarians of all countries."

The year 1905 was made to look like a breakthrough in the historical map of these struggles—as a moment of great revolutionary upsurge against the tyranny of the Russian Empire. In the memoirs of communist women, this date was of key significance, of founding importance for combining the ideas of class struggle and the struggle for freedom, internationalism and patriotism:

> There came the year 1905, a year of historical events. A rebellion breaks out in the rotten tsarist state. [. . .] Overthrowing tsarism becomes the premise of the victorious struggle for social and national liberation.[29]

In the historical narrative the Polish communist women authors constructed in the 1960s, the Revolution of 1905 became the great predecessor of the October Revolution, but also—which is particularly important in the context of my reflections about the identity and roots of the revolutionary movement in Poland—a moment of cooperation between various leftist forces, especially among the radical ones—the SDKPL and the Polish Socialist Party-Left, whose merger in December 1918 resulted in the establishment of the Communist Workers' Party of Poland (in 1925, its name was changed to the CPP).

In communist women's memoirs, the year 1905 was important also because it was de facto the last moment in the history of the radical Polish left for which it did not have to provide any explanations later on—a moment about which there were no doubts, no need to maneuver around it, to self-criticize or to self-flagellate. Later events no longer seemed this simple and unambiguous, and the authors of the memoirs did not always inform their readers about these complexities; they often mentioned them grudgingly, hesitantly—or, on the contrary, they recited the currently binding directives in an attempt to toe the latest party line.

From the perspective of the 1960s—i.e., the time these memoirs were published—one of the most difficult issues to explain to readers seemed to be the attitude of the Communist Workers' Party of Poland (CWPP) toward the independence of Poland. In 1918, the CWPP shared Rosa Luxemburg's (1871–1919) position that if the Polish proletariat focused on the fight for independence, its attention would be diverted from a more important goal: the social revolution.[30] While waiting for the Bolsheviks and German communists to join them, members of the CWPP did not recognize Poland's independence and boycotted the first parliamentary elections in January 1919. Years later, when Lenin's concept of the "right of nations to self-determination" had become the approved party outlook, Polish communists practiced self-criticism and admitted to having erred, which in party terminology became known as "the error of Luxemburgism" or the "left error." From Dzerzhinskaya's memoirs, it follows that her husband had also made this mistake:

> Dzerzhinsky took the correct position in supporting Lenin. However, as regards the national issue, Felix adopted an erroneous, Luxemburgist stance and he opposed the "right of nations to self-determination" in the program of the RSDLP(B) [Russian Social Democratic Labor Party (Bolsheviks)]. [. . .] later on, he criticized the Luxemburgist views of the SDKPL and his own [view] regarding the national issue, emphasizing that the only correct stance in this matter is that of Lenin, as it is the only one that "leads to victory."[31]

Kamińska, on the other hand, asserted that even though she felt hurt when she opposed a party directive for the first time, she managed to avoid the "error of Luxemburgism," and she did participate in the first Polish elections.[32]

The memoirs presented the question of Poland's independence and of the communists' attitude toward it as one of the internal party disputes, stemming from uncertainty about the direction of the development of the European situation in the early twentieth century. From the perspective of the 1960s, the question of the degree to which the party should have remained faithful to its own social program—class struggle on a world scale—and to what extent it should have adjusted this program to the political context and account for the growing significance of the category of nation and national relations seemed irrelevant.[33] Nevertheless, the authors asked this question. They strove to maintain the delicate balance between the then current party line (under Gomułka) and the lines that had changed many times even before World War II in order to reconcile their own decisions and choices in (different moments of) the past with the later assessment of past events, especially since communists in all circumstances were obliged to follow party discipline.

The memoirs of Maria Kamińska, but also those of Romana Granas (*Gruba Ceśka* [Fat Ceśka, 1958]), Janina Broniewska (*Dziesięć serc czerwiennych* [Ten Red Hearts, 1964], *Maje i listopady* [Mays and Novembers, 1967], *Tamten brzeg mych lat*, [The Other Bank of My Years, 1973]), Jadwiga Sabina Ludwińska (*Drogi i ludzie* [Roads and People, 1967]) and Edwarda Orłowska (*Pamiętam jak dziś* [As If It Was Yesterday, 1973]), offered an image of a "zigzagging" history of the CPP in the 1920s and 1930s, whose line in social and national questions hinged as much on the evaluation of the situation in the country as on the decisions of the Communist International. Internal disputes, factional clashes, mutual accusations of "errors," "provocations," rightist or leftist "deviations," after all the years that had passed, came across as either grotesque or tragic—particularly in the context of the event that was still not to be mentioned straightforwardly, i.e., the disbanding of the CPP in 1938 (after its leading cadres had been murdered on Stalin's orders): "So who exactly was a provocateur? A normal person could not understand it. The deeply-rooted discipline made it unthinkable to rebel against a decision of the International."[34] At the same time, the crux of these disputes seemed still topical in the form of the old/new question of the relation between internationalism and patriotism, between class and independence struggles; it recurred in musings on "the new Marxist Party," no longer with the adjective "communist." These reflections were taken up primarily by Ludwińska, who was one of the few authors of memoirs (besides Orłowska, Fornalska and Duraj) who continued her narrative up to 1945:

> Patriotic tasks had to take center stage, but we thought that in any diversion from the internationalist core of Marxism-Leninism there may have lurked the danger of nationalistic, bourgeois deviation. We

had to continue the line of the CPP and work out a new one, adapted to the changed circumstances of occupied Poland.[35]

Ludwińska's memoirs, alongside Kamińska's, gave the readers the fullest picture of what had happened behind the scenes of the Communist Party in Poland, where its strategy was hammered out; they revealed how this strategy was manipulated to fit the external circumstances. It is difficult to tell to what extent Ludwińska made a conscious, intentional gesture here and to what extent she unintentionally exposed the internal party disputes, racked by doubts regarding the party program. Ludwińska kept returning to the ideological profile of the PWP established in 1942, asking about the relations between the old CPP internationalist ethos and the patriotic, nationalistic program trimmed to fit the new times. She brought up her own doubts and those of other members of the old CPP, as well as the responses of the founders and leaders of the PWP—Marceli Nowotko (1893–1942) and Władysław Gomułka—who, as part of imposing discipline on the activists, recommended that they abandon "orthodox debates over minutiae and stop clinging to traditional mental patterns,"[36] reject "all avant-gardism" and "detachment from the tragic present,"[37] "sectarianism" or the "lingering ghost of the Seventeenth Republic."[38] Even though Ludwińska admitted that "the sense of responsibility and patriotic duty"[39] ultimately had the upper hand, and that they weighed on the pre-war communists finally accepting the program of the PWP, her stubborn repetition of the question about the ideological sources and foundations of the left ethos showed that, even though stifled, old doubts were still smoldering in people close to the party like herself.

Kamińska's memoirs preceded Ludwińska's by nearly a decade, with the antisemitic campaign of March 1968 occurring between them, yet the difference between them evidenced a change in the public self-identification of Polish communist activists that was difficult to miss. In 1960, Kamińska wrote about the CPP of the 1920s:

> The Party would not be pushed off its track. Bravely, despite the incessant arrests, it faced the wild nationalism spreading from all sides. It stood unwavering on the ground of proletarian internationalism, international workers' solidarity. They shouted "traitors!" at us. We were never that. We dreamt of a Polish Soviet Republic, the homeland of the Polish people, and we acted in its name.[40]

But in 1969, Ludwińska only emphasized the "ardent Polish patriotism" of the PWP communists, including its Jewish activists.[41]

Vouching for "Polishness," asserting the "deep sense of national belonging"[42] of communists while simultaneously pointing out their Jewish origins, became the hallmark of the nationalistic turn within the revolutionary movement in Poland.[43] At the same time, it was also a confirmation of the bankruptcy of a universalist historiographic project, which the communist life writers discussed here undertook. And so their attempt at telling the story of the revolutionary movement in Poland, or, better yet, at creating this story based on new foundations, failed, owing to the changing context of the 1960s: The post-revolutionary situation in a way enforced intertwining the history of the communist movement with the history of the nation, turning the latter into a sort of support, a prosthesis that was to keep the entire construction from toppling over. Or, perhaps, the very conviction that such a "support" was necessary was a manifestation of the fragility of this construction and contributed to its erosion. The latter is, I think, what Karl Marx had in mind when he wrote:

> Men make their own history, but they do not make it as they please; they do not make it under self-selected circumstances, but under circumstances existing already, given and transmitted from the past. The tradition of all dead generations weighs like a nightmare on the brains of the living. And just as they seem to be occupied with revolutionizing themselves and things, creating something that did not exist before, precisely in such epochs of revolutionary crisis they anxiously conjure up the spirits of the past to their service, borrowing from them names, battle slogans, and costumes in order to present this new scene in world history in time-honored disguise and borrowed language.[44]

In one way or another, the failure of the historiographic project of the life writers—especially the project constructed in the late 1960s—became a confirmation of the failure of the political project they carried out while in power.

"As These Are Memories, Not History"[45]

Even though these memoirs were part of a certain historiographic project, which they co-created at the same time, one could hardly call them historiographical works. The authors were not professional historians and did not avail themselves of historical sources to support their narratives (Dzerzhinskaya was an exception here, as she quoted various documents, both official and unofficial, from the collections of mostly Soviet archives). The status of their utterances was more that of memory texts, which, unlike historical texts, were "capable of storing 'small narratives'" and as such may have "acted as a counterbalance to the official history."[46]

The authors declared that they had no ambitions to write history. Their aim was to rekindle in their memories events in which they participated, places where they used to be and, especially, the people they once knew. They spoke of this in their forewords:

> The human memory is not infallible. Yet there are events which cannot be forgotten until one's death. There are people whom I met over

my more than half a century of revolutionary and social activity, who are no longer alive, but whose memory deserves to be rescued from oblivion.[47]

Authors who referred to themselves as "witnesses of the times" did not set for themselves the goal of exhausting the topic or of painting a full picture. They called their utterances "cards of the past," thus emphasizing the randomness, fragmented quality and openness of what they wrote. Such a construction, encapsulating a specific time, place and people, along with a number of other narrative and compositional solutions, such as giving exact dates, surnames, names of towns, quoting letters, notes and fragments of diaries written on an ongoing basis, was, to the authors' minds, meant to confirm the authenticity of their memories, to emphasize their documentary character and to protect them against accusations of "fantasizing" or slipping into "literary fiction":

> When I started writing this *Diary*, I eschewed at the outset the greatest aid to a writer, i.e., the right to employ fiction and fantasy. [. . .] *Accuracy in the description* of events and *real* people was precisely what I was after. I cite real names and historical dates. [. . .] My life unfolded such that I found myself in the very midst of great events. I have tried to convey the *unmistakable atmosphere* of those years.[48]

The reference to memory underlines the individual quality of memories: "Only individuals 'have' memory," observes Jan Assmann, while also noting, after Maurice Halbwachs, that the "memory of individuals is created collectively," organized within certain "frameworks" or "horizons."[49] Aleida Assmann also points this out:

> As individuals, we are trapped between different memory horizons and these horizons overlap in increasingly wide circles: the memories of the family, of the generation, of the society, of culture.[50]

The relationship between the memory of individuals and collectives is, however, reflexive, which is to say that the memory of individuals, which is formed within "social frameworks of memory,"[51] participates simultaneously in the process of (re/de)coding these frameworks, of transforming them and changing their scope. Of particular significance in this process is the memory of public figures, of those in power and making decisions. The memory of such individuals is important insofar as, being part of the memory of the dominant groups with which it shares a certain "community of interests and thoughts,"[52] it becomes its "relay," advocate and expression within a larger collective. To paraphrase the words of *The German Ideology* by Karl Marx and Friedrich Engels,[53] we could say that the memory of dominant groups becomes dominant owing, among other things, to the memory of influential individuals who belong to these groups. However, when the memory of such individuals no longer overlaps with the memory of the dominating groups, when it starts to diverge from this "community of interests and thoughts," then it becomes subject to the same mechanisms of control and/or processing as the memory of subordinate groups. Simultaneously, it may start to put up resistance in a similar or identical way.

These mechanisms of (co-)operation and friction/clashes of memory are well illustrated by the example of the memoirs of "retired" Polish communist activists. Belonging to a certain ideological formation—to this dominant group with which they were still linked by a "community of interests and thought" despite some differences—the authors painted a picture of the past that legitimized the present authority of the party. At the same time, however, they tried to negotiate this picture—through their selection of contents, composition and background—to clarify the reasons behind the choices and decisions they made when they were in the power structures, and for which they were now paying the price of political marginalization.

And so the entire "work of narrative configuration" was organized in memoirs around, as Paul Ricoeur put it, "remembrance of those events belonging to the common history that were held to be remarkable, even founding, with respect to the common identity."[54] However, this "remembrance of common history," or, in fact, the fabrication or invention of this common quality, was not always possible. This is because the process was impeded by the memory of subsequent events in authors' life stories and political choices they made during and after the Second World War (that is, affiliation with Stalinism and the Soviet Union), which must have found their reflection on the map of common memory. Therefore, the authors strove to maneuver between the memory of what they considered absolutely common for their ideological and political formation—thus staking out a core, the very heart of this "community of interests and thoughts"—and what fell beyond the framework of this community.

One of the supporting pillars of the construction of the "common history of the communist formation" in the memoirs seemed to be the coherent, unambiguously negative image of the *Sanacja* [sanation][55] authorities, which employed practices similar to the tsarist regime and to Adolf Hitler's. The *Sanacja* authorities were characterized as those responsible for the bad economic situation in the country—for the abject poverty and unemployment. It was also an authoritarian and despotic rule. Lastly, it was an authority born out of an alliance between right-wing politicians and the clergy, factory owners and eastern feudal landholders, reproducing and strengthening national, class, gender and religious inequalities.

Conjuring up a coherent picture of the enemy ("them") made it easier for the authors to construct an equally coherent picture of a force capable of putting up a resistance—i.e., of their own camp ("us"). The memoirs created the radical, communist left as an alternative to the rule of *Sanacja*. That communist left may have been feeble in terms of numbers (as its members were continuously watched over or imprisoned), yet it was infused with ideology, committed and feisty. The tale of the revolutionary ethos of the communists, which recurred in nearly all these memoirs, of their bravery, self-discipline and unwavering capacity for sacrificing their own happiness in the name of a greater idea—was the second solid pillar of the history perceived as "common." The authors emphasized that this ethos was shaped as much in the process of reading revolutionary literature, singing songs and watching and producing dramatic plays, as it was through participation in political manifestations and party meetings, in agitation in factories and in serving long prison sentences for illegal political activity. Always careful to not let the intelligentsia side outweigh the working-class elements, the authors emphasized the cooperation between the two groups and how they strove to learn from each other; they were complementary rather than different:

> After all, these were times of a struggle which would intensify with each passing year. The party led us in this struggle. We felt not only attached to it, but also subordinate to it. Consciously so. There was no third side of the barricade in those years. So "proletarian" poetry and art were also among the party's weapons in this struggle.[56]

Youth, love and revolution acted as threads weaving together the stories of various lives into a single common life of a specific generation—a generation having risen up against the power of capital, religion and bourgeois customs, ready to fight against this power both in the public and private sphere:

> We were connected by love and by fascination for the revolution. [. . .] Internationalism, the sense that we were on a mission, never left us, it also accompanied us at home. It was hard to tell where Party matters ended and personal matters started. It was all tangled up: Party, family, friendships.[57]

Thanks to these threads, there emerged a coherent, romantic picture of a community—of a joint struggle and joint life. This was a very alluring image, which was as nostalgic as it was persuasive. And so the authors, while spinning the yarn of their memories, also spun a determined project of life and struggle—still relevant and still calling for continuation in the new circumstances to be taken up by the new generation.[58]

Yet this image of "common history" and "common experiences" was lined with fissures and cracks, which the authors later indicated in their memoirs as the cause of disagreement that subsequently produced various divergences. Or, in other words, the authors of the memoirs sought justification for their later decisions, choices and steps, determined along the way by a series of factors, in the divergences from a more distant past. Their determined action and behavior in the war and postwar years seemed to stem directly from the pre-war lack of unambiguous answers to certain questions.

A particularly difficult and complex matter that the life writers attempted to tackle after all these years was the issue of "having bet" on the USSR and of having trusted Stalin in times when Polish communists were being murdered and when the CPP was disbanded at his orders. The most difficult topic to broach was that of Stalinist crimes, because when the memoirs first appeared, this topic was still taboo. Although in his speech "On the Cult of Personality and Its Consequences" (1956), Soviet leader Nikita Khrushchev denounced the scale of those crimes, thus shaking up communist men and women in various countries and setting in motion the process of de-Stalinization, his speech did not initiate public and open debate on this subject. The historian Ludwik Hass found that no scientific publication dealing with the purges of 1937–1938, with the disbanding of the CPP in August 1938, or with the reactions of Polish communists to these events appeared in Poland until the latter half of the 1980s.[59] Censorship ensured that this subject, even if brought up, was discussed in the language adopted by the relevant party directives.[60]

The atmosphere of cautiousness must have also infected the authors of the memoirs, which is noticeable in certain fragments that mention the purges and the disbandment of the CPP. In these passages, the authors avail themselves of party language, writing the whole matter off as "provocation," or they use "Aesopic," encoded speech. This code is signaled, for example, by the date (years 1937–1938) and place (Moscow) of the last meeting with the victims of purges or of the last news heard from/about them (this piece of information is often followed by ambiguous points of ellipsis):

> I last saw Ceśka in 1933 in Moscow. . . [. . .] And then came 1937. . .[61]
>
> In mid-September 1937, "Luba" was suddenly called to Moscow. She was surprised and nervous, which made me very anxious. [. . .] "Luba" never returned to the country, although we all kept waiting for her.[62]
>
> The year 1937, sad and tragic to me, was approaching. Three of my children—Fela, Oleś and Staś—fell victim to a horrid provocation or mistake, and, as with many other comrades, they were arrested.[63]

This language—elliptical, sparse, encoded—lends an atmosphere of fear to the memoirs: There are people disappearing in Moscow, while their party comrades receive only shreds of information, and this information casts the "missing" people in a bad light, presenting them as "provocateurs" or "traitors."[64]

Some authors, however, remind us that the deep shock that left a mark on people's memories was an ex post reaction—a reaction to the denunciation of Stalin's crimes, which happened at a specific historical moment and which was used as a tool of political games at the top:

> The violent reaction to the revealed unhealthy phenomena in the international workers' movement, especially after the Twentieth Congress of the Communist Party of the Soviet Union, woke the proverbial beast, i.e., gave rise to revisionism. However, the very shock caused by the Twentieth Congress was a healing factor for the international workers' movement. Yet, as with every shock, the weak and the unsteady were taken over by defeatism, by lack of faith in socialism.[65]

Without diminishing the scale of the crimes, the authors of memoirs attempted to reconstruct the atmosphere of events of the 1930s and their own emotions of those times, as well as their contemporary knowledge: "During my stay in Grodno in May 1938, a Bundist newspaper published a release naming Leński as a traitor. We still treated it as a provocation."[66] The authors wrote not only about a climate of mutual distrust and suspicion exacerbated by the conspiratorial conditions, about intrigues and provocations of the Polish political police, but also about the strong party discipline, which obscured their view of the situation. Their comments on these situations are important to bear in mind, but with the caveat that both claiming a lack of knowledge about particular events, caused by the uncertainty of circumstances in which these events transpired, and appealing to the emotions felt as a result of information acquired with time may be used to justify certain choices and decisions and the reasons underlying them. This gesture, in the individual dimension, may be connected to the wish to give one's own life meaning—to integrate the present "I" with past "I(s)"—and, in the supra-individual dimension, to the desire to ascribe sense to political and social processes in which the authors not only participated but also whose direction they set.[67]

"Women Deserve a Mention?"[68]

In the discussed memoirs, the distant, pre-war past is the subject of particularly meticulous manipulations. Its images are a type of connection between the present and past "I" of the authors; they are a sort of screen onto which they "project" their reasoning, indirectly expressing what is subject to a real prohibition: the memory of the beginnings of the new system, of laying the foundations of the new order, in which the authors had actively participated. An elaborate tale of the pre-war past has a compensatory function: It is a counterbalance to the lack of memories of wartime and especially of the postwar years (the memoirs cover the period up to the beginning of World War II, sometimes until its end). The telling absence of the Stalinist period in these memoirs—a kind of amputation—shows that in the new circumstances, under the rule of Gomułka, the genesis of People's Poland was impossible to articulate.

The question is, what was it that could not be expressed, as far as Stalinism was concerned? In a literal sense, the figure of Stalin has been effaced from the memoirs. The names of people who decided the fate of Poland during and after the war are also veiled in silence: Broniewska did mention Wasilewska, but only as a pre-war writer and activist of the Polish Teachers' Union, and not the wartime leader of the Union of Polish Patriots; Fornalska brought up Bierut's name, but mainly in a private context.[69]

It seems, however, that the thing that could not be expressed was not (just) the names but rather a determined social and political project associated with specific people, or its dimensions that did not fit into the new post-Stalinist order. This involves, for example, the specific "excess of femininity" associated with Stalinism—a type of transgression in which the authors of memoirs took part during the war and later, consisting of the overstepping of boundaries of gender roles in the private and public sphere (for example, being soldiers, political officers, officials and politicians rather than traditional wives and mothers). This led to the redefining of these roles, similarly to the model of the family or the concept of patriotism, redefinitions that were not—and could not be—expressed in the memoirs because they were threatening to the Polish gender and national imaginarium.[70] The authors were silent about their war and postwar public lives (service in the Polish Army in the USSR, holding public functions in postwar Poland), and as to their private lives, they trimmed them to the currently binding models, infusing them with senses that they probably did not have in the past. One fitting example was the polished self-portrait of Dzerzhinskaya as a faithful wife of "Iron Felix" and a caring mother of his son, in which there was no space for her autonomous intimate life, including the long-term affair she had with Adolf Warski (1867–1937), one of the founders of the SDKPL.[71]

A careful reading of these memoirs, however, reveals that the authors did not entirely succeed in keeping silent about things inconvenient from the perspective of the new balance of forces. The suppressed, denied elements often stick out from underneath these texts; they lurk in various crevices, return in persistent repetitions or unintentional mentions—various remarks uttered in a seemingly matter-of-fact way but which in reality are significant. Thus the memoirs illustrate the old Freudian thesis that the forgetting is never innocent or complete:

> Content suppressed into the unconscious echoes in compulsive actions, recurring nightmares and even verbal slips. Besides the *conscious* memory, there is also the sphere of forgetting which finds its way into our imagination in a transformed, "encoded" form.[72]

Examples supporting this diagnosis abound. Broniewska, at the beginning and end of her memoirs, says that *Z notatnika korespondenta wojennego*

[From the Notes of a War Correspondent, 1953], in which she described the war trail of the Polish First "Tadeusz Kościuszko" Infantry Division from USSR to Warsaw, was the "book of her life." Here and there, she also referred to topics outside of the interwar reality, "flashing" images of war-ravaged Warsaw or of herself in the uniform of a Polish Army soldier, which indicated her attachment to the concept of female identity as created and defined in the public rather than in the private sphere. As did other authors, Broniewska also dropped dispersed yet memorable remarks about family being a community based not necessarily on blood ties but rather on shared experiences and views, with the cementing bond of friendship and trust, not of tradition and conventions.[73] Finally, many of these texts were marked by a noticeable tension between the role of a woman as a political activist and her role as a mother, with the greatest taboo embodied in those situations in which public tasks may be more important than the private ones.

According to historian Małgorzata Fidelis, along with the "thaw" in Poland, a gradual return to traditional gender roles began to set in. From the middle of the 1950s, women removed from so-called masculine professions (miners, steelworkers, bricklayers and welders)—which symbolized the "barbaric times of Stalinism"—were directed to work in feminine professions (teachers, nurses, preschool caretakers, etc.), and it was recommended that they combine professional careers with housework and child rearing.[74] The gradual return to traditional values may also be confirmed by the already mentioned removal of women from high-ranking positions in public institutions.[75] Somewhat against the current of the reassignment of traditional gender roles occurring under Gomułka's rule, the female authors who wrote until the mid-1960s focused on exposing women's public agency: They accentuated their pre-war activity in the party, in social and cultural organizations, their participation in strikes and demonstrations, their writing, publishing and propaganda activities (including delivering speeches at meetings and manifestations, which was traditionally considered a male domain owing to men's easier access to public space). Their writing about family life was sparse, on the other hand. However, the memoirs published in the second half of the 1960s had different accents, which may indicate that the conservative turn in Polish gender politics had affected them more strongly: Their authors devoted significant sections of their works to the men to whom they had been close, so much so that at times their own stories were overshadowed by the male biographies. This was particularly the case with Marchlewska, who wrote at length about her father; with Duraj, who paid homage to her brother, Aleksander Zawadzki (1899–1964), a high-ranking postwar political activist (whose offices included deputy prime minister of Poland on two occasions, in 1949 and in 1950–1952); and with Dzerzhinskaya, whose memoirs ended abruptly with information about her husband's death, although she survived him by over 40 years!

Nonetheless, the analyzed publications were not a gender-traditional homage of life writers to the great male heroes of the communist movement.

These books kindled the memory of women involved in radically left political and social activities as much as that of men, and sometimes the former came across as more vivid, easier to grasp, almost physically tangible. The pages of these memoirs were populated with names of prominent women activists of the workers' movement, such as Rosa Luxemburg, Maria Koszutska (1876–1939), Clara Zetkin (1857–1933) and Dolores Ibarruri (1895–1989), but also with names of lesser-known comrades, often from the authors' closest family and social circles: their mothers, aunts, sisters and female friends. The stories of their lives bore the characteristics of feminist herstories, the task of which was to preserve for posterity the memory of relentless fighters for emancipation.

"Women's topics" penetrated these memoirs not only through the spirits of great female ancestors called up in these works but also through the issues raised that were important from the perspective of female narrators and readers. Many authors stressed that what attracted them to the communist movement was their bitter conclusions about the position of women in society:

> The issue of equal rights for women was key for me. Raised among boys, I thought it a matter of honor not to be outdone by them. [. . .] Later, I read books by Karin Michaelis and Ellen Key, and Bebel's seminal *Woman and Socialism*. Equality of rights for women became one of the nodal points of my life program: after all, it promised my own personal liberation, too.[76]

The so-called woman question—i.e., the problem of sexual violence, prostitution, unequal treatment of women at home, school, work, etc.—recurred in the memoirs of female communists both as a theoretical problem, as a task to be tackled by the communist movement, and as a practical one, when it touched their own lives, brutally reminding them of their own "inferior sex."

Not always explicitly, the authors mentioned the fact that despite the lofty slogans of equality between men and women, raising children and housekeeping were still women's domain in the relationships of communists: "There was only one subject we kept silent about, namely, that equality of women was not quite in keeping with Clara Zetkin's guidelines even in our own flock."[77] They concluded that even in relationships with men who had declared their support for emancipation, women could never be certain that their plans and ambitions would be treated with respect:

> Now is the time for a cold assessment of the last few years, when I lived mostly *for him*. Even my child did not absorb me as much as this restless man, who was simultaneously pursuing a doctorate in philosophy and a diploma at the Tharandt Forest Academy near Dresden, who was

always on his way to Party conventions, to meetings with comrades in Leipzig, to Krakow and to Prague. [. . .] Everything throughout these years of my life was circumstantial, hinging on [. . .] him, caught up in the frenetic pace of his life. It is with horror that I now look back at *my* balance sheet of those years.[78]

The authors also raised the issue of double moral standards within the party and of men's disregarding attitude toward them as party comrades: From the memoirs, it follows that crude jokes and patronizing comments were not scarce in the Communist Party and that the party hierarchy was clearly gender-driven.

What we would today call classic discriminatory practices and would condemn, the authors described with caution, often escaping into a light-hearted tone, at times even joking or ironic. These descriptions were marked by a sort of astonishment, embarrassment and shame that they, for whom communism bore the promise of universalism, of equal treatment of all people regardless of sex, religion or ethnic background, were blindsided by gender inequality precisely in the bosom of the communist movement. In the awareness of this fact, there was something of an epiphany, or "awakening," described in a similar way by members of feminism's "second wave," whose beginnings are traced back to the 1960s in the West.[79] However, in opposition to the verbatim message of the young generation of Western feminists, who started to speak of these issues openly, the message of the Polish female communists remained encoded, muted under the surface of the officially sanctioned narrative.

The memoirs of these female Polish communists, similar to nineteenth-century Victorian novels, more resembled women's palimpsests than feminist manifestos: In both these genres, under a layer of meanings compatible with the official discourse on gender there lurked deeply hidden contents that contested the official discourse. Sandra M. Gilbert and Susan Gubar explored this subversive potential in the context of women's Victorian literature:

> Women from Jane Austen and Mary Shelley to Emily Brönte and Emily Dickinson produced literary works that are in some sense palimpsestic, works whose surface designs conceal or obscure deeper, less accessible (and less socially acceptable) levels of meaning. [. . .] in publicly presenting acceptable facades for *private* and dangerous visions women writers have long used a wide range of tactics to obscure but not obliterate their most subversive impulses.[80]

The case of communist memoirs was, however, more complicated, as the visions "smuggled" in by their authors were not private but very much public and political, and as such, they related to models, attitudes and ideals of women's political and public involvement. They were a reservoir of memory of/about the revolution in post-revolutionary times, from which generations of women to come were to draw in new and more favorable circumstances.

Conclusions

In this chapter, I have focused on the analysis of the mechanisms of constructing the history of the left in the memoirs of Polish communist women in the 1960s. I have examined both the contents overtly expressed by life writers and those passed over in silence or hinted at indirectly, in monosyllables, Aesopian language, ironically, sarcastically. I have indicated that most of the memoirs ended abruptly with the description of the outbreak of the Second World War, or its end in 1945, which means that the entire postwar period, when the new, socialist order was established, was left out. I have argued that in the post-Stalinist period, the memory of Stalinism was uncomfortable not only because of the reminiscence of the violence used by the authorities of that time but also because of the reminiscence of values and attitudes they sought to bring to life: internationalist, egalitarian (including in the area of gender policy) and materialistic. In the post-1956 period, marked by the slogan of "building the Polish road to socialism" and by the return to traditional gender roles, the memoirs of female communists, ex-dignitaries of the Communist Party, "smuggled in" the contents that were inconsistent with the party line but still present at the horizon of the memory of "old communists," being part of their pre-war ethos. Thus I have considered the memoirs of female communists as a sort of palimpsest in which some prohibited contents were hidden under the official layer and whose contents were inconvenient for the authorities, as they disturbed the coherence of their message.

Analyzing the memoirs of Polish communist women, which reflected a wider European phenomenon, I have followed traces of the memory of revolution into post-revolutionary times, wondering if it still had its place in the new order of the 1960s.

Notes

1 Marcjanna Fornalska, *Pamiętnik matki* (Warszawa: Książka i Wiedza, 1960), 664.
2 Bronisław Gołębiowski, *Pamiętnikarstwo i literatura: Szkice z socjologii kultury* (Warszawa: Ludowa Spółdzielnia Wydawnicza, 1973), 200.
3 Historian Marcin Zaremba notes that after Gomułka rose to power, "a process of 'dilution' of non-Aryan cadres was initiated, although the scale of this action was not massive. The spotlight was only on the 'Jewish comrades' removed from the security forces, while purges in other institutions took place quietly, without publicity. Many were moved to other positions owing to their background, which was the so-called cadre carousel." Marcin Zaremba, *Komunizm, legitymizacja, nacjonalizm: Nacjonalistyczna legitymizacja władzy komunistycznej w Polsce* (Warszawa: TRIO, 2005), 238. On the other hand, the memoirs

published many years later by the male participants in the "Polish October" of 1956, gathered around the student weekly *Po Prostu* [In Plain Words], one of the central media of the "thaw" period, attested that de-Stalinization in Poland was occurring in the form of removing female party activists from important positions in public institutions of culture, science and education. The figure of a 40–50-year-old communist woman, most frequently of Jewish background, clad in the characteristic party uniform, dogmatic and obligatorily ugly, functioned in these accounts as relics of the loathed Stalinist period. Dubbed "aunts of the revolution," the communist women removed from their positions were alternately depicted as horrific and laughable. Seen as very "unfeminine," they were the opposite of girls connected to *Po Prostu*, characterized as young and pretty, and thus "feminine." These girls were to be the harbinger of the post-Stalinist, "normal," era. See Stefan Bratkowski, ed., *Październik 1956—pierwszy wyłom w systemie: Bunt, młodość, rozsądek* (Warszawa: Prószyński i S-ka, 1996). The figures of the "aunts of the revolution," who were losing power, were also present in the pages of Polish post-thaw literature (Leopold Tyrmand, *Diary 1954*, 1980; Tadeusz Konwicki, *Nowy Świat i okolice* [Nowy Świat Street and Around], 1986). Interestingly, their caricatured portraits were present not only in the works by anti-communist writers (Tyrmand, Konwicki) but also by those involved in communism (Jerzy Putrament, *Małowierni* [Those of Little Faith], 1967).

4 In Douglas's words, "Uncleanness or dirt is that which must not be included if a pattern is to be maintained." Mary Douglas, *Purity and Danger: An Analysis of Concepts of Pollution and Taboo* (London and New York: Rutledge, 2001), 41.

5 It should also be noted that the Polish case, characterized by the relatively large representation of women in the leadership of various public institutions (especially in the sectors of science, culture and education, but also of the economy and even security), in the period immediately following the war and in the Stalinist period, and by the considerable weakening of their position during the "thaw," was not always in sync with the situation of other countries of Central and Eastern Europe. For example, in Czechoslovakia or Romania, the process of removing communist women from their positions had already started during Stalin's lifetime. The most striking example can be found in the biography of Ana Pauker (1893–1960), a Romanian communist of Jewish descent, a deputy prime minister and minister of foreign affairs (1949–1952), whose political role waned in 1952 and who was put under house arrest soon after Stalin's death (earlier, in February 1953, she was imprisoned). See Robert Levy, *Ana Pauker: The Rise and Fall of a Jewish Communist* (Berkeley and Los Angeles: University of California Press, 2001). Marie Švermova (1902–1992), a high-ranking Czechoslovakian politician, a deputy and member of the Political Bureau of the Central Committee of the Communist Party of Czechoslovakia, had a similar fate: On the wave of purges, she was first expelled from the party in 1951 and subsequently imprisoned and questioned with the use of violent methods; she was not released until 1956. (I would like to express my gratitude to Stanislav Holubec from Imre Kertész Kolleg in Jena for this information.) As pointed out by Barbara Evans Clements, in the Soviet Union, on the other hand, Stalin's death was welcomed by the "old Bolshevik" women who had distinguished achievements in the times of the October Revolution as their opportunity to reclaim their status of "founding mothers" of the Party. Barbara Evans Clements, *Bolshevik Women* (Cambridge: Cambridge University Press, 1997), 296–297.

6 See Andrea Pető, "A Missing Piece? How Hungarian Women in the Communist Nomenklatura Are Not Remembering," *East European Politics and Societies* 16.3 (2002): 948–958; Clements, *Bolshevik Women*.

7 See Chiara Bonfiglioli, "Red Girls' Revolutionary Tales: Anti-fascist Women's Autobiographies in Italy," *Feminist Review* 106.1 (2014): 60–77.
8 See Gina Herrmann, *Written in Red: The Communist Memoir in Spain* (Urbana and Chicago: University of Illinois Press, 2010).
9 I omit her case here, mainly because the present analysis is meant to cover only memoirs published as separate books. The memoirs of Wasilewska, which were a record of interviews conducted by historians from the Institute of Party History run by the Central Committee of the Polish United Workers' Party in January 1964, were released in two instalments: In 1968, the magazine *Z Pola Walki* [From the Battlefield] published her memoir up to World War II, while in 1982, the magazine *Archiwum Ruchu Robotniczego* [Archive of the Polish Workers' Movement] published her wartime memoirs, up to 1944. I cover Wasilewska's story in detail in my article "Crossing Boundaries: The Case of Wanda Wasilewska and Polish Communism," *Aspasia: The International Yearbook of Central, Eastern, and Southeastern European Women's and Gender History* 11 (2017): 19–53.
10 For example, Edwarda Orłowska until 1953 had been the head of the Women's Department of the PWP/PUWP and a long-term deputy to Parliament. Janina Broniewska, prior to 1950, had been editor-in-chief of *Kobieta* [Woman] magazine and until 1953 a secretary of the Basic Party Organization in the Council Board of the Polish Writers' Union. Jadwiga Siekierska had been a member of the Council on Culture and Art until 1956, and until 1957, she headed the chair of Dialectical and Historical Materialism at the Institute for the Education of Research Staff. Maria Kamińska, in the years 1947–1949 was the director of the Training Department of the Ministry of Public Security; from 1949 to 1952, she was editor-in-chief of a farmer magazine *Gromada* [Community] and until 1953 served as undersecretary of state at the Ministry of State Agricultural Holdings. Romana Granas, in the years 1950–1957, had been the principal of the two-year Party School of the Central Committee of the Polish United Workers' Party. See Feliks Tych, ed., *Słownik biograficzny działaczy polskiego ruchu robotniczego*, vol. 1 (A-D) (Warszawa: Książka i Wiedza, 1985); vol. 2 (E-J) (Warszawa: Książka i Wiedza, 1987); vol. 3 (K) (Warszawa: Muzeum Niepodległości w Warszawie, 1992).
11 Here is a list of the texts in the chronological order of their publication: Halina Krahelska, *Wspomnienia rewolucjonistki* (Warszawa: Książka i Wiedza, 1957) (first edition, 1934); Romana Granas, *Gruba Ceśka* (Warszawa: Iskry, 1958); Marcjanna Fornalska, *Pamiętnik matki* (Warszawa: Książka i Wiedza, 1960); Jadwiga Siekierska, *Kartki z przeszłości* (Warszawa: Iskry, 1960); Maria Kamińska, *Ścieżkami wspomnień* (Warszawa: Książka i Wiedza, 1960); Helena Bobińska, *Pamiętnik tamtych lat, cz. 1* (Warszawa: Państwowy Instytut Wydawniczy, 1963); Janina Broniewska, *Dziesięć serc czerwiennych* (Warszawa: Iskry, 1964); Anna Jędrychowska, *Zygzakiem i po prostu* (Warszawa: Czytelnik, 1965); Janina Broniewska, *Maje i listopady* (Warszawa: Iskry, 1967); Zofia Marchlewska, *Piórem i pędzlem* (Warszawa: Ludowa Spółdzielnia Wydawnicza, 1967); Wanda Duraj, *W smudze czerwonych iskier* (Warszawa: Czytelnik, 1968); Zofia Dzerzhinskaya, *Lata wielkich bojów* (Warszawa: Książka i Wiedza, 1969); Jadwiga Ludwińska, *Drogi i ludzie* (Warszawa: Książka i Wiedza, 1969); Edwarda Orłowska, *Pamiętam jak dziś* (Warszawa: Książka i Wiedza, 1973); Janina Broniewska, *Tamten brzeg mych lat* (Warszawa: Książka i Wiedza, 1973).
12 See Małgorzata Fidelis, "Are You a Modern Girl? Consumer Culture and Young Women in 1960s Poland," in *Gender Politics and Everyday Life in State Socialist Eastern and Central Europe*, eds. Shana Penn and Jill Massino (New York: Palgrave, 2009), 171–184; Małgorzata Fidelis, "Red State, Golden Youth: The

Student Culture and Political Protest in Poland in the 1960s," in *Between the Avant Garde and the Everyday: Subversive Politics in Europe, 1958–2008*, eds. Timothy Brown and Lorena Anton (Oxford and New York: Berghahn Books, 2011), 145–153.
13 Krahelska, *Wspomnienia rewolucjonistki*, 275.
14 See Georges Gusdorf, "Conditions and Limits of Autobiography," in *Autobiography: Essays Theoretical and Critical*, ed. James Olney (Princeton: Princeton University Press, 1980), 28–48; Stuart Tannock, "Nostalgia Critique," *Cultural Studies* 9.3 (1995): 453–464.
15 See John L. Austin, *How to Do Things with Words: The William James Lectures Delivered at Harvard University in 1955* (Oxford: Clarendon Press, 1962).
16 See Kazimier Szczuka, *Kopciuszek, Frankenstein i inne: Feminizm wobec mitu* (Kraków: Wydawnictwo eFKa, 2001), 27–44.
17 The model readers of those memoirs were primarily the (former) party comrades of the authors, although the total targeted reception (especially among women) was broader, as evidenced by the considerable print runs, repeated new editions and reprints of fragments in women's magazines. For example, the memoirs of Marcjanna Fornalska, daughter of a landless peasant and a serf, who taught herself to read and write at a mature age, and a mother of six communists of whom only one survived the Stalinist purges and Nazi genocide, were published in installments in the women's magazine *Przyjaciółka* [Girlfriend]. I would like to thank Katarzyna Stańczak-Wiślicz from the Institute of Literary Research of the Polish Academy of Sciences in Warsaw for this information.
18 Dzerzhinskaya, *Lata wielkich bojów*, 453.
19 See, for example, Hedda Bartoszek, Stefan Marody and Jan Szewczyk, eds., *My z głodujących miast: Wspomnienia ZWM-owców z lat okupacji* (Warszawa: Wydawnictwo MON, 1961); Henryk Smolak, ed., *Taki był początek: Wspomnienia działaczy PPR Dolnego Śląska* (Wrocław: Zakład Narodowy im. Ossolińskich, 1962). Historian Tomasz Siewierski notes that within the Institute of Party History, the research interests coincided with the fault lines of generational divides: "The younger generation of Party historians was interested in the period of time closer to their own Party activity, while the older generation cared more about the distant past." Tomasz Siewierski, "Specyfika badań nad tzw: ruchem robotniczym w historiografii PRL: Zarys problemu," in *Letnia Szkoła Historii Najnowszej IPN: Referaty 2012*, eds. Kamil Dworaczek and Łukasz Kamiński (Warszawa: Instytut Pamięci Narodowej, 2013), 181. Therefore, besides the collections of memoirs involving communists during the war and afterward, volumes on the activity of the pre-war CPP were also published. See, for example, Leonard Borkowicz, ed., *Komuniści: Wspomnienia o Komunistycznej Partii Polski* (Warszawa: Książka i Wiedza, 1969).
20 Jerzy Eisler, *Siedmiu wspaniałych: Poczet pierwszych sekretarzy KC PZPR* (Warszawa: Czerwone i Czarne, 2014), 221–222.
21 As a result of the antisemitic witch hunt of 1967–1968, with its culmination in March 1968, a few thousand Jewish activists were expelled from the PUWP and over 15,000 Polish Jews left the country. See Jerzy Eisler, *"Polskie miesiące," czyli kryzys(y) w PRL* (Warszawa: Instytut Pamięci Narodowej, 2008), 34.
22 Zaremba, *Komunizm, legitymizacja, nacjonalizm*, 290.
23 Helena Bobińska was the first, and Jadwiga Siekierska the second, wife of Stanisław Bobiński (1882–1937) who in 1918 was deputy head of the Polish Commissariat of the People's Commissariat for Nationality Affairs and in 1920 a member of the Provisional Polish Revolutionary Committee (Polrevkom) for agriculture. Zofia Dzerzhinskaya was married to Felix Dzerzhinsky (1877–1926), founder and chief of the Cheka and member of Polrevkom. Zofia Marchlewska

was the daughter of Julian Marchlewski (1866–1925), cofounder of the Communist International in 1919 and chair of Polrevkom. Marcjanna Fornalska was the mother of Aleksander Fornalski (1899–1937) and soldier of the Revolutionary Division of the Red Guards in Tsaritsyn. Interestingly, Fornalska devoted about the same space in her memoirs to the service of her daughters—Felicja Fornalska (1893–1987) and Małgorzata Fornalska (1902–1944)—in the First Tsaritsyn Communist Battalion, their political activity in the Russian Communist Party (Bolsheviks) and the Social Democracy of the Kingdom of Poland and Lithuania (SDKPL), and their social activity within the Party, e.g. organizing and volunteering in orphanages.

24 Bobińska, *Pamiętnik tamtych lat*, 196.
25 Siekierska, *Kartki z przeszłości*, 72. For more about the activities of Polish communists during the October Revolution, see Konrad Zieliński, *O Polską Republikę Rad: Działalność polskich komunistów w Rosji Radzieckiej 1918–1922* (Lublin: Wydawnictwo UMCS, 2013).
26 Siekierska, *Kartki z przeszłości*, 51.
27 Marcin Zaremba points out that under Gomułka's rule, there were lively discussions within the PUWP about national and internationalist traditions in the Polish workers' movement. Zaremba brings up, for example, the heated disputes sparked by Zbigniew Załuski's book *Siedem polskich grzechów głównych* [Seven Polish Cardinal Sins, 1963] and his lecture for the Party apparatus entitled *Tradycje patriotyczne a współczesny kształt patriotyzmu socjalistycznego* [Patriotic Traditions and the Contemporary Shape of Socialist Patriotism, 1967]. Zaremba, *Komunizm, legitymizacja, nacjonalizm*, 291–298.
28 Dzerzhinskaya, *Lata wielkich bojów*, 6. The manipulations of Dzerzhinskaya around the memory of her husband were to be a response to the request made by the publisher of her memoirs. In the *Note from the Publisher*, we read, "The entire work differs somewhat from the Russian book: we have eliminated from it the fragments of less significance to the Polish reader. Some passages have also been moved to different places, and material dispersed throughout the book has been collated into a new separate chapter entitled: 'Felix Dzerzhinsky and the Communist Party of Poland.' All the changes have been agreed upon with the author." Dzerzhinskaya, *Lata wielkich bojów*, 6.
29 Marchlewska, *Piórem i pędzlem*, 49.
30 See, for example, Rosa Luxemburg, "Foreword to the Anthology *The Polish Question and the Socialist Movement*," in *The National Question: Selected Writings by Rosa Luxemburg*, ed. Horace B. Davis (New York and London: Monthly Review Press, 1976), 60–100.
31 Dzerzhinskaya, *Lata wielkich bojów*, 310–311.
32 Kamińska, *Ścieżkami wspomnień*, 155–156.
33 See Eric J. Hobsbawm, *Nations and Nationalism Since 1780: Programme, Myth, Reality* (Cambridge: Cambridge University Press, 1992), 131–162.
34 Ludwińska, *Drogi i ludzie*, 42.
35 Ludwińska, *Drogi i ludzie*, 67.
36 Ludwińska, *Drogi i ludzie*, 81.
37 Ludwińska, *Drogi i ludzie*, 84.
38 Ludwińska, *Drogi i ludzie*, 159. Turning Poland into the Seventeenth Soviet Republic, instead of an independent state, was one of the elements of the "Luxemburgist" vision of the country's fate, popular in some circles of the pre-war CPP.
39 Ludwińska, *Drogi i ludzie*, 159.
40 Kamińska, *Ścieżkami wspomnień*, 208.
41 Ludwińska, *Drogi i ludzie*, 127. The so-called Jewish Question, or the matter of the authors' Jewish self-identification, of the communists' attitude toward the "Jewish Question," including especially the issue of how to be active among the

Jewish masses, and how to deal with antisemitism in Poland, merits a lengthier exploration. Here, I only present a few brief diagnoses. First, although we know from many academic sources that Dzerzhinskaya (née Muszkat), Bobińska (née Brun), Kamińska (née Eiger), Ludwińska (née Goldszlak), Orłowska (née Mirer) and Granas were all of Jewish descent, the authors themselves did not usually bring this up. It is difficult to assess whether they were silent because the issue seemed irrelevant to their sense of communist identity, or if it was a defense strategy. Only Kamińska wrote that she had been born in a family of Polish Jews, yet, at the same time, she emphasized that it was a fully assimilated, bourgeois family, far removed from the orthodox Jewish masses "still stuck in the depths of the Middle Ages." Kamińska, *Ścieżkami wspomnień*, 187. Second, the memoirs revealed divergent views at the core of the Communist Party about the methods of work to adopt among the Jewish masses. Kamińska wrote that members of the SDKPL and of the Polish Socialist Party-Left were against the "organization of lectures and talks in the Jewish language. In their fight against the separatism of the Bund, they were of the opinion that Yiddish will make it difficult to build a common front of Polish and Jewish workers." Kamińska, *Ścieżkami wspomnień*, 188. Orłowska, on the other hand, mentioned activists from the CPP who, "wishing to remove language barriers impeding communication, clarification of the Party line, and winning over honest people," intensively studied various languages, including Yiddish. Orłowska, *Pamiętam jak dziś*, 94. Ludwińska, who mostly dealt with the beginnings of the PWP, did not pay any attention to the party's attitude toward the "Jewish Question." She only emphasized the "sense of national belonging" and the "heartfelt Polish patriotism," which bound Polish and Jewish communists together and which was manifested in the "joint fight against the occupier." Ludwińska, *Drogi i ludzie*, 126, 133–134. Third, the phenomenon of antisemitism in pre-war and wartime Poland was not a major topic in these memoirs. Kamińska recalled that she was aware of antisemitism more through the newspapers than through her own experience; at the same time, she distinguished between the internationalism of the popular and working masses and the antisemitism of the moneyed class. Kamińska, *Ścieżkami wspomnień*, 157, 187–192. Broniewska devoted the most space to antisemitism. She too insisted on the "genuine proletarian internationalism, the solidarity of young Polish workers, who punished the beating up of Jews with 'butt-kickings' administered to uniform-clad members of student societies, richly adorned in gold and silver after the fashion of German academics." Broniewska, *Dziesięć serc czerwiennych*, 107. She also brought up rural pogroms but presented them as a sad example of the policy practiced by the rich who had succeeded in harnessing the frustration of the poor and in directing it against Jews. Broniewska, *Tamten brzeg mych lat*, 135–137. Ludwińska associated antisemitism exclusively with the pre-war rhetoric and practice of the National Radical Camp and with the wartime pursuits of the National Armed Forces, which she compared to the politics of Hitler. She kept quiet about the antisemitism of Poles, yet at the same time, she did mention the relentless "cross-fire" of looks that she had been subjected to during the war owing to her "suspicious appearance." Ludwińska, *Drogi i ludzie*, 103, 107, 113. What she did emphasize was the wartime heroism of Poles who saved Jews. Ludwińska, *Drogi i ludzie*, 132.

42 Ludwińska, *Drogi i ludzie*, 127.
43 Marcin Zaremba reports that in 1969, "for the first time in the history of the Polish Communist Party the personal survey, which formed part of the system of evaluation and recording of party cadres, was extended to include the rubric 'nationality.'" Zaremba, *Komunizm, legitymizacja, nacjonalizm*, 351–352.
44 Karl Marx, *The Eighteenth Brumaire of Louis Bonaparte*, trans. Saul K. Padover et al. (Moscow: Progress Publishers, 1972), 10.

45 Orłowska, *Pamiętam jak dziś*, 7.
46 Marcin Napiórkowski, "Jak społeczeństwa pamiętają Paula Connertona na tle współczesnych badań nad pamięcią zbiorową," in Paul Connerton, *Jak społeczeństwa pamiętają*, trans. Marcin Napiórkowski (Warszawa: Wydawnictwo Uniwersytetu Warszawskiego, 2012), 23.
47 Orłowska, *Pamiętam jak dziś*, 5.
48 Bobińska, *Pamiętnik tamtych lat*, on the jacket flaps. Emphases in original.
49 Jan Assmann, *Cultural Memory and Early Civilization: Writing, Remembrance, and Political Imagination* (New York: Cambridge University Press, 2011), 22.
50 Aleida Assmann, "1998—między historią a pamięcią," trans. from the German Magdalena Saryusz-Wolska, in *Pamięć zbiorowa i kulturowa: Współczesna perspektywa niemiecka*, ed. Magdalena Saryusz-Wolska (Kraków: Universitas, 2009), 158.
51 See Maurice Halbwachs, *On Collective Memory*, trans., ed. and introduction Lewis A. Coser (Chicago: University of Chicago Press, 1992).
52 Paul Connerton, *How Societies Remember* (Cambridge: Cambridge University Press, 1989), 37.
53 The original words are: "The ideas of the ruling class are in every epoch the ruling ideas." Karl Marx and Friedrich Engels, *The German Ideology*, trans. Clemens Dutt, William Lough and Charles Philip Magill, ed. and introduction Chris J. Arthur (London: Lawrence and Wishart, 1970), 64.
54 Paul Ricoeur, *Memory, History, Forgetting*, trans. Kathleen Blamey and David Pellauer (Chicago and London: University of Chicago Press, 2004), 85.
55 *Sanacja*, after the Latin word *sanatio* [healing], a political movement of Józef Piłsudski's associates who came to power in May 1926 and remained influential until 1939. Józef Piłsudski (1867–1935) was a national political leader who played the key role in securing Polish independence in 1918 and who in 1926 became the dictator of Poland.
56 Broniewska, *Dziesięć serc czerwiennych*, 292. Most of my protagonists originated from intelligentsia families with landed gentry or bourgeois pedigree. Only Fornalska was of peasant background, and Duraj was born into a workers' family. Most of them lived in central and western Poland prior to the war (Warsaw, Łódź, Zagłębie Dąbrowskie), although there was no shortage of those who had tied their fates to eastern Poland (Fornalska with Lublin, Orłowska with Białystok), including also the so-called Eastern Borderlands (Jędrychowska with Vilnius, Orłowska with Grodno), incorporated into Lithuania and Belarus according to the stipulations of the Yalta Conference of February 1945. Dzerzhinskaya, Bobińska, Siekierska, Marchlewska and Fornalska (for a significant part of her lifetime) lived and worked in the USSR following the October Revolution, mainly in Moscow.
57 Siekierska, *Kartki z przeszłości*, 27, 64.
58 The memoirs of communists fit into the lively discussion on the issue of generation and the generation gap that took place in Poland in the 1960s. The wave of youth protests that rolled through Europe and the rest of the world at the time had also reached Poland. See Małgorzata Fidelis, "The Other Marxists: Making Sense of International Student Revolts in Poland in the Global Sixties," *Zeitschrift für Ostmitteleuropa-Forschung* 62 (2013): 425–449. The utterances of older-generation communists, centered on ideas of youth, love and revolution, pointed to both differences from and similarities to the experience of the newer generation; the authors declared their sense of separateness but also proximity to the new generation. Janina Broniewska gave the fullest expression of this: "I dedicate the issues contained in these old letters, which nevertheless remain eternally common to all generations, [. . .] along with everything that is yet to come, [. . .] to an entire generation, so that it may confront its own youth with

our distant youth. Radically different, in both its difficulties and joys, yet youth all the same." Broniewska, *Dziesięć serc czerwiennych*, 11.
59 Ludwik Hass, "Reakcje komunistów w Polsce na rozwiązanie KPP (1938 r.)," *Dzieje Najnowsze* 1.2 (1990): 159–168.
60 Regarding the trope of purges, the censorship interfered with Kamińska's text. It was recommended that the author change the following original phrase: "He then shared the fate of Polish comrades in the USSR" to "He later fell victim to provocation." See Archive of New Records, Main Office for Control of the Press, Publications and Public Performances, 645, file 68/59, sheet 49. The censors were also worried about the "excessive exposure" by Fornalska of the theme of Stalinist repression suffered by her three sons and daughter. In the end, the author was not required to make adjustments, as it was understood that her anxiety about the fate of her children did not affect her attitude toward communism. See Archive of New Records, Main Office of Control of Press, Publications and Public Performances, 645, file 68/59, sheet 42.
61 Granas, *Gruba Ceśka*, 10, 113.
62 Orłowska, *Pamiętam jak dziś*, 320.
63 Fornalska, *Pamiętnik matki*, 539.
64 It was not until after 1989 that the Stalinist purges of the 1930s could be spoken of openly. The transformation was followed by the publication of many memoirs either by communist men and women who had personally suffered from the repression in the USSR (for example, Celina Budzyńska, *Strzępy rodzinnej sagi* [Shreds of a Family Saga], 1997) or by the children or grandchildren of victims (for example, Joanna Olczak-Ronikier, *W ogrodzie pamięci* [In the Garden of Memory], 2001; Witold and Stefan Leder, *Czerwona nić* [The Red Thread], 2005; Karol Modzelewski, *Zajeździmy kobyłę historii* [We'll Ride the Mare of History into the Ground], 2013). Sadly, especially in the accounts by descendants of victims of Stalinist purges, instead of an attempt at understanding and respecting the life choices of their relatives, even if they had a tragic end, we find judgmental evaluations of both their attitudes and the movement they were involved in. The compassion for relatives who had been painfully tested by history is intertwined in these accounts with a condemnation of their role in creating this very history; the distinctly moralizing tones are very much in line with the dominant Polish discourse on communism, and at times they are even more critical than mainstream opinion is. I have written about the memory of communism in Polish families in my article " 'Dziadek (nie) był komunistą': Między/transgeneracyjna pamięć o komunizmie w polskich (auto)biografiach rodzinnych po 1989 roku," *Teksty Drugie* 1 (2016): 46–67.
65 Siekierska, *Kartki z przeszłości*, 76.
66 Orłowska, *Pamiętam jak dziś*, 322. Julian Leszczyński-Leński (1899–1939), leader of the Stalinist faction in the CPP, led the party in the 1930s, and himself fell victim to Stalin's purges.
67 Gusdorf, "Conditions and Limits of Autobiography," 28–48.
68 Broniewska, *Dziesięć serc czerwiennych*, 246.
69 The author's granddaughter, Ola, was born in 1932 from the informal relationship of Bierut and Fornalska's daughter Małgorzata, a member of the Second Initiative Group of the PWP. A query conducted at the Archive of New Records reveals that Marcjanna Fornalska's public disclosure of the information regarding Bierut's illegitimate child at first caused considerable misgivings among the censors. Ultimately, however, the censors who expressed opinions on this text prior to its publication did not recommend any adjustments. See Archive of New Records, Main Office of Control of Press, Publications and Public Performances, 645, file 68/59, sheet 42.

70 See Alicja Kusiak-Brownstein, "Płeć kulturowa, 'doświadczenie' i wojna—kilka metodologicznych uwag o wykorzystaniu relacji wspomnieniowych," in *Kobieta i rewolucja obyczajowa: Społeczno-kulturowe aspekty seksualności: Wiek XIX i XX*, eds. Anna Żarnowska and Andrzej Szwarc (Warszawa: Wydawnictwo DiG, 2006), 421–436.

71 The story of Dzerzhinskaya's affair with Warski is told in unpublished letters. See Sylwia Frołow, *Dzierżyński. Miłość i rewolucja* (Kraków: Znak, 2014), 140–142, 313.

72 Napiórkowski, "*Jak społeczeństwa pamiętają* Paula Connertona," 15. Emphases in original.

73 In her memoirs, Broniewska recalled a picture of the "patchwork family" that she formed in the late 1930s with the revolutionary poet Władysław Broniewski (1897–1962), her husband from whom she was separated; her new partner, a communist activist Romuald Gadomski (1905–1974); and Broniewski's new partner, actress Maria Zarębińska (1904–1947). There were also children involved in this arrangement: Anka (1929–1954), the daughter of Broniewskis, and Majka (born 1931), daughter of Zarębińska and of Zbigniew Kornacki (deceased in 1933), whom Broniewski later adopted. Prior to the onset of the war, they all lived in the same building in the Warsaw district of Żoliborz. Broniewska, *Tamten brzeg mych lat*, 302–303. In another fragment, she also described her "family of choice," which she formed with her best friend Wanda Wasilewska and her second husband, a bricklayer and activist, Marian Bogatko (1906–1940). Broniewska, *Maje i listopady*, 242, 244.

74 Małgorzata Fidelis, *Women, Communism, and Industrialization in Postwar Poland* (Cambridge: Cambridge University Press, 2010).

75 Historian Mirosław Szumiło observes that "in the period of Gomułka's rule, the role of women in the party apparatus decreased radically. In the 1960s, not a single woman held the function of department head in the Central Committee." Mirosław Szumiło, "Kadra kierownicza aparatu kierowniczego KC PPR-PZPR w latach 1944–1956," in *Dzieje biurokracji na ziemiach polskich*, vol. 1, eds. Artur Górak, Ireneusz Łuć and Dariusz Magier (Lublin-Siedlce: Stowarzyszenie Inicjatyw Lokalnych, 2009), 584.

76 Kamińska, *Ścieżkami wspomnień*, 128–129.

77 Broniewska, *Dziesięć serc czerwiennych*, 242.

78 Bobińska, *Pamiętnik tamtych lat*, 70–71. Emphases in original.

79 See, for example, Rachel Blau DuPlessis and Ann Snitow, eds., *The Feminist Memoir Project: Voices from Women's Liberation* (New Brunswick: Rutgers University Press, 2007).

80 Sandra M. Gilbert and Susan Gubar, *The Madwoman in the Attic: The Woman Writer and the Nineteenth-Century Literary Imagination* (New York: Yale Nota Bene, 2000), 73, 74. Emphasis mine.

9 Romanian Communists Under Gheorghiu-Dej

Legitimation Before 1965 and Its Memory as Opposition to Ceauşescu

Monica Ciobanu

It is significant that in their analysis of recent Romanian history, memory studies and transitional justice scholars in general emphasize two important variables that shaped (and to a degree still explain) the country's post-1989 reckoning with its past. In the first place, the communist regime was characterized by the personalized rule of Nicolae Ceauşescu, which had been based on a nationalist-xenophobic ideology and the control of a repressive secret police (Securitate). Second, a chaotic transition to democracy following an abrupt and violent popular uprising and the execution of Ceauşescu and his wife, resulting in a takeover by a provisional political body—the National Salvation Front (FSN)—dominated by former lower-echelon communist activists and other elements associated with the regime.[1] In contrast to a wide range of state and non-state projects to preserve the memory and reconstruct the history of communist repression and the 1989 popular revolt, no systematic attempt has been made to recover the early history of the Romanian Communist Party (PCR) within the wider project of manufacturing an official narrative. Little or no attention has been paid to how the political socialization of an older generation of communists under Ceauşescu's predecessor Gheorghe Gheorghiu-Dej, who wielded power between 1948 and 1965, has influenced either memory politics or the political performance of the FSN as the heir to the PCR.

This chapter attempts to fill the gap by addressing two distinct but interrelated issues: first, why the memory of communism has remained marginal in the post-1989 left and second, how this has affected the ability of former communists to reinvent and represent themselves as credible democratic actors during the first decade of the democratic transition.

The framework for this analysis begins with a brief overview of the December '89 revolution and its political aftermath, which has shaped the nature of post-communist memory politics. This is followed by a reexamination of the history of the first two decades of the PCR in the context of the post-1989 politics of memory—a period covering the beginning of the country's transformation into a socialist satellite of the Soviet Union after

World War II until the withdrawal of Soviet troops in 1958. In the following years, the party's history was revised from a national communist perspective, and a cult of personality emerged under Gheorghiu-Dej, the then party leader until his death in 1965. But Dej's image as the true Romanian communist was quickly dismantled and appropriated in even more extreme forms by Ceaușescu, his successor. Ceaușescu skillfully built his own apparatus of loyalists and marginalized the Dej-era, first-echelon party apparatchiks. Unable to transform themselves into a reformist faction within the party, they did little more than engage in belated criticism of Ceaușescu's policies and his cult of personality. This is the case of the "Letter of the Six" (*Scrisoarea celor șase*) signed by several older communists and released by Radio Free Europe in 1989, which deplored the severe decline in living standards and the country's international isolation. Finally, I will examine the position some of these former party officials took on the communist past in putting most of the blame on Ceaușescu for its misdeeds. In the process, they aimed to restore the memory of Dej as a genuine communist and a patriotic leader. However, this attempt failed to resonate in post-communist public rhetoric, nor did it result in any significant efforts by members of previous political elites to manufacture a new identity for the left that could be grounded in the memory of this earlier communism.

The December 1989 Revolution and the Politics of Memory

By the 1980s, the communist regime in Romania had become entirely dominated by Ceaușescu's clan and a small group of loyalists. At the same time, the standard of living had significantly declined, and the country began to experience the full effect of an imposed economy of shortages. This had resulted from ill-conceived and inefficient economic policies geared to over-industrialization combined with the PCR's strategy of national economic independence, which was realized by paying off the large foreign debt accumulated in the 1970s. This was done at the population's expense. The regime attempted to justify the resulting harsh living conditions with nationalist-xenophobic propaganda. This use of an extremist ideology of national survival together with a repressive Securitate was the principal foundation of the regime and prevented the emergence of any organized civil-society opposition movement. Acts of dissidence were disparate and isolated.[2]

At the time, the country seemed almost immune to the political upheavals and changes occurring elsewhere in the region as well as in the Soviet Union. But in 1989, seen as an *annus mirabilis* across Eastern Europe, state socialism collapsed, and the future suddenly seemed to belong to democratic liberalism and the prospect of free markets. Regime change in Hungary and Poland was peaceful and followed a roundtable model. After communists in Poland initiated negotiations in February 1989 with the opposition represented by the working-class Solidarity movement, similar developments (following slightly different scenarios) occurred shortly afterward in Hungary, East Germany, Czechoslovakia and Bulgaria.³ At the same time, the policies of *glasnost* and *perestroika* initiated by Soviet leader Mikhail Gorbachev in the mid-1980s, which sought reform of the socialist economy and public life as a whole, were still unfolding. Although many believed that the end of the regime was imminent, given the lack of credible alternatives, it was not clear when and how it would occur.

But on December 15, 1989, the revolution began in Timișoara (a large multiethnic city in the western part of the country). Here the local population rallied against the police's attempt to remove the Hungarian reformist priest Laszlo Tokes forcibly from his parish, which turned a small-scale ethnic and religious protest into a broad anti-Ceaușescu movement. It is no coincidence that popular dissatisfaction and frustration exploded in this part of the country. It was historically more prosperous, more exposed to outside influences and possessed a long tradition of multicultural coexistence. Violent encounters between protesters and the military forces sent to reestablish order led to a significant death toll. Unrest then spread to the capital after Ceaușescu called a mass meeting in Bucharest's Republic Square on December 21 to rally support against a so-called anti-national plot allegedly organized from abroad by the East and the West. The rally, however, quickly turned into an anti-Ceaușescu protest.⁴ Immediately, a new provisional political body, the National Salvation Front (FSN) and its leadership body, the National Council (CNFSN), emerged virtually spontaneously. The execution of Ceaușescus followed on December 24 after a mock military trial.⁵ Still, street fighting continued until the end of December. Casualties of the uprising included 1,142 deaths, 3,138 wounded and 760 imprisoned.⁶

This brief excursion into the Romanian Revolution and its extraordinary *mise-en-scène* is crucial for understanding the way in which memory politics was shaped after 1989 by the principal political actors. These were represented by both former communists and the newly reestablished pre-World War II historical parties, the National Liberal Party (PNL) and the National Peasant Christian-Democratic Party (PNȚCD). It also explains the subsequent public identification of the former dictator, whose image was quickly vilified and demonized, with the communist regime in general. The CNFSN, the new leadership of the FSN, was predominantly staffed by former lower-echelon party activists and officials. Former dissidents and intellectuals who were initially included in the CNFSN, such as Ana Blandiana, Mircea Dinescu, Radu Filipescu and Doina Cornea, realizing this, quickly withdrew their support. Throughout the 1990s, the legitimizing rhetoric of the FSN became rooted in the revolutionary ethos of December 1989 as the defining moment for the break with the regime. Some of the important figures in the council included Silviu Brucan (a former managing editor of *Scînteia* [Spark]—the official newspaper of the PCR between 1944 and 1947, ambassador to the US between 1955 and 1959 and to the United Nations from 1959 to 1962), Alexandru Bârlădeanu (a well-known Marxist economist who held key positions including minister of foreign trade from 1948 until 1954, president of the State Planning Committee from 1955 to 1957 and first deputy prime minister, 1965–1967) and Corneliu Mănescu (a former diplomat who served as minister of foreign affairs from 1961 to 1972 and president of the United Nations General Assembly in 1967–1968). All three were signatories of the aforementioned "Letter of the Six." Ion Iliescu himself, the newly proclaimed leader of the FSN, had been a member of the PCR since 1953, became part of its Central Committee in 1965, and served as minister of youth from 1967 until 1971. Since the early 1970s, he had been marginalized by Ceaușescu who regarded him as a potential rival and relegated him to secondary positions in the party.

In fact, on December 22, in the first communiqué of the CNFSN on national television, Iliescu announced the dismantling of the existing power structure, including the State Council, and the subordination of all state institutions to the FSN.[7] And so the PCR, which was one of the largest mass parties in the region (estimated at four million members), and all the other state institutions associated with it, disappeared overnight. In this way, the FSN appealed to a majority who neither opposed nor supported the regime but were willing to be counted among those who overthrew the dictator. Also, given the difficulties of daily existence, minimal measures taken by the NSF, including shortening the work week from six to five days, legalization of abortion and increasing the availability of goods in markets, brought a sense of normalcy and security. While many had experienced in their lifetime little else but the hardships of late socialism, there was a wave of nostalgia for the more prosperous days of socialism in the late 1960s and early 1970s among a large segment of the population that remembered them, and the FSN's rhetoric contributed to this.[8]

In this context, the first transitional justice measures undertaken by the FSN were to erase communist symbols and erect new ones celebrating the victors and heroes of the revolution. The FSN legitimized itself as the direct heir of the December revolution. It also manufactured the myth of the December popular uprising as a national revolution. In addition, it also granted generous financial and social compensation to those who had participated and were wounded in the revolution (celebrated as hero-martyrs), as well as their families and the families of the dead.[9] But despite this celebration of the revolution and its heroes, legal prosecutions against those in the senior ranks of the PCR directly responsible for the attempt to suppress the events of December 1989 were minimal. The sentences given in 1990 at the trial of 24 members of the Political Executive Committee of the party who approved Ceaușescu's decision to use force were, by the mid-1990s, reduced or annulled.[10] Upon their release, two of the latter—Paul Niculescu-Mizil and Dumitru Popescu—became staunch defenders of communism and quite vocal in rehabilitating the image of the party.[11] But the new political authority showed little interest in investigating the violence that had occurred after the execution of the Ceaușescus or in establishing the responsibility of Securitate officers and army factions for some of this violence.[12]

As for the newly emerging opposition represented by the historical parties, some civic associations, of which the most significant were the Civic Alliance, former dissidents associated with the Group for Social Dialogue and political prisoners represented by the Association of Former Political Prisoners, immediately engaged in virulent anti-communist rhetoric. The unwillingness of the FSN and its various successors to address the crimes and abuses committed by the communist regime has shaped the ideological polarization between the two opposing forces. From 1989 to 2004, these two main political actors showed no interest in constructive dialogue or compromise and instead engaged in confrontational politics that reinforced a violent political climate.[13]

The front's decision to participate in the first elections on May 20, 1990, deepened the conflict between the historical parties and the ex-communists. From January through May, inflammatory language and street violence indicated a serious lack of interest in any reconciliation and dialogue between both sides. While anti-communist actors demanded the banning of the PCR and all previous officials from key positions in public life, the ex-communists called the opposition fascists, greedy heirs of the bourgeoisie and landowners, and destined to sell the country's assets to Western capitalists. This rhetoric appealed to the industrial working class and particularly to those working in mining and heavy industry. For them, December '89 meant the overthrow of the dictator and not a change in the system. Given their fear of losing socialist benefits, they were easily incited by an anti-capitalist and intellectual message.[14] The elections resulted in an overwhelming victory for the FSN with almost 67 percent of the votes, followed by the Hungarian Democratic Alliance of Hungarians in Romania with no more than 7 percent. The historical parties' gains were rather modest (the PNL scored less than 7 percent overall and PNȚCD garnered 3 percent). Iliescu's victory in the presidency further deepened the current trend to political polarization. On June 13, 1990, he called in the security forces and 10,000 miners from the Jiu Valley to defend democracy from the threat of "fascists" and "hooligans" in Bucharest. Anti-communist demonstrators in University Square, who had refused to vacate it after the elections, were beaten, arrested and a few shot. The miners and some security forces terrorized citizens in the capital for several days. They particularly targeted students, intellectuals, members of the opposition parties, civic activists and journalists. This climate of suspicion and intolerance was very reminiscent of post-1944 Romania when the country withdrew from its military alliance with Nazi Germany. At that time, a small Communist Party backed by the Soviet authorities took over the government and imposed its hegemony over the country, deploying terror exercised by revolutionary vigilantes.

The Romanian Communist Party (1944–1965): From Soviet Subservience to the Myth of National Independence

During the interwar period, Romania was a constitutional monarchy. A smooth alternation in power between the two historical parties ensured a relatively stable political system. Given the predominantly agrarian nature of the economy and the relatively low level of urbanization, the Social Democratic Party (PSD)—the biggest party of the left—lacked a strong base. In addition, especially since the 1930s, an extremist right-wing nationalist, fascist and antisemitic legionary movement with strong mystical-Christian roots—the Iron Guard—gained a robust foothold in rural areas and among students, intellectuals and some segments of the Orthodox Church.[15] Moreover, the creation of the Communist (Third) International (Comintern) in March 1919 weakened the PSD further as the party split into two principal factions. The first, which indiscriminately adhered to the Bolshevik line, advocated revolution and immediate affiliation with international communism. Among the members of the "maximalist" group, the presence of Ana Pauker was crucial. She would play a major role in the Sovietization process after 1944. Her rise to power and later marginalization in the party is discussed next. By contrast, the "minimalist" faction was willing to comply with the democratic process and advocated independence from the Comintern. Eventually, the minimalists withdrew from the party in May 1921 after pro-Moscow supporters decided to transform the PSD into a communist party: the PCR. This congress was regarded as the PCR's first congress.

From the very beginning, the government defined the PCR and its members as traitors and criminals for subscribing to the Bolshevik line that Romania was a multinational imperialistic state. As a result, 800 members were arrested, and for the next two decades, the PCR operated clandestinely.[16] Researchers of Romanian communism emphasize the determining influence of the long experience of political illegality and the effect incarceration of PCR leaders had upon its future development after its accession to power in 1947 until its collapse in December 1989. They became masters in the art of manipulation and skilled at acting in secrecy. Factionalism, distrust and inter-personal power struggles also influenced the evolution of the PCR both before and after the war.[17]

Three major groups contended for the leadership of the party. In the first place, the "Romanian faction," which eventually emerged victorious and coalesced around activists involved in the 1930s workers' strikes, then jailed in Doftana Prison and interned in the labor camp at Târgu-Jiu. They were led by Gheorghe Gheorghiu-Dej (1901–1965) and included Gheorghe Apostol (1913–2010), Alexandru Moghioroș (1911–1969), Teohari Georgescu (1908–1976), Miron Constantinescu (1917–1974) and the youngest of them Nicolae Ceaușescu (1918–1989). For them, prison was a university where they learned basic Marxism, Russian and, most importantly, survival skills and the art of deceit. Gheorghiu-Dej was a unique figure among the pre-war generation of communists. He had real working-class roots and unlike many others spent no time in Moscow before the war. Especially after 1958, Dej played a crucial role in shaping a Romanian brand of communism and became a deeply respected leader in the country. His predilection for a cult of personality became even more pronounced under his successor Ceaușescu.

Ana Pauker, who held a position in the executive committee of the Comintern and was head of the external bureau of the PCR, led the second group, known as the "Moscow group." Born in 1893 as Hannah Rabinsohn to a poor Orthodox Jewish family in Codăești, Vaslui County, in the Moldova region, Pauker became active in the Romanian communist movement and the Comintern during the interwar period. In 1941, after spending six years in prison for illegal communist activities, she was sent to Moscow and became the leader of the Romanian exiles there. Ironically, it was her imprisonment in Romania that saved Pauker from sharing the same fate of many of her comrades, including that of her own husband, Marcel Pauker (1896–1938), who were executed during the 1937–1938 purges in the Soviet Union. Other prominent communist leaders killed in the purges included Alexandru Dobrogeanu-Gherea (1879–1937), Ecaterina Arbore (1873?–1937), Eugen Rozvan (1878–1938) and Elek Kőblös (1887–1938). The "Moscow group" also included Vasile Luca (1898–1963), Leonte Răutu (1910–1993), Valter Roman (1913–1983) and others, all of whom had at various times sought to escape arrest and imprisonment in Romania. It is important to note that all three changed their names: Luca was Hungarian and his first name had been Laszlo. Both Răutu and Roman were Jewish and their original names were Lev Oigenstein and Ernst Neulander. This was common practice after the war when communist officials, to avoid being perceived as agents of the foreign Soviet occupation, took on Romanian names. Some in this group fought in the Spanish Civil War and during World War II were active in the French Resistance.

After 1944, Pauker came back to Romania with Soviet troops and in 1947 became the first female minister of foreign affairs and the most powerful woman in the so-called Eastern Bloc. Her meteoric rise to power was also acknowledged at the time by some Western media outlets that ranked her with well-respected anti-fascist and communist leaders such as Josip Broz Tito and Georgi Dimitrov. However, her image was not always flattering, as she was equally portrayed as a ruthless power-hungry, Soviet-style communist.[18] Although Pauker was formally the second deputy in the four-person Secretariat of the Central Committee, many considered her the de facto leader of the PCR until her political demise in 1952. From 1945 to 1953, she was also the only woman in the Romanian Political Bureau—a position that no other woman held before 1973.[19] Among communist leaders, Pauker was perhaps the most vilified in public opinion and among her own comrades. They resented her power and influence. As a woman in a male-dominated and traditional agrarian society, Pauker perfectly fit the stereotype of the masculine woman or, as some named her, "Stalin in skirts." Moreover, in the context of antisemitism, which had deep roots during the interwar period, and the Stalinist purges of 1952–1953 in the USSR targeting Zionists, Pauker's image became doubly exceptional as a communist, a woman and a Jewess. This negative image was used both under socialism in the 1960s and 1970s when the regime attempted to dissociate itself from the Soviet system and after 1989 when communism was presented as a foreign and alien regime.[20]

Lastly, a third group consisted of veteran communists led by a Hungarian Ştefan Foriş (1892–1946) and also by Remus Koffler (1902–1954), Constantin Pîrvulescu (1895–1992) and Lucreţiu Pătrăşcanu (1900–1954). Before the war, they spent time in the Soviet Union as well as in Romanian prisons. In 1940, the Comintern confirmed Foriş as secretary general of the PCR. However, members of the three groups often ignored intergroup loyalties and competed for power or found allies when necessary to remove common rivals. This happened in 1946 when the Moscow and Romanian groups orchestrated the murder of Foriş based on the dubious allegation that he was a police informer for the bourgeois state.[21]

The August 23, 1944, coup d'état orchestrated by King Michael and the historical parties resulted in Ion Marshal Antonescu's arrest (Adolf Hitler's wartime ally) and the appointment of a military government led by General Constantin Sănătescu. A few days later, the Soviets entered Bucharest. Slowly, the communists took over the government, and with Soviet backing, they managed to weaken the historical parties. The forced abdication of King Michael on December 30, 1947, meant the end of the democratic regime. By 1948, the communization and Sovietization of the country was already well advanced. As minister of justice from 1944, Pătrăşcanu laid the basis of the communist legal system by a complete purge of the justice system, the state administrative apparatus and the local administration. He also set up People's Tribunals with the task of prosecuting and punishing class enemies and traitors. Paradoxically, or ironically, Pătrăşcanu's own fate was sealed by the very system he established. Intensive communization aimed at the collectivization of agriculture and the dismantling of private property was forcefully pursued. It is estimated that the victims of direct Stalinist repression in Romania included 600,000 political detainees, 200,000 administrative internees, 80,000 peasants who refused to submit to collectivization, deportees, prisoners of war and more than a half million young people forced into labor.[22] Later, starting in the early 1960s and after 1989, communists of the Dej era argued that the Moscow faction led by Pauker and Luca under direct orders from Joseph Stalin solely perpetrated repression. Some even went so far as to create a narrative of victimization of Romanian communists by those alien forces. The gesture of purification of national communism was thus achieved through denunciation and expulsion of an "evil" containing a "foreign" element. The previously mentioned Hungarian and Jewish origins of Luca and Pauker fit well into the concept of the stranger, the "Other" who infiltrated the ranks of good—that is, indigenous Romanian communists, abusing their trust and that of the Romanian nation.

In fact, the Romanian communist regime never carried out a process of de-Stalinization such as other communist parties initiated after Stalin's 1953 death. Under the mantle of de-Stalinization and reform, Dej and his acolytes emerged all-powerful and eliminated the two rival factions. First, Pătrășcanu was removed from power in 1948 and later tried and executed in 1954.[23] It is important to emphasize that unlike Laszlo Rajk in Hungary or Traicho Kostov in Bulgaria, whose trials and executions in 1949 were ordered by Moscow, Pătrășcanu never confessed to the alleged crimes. The second purge in the party occurred in 1952 with the removal of Ana Pauker, Vasile Luca and Teohari Gerogescu from the Politburo after two Central Committee plenary meetings. Accused of right-wing deviation related to serious mistakes while he presided over currency reform, Luca was expelled from the party. He died in 1963 in Aiud Prison. Pauker and Georgescu were accused of shielding Luca. Georgescu lost all his party positions. As for Pauker, she was simultaneously accused of left-wing and right-wing deviation. One of the main accusations against her involved her position on the collectivization of agriculture since she simultaneously failed to establish the collective farms and to allow peasants to join these state enterprises. Pauker was also accused of allowing Jews to immigrate to Israel and of opening the doors to "hostile elements" (including former Iron Guard members) to join the party in 1945–1946. After 1954, Pauker was relegated to a minor post at the Editura Politică (publishing house). Although she remained marginalized and mostly abandoned by her former comrades until her death in 1960, she continued to believe in the party and avoided any action that would jeopardize its image.[24]

As a result of the two purges, the party leadership did become more cohesive, and Dej's clique managed to consolidate his power. After his appointment in 1952 as president of the Council of Ministers and his re-election as the first secretary of the Romanian Workers' Party (RWP; as the PCR was named from 1948 until 1965) in 1955, Dej concentrated both state and party power in his hands.

Dej's ability to emerge as the undisputed leader after Stalin's death in 1953 and then to avoid de-Stalinization after the secret report issued by the new Soviet leader Nikita Khrushchev in 1956 at the Communist Party of the Soviet Union's Twentieth Congress was quite remarkable. Dej and loyalists managed to preempt any potential moves to de-Stalinization. The attempts by Iosif Chișinevschi and Miron Constantinescu to discuss the recommendations of Khrushchev's report during the plenums of the Central Committee meetings in 1957 had no effect. Both were removed from their posts. The issue was settled and closed once and for all by Romanian communists who argued that de-Stalinization had been achieved in 1954 with the removal of the Pauker-Luca-Georgescu Moscow triumvirate! While the Polish, Hungarian and Yugoslav communists introduced some measures of economic liberalization and cultural liberalism, Dej continued to promote Stalinist policies of industrialization and forced collectivization as a means of opposing Soviet hegemony.[25]

In 1962, during the meeting of the Council for Mutual Economic Assistance (COMECOM)—a supranational institution aimed at the economic integration of all socialist countries—the RWP refused the role assigned to Romania of being merely a source of cheap agricultural produce in the region. This unexpected move boosted Dej's popularity at home and also reestablished Romania's trade relations with West Germany, Austria, the US, Yugoslavia and China. Similar independent policies were pursued in the area of foreign affairs by establishing diplomatic relations with capitalist countries (Germany, France and the US) and their reestablishment with socialist countries (China, Yugoslavia) who were out of favor with the USSR.

After the withdrawal of Soviet troops from the country in 1958, the party identified itself with the cause of national independence and history was to be rewritten. By 1960, the Maxim Gorki Institute of History in Bucharest was abolished and the study of the Russian language eliminated as a school requirement. Some bourgeois intellectuals and professional cadres were rehabilitated, and Dej's 1964 "Declaration of Independence" (*Declarația de independență*) that criticized the USSR's hegemony in the bloc and its threat to national independence seemed to legitimize a national communism.[26] The same year, Soviet advisors who had been present in the country since 1950 and who played an instrumental role in the process of communization by holding key positions in the military, the Ministry of Internal Affairs and the economy were asked to leave.[27] Following this, the security and intelligence services became indigenous, although still engaged in political repression. According to contemporary witnesses, a state of collective enthusiasm characterized the general mood at the time, even among some who initially opposed the regime.[28] In 1964, for the first time, the status of Bessarabia (the eastern province lost to the Soviet Union in 1940) was addressed. Without minimizing the role of official propaganda, which at the time capitalized on these important political changes to enhance the legitimacy of the regime, it is quite likely that many genuinely thought that some kind of national independence had been restored.

Before the war, communists were active either outside the country or clandestinely from inside prisons and thus were little known by a public that chiefly viewed them suspiciously or with outright hostility. After 1947, both the party and its leaders found they had to manufacture a new memory and new biographies in order to connect them to society and claim an important role in recent history. Several dominant narratives were developed by official propaganda. The following themes have constantly recurred in public discourse: involvement of the party in the struggle for justice for the working class and the unions during the interwar period; the courageous and heroic behavior of communists unjustly imprisoned by capitalists and their fascist allies during the war; the instrumental role played by communists in the anti-fascist front and during the August 23, 1944, coup d'état that led to the overthrow of Marshal Antonescu; and, after 1958, the concerted efforts to revisit the ideology of the party and attune it to key national traditions.[29]

The party's role in the labor movement during the 1930s, as well as its involvement in the anti-fascist front during the war, was very exaggerated by postwar communist historiography.[30] In fact, given that so many communists were either imprisoned or in exile during the interwar period, they had limited contact or capacity to cooperate with other political actors, whether socialists, social democrats or the two historical parties: PNL and National Peasant Party (*Partidul Național Țărănesc*, PNȚ). Within the labor movement, communists clashed with socialists over political strategy. This happened, for example, during the 1933 strikes at the Grivița railroad workshops in Bucharest and also at the Ploiești refineries, where the communists pursued radical tactics while socialists favored dialogue and negotiation. However, the 1933 trials that led to the imprisonment of many communist leaders, including Gheorghiu-Dej, Constantin Doncea and Dumitru Popescu, were to become one of the central narratives of postwar historiography in its attempt to tie the working class to the PCR.[31] It was achieved at the cost of marginalizing the socialists. In the 1960s, when Dej's cult of personality reached its peak, his role was disproportionately emphasized, while the names of other communist leaders were erased from official propaganda.[32]

Like Grivița, Doftana Prison (located in Doftana village in Prahova County, an hour away from Bucharest) was to become one of the principal *lieux de mémoire* in party history. It was in Doftana, according to communist historiography, that revolutionary heroes fought capitalist oppression and prepared to build a free and fair socialist society through the study and discussion of the teachings of Karl Marx and Vladimir Lenin. A museum was built there in 1960, and schoolchildren were regularly taken for visits to sing the Doftana Hymn.[33]

Communist propaganda also exaggerated the role of the PCR and Dej in the coup d'état of August 23, 1944, that led to the abrogation of Romania's military alliance with Nazi Germany. In fact, historians as well as contemporaries of Dej have shown that although his escape from the labor camp of Târgu-Jiu, where he was held from 1943 to 1944, took place sometime in August, he was not in Bucharest on the twenty-third, which means that he could not have participated in these events.[34] In reality, the only communist who took part in a broader coalition, which was dominated by the monarchy (King Michael was still head of state) and the historical parties (PNL and PNȚ) and ultimately led to overthrow of Antonescu as Hitler's ally, was Pătrășcanu.[35] But both Pătrășcanu's middle-class intellectual background and his reputation as an independent communist triggered the jealousy of his comrades, including Dej's; as he also did not fit the general pattern of a working-class communist activist close to the people, his role in these events was erased.

As for the party's contribution to the anti-fascist coalition before and during the war, it was as early as the 1930s that communists attempted to portray their trials and imprisonment as the work of a bourgeois-fascist alliance against the anti-fascist, pro-working-class activists and progressive intellectuals. This was particularly the case with the 1936 trial against 19 communists accused of treason. The accused—including Pauker who was the most vocal—and their defendants used it as an opportunity to condemn fascism.[36] Although during the 1950s, the fascist label was often used against the so-called enemies of the state regardless of their political affiliations or convictions, after 1989, many old communists still explained their entry into the communist movement as a reaction against fascism and antisemitism.[37] Strikingly, the involvement of Romanian communists in the Spanish Civil War (estimated at 400 *brigadistas*) and in the French Resistance is met by an almost complete silence in both communist and post-1989 historiography.[38] After 1952, they were marginalized by Dej. But after 1989, and especially in the 1990s when anti-communist discourse became dominant, they were consigned to oblivion.

Parallel and in harmony with the rewriting of the history of Romanian communism, Dej's cult of personality enjoyed a major boost. In 1964, two interconnected myths became the basis for an official master narrative. While the first asserted the leading role of the PCR in the national arena, the second elevated Dej as the supreme leader of the party. As Alexandra Toader shows, from 1944 to 1952, several leaders (including Dej, Pauker and Luca) shared the party's center stage.[39] Between 1947 and 1950, letters received by Pauker on International Women's Day described her as a "beloved comrade," "a courageous fighter" and a model for working-class women.[40] One of the most popular slogans of the time "Ana, Luca and Dej frighten the bourgeoisie" (*Ana, Luca și cu Dej bagă spaima in burghezi*) celebrated the role of the collective leadership in destroying the capitalist system.

However, after the purges and primarily after 1958, Dej became the only dominant figure in the party. His numerous visits (*vizite de lucru*) to factories, construction sites and schools became occasions for public adulation. Through official propaganda (biographies, novels, poems and exhibitions), regime sycophants constructed an image of Dej as the father, teacher, theoretician, autodidact, humble worker and first railroad worker of the nation. This last image was aimed at emphasizing the role of the party as an agent of modernization through the electrification of the countryside, as if only Dej, a former highly qualified electrician, could have accomplished this. The propaganda machine attributed exceptional accomplishments to Dej during the 1933 Grivița strikes—undeservedly as we have seen. Later in the 1960 volume dedicated to Doftana Prison, he was presented as the supreme leader of the communist organization. At his sixtieth birthday in 1961, Dej was called for the first time the genial leader (*conducător genial*).⁴¹

His death in 1965 was followed by widespread national mourning. He was given a spectacular funeral and laid to rest at the Liberty Park Mausoleum in Bucharest alongside other communist leaders. Interestingly, the idea of embalming Dej that was circulating was opposed by his successor Ceaușescu. In her 1999 book, *The Political Lives of Dead Bodies: Reburial and Postsocialist Change*, Katherine Verdery demonstrates how the continued existence of such bodies has an unusual power in socializing authority.⁴² It seems that Ceaușescu understood this quickly and preempted many of the commemorative measures agreed upon in March 1965 at the joint meeting of the Central Committee, the State Council and the Council of Ministers after Dej's death. No statue in his honor was erected; no special room was dedicated to Dej at the museum of the history of the party, and his biography was not republished.⁴³ Dej was quickly forgotten, and Ceaușescu usurped his place in the communist pantheon. Very like Dej himself, Ceaușescu, in the next 25 years, proclaimed himself the uncontested leader of the PCR and the party as the true heir of the national tradition. Again, like Dej, he pursued a similarly independent path in foreign affairs, adopted ill-conceived economic policies and imposed a regime of mass surveillance and terror.

The Letter of the Six and Its Aftermath

In 1989, major political upheavals and fundamental changes occurred across communist Europe. However, in Romania, Ceaușescu's reelection as general secretary at the Fourteenth Party Congress in November dashed any hope for political change. In May 1987, during his visit to Romania, Mikhail Gorbachev had expressed concerns about how much the country was under the sole control of Ceaușescu and his inner family circle. A year later, because of criticism leveled by the US president and Congress at Romania for human rights violations, Romania's eligibility to receive American trade benefits granted to communist states was withdrawn. A few months after Gorbachev's visit, a workers' uprising in the city of Brașov, which was ultimately suppressed, represented yet another blow to the regime.

It is in this context that we can situate the "Letter of the Six" released on March 11, 1989, and broadcast by the BBC and Radio Free Europe. The six signatories were all party veterans involved with the communist movement since its early clandestine days. We have already given a brief account of three of them (Alexandru Bârlădeanu, Silviu Brucan and Corneliu Mănescu) and their participation in the FSN. The others were Gheorghe Apostol, Constantin Pîrvulescu and Grigore Ion Răceanu. Apostol was the most prominent and loyal of Dej's associates. The two became close in 1937 when they were imprisoned in connection with the railway workers' strikes.⁴⁴ As a member of the Politburo since 1948 and briefly as first secretary of the party (1954–1955) when Dej appeared to imitate the Soviet style of collective leadership, Apostol was groomed as Dej's successor. However, in a byzantine conspiracy within the party's inner circle after Dej's death, Ceaușescu seized power. Pîrvulescu was one of the founders of the PCR who supported unconditional affiliation with the Comintern. Dej briefly expelled him from the party in 1960 for alleged involvement with the Chișinevschi and Constantinescu faction that advocated de-Stalinization after Khrushchev's secret speech in 1956. In 1974, he was readmitted to the party but barred from exerting any major influence. However, in 1989, Pîrvulescu was chiefly known to the public for his courageous stand during the Twelfth Party Congress in 1979 when he asked Ceaușescu to step down from the party's leadership. Lastly, Răceanu was also a pre-World War II communist activist involved with the workers strikes, but in 1958, Dej and his acolytes accused him of deviation. However, unlike Pîrvulescu, who at the time distanced himself from the pro-Khrushchev group to preserve his party status, Răceanu chose to stand by his views with the result that Dej marginalized him. His stepson Mircea Răceanu, a high-level diplomat, was instrumental in facilitating communication between the Six, for which he was accused of treason and sentenced to death, but the December '89 revolution saved his life.⁴⁵

The political background and life trajectories of the Six are significant in understanding the limitations of their protest. Perhaps with the exception of Brucan, who later criticized the FSN for its limited reforms and advocated Western-type capitalism, all were devoted communists. In the five points of the letter, Ceaușescu was strongly condemned for the current state of the economy and decline in living standards, for the violation of constitutional rights, for his dictatorial practices and for the country's international isolation. Some of the language is clearly reminiscent of Dej's earlier rhetoric extolling internal political autonomy and national independence in the international arena. They deplored the transformation of the Securitate, "which we created to defend the socialist order against the exploiting classes [. . .] now directed against workers demanding their rights." Finally, they decried the country's loss of prestige in the world and warned the dictator that "Romania is and remains a European country [. . .] you cannot remove Romania to Africa."⁴⁶ Shortly after the release of the letter, at a meeting of the Politburo, Ceaușescu attacked them as political bandits, morally depraved and treasonous.⁴⁷ With their families, they were all arrested, interrogated, forcibly taken from their homes and then confined to compulsory domicile. Their advanced age, however, proved disadvantageous in terms of their ability to initiate a true reform movement within the party or in general on the left. Clearly, they were advocating some reform of the regime but without basic structural or systemic change.

In fact, in memoirs and interviews after 1989, Apostol, Bârlădeanu, Brucan and Mănescu emphasized the lessons for the present and future of the important economic achievements and foreign policy successes of the Dej era to which they themselves had directly contributed. For example, Bârlădeanu, as former deputy minister for economic issues between 1955 and 1965, took credit for the relaxation in economic policies that had resulted in the higher standard of living enjoyed by Romanians from 1960 to 1965.[48] Apostol went so far as to speculate that if Dej had not died prematurely and had remained in power for at least five more years, the country could have adopted an economic model based on a combination of both state and private capital.[49] Bârlădeanu also proudly recalled his position as the representative at COMECOM when the Western media referred to him as "the man who said no to Khrushchev" by refusing to accept the relegation of Romania to the status of "a colony of the most industrialized countries" of the socialist bloc.[50] Mănescu and Apostol presented Dej's achievements in foreign policy that had allegedly preempted open military intervention against Romania in 1956 and secured its national independence after 1960. Apostol denounced current political leaders who in the early 2000s were not shrewd enough to balance national interests with NATO membership.[51] In the same vein, Brucan described Dej's independent foreign policy as "Stalinist desatellitization."[52] Others, including Paul Niculescu-Mizil, Gheorghe Maurer, Dumitru Popescu and Paul Sfetcu, presented the last stage of Dej's leadership in similarly reverent terms.[53] Although they were not among the signatories of the letter, they belonged to the same generation of communists and worked closely with Dej. An examination of their writings clearly suggests that they saw the final stage of the Dej regime as the true golden era of communism that reintroduced Romanian pride and dignity, all of which followed from an autonomous foreign policy, the liberalization of public life and the economy and the rediscovery of a national culture and its traditions.

What is most prominent in these memoirs is the image of Dej as a gifted leader. He is remembered as an avuncular figure ("the old man") who possessed a "native intelligence," as a "good psychologist" and "shrewd" in human relationships, but also compassionate and ready to listen to advice.[54] But, above all, Dej is considered to be a true patriot, and, according to Niculescu-Mizil, the 1964 "Declaration of Independence" represents his great political testament. Brucan, Bârlădeanu, Maurer, Mănescu and Mizil acknowledge that Ceaușescu's independent foreign policy of the 1970s was in fact built on the legacy of Dej who challenged the Soviet hegemony. Dej's loyalists have, after 1989, been celebrating the same images and themes that made up his cult of personality in the late 1950s and early 1960s, these being the very qualities that distinguished him from what they thought of as the ignorance, self-righteousness and dogmatism of Ceaușescu. As Lucian Boia and Vladimir Tismăneanu have shown, the old guard was engaged in reviving the Dej myth.[55] As communists of the pre-war generation, they were reasserting what they believed to be the true ideals of communism that the next generation led by Ceaușescu had betrayed.

However, as scholars of memory studies emphasize, the act of remembering is selective and is shaped by the need of social actors to redefine and reassign meaning to past events or individual and group actions in light of currently changing circumstances.[56] Given their pre-war generational identity and commitment to communist ideology, these six former officials and others who have identified with them attempted to transmit to younger audiences *their own truth*. By doing so, they often indulged in what Paul Ricoeur called "manipulated memory" that simultaneously "abuses" and blocks out specific aspects of the past.[57] While certain events are reinterpreted for instrumental purposes, others are intentionally reduced in significance or simply eliminated. In this case, the habitual over-emphasis of the positive aspects of the Dej era on the part of former leading Stalinists included episodes such as the withdrawal of Soviet troops in 1958, the 1964 "Declaration of Independence," the release of political prisoners in 1964 and Romania's position in COMECOM and in international relations. Meanwhile, other significant aspects of this history such as widespread gulag-style repression and the execution of Pătrășcanu and many others were either minimized or presented as simply by-products of Soviet occupation. In so doing, they offered lessons to the post-1989 political establishment now represented by communist era officials who chose to promote anti-communist rhetoric out of sheer opportunism. At the same time, former political prisoners and their descendants sought justice for the Soviet-era repression that had victimized them.[58]

To a significant degree, such representations of both the past and present reflected the FSN's, and its various successors', record in government throughout the 1990s. From the very beginning, the reformist wing of the FSN led by Prime Minister Petre Roman encountered opposition from the central conservative group rallied around Ion Iliescu. This led to the split of the FSN into two rival political parties: The Democratic Party led by Roman from February 1990 to 2001 and the Democratic Front of National Salvation (DFSN) established in March 1992 by Iliescu and his loyalists. The DFSN and Iliescu won the elections again in 1992. Despite its alleged commitment to democracy and a market economy, in order to ensure a parliamentary majority from 1992 to 1996, former communists organized as the FDSN entered into coalition with extreme right-wing nationalist parties (the Greater Romania Party (PRM) and the Party of National Unity Support, along with the hardline communists who were organized as the Socialist Party of Labor).

The historical legacy of the PCR was never explicitly articulated by these successors to the party during the 1990s and early 2000s.[59] As noted earlier, December '89 became the defining moment for the FSN to manufacture its revolutionary identity in opposition to the years of late communism under Ceaușescu's dictatorship. Dej's legacy was primarily revived in individual memoirs but not as part of a coherent socialist or political program. In 1991, Dej was "killed" for the second time after his body was exhumed from the Liberty Park Mausoleum and reburied in Bellu Cemetery in Bucharest entirely without ceremony. His former comrades neither publicly opposed this nor expressed any regret for this symbolic and somewhat ignominious reburial. At the time, the country inaugurated a new memory politics that attempted to make a clean break with the past. In this framework, the FSN succeeded in avoiding any formal association with the PCR.

It was as late as 2001 that the Party of Social Democracy, which emerged out of the FDSN, took a decisive step in reinventing itself and asserting a clear socialist identity by joining the Socialist International after first merging with the reestablished pre-war Social Democratic Party. It then became the current PSD. From 2000 to 2004, the PSD embarked on a sustained program of reform under the close guidance of the EU. But in 2007, when Romania joined the European Union and the Presidential Commission for the Analysis of Communist Dictatorship condemned the former regime as criminal, illegal and illegitimate, with a list of individual perpetrators that included Iliescu and other post-1989 politicians and a characterization of the FSN as continuing undemocratic communist practices, PSD representatives in the Parliament virulently criticized the report. Together with supporters of the PRM, they verbally assaulted and even physically threatened some members of the commission.[60] As of this writing, the PSD continues to define its ideological identity as rooted in pre-war socialist traditions and makes no references to its communist past.[61]

But vernacular and localized images of the past cannot be expected to follow the logic of the political elites, which needs to orient the official politics of memory to the project of Europeanization. In 2009, a group of local officials and historians in the city of Dej's birth (Bârlad) began organizing annual conferences exploring the history of communism. Some historians have attempted to critically reassess the Dej period and emphasize its "positive aspects."[62] At present, the local city council in cooperation with the Institute for the Investigation of Crimes of Communism and the Romanian Exile are seeking to restore Dej's house as a museum.[63] It still remains unclear to what extent this local initiative could have an effect on the historical reconstruction of the left's identity.

Conclusions

This analysis of the PCR's history from 1944 to 1965, and the ongoing struggle to construct and link its identity to a national narrative both before and after 1989, leads us to several conclusions regarding the marginal status of the memory of communism on the political left and the latter's inability to reinvent itself as a genuine social democratic political actor. In order to understand the extraordinary nature of the dynastic and nationalist regime of the 1980s under Ceauşescu and its later effect on the sudden appearance of a revolutionary moment or situation, it is important to examine it as a continuation and amplified version of an autonomous "national version of socialism," as had already been fully articulated in the early 1960s by the Dej regime. It is in this context that we need to analyze the significance of the dissident protest of the six party veterans. Unlike Hungary and Poland (and to a certain extent Bulgaria), Romanian communists did not attempt regime change as a kind of rapprochement with opposition forces in 1989. In fact, in the aftermath of the December popular revolt, many felt that former communists stole the revolution and derailed its course in favor of a mere anti-Ceaușescu reform. It is this ambiguity of the Romanian Revolution and its aftermath that has inhibited political reconciliation between former communists and anti-communists. It is a division that has remained to the present day.

The post-1989 instability and volatility of public opinion and emotions partly explain why current official representations of the past are so embedded in a narrative of trauma, national suffering and victimization very reminiscent of pre-1989 official propaganda. However, their meaning should also be read in the present international political context dominated by growing Euroscepticism and the rise of extreme right-wing populist movements, which stand in sharp and ominous contrast to the enthusiasm and commitment to the liberal democratic project of the first years after 1989. At the time, this was understood by many as a necessary change following the deprivations of the Ceaușescu dictatorship. But because this desired political liberalization was coupled with neoliberal economics, it is likely to generate a more sympathetic feeling for the communist past among a significant section of the population. It is not hard to imagine a second exhumation of Dej and a restoration of his legacy.

Notes

1 Lavinia Stan, *Transitional Justice in Post-Communist Romania* (Cambridge: Cambridge University Press, 2013); Monica Ciobanu, "Post-Communist Transitional Justice at 25: Unresolved Dilemmas," *Analele Universității din București: Seria Științe Politice* 16.2 (2014): 119–136.
2 Dennis Deletant, *Ceaușescu and the Securitate: Coercion and Dissent in Romania, 1965–1989* (Armonk, NY: M. E. Sharpe, 1995). For Romania in the 1980s and the nationalist ideology see Katherine Verdey, *National Ideology Under Socialism: Identity and Cultural Politics in Ceaușescu's Romania* (Berkeley and Los Angeles and London: University of California Press, 1991).
3 For the roundtables of 1989, see John Elster, ed., *The Roundtable Talks and the Breakdown of Communism* (Chicago and London: University of Chicago Press, 1996).
4 For a vivid description of the Romanian revolution and its aftermath, see Peter Siani-Davies, *The Romanian Revolution of December 1989* (Ithaca and London: Cornell University Press, 2005), which examines both the revolution and its political aftermath.
5 See "Transcript of the Closed 'Trial' of Nicolae Ceaușescu and Elena Ceaușescu," www.ceausescu.org/ceausescu_texts/revolution/trial-eng.htm, accessed December 22, 2016.
6 Siani-Davies, *The Romanian Revolution of December 1989*.

7 "Revoluția Română: Ion Iliescu prezintă comunicatul catre țară al CFSN," December 22, 1989, www.youtube.com/watch?v=pFWe8G3QdcI, accessed December 22, 2016.
8 Liviu Țăranu, *Românii în 'epoca de aur': Corespondență din anii '80* (Târgoviște: Editura Cetatea de Scaun, 2012).
9 Monica Ciobanu, "The Challenge of Competing Pasts," in *Post-Communist Transitional Justice: Lessons from Twenty-Five Years of Experience*, eds. Lavinia Stan and Nadya Nedelsky (Cambridge: Cambridge University Press, 2015), 148–166.
10 Raluca Grosescu and Raluca Ursachi, *Justiția penală de tranziție: De la Nuremberg la Postcomunimul românesc* (București: Institutul de Investigare a Crimelor Comunismului din România, 2009).
11 Both Paul Niculescu-Mizil and Dumitru Popescu published their memoirs. See Paul Niculescu-Mizil, *O istorie trăită: memorii* (București: Editura Enciclopedică, 2002); Dumitru Popescu, *Am fost și cioplitor de himere: un fost lider comunist se destăinuie* (București: Expres, 1993).
12 In 1992, representatives of the December '89 revolutionaries initiated legal action regarding the crimes of the revolution. Until 2004, there were no prosecutions in the "Revolution File." However, in 2011, thanks to civil-society activism and consistent pressure from the European Court of Human Rights, the case was reopened. After the file was closed again in 2015 on the grounds that there was no evidence of crimes against humanity, it was reopened for the third time in June 2016. The case is still pending. See Ondine Ghergut, "Procurorii redeschid a patra oară dosarul Revoluției: Parchetul militar recunoaște lovitura de stat din 22 decembrie 1989," *România libera*, November 3, 2016, http://romanialibera.ro/special/dezvaluiri/procurorii-redeschid-a-patra-oara-dosarul-revolutiei—parchetul-militar-recunoaste-lovitura-de-stat-din-22-decembrie-1989–432077, accessed August 25, 2017.
13 John Gledhill, "Three Days in Bucharest: Making Sense of Romania's Transitional Violence, 20 Years On," *Europe—Asia Studies* 63.9 (2011): 1639–1669.
14 Monica Ciobanu, "Reconstructing the Role of the Working Class in Communist and Postcommunist Romania," *International Journal of Politics, Culture and Society* 22.3 (2009): 315–335.
15 Roland Clark, *Holy Legionary Youth: Fascist Activism in Interwar Romania* (Ithaca and London: Cornell University Press, 2015).
16 For the early history of communism in Romania see Dennis Deletant, *Gheorghiu-Dej and the Police State (1945–1965)* (London: Hurst and Company, 1999), 1–33; Vladimir Tismăneanu, *Stalinism for All Seasons: A Political History of Romanian Communism* (Berkeley: University of California Press, 2003), 37–84.
17 Deletant, *Gheorghiu-Dej and the Police State (1945–1965)*; Tismăneanu, *Stalinism for All Seasons*. Also see Ghiță Ionescu, *Communism in Romania: 1944–1962* (London and New York: Oxford University Press, 1964).
18 Ion Calafeteanu, *Scrisori către tovarăşa Ana* (București: Editura Universul Enciclopedic, 2005), 11–12.
19 Luciana Jinga, *Gen și Reprezentare în Romania Comunistă: 1944–1989* (București: Polirom, 2015), 266.
20 Marius Mircu, *Dosar Ana Pauker* (București: Editura Gutenberg, 1991). For a comprehensive monograph on Ana Pauker in English see Robert Levy, *Ana Pauker: The Rise and Fall of a Jewish Communist* (Berkeley and Los Angeles: Berkeley University Press, 2001).
21 Lavinia Betea, ed., "Ștefan Sârbu, nepotul lui Foriș, despre trei generații în vîrtejul politiii," in *Povești din Cartierul Primăverii*, (București: Curtea Veche, 2010), 61–80.

22 Romulus Rusan, *The Chronology and the Geography of the Repression in Communist Romania: Census of the Concentration Camp Population 1945–1989* (București: Editura Fundației Academia Civică, 2007).
23 Lavinia Betea, *Lucrețiu Pătrășcanu: Moartea unui Lider Comunist* (București: Humanitas, 2001).
24 Lavinia Betea, ed., "Tatiana Brătescu, fiica lui Marcel și a Anei Pauker, despre copiii Cominternului," in *Povești din Cartierul Primăverii* (București: Curtea Veche, 2010), 93–115.
25 For the processes of industrialization see Stelian Tănase, *Elite și Societate: Guvernarea Gheorghe Gheorghiu-Dej 1948–1965* (București: Humanitas, 1998); for the collectivization of agriculture see Gail Kligman and Katherine Verdery, *Peasants Under Siege: The Collectivization of Romanian Agriculture* (Princeton: Princeton University Press, 2011).
26 Vlad Georgescu, *Politică și Istorie: Cazul Comuniștilor Români (1944–1947)* (București: Humanitas, 2008).
27 Florin Banu and Luminița Banu, "Consilierii sovietici și acțiunile organelor repressive ale regimului comunist din Romania," *Analele Universității Dunărea de Jos* 1 (2008): 197–222.
28 Niculescu-Mizil, *O istorie trăită: memorii*, 42–43.
29 *Eroi și martiri ai clasei muncitoare* (București: Federația Națională a foștilor deținuți și internați politici antifasciști, 1949); *Grivița Roșie: Cîntece de masă* (București: Editura Muzicală a Uniunii Compozitorilor din RPR, 1963); Mihai Novicov, *Povestiri despre Doftana* (București: Editura Tineretului, 1957); Augustin Deac, Gheorghe Matei, *Mișcarea de solidaritate cu luptele eroice ale ceferiștilor și petroliștilor din 1933* (București: Editura Științifică, 1967).
30 Deac and Matei, *Mișcarea de solidaritate cu luptele eroice ale ceferiștilor și petroliștilor din 1933*.
31 Cristina Diac, "Liderul nevăzut: Gheorghe Gheorghiu-Dej și grevele de la Grivița," in *Spectrele lui Dej*, eds. Ștefan Bosomitu and Mihai Burcea (Iași: Polirom, 2012), 31–49.
32 Alexandra Toader, *Cultul Personalității lui Gheorghe Gheorghiu-Dej (1945–1965)* (Iași: Universitatea "Al. I. Cuza," 2015), 135–137.
33 Vladimir Tismăneanu, *Lumea secretă a nomenclaturii: amintiti, dezvăluiri, portrete* (București: Humanitas, 2012), 114.
34 Dumitru Lăcătușu, "Fuga spre putere: Evadarea lui Gheorghe Gheorghiu-Dej din lagărul de la Târgu-Jiu," in *Spectrelelui Dej*, eds. Ștefan Bosomitu and Mihai Burcea (Iași: Polirom, 2012), 76–101.
35 Betea, *Lucrețiu Pătrășcanu*.
36 Dumitru Lăcătușu, "Procesul Anei Pauker de la București și Craiova," in *Comuniștii Înainte de Comunism: Procese și Condamnări ale Ilegaliștilor din Romania*, ed. Adrian Cioroianu (București: Editura Universității din București, 2014), 168–256.
37 Lavinia Betea, ed., "Maurer și lumea de ieri," in *Partea lor de adevăr*, (București: Compania, 2008), 268; Lavinia Betea, ed., "Alexandru Bârladeanu despre Dej, Iliescu ș Ceaușescu," in *Partea lor de adevăr*, (București: Compania, 2008), 11–37; Gheorghe Apostol, *Eu și Gheorghiu Dej* (București: PACO, 2011); Silviu Brucan, *The Wasted Generation: Memoirs of the Romanian Journey from Capitalism to Socialism and Back* (Boulder: Westview Press, 1993).
38 Mihai Burcea, "Recalling the Memory of the Romanian Interbrigadists and Maquisards: A Case Study—Ion Călin (I)," *Analele Universității din București: Seria Științe Politice* 15.1 (2013): 86–118. A notorious case involves Olga Bancic, born in 1912, who was killed in 1944 in France by the Nazis. See Jinga, *Gen și Reprezentare în Romania Comunistă: 1944–1989*, 56–58.

39 Toader, *Cultul Personalității lui Gheorghe Gheorghiu-Dej (1945–1965)*, 135–137.
40 Calafeteanu, *Scrisori către tovarășa Ana*, 22–31.
41 See Elis Pleșa, *Gheorghe Gheorghiu-Dej: Cultul Personalității* (Târgoviște: Editura Cetatea de Scaune, 2015), 223–250.
42 Katherine Verdery, *The Political Lives of Dead Bodies: Reburial and Postsocialist Change* (New York: Columbia University Press, 1999).
43 Pleșa, *Gheorghe Gheorghiu-Dej*, 297–310.
44 About Apostol see Toader, *Cultul Personalității lui Gheorghe Gheorghiu-Dej (1945–1965)*.
45 Mircea Răceanu, *Infern '89: Povestea unui Condamnat la Moarte* (București: Silex, 2000).
46 For the text of the letter see "Scrisoarea celor sase—text integral," www.hetel.ro/index.php/2011/01/1603, accessed August 25, 2017.
47 Ilarion Țiu, "Martie 1989: șase veteran comuniști au protestat față de dictatura lui Ceaușescu," *Sfera Politicii* 22.2 (2014): 100–106.
48 About Bârlădeanu see Toader, *Cultul Personalității lui Gheorghe Gheorghiu-Dej (1945–1965)*, 85.
49 About Apostol see Toader, *Cultul Personalității lui Gheorghe Gheorghiu-Dej (1945–1965)*, 140.
50 Abiut Bârlădeanu see Toader, *Cultul Personalității lui Gheorghe Gheorghiu-Dej (1945–1965)*, 129–130.
51 About Mănescu see Toader, *Cultul Personalității lui Gheorghe Gheorghiu-Dej (1945–1965)*, 468–488; and about Apostol see Toader, *Cultul Personalității lui Gheorghe Gheorghiu-Dej (1945–1965)*, 128.
52 Brucan, *The Wasted Generation*, 60.
53 Niculescu-Mizil, *O istorie trăită*; Popescu, *Am fost și cioplitor de himere*; "Maurer și lumea de ieri." Also see Paul Sfetcu, *13 Ani în Antecamerului Dej* (București: Fundația Culturală Romană, 2000).
54 Maurer, "Maurer și lumea de ieri," 304; Sfetcu, *13 Ani în Antecamerului Dej*, 54–55.
55 Lucian Boia, *History and Myth in Romanian Consciousness*, trans. James Christian Brown (Budapest: Central European University Press, 2001), 214–226; and Vladimir Tismăneanu, *Fantoma lui Gheorghiu-Dej* (București: Humanitas, 2008).
56 Aleida Assmann and Linda Shortt, eds., *Memory and Political Change* (New York: Palgrave Macmillan, 2012); Peter Berger, *Invitation to Sociology: A Humanistic Perspective* (New York: Anchor, 1963); Maurice Halbwachs, *On Collective Memory*, trans., ed. and introduction Lewis A. Coser (Chicago: Chicago University Press, 1992).
57 Paul Ricoeur, *Memory, History, Forgetting*, trans. Kathleen Blamey and David Pellauer (Chicago: University of Chicago Press, 2004).
58 Niculescu-Mizil, *O istorie trăită: memorii*, 463.
59 Alexandru Gussi, "The Ex-Communist's Policy of Forgetting in Romania After 1990," *Studia Politica: Romanian Political Science Review* 9.2 (2009): 273–290.
60 Vladimir Tismaneanu, Dorin Dobrincu and Cristian Vasile, eds., *Raport Final: Comisia Prezidențială pentru Analiza Dictaturii Comuniste din România* (București: Humanitas, 2007); Monica Ciobanu, "Criminalising the Past and Reconstructing Collective Memory: The Romanian Truth Commission," *Europe—Asia Studies* 61 (2009): 313–336.
61 See Istoric, www.psd.ro/istoric, accessed February 20, 2017.
62 Personal communication with Dr. Liviu Țăranu, February 6, 2017.
63 See Casa Gheorghe Gheorghiu-Dej și Centrul de Documentare Antitotalitară, www.reteauamemoriei.ro/casa-gheorghe-gheorghiu-dej-si-centrul-de-documentare, accessed February 7, 2017.

10 Constructing New Friends and Enemies
Rewriting Czechoslovak History After the Communist Takeover

Darina Volf

Introduction

Radical political changes bring about not only shifts in political power and transformations of the social and economic order but also they are often accompanied by new narratives of the past and redefinitions of the national self-image for the purpose of legitimizing the changes. In many cases, the new understanding of the nation, its beliefs, values and aspirations entails the reshaping of views regarding other national groups—friends, allies, enemies.

The idea of the nation as an imagined, socially constructed entity was put forward in the influential works of Benedict Anderson, Ernest Gellner and Eric Hobsbawm and Terence Ranger.[1] Based on these ideas, Montserrat Guibernau, studying the creation of a shared sense of national identity as a significant part of nation-building processes, emphasizes two fundamental elements of national identity: continuity over time and differentiation from others. While continuity springs from the conception of the nation as a historically rooted entity, differentiation stems from the consciousness of forming a distinct community with a shared culture, past, symbols and traditions attached to a limited territory.[2]

Both elements—continuity and differentiation—are reinforced by historical narratives and images. Analogously to the concept of national identity, whose persuasive power rests on the presentation of the nation as a natural, eternal entity, the credibility of the lines drawn between the national community, on the one hand, and its friends and enemies, on the other, can be reinforced by emphasizing their historical continuity. Therefore, the elites attempt to highlight those historical events that fit into the narrative of long-lasting friendship or enmity and suppress memories that are at odds with this outlook.

The purpose here is to point out changes in the historical images of the US and the Soviet Union[3] that occurred with the enforced establishment of the communist interpretation of Czechoslovak history and that were functionally related to the foreign policy of postwar Czechoslovakia. The new foreign policy line was coordinated with the foreign policy of the Soviet Union, which was declared to be the best friend and helper of Czechoslovakia and the guarantor of Czechoslovak independence. As this study will demonstrate, the legitimation of the postwar drift to the East rested on a twofold historical argument. On the one hand, the communist historians tried to disprove the interwar interpretation that emphasized the role of US President Woodrow Wilson in the founding of the First Czechoslovak Republic. Instead, the links of the interwar elites to the West were blamed for the loss of sovereignty and destruction of the Czechoslovak state in 1938. On the other hand, the long tradition of friendship between Russians, on the one hand, and Czechs and Slovaks, on the other, was highlighted by tracing the roots of their contacts and cooperative efforts back to the Middle Ages and showing their persistence up to the present day.

The chapter starts with a short overview of developments leading to the establishment of communist rule in February 1948, in consequence of which the communists were able not only to shape foreign and memory policy but also to wipe out alternative interpretations from the public discourse.[4] The four following sections analyze the changes in historical interpretations of some important events in Czechoslovak history related to the US and the Soviet Union. They focus on the construction of communist historical narratives and on the spread of these narratives through different commemorative practices. Finally, the chapter poses the question of the extent to which the communists succeeded in enforcing their interpretations within society. Although there are only a few sources dealing with public opinion regarding images of other nations in the early phase of communist rule, the existing research on collective images, together with reflections on the historical context and the taking into account of later developments, allows us to draw some conclusions about the persuasive power of the communist narratives.

The "Victorious February": "Flooding" the Public Discourse with Communist Interpretations

From 1945 to 1948, Czechoslovakia was governed by a coalition of all existing political parties. Since many parties were banned or prevented from resuming their activities after the war, the communist and socialist parties already dominated the coalition before the communist takeover. However, on February 25, 1948, the Communist Party of Czechoslovakia (KSČ) gained full control of the government after President Edvard Beneš accepted the resignations of the non-communist ministers. The resignations were intended as a protest against the policies of the communist minister of the interior Václav Nosek, but the non-communists expected Beneš to refuse the resignations and enable a caretaker government. Beneš's acceptance allowed Communist Party leader Klement Gottwald to form a new government, which purportedly was still a coalition of different parties. However, the communists assumed a dominant position and managed to empower their loyal supporters in other parties, while the opponents who were unwilling to accept the new power relations (for example, Petr Zenkl and Hubert Ripka) were forced to leave the country or later sentenced in show trials as, for example, in the case of Milada Horáková. In April 1948, two months after the takeover and shortly before the elections that were intended to confirm the leading role of the Communist Party, the communist minister of the interior Václav Kopecký described the new situation as follows: "In fact, decisions on how to elect candidates, what the candidate lists will look like, and what happens to other parties, lie entirely in our hands."[5]

It was not only the political framework that the communist takeover changed. It also had far-reaching consequences for the economic and social order, and altered the media landscape in a very fundamental way. Although it was common to exercise press censorship before 1948 as well, its intensity and manner changed. The Communist Party gained control over all media. Libraries were cleansed of literature classified as subversive, reactionary or anti-Soviet.[6] Many periodicals, including the weeklies *Dnešek* [Today], *Obzory* [Horizons] and *Vývoj* [Development], as well as some regional and Catholic periodicals, were forced to cease publication, and several journalists—the best-known being Ferdinand Peroutka and Pavel Tigrid—went into exile. The books published under the control of the Communist Party disseminated similar news, pictures and comments, deploying in many cases a very similar vocabulary. Once again, it was Minister of Interior Kopecký who commented on these changes by pointing out the outstanding position held by the Communist Party, which would make it possible to "flood" public discourse with Marxist writings and communist narratives.[7]

Turning now to foreign policy, the abandonment of the interwar republic's Western orientation and the growing orientation to the Soviet Union emerged not as a consequence of the takeover but had already been evident shortly after the war. Despite the initial communist rhetoric of a specific Czechoslovak road to communism and despite the quite popular idea of Czechoslovakia as a bridge between the East and the West,[8] the actual policies showed a clear tendency in a particular direction. Already in 1947, the refusal to participate in the Marshall Plan showed what Czechoslovak foreign policy would become, with its one-sided orientation to the Soviet Union. Therefore, the policy change brought about by the communist takeover and the outbreak of the Cold War was more one of degree than kind. Communist Party officials used their domination of public discourse to legitimize their foreign policy by radicalizing their anti-West and especially anti-US rhetoric, depicting the US and its allies as enemies and as threats to Czechoslovak sovereignty.

Apart from the legitimation based on fear in Czechoslovak society grounded in the memory of the very recent loss of sovereignty, there were legitimation narratives drawing from a specific interpretation of the past. In these narratives, emphasis was put on the past experience of Czechs and Slovaks with the Soviet Union and its predecessors and with the US, or the West in general. The meaning of the historical encounters with the East and the West was reinterpreted to fit into the communist friend-enemy dichotomy; all memories that were at odds with the newly drawn image were to be erased. The aim of the new memory policies was to strengthen the persuasive power of the historical argument for the eastern-oriented foreign policy and to naturalize the constructed images of friendship and enmity by demonstrating the long continuity of Soviet or Russian-Czechoslovak cooperation and of a Western hostile attitude toward Czechoslovakia. In other words, the Communist Party attempted to persuade the Czechs and Slovaks that the US had always been and still was an enemy of Czechoslovak sovereignty, while the Soviet Union had acted and was still acting as a friend and helper of Czechoslovakia.

A Thousand Years of Struggle for Slavic Unity

> The Slavic policy of our republic is often explained as a result of the international constellation that has emerged during the war against Hitler's Germany and after this war. But this is only one side of the story. Our Slavic policy has to be understood as the accomplishment of a long-term process involving the efforts of the Slavic nations to cooperate, to pool their strengths, and to achieve unity backed up by the great Russia. The aim of this unity was always joint defense against the common enemy—German expansion—as well as economic and cultural rapprochement.[9]

The introductory words of the 1947 publication *1000 let: Kronika československo-ruských styků slovem i obrazem* [1000 Years: The Chronicle of Czechoslovak-Russian Relations in Words and Pictures] emphasize an important aspect of the communist narrative legitimizing the eastern-oriented foreign policy during the early postwar years. The perception of the German threat and the need to secure the sovereignty of Czechoslovakia was not the only argument used in support of close cooperation with the Soviet Union. Its second and even more important foundation was the stress laid on the long-term character of the relations with Russia and other Slavic nations. While the perceived threat reinforced by the recent experience with Germany provided arguments valid for the duration of that particular threat, which would disappear with the end of it, the emphasis on the long-lasting cultural and economic links justified cooperation regardless of geopolitical concerns.

On the one hand, the Communist Party stressed continuity with the traditional national idea of Slavic unity and friendship among the Slavic nations. It congratulated itself for having realized the dreams of the "best sons of our nation"[10]—that is, representatives of the national movement, who in the nineteenth century envisioned a united Slavic world under the leadership of Russia. But at the same time, the communist historians and politicians, for example, historian Václav Čejchan or Minister of Education and National

Enlightenment Zdeněk Nejedlý, drew a clear demarcation line between them and the national movement. While nineteenth-century tsarist Russia was unable to meet the expectations of Czech and Slovak national figures because of its imperialistic policy, the socialist Soviet Union with its peaceful and cooperative policies would lay the foundations for true Slavic unity.[11]

The most visible expression of this ideal of unity in public space was the so-called Slavic Day celebrated since 1945 close to Saints Cyril and Methodius Day (July 5) at Devín Castle. The choice of this symbolic place, which had become a meeting point for the Slovak national movement in the nineteenth century, underlined the continuity of Czechoslovak postwar foreign policies with national traditions. The "Victorious February" was presented as a turning point in the history of Slavic unity, and the significance of the celebrations in July 1948 was underlined by the presence of the Czechoslovak president Klement Gottwald.[12]

However, the development of Slavic Day in succeeding years demonstrated the fading of the idea of Slavic unity in the communist narrative. In 1951, the name of the celebration was changed to "Peace Manifestation," media coverage decreased and the highest state officials stayed away. By 1952, the event disappeared completely. In Czechoslovak propaganda since 1948, Slavic unity and friendship was replaced by the idea of proletarian internationalism, which corresponded more closely to the new political situation in which the socialist world led by the Soviet Union encompassed non-Slavic states such as the German Democratic Republic and Hungary, while at the same time a significant part of the Slavic world—the Yugoslavs—was rhetorically and institutionally excluded from the socialist community. But the recourse to traditions of the nineteenth-century national movement with its hopes for unity among Slavic nations did play an important role in the legitimization of the country's foreign policy in the early postwar years.

Reinterpreting the Role of the US and the Soviet Union in the Czechoslovak Independence Struggle: From Wilson to the Revolutionary Example

> To remove the remnants of the legends, myths, and superstitions of cosmopolitanism from the thought and feelings of Czechs and Slovaks is an important task. As the Wilson legend is the most comprehensive attempt at a cosmopolitan falsification of our history, and as it played an important role in the introduction of the cult of America and of Western imperialism in general in our lives, the destruction of the legend is an important contribution to fulfilling our patriotic task.[13]

With these words, Jiří Hájek, rector of the University of Economics in Prague, member of the Central Committee of the Communist Party and author of 1953 *Wilsonovská legenda v dějinách ČSR* [The Wilson Legend in Czechoslovak History], described his mission. It was apparently managed from the higher ranks of the Communist Party, as could be understood through the foreword, which stated that the initiative for the publication came from the Institute of History of the Communist Party of Czechoslovakia, closely tied to the party's political elites. The importance of producing such a book was also discussed at the First Ideological Conference in Brno in March 1952, as Hájek pointed out.[14] Moreover, the relatively high print runs of this publication indicated state support, since production and distribution of books was planned, regulated and controlled by the Central Administration for Publishers, Printers and Booksellers—a department of the Ministry of Culture. Finally, Hájek's book was not the only attempt to revise historical interpretations widespread during the First Republic. Many articles in newspapers and magazines were aimed at reinterpreting the role of the US and the Soviet Union in the beginnings of the independent Czechoslovak Republic as well[15] and were consistent with the new memory policy termed by President Gottwald as "the end of a false historical fiction."[16]

The arguments used by the communist historians to disprove the positive role of President Wilson in founding Czechoslovakia[17] were quite diverse and ranged from Wilson's "undemocratic" attitude in domestic politics exemplified by the problem of racism in the US to Wilson's foreign policies denounced as "dollar imperialism."[18] Wilson's views on the independence of Czechoslovakia were interpreted in accordance with the image of American imperialism. Not only Hájek but also all historians dealing with this topic emphasized the change in Wilson's attitude: While initially Wilson supported the preservation of the Habsburg monarchy and was not interested in an independent Czechoslovak state, under the pressure of events, he changed his mind and presented himself as a liberator of the small central European nations, thus spreading the political, economic and cultural influence of the US in this part of the world.

At the same time, the book by Hájek provided some insights into the attitudes of Czechoslovak society toward Wilson before the Second World War, indicating that the task of removing Wilson from Czechoslovak history would be difficult notwithstanding communist dominance in the public sphere. Hájek spoke of the mass circulation of Wilson's portraits among the Czechoslovak population in the interwar period. Moreover, all the political forces in interwar Czechoslovakia reinforced the "Wilson legend" in their speeches, and even the Catholic Church invited Catholic Czech and Slovak émigrés living in the US to speak in Czechoslovakia in order to boast of Czechoslovakia's connection to the "American benefactor," as Hájek described.[19] The popularity of President Wilson in interwar Czechoslovakia was reflected in public space through the naming of streets, squares and buildings—for example, the main railway station in Prague—after Wilson. On the occasion of Wilson's funeral in 1924, there were memorial services in Czechoslovakia as well, and in 1928, Wilson was honored with a statue in Prague.[20]

The widespread popularity of the US in Czechoslovak society enforced by the role of the US in the Second World War and afterward (for example, by aid distributed by United Nations Relief and Rehabilitation Administration) was clearly at odds with communist attempts to establish an enemy image of the US and to show the long continuity of a hostile relationship between the US and Czechoslovakia. At the same time, the "Wilson legend" was an impediment to the emerging narrative aimed at legitimizing the eastward orientation of Czechoslovak foreign policy by emphasizing the eternal tradition of Czech/Slovak-Russian friendship. The evidence for the huge effect of this friendship was sought not only in nineteenth-century Pan-Slavic projects, as described earlier, but also in the initial phase of the independent Czechoslovak Republic.

The narrative of President Wilson as a liberator of small central European nations from Habsburg rule was displaced by stressing the importance of the "revolutionary example of the Soviet Union" for Czechoslovakia's struggle for independence. President Gottwald described the main outlines of this new interpretation in an article for the communist daily *Rudé Právo* [Red Justice] on the occasion of the thirtieth anniversary of the October Revolution. In Gottwald's view, the 1917 Bolshevik revolution in Russia dealt the deathblow to the Habsburg monarchy, posed the issue of self-determination of the peoples and inspired the Czechs and Slovaks in their struggle for independence.[21] After February 1948, this narrative entered the school curricula and became the official view. In a history textbook published in 1953, the group of authors led by Jan Dědina emphasized the strikes and protest actions of Czechoslovak workers inspired by the Soviet example and organized in Czech cities (Prague, Pilsen, Kladno and Ostrava) in October 1918 as the main driving force in the struggle for national sovereignty. At the same time, the authors countered the "Wilson legend" by pointing to the initial reluctance of Wilson to dismantle the monarchy.[22]

This rewriting of the history of the Czechoslovak Republic's foundation[23] was manifested in the altered meaning of the national holiday on October 28, originally commemorating the declaration of Czechoslovak independence in 1918. The commemoration of the foundation of the "bourgeois" First Republic was not in the interest of the Communist Party, especially since gratitude expressed to the allies, and to President Wilson in particular, was a regular part of the commemoration ceremonies between 1918 and 1938.[24] Therefore, October 28 was celebrated as "Nationalization Day" since 1952, recalling the nationalization of major industries in October 1945 (although this did not occur exactly on the twenty-eighth). While in the first years after the communist takeover, articles in the official press tried to establish a connection between the two commemorations, in later years, the earlier association was overshadowed entirely by the newer meaning. On October 28, 1950, *Rudé Právo* published an article by Minister of Industry Gustav Kliment remembering both events and interpreting the nationalization of industries as a completion of the efforts that had begun in 1918.[25] One year later, the same author in the same newspaper did not even mention 1918 and referred only to the nationalization of industry.[26] Brief mention was made of 1918 later on in the same issue, but only in order to assert that independence in 1918 could not be the actual basis for commemorating the day as a significant turning point in Czechoslovak history.[27]

Thus the communist narrative of the foundation of the Czechoslovak Republic in 1918 had two important aspects reflecting shifts in foreign policy. First, it denied the US contribution to Czechoslovakia's independence, breaking with Tomáš Garrigue Masaryk's attitude of gratitude, as expressed in interwar Czechoslovak celebrations of the US and Wilson.[28] Second, stress was laid on the role of the USSR and of the Bolshevik revolution in the Czechoslovak struggle for independence, thus redirecting gratitude toward the new hegemon. The celebrations of the fortieth anniversary of the foundation of the Czechoslovak Republic in 1958 took place under the slogan "there would not be an independent Czechoslovakia without the Great October Socialist Revolution" (*Bez Velké říjnové socialistické revoluce by nebylo samostatného Československa*), thus shifting attention from declaration of independence to the Bolshevik revolution—i.e., to the historical link between Czechoslovakia and the Soviet Union. At the same time, the links between Czechoslovakia and the West were reduced to a master/slave dichotomy, with Czechoslovakia as a mere object of the US's political, economic and cultural interests.

Betrayal by the West and the Threat of a "New Munich"

> The servitude and kowtowing to America, and to the capitalist West in general, the humiliation and suppression of national pride, ostentatious ignorance towards the Soviet Union, and even the attack and defamation of it [. . .] were part of the ideological and moral preparation for the Munich Betrayal.[29]

This citation from Hájek's book on Wilson illustrates the second function of the "Wilson legend" in the communist past narrative. Beyond disproving the role of the US in Czechoslovakia's winning of independence, party historians attempted to establish a causal link between the influence of the US in the First Republic and the loss of sovereignty through the Munich Agreement.[30] The "Western Betrayal" in Munich was primarily associated with France and Great Britain, the two signatories of the Agreement with Nazi Germany and Fascist Italy from 1938. Considering the traumatic nature of this event for the Czechoslovak people,[31] the Communist Party was eager to displace onto the US the negative feelings about the Western abandonment of Czechoslovakia. Since the US did not participate in the Munich conference, the link was established indirectly and supported with two arguments.

The subordinate position of Czechoslovakia vis-à-vis the US and the interwar Czechoslovak elites' ignoring of the Soviet Union and consequent failure to accept its alleged offer of assistance constituted one part of Hájek's explanation. But there was also another point used by the communist narrative to demonstrate the involvement of the US in the Munich Agreement. Several articles in the communist weekly *Tvorba* [Creation], which was regarded as the voice of Gustav Bareš, director of the Central Committee's Department of Culture and Propaganda, used a number of arguments to demonstrate the role of the US in the rearmament of interwar Germany, which was said to have laid the basis for the Munich Agreement.[32] The historians Karel Bartošek and Karel Pichlík even concluded that the US had "the decisive share in selling out Czechoslovakia to Hitler" in Munich.[33] The claim of American participation in the so-called Munich betrayal was in line with the general tendency of historical interpretations disseminated during the rule of the Communist Party in Czechoslovakia, which stressed the long-standing continuity of a hostile Western attitude, in particular of the USA, toward Czechs and Slovaks.

However, the constantly repeated claims of US involvement in the Munich Agreement played yet another role in legitimizing Czechoslovak foreign policy shortly before and after the communist takeover. Proceeding from this assumption, the postwar cooperation with and reliance on the US were presented as steps toward the so-called New Munich. The "New Munich" became a key concept in legitimizing the orientation of communist foreign policy. Before the takeover, it was used to justify Czechoslovak rejection of the Marshall Plan. The persuasive power of this argument was recognized even by non-communist politicians who approved the establishment of stronger ties to the East, although they did not want to break with the West entirely.[34] After the takeover, the "New Munich" remained an important allegory for the impending loss of sovereignty. In the course of the Korean War, 1950–1953, the communist media stressed the similarities between the small Korean and Czechoslovak nations in order to evoke a sense of danger posed by the US.[35]

As to the theme of the Soviet offer of help refused on ideological grounds by the elites, underscored by all the cited historians, the claim was that the Soviet Union would have helped Czechoslovakia even in the traumatic Munich settlement if only the Czechoslovak "bourgeoisie" had accepted it. The argument implied comparability with the postwar development, especially after the outbreak of the Cold War. In this view, the West threatened Czechoslovakia and the East offered help. But now, because of the "Victorious February" and the communist eastward-oriented foreign policy, the outcome would be different, as the Soviet Union would guarantee Czechoslovak independence.

The two images—of Soviet help, on the one hand, and the American threat, on the other hand—were structurally interconnected and worked in

Liberation from the East, Occupation from the West

The model of the Soviet Union as a friend of Czechoslovakia and the US as enemy also affected the interpretation of the end of the Second World War. In the agreement between the Soviet and US militaries dividing Czechoslovak territory, a demarcation line was drawn through Bohemia. Accordingly, the Third US Army of General George Patton liberated West Bohemia. After the war, there were annual celebrations commemorating this event, and several cities (Klatovy, Sušice, Sokolov) installed commemorative plaques. In Pilsen, the largest city liberated by the Americans, there was a collection of donations to erect a memorial to the US Army. However, this kind of commemoration clearly did not fit into the communist narrative stressing the hostility of the US toward Czechoslovakia, and, consequently, it was not desirable after 1948.

In the first years after seizing power, the Communist Party chose to ignore the memory of the liberation by the US Army in order to not draw undue attention to it. In 1948, the party abolished and banned the celebrations of the liberation in Pilsen. However, the association uniting anti-fascist fighters called Union of National Revolution (*Svaz národní revoluce*) and the regional cultural council (*Osvětová rada*) organized a commemorative event that—in the view of communist officials—got out of hand and developed into an anti-communist "provocation."[36]

The regional committee of the party later met to discuss the event. As the archival material shows, there was no agreement in the party on how to deal with the undesirable memory. Some party officials criticized the party's omission of the US role in liberation and saw the ban as having triggered political protest. Karel Štekl, secretary of the regional committee of the party in West Bohemia (*Západočeský krajský výbor*), said,

> I have the impression that we should not have concealed from the people that the Americans came here; we should have displayed the American flag on the city hall. The consequences would have been less serious than the consequences of it not being there. Lots of reasonable people noticed it, and they [the reactionaries] told them that it is an infringement of ceremonial propriety.[37]

And Štekl continued by proposing that the achievements of the US Army in liberating the city be recognized simultaneously with an expression of disapproval of current US foreign policy. Similarly, Josef Dvořák, member of the Presidium of the West Bohemian regional party committee, acknowledged the party's tactical mistakes and reasoned that it would have been better to use the ceremonies for communist agitation than to forbid the American flag, which created space for "reactionary forces."[38]

However, these proposals were not adopted in the strategy deployed in the following years. Although the Communist Party did not deny the fact that the Americans came to West Bohemia in 1945, there were no celebrations; this had to do with the reinterpretation of the events in which the US presence on Czechoslovak territory was conceived not as liberation but as occupation. The already existing commemorative signs were removed from public space—for example, the plaques in honor of the US Army in the towns of Sušice and Klatovy. The money collected for the memorial in Pilsen was sent to Korea after the outbreak of the Korean War in June 1950.

Moreover, in order to justify the characterization "occupation," several articles and publications were dedicated to explaining the "actual" role of Americans in West Bohemia. This effort was initiated in 1951 with the article "Shameful Role of the American Occupiers in West Bohemia in 1945" (*Hanebná role amerických okupantů v západních Čechách v r. 1945*)[39] by the young historians Karel Bartošek and Karel Pichlík.[40] It was considered so important that an expanded version appeared as a book in the same year through the publishing house Svoboda, controlled by the Department of Culture and Propaganda of the Central Committee of the party. The huge edition of more than 50,000 copies indicated the importance attached to the book. Moreover, there was a second enlarged edition two years later with the somewhat milder sounding title *Američané v západních Čechách v roce 1945* [Americans in Western Bohemia in 1945].[41] However, the argumentation and the biased, emotionally charged vocabulary remained.

The book began by presenting the conduct of American soldiers toward Czechs in 1945 as the manifestation of a US foreign policy that endangers the freedom of the peoples. Bartošek and Pichlík then described the developments up to the Second World War, refuting the "Wilson legend" and pointing to US involvement in rearming Germany and in the Munich Agreement. In the chapters dealing with the US Army in West Bohemia, US soldiers were called "protectors of the Nazis," "destroyers of our economy" and "carriers of the American way of life," whose image was purely negative. Needless to say, the book portrayed the Red Army as the "true liberator." The text was supported by visual material showing—for example, buildings (a school and workers' houses) destroyed by American bombs during the war. The contrast between the Americans and the Soviets was especially striking in an illustration in the book by caricaturist and artist Lev Haas, which depicted a Soviet soldier lifting a smiling child, with a second child running toward him with a bunch of flowers; in stark contrast, the same drawing showed an American soldier aiming his gun at a Czech girl.[42]

The role of the US Army and the Red Army in the liberation of Czechoslovakia in 1945 implied symmetry in these two countries' relationship to

Czechoslovakia. Obviously, the notion of liberation from both East and West contradicted the newly drawn line between friends and enemies. Therefore, the Communist Party looked for suitable strategies to avoid possible analogies and to erase the image of the US as a liberator of Czechoslovakia. First, it tried to retain silence about the US Army presence in Czechoslovakia in 1945. However, the strategy was problematic since the silence around the event had the effect of drawing even more attention to it. That is why a shift occurred in 1951. The Communist Party turned to stressing the negative role of Americans and this reinterpretation was reflected in the semantics distinguishing strictly between the American "occupation" and the Soviet "liberation."

The Persuasive Power of the New Historical Narratives

> The propaganda overemphasizes the influence of the Soviet Union on our history, our political and cultural life, and our industry. It goes so far that it appears as if everything our people achieved was the result of the Soviet influence.[43]

This quote is from a resolution adopted in May 1956 during the de-Stalinization process[44] by the students of the Faculty of Education at the Charles University in Prague, and it illustrates the kinds of reservations generated by the omnipresence of the Soviet influence in communist interpretations. The question that arises is that of the extent to which the communist interpretation was able to become hegemonic in the society. There can be no definitive answer because of the lack of a reliable source dealing with historical consciousness during the communist period and with public opinion vis-à-vis the role of other nations in Czechoslovak history. Nevertheless, based on research on collective images, and by taking the later developments into account, one can form an idea of the persuasive power of communist narratives.

Speaking of the persuasive power of images of the self and the other, sociologist Bernhard Giesen claims that the constructed images need to be embedded in the general cultural images of a society in order to be perceived as eternal and natural so that their constructedness remains unrecognizable.[45] Similarly, historian Paulina Bren, writing about Czechoslovak culture in the so-called normalization period of the 1970s and 1980s, points to the "Herculean task" that the normalization regime faced when it tried to "re-create a nation as a blank slate without history or memory, to white-wash an entire image rather than merely erase a small part of it."[46] Finally, a study by historian Jan Behrends on the importing of Soviet anti-Americanism to Poland and the German Democratic Republic (GDR) comes to the conclusion that the anti-Americanism in the Stalinist period was more effective in the GDR because of the existing national tradition of anti-Americanism there.

By contrast, in Poland, without a similar tradition, the anti-Americanism remained a foreign element.[47]

The following reflection on the embeddedness of the communist images in Czech culture is based on these considerations. The interpretation of the Soviet Union as a friend and helper of Czechoslovakia was compatible with the significant tradition of Pan-Slavism. Moreover, unlike in Poland, Czech-Russian relations were not affected by a traumatic national experience comparable to the Partitions of Poland in the eighteenth century, the Polish-Soviet War in 1920 and the Soviet invasion in 1939. The disillusionment with the West caused by the Munich "betrayal" contributed to the support for an eastward orientation in Czechoslovak society. As has been said, even opponents of the communists did not doubt the need to have friendly relations with the Soviet Union. Finally, the liberation of Czechoslovakia by the Red Army reinforced the friendship narrative. Hence the images of the Soviet Union disseminated through historical narratives could develop strong persuasive power despite the criticism of some aspects of the Czechoslovak-Soviet relationship expressed since the mid-1950s, especially among students and intellectuals exemplified in the earlier cited students' resolution. Until in 1968, there was far more criticism of the idealized images of the domestic situation in the Soviet Union and the idea of the Soviet Union as a role model for Czechoslovakia than criticism of the image of the Soviet Union as a friend, or at least an ally, of Czechs and Slovaks.[48]

It was only after the invasion of the Warsaw Pact in 1968 that the Czechoslovak-Soviet relationship was shaken to its very foundations. In August 1968, and the following months, a great deal of the opinion expressed in public—for example, in the country's media, but also through signs, leaflets and graffiti—articulated dismay about actions of the former "brotherly nation" and proclaimed the end of the Czechoslovak-Soviet friendship, implying the real existence of this friendly relationship before the invasion.[49]

Turning now to the images of the negative role of the US in Czechoslovak history, we can assume that their persuasive power was hampered by the persistence of images prevalent in the previous periods of Czechoslovak history.[50] In the eighteenth and nineteenth centuries, America had become a dreamland for many immigrants from Czech lands fleeing religious persecution and poverty in the Austro-Hungarian Empire. In the First Czechoslovak Republic (1918–1938), the attitude of President Masaryk, who highly valued American democracy and culture, and the emphasis on the US role in gaining independence enhanced the positive image of America. Despite reservations toward some aspects of American policy, its economy and culture, especially expressed by Catholic intellectuals, who criticized its materialistic culture, and among communists, who disapproved of the capitalist system, one can hardly speak of a pronounced tradition of anti-Americanism in Czechoslovak culture. Even the communist authorities admitted the strong influence of America in Czechoslovak society and considered eliminating the positive images of the US to be a difficult task.[51]

This is not to say that the anti-American campaigns of the 1950s in the communist media had no effect at all. First, the media focused on the links between Germany and the US—i.e., Nazism and US capitalism—trying to recast the existing enemy image so as to encompass the US as well. Given the potency of the German enemy image in postwar Czechoslovakia, the projected connection between Germany and the US effectively damaged the US's image. Second, the strategies of visual representations of the US, spread through posters, photographs and comics—especially after the outbreak of the Korean War—dehumanized Americans in an especially effective way[52] by portraying them as disgusting insects, or as practicing violence against the most vulnerable—children, women and elderly people.[53]

Nevertheless, even the aggressive campaign during the Korean War did not have its intended effects. Some regional party organizations—for example, in the Carlsbad region—pointed to the geographic distance from the war and its consequent scant interest for the Czechoslovak people. But beyond this, the factual representation of US responsibility for the Korean War also met with mixed public response, as some people attributed responsibility for it to both the US and the Soviet Union.[54] The aforementioned resolution of the students criticized the official image of the West as well, indicating that the coverage of the US and the Soviet Union by the state media was, at least partially, counterproductive.

Moreover, the positive images of the US role in Czechoslovak history did not disappear from the collective memory. During the liberalization of the Prague Spring, the media revised some historical images from the 1950s, including the role of the US in the liberation of West Bohemia. In 1968, the commemorative plaques were reinstalled in Sušice and Klatovy, and historians from the Institute of History of the Communist Party of Czechoslovakia (*Ústav dějin Komunistické strany Československa*) drafted a proposal to celebrate the liberation of West Bohemia by the US Army on a par with that of the cities liberated by the Red Army.[55] Even though these proposals were not realized because of the cancellation of reform policies after the invasion of the Warsaw Pact, the memory of liberation by the US Army prevailed and become powerful in the 1980s, when some petitions demanded the reinstallation of the commemorative plaques and a demonstration took place in Pilsen in May 1989 to commemorate the forty-fourth anniversary of liberation by the US Army.

Conclusions

Many scholars in the field of memory studies emphasize the selective nature of collective memory: What is remembered in a society always results from processes of selection, recomposition and reinterpretation of events, images and figures, as well as the forgetting and erasing of incongruent elements.

The selection criteria are neither clear nor uncontested, and they are closely linked to the current needs and power relations of political actors, regardless of the political system.[56] Further, some scholars emphasize that the actors' capacities to reconstruct the past according to their present interests are limited, as the number of available pasts is not infinite, and some inconvenient elements persist.[57] Thus beyond showing the processes of reconstruction of the past in terms of the images of the US and the Soviet Union after the communist takeover in Czechoslovakia, my purpose here was also to point out the limitations of the new past narratives. Indeed, as a result of the weakness of these new narratives, the banned historical images reemerged as soon as party control over public discourse was relaxed, as was the case in the course of the Prague Spring. In the end, it proved impossible to erase all positive memories of the US role in Czechoslovak history. And the 1968 Warsaw Pact invasion and consequent destruction of the narrative of Soviet-Czechoslovak friendship made the narrative of long-lasting US-Czechoslovak enmity still more fragile.

Notes

1 Benedict Anderson, *Imagined Communities: Reflections on the Origin and Spread of Nationalism* (London: Verso, 2006); Ernest Gellner, *Nations and Nationalism: New Perspectives on the Past* (Ithaca: Cornell University Press, 1983); Eric J. Hobsbawm and Terence O. Ranger, eds., *The Invention of Tradition* (Cambridge: Cambridge University Press, 1983).
2 Maria Montserrat Guibernau i Berdún, *The Identity of Nations* (Cambridge: Polity, 2007), 10.
3 The focus on the Soviet Union and the US had two bases. First, in the postwar debates in Czechoslovakia, the two countries standing for East and West, respectively, were presented as two foreign policy options to choose between. Other countries tended to appear merely as allies or enemies of the two major powers. Second, it had to do with Germany, which played a specific role in the postwar debates because of the experience of the war; this has been discussed by historian Christiane Brenner for the period from 1945 to 1948. See Christiane Brenner, *"Zwischen Ost und West": Tschechische politische Diskurse 1945–1948* (München: Oldenbourg, 2009). As for the later period, the communist elites tried to transfer the enemy image of Germany to the US in the early 1950s, as Hans Henning Hahn has shown, thus enforcing the bipolar image of the world. See Hans Henning Hahn, "Stereotypen auf der Wanderschaft: Amerikaner und Deutsche in der Stereotypenwelt des Kalten Krieges," in *Nationale Wahrnehmungen und ihre Stereotypisierung: Beiträge zur historischen Stereotypenforschung*, eds. Hans Henning Hahn and Elena Mannová (Frankfurt am Main: Lang, 2007), 443–472.
4 For studies on memory policy during the Stalinist period in Czechoslovakia see Ján Randák, *V záři rudého kalicha: politika dějin a husitská tradice v Československu 1948–1956* (Praha: Nakladatelství Lidové noviny, 2015); Stanislav Holubec, "Golden Twenty Years or Bad Stepmother? The Czech Communist and Post-communist Narratives on Interwar Czechoslovakia," *Acta Poloniae Historica* 110 (2014): 23–48.
5 "Diskuse na zasedání ÚV KSČ," April 9, 1948, min. Kopecký. Coll. KSČ-ÚV-01, no. 1261/0/1, vol. 5, item 17 (2), 79, Národní archiv Praha.

6 For an extensive overview of this topic including the list of the banned books, see Petr Šámal, *Soustružníci lidských duší: Lidové knihovny a jejich cenzura na počátku padesátých let 20. století: s edicí seznamů zakázaných knih* (Praha: Academia, 2009).
7 "Diskuse na zasedání ÚV KSČ," November 17–18, 1948, min. Kopecký. Coll. KSČ-ÚV-01, no. 1261/0/1 vol. 5, item 20 (4), 141, Národní archiv Praha.
8 For a comprehensive inquiry into this issue see Brenner, *"Zwischen Ost und West."*
9 Václav Čejchan, *1000 let: Kronika československo-ruských styků slovem i obrazem* (Praha: Ministerstvo informací, 1947), 5.
10 Čejchan, *1000 let*. The most frequently mentioned names in this context were those of the poet Jan Kollár and the scientist Pavel Jozef Šafařík, both supporters of the idea of Slavic unity in the nineteenth century. See, for example, a speech by Zdeněk Nejedlý, "Oživenie tradície Devína," in *Prvá cesta na Slovensko: Prejavy, články a fotografie z cesty prezidenta republiky Klementa Gottwalda na IV: Slovanský deň na Devíne 11.VII. 1948*, ed. Povereníctvo informácií (Bratislava: Tatran, 1948).
11 Nejedlý, "Oživenie tradície Devína"; Zdeněk Nejedlý, "Slované dnes a jindy," *Májový list KSČ* (1948): 7.
12 For a report on the "Slavic Day" see *Prvá cesta na Slovensko*.
13 Jiří Hájek, *Wilsonovska legenda v dějinách ČSR* (Praha: SNPL, 1953), 17.
14 Hájek, *Wilsonovska legenda v dějinách ČSR*, 7.
15 See, for example, Čestmír Císař, "Kořeny naší samostatnosti," *Tvorba* 19 (1950): 433–434; Josef Čihák, "Vliv Velké říjnové socialistické revoluce na naše osvobození," *Rudé Právo*, November 4, 1952, 2.
16 Čihák, "Vliv Velké říjnové socialistické revoluce na naše osvobození," 2.
17 For Wilson's policy towards Czechoslovakia see Betty M. Unterberger, *The United States, Revolutionary Russia, and the Rise of Czechoslovakia* (Chapel Hill: University of North Carolina Press, 1989).
18 Hájek, *Wilsonovská legenda*; Vladimír Bernášek and Vladimír V. Bernášek, *Bez slávy a bez ilusí: ČSR a USA v letech 1918–1938* (Praha: Mladá Fronta, 1956), 50–66; Karel Bartošek and Karel Pichlík, *Američané v západních Čechách v roce 1945* (Praha: Mladá fronta, 1953), 7–31.
19 Hájek, *Wilsonovská legenda*, 13.
20 For the image of Wilson in interwar Czechoslovakia see Halina Parafianowicz, "Restoration of Poland and Czechoslovakia in Woodrow Wilson's Policy: The Myth and the Reality," in *From Theodore Roosevelt to FDR: Internationalism and Isolationism in American Foreign Policy*, ed. Daniela Rossini (Staffordshire: Ryburn, 1995), 55–68.
21 Klement Gottwald, "Dík SSSR můžeme dnes kráčet k socialismu pokojnou cestou," *Rudé Právo*, November 7, 1947, 1.
22 Jan Dědina, *Dějiny novověku* (Praha: Státní pedagogické nakladatelství, 1953), 81–82.
23 For the changes in the image of the First Czechoslovak Republic during communist rule, see Holubec, "Golden Twenty Years or Bad Stepmother?" 28–38.
24 See, for example, "Speech by President Masaryk on the Tenth Anniversary of Czechoslovak Independence, October 28, 1928," www.aic.cz/documents/Masaryk_Speech_1928.pdf, accessed April 14, 2017.
25 Gustav Kliment, "Slavné výročí," *Rudé Právo*, October 28, 1950, 1.
26 Gustav Kliment, "Projev ministra těžkého strojírenství Gustava Klimenta," *Rudé Právo*, October 28, 1951, 1.
27 Ludvík Frejka, "Znárodnění: základ rozmachu naší vlasti," *Rudé Právo*, October 28, 1951, 3.
28 Woodrow Wilson recognized the Czechoslovak National Council, an exile organization led by Tomáš Garrigue Masaryk and working for the independence of

Czechs and Slovaks from Austria-Hungary, as a provisional government in 1918. Therefore, and for supporting an autonomous development for the people of Austria-Hungary in his Fourteen Points, Wilson was celebrated as an advocate of independent Czechoslovakia.

29 Hájek, *Wilsonovská legenda*, 16–17.
30 The 1938 Munich Agreement signed by the United Kingdom, France, Germany and Italy permitted Adolf Hitler to annex Czechoslovak territories inhabited mainly by Germans.
31 For the effects of the Munich Agreement on Czechoslovak society, see Hildegard Schmoller, "Der Gedächtnisort 'Münchner Abkommen' als Manifestation tschechischer Selbstbildnisse," in *Nationen und ihre Selbstbilder: Postdiktatorische Gesellschaften in Europa*, eds. Regina Fritz et al. (Göttingen: Wallstein, 2008), 90–107.
32 Michail Gus, "Američtí Mnichované: Jak se připravovala druhá světová válka," *Tvorba* 18 (1949): 771–773; Kamil Winter, "Po stopách Mnichova," *Tvorba* 18 (1949): 915; Oldřich Říha, "Partneri mnichovského diktátu," *Tvorba* 19 (1950): 928–929.
33 Bartošek and Pichlík, *Američané v západních Čechách*, 29.
34 Brenner, "Zwischen Ost und West," 406–407.
35 See, for example, "Provolání I. československého sjezdu obránců míru," *Rudé Právo*, January 23, 1951, 1. For a visual representation of the parallel between Czechoslovakia and Korea, see a cartoon by Otakar Štembera, "Síla lidu je mocnější než zločinné plány imperialistů," *Mladá Fronta*, July 23, 1950, 3.
36 "Zápis ze schůze KV KSČ," May 10, 1948. Coll. KSČ Západočeský krajský výbor Plzeň, no. 457, 212/2, item 13a, 1, Státní oblastní archiv Plzeň.
37 "Zápis ze schůze KV KSČ," 1.
38 "Zápis ze schůze KV KSČ," 1–3.
39 Karel Bartošek and Karel Pichlík, "Hanebná role amerických okupantů v západních Čechách v r. 1945," *Tvorba* 20 (1951): 856.
40 Pichlík was 23 years old, Bartošek only 21. However, both historians soon distanced themselves from this work.
41 Karel Bartošek and Karel Pichlík, *Hanebná role amerických okupantů v západních Čechách v r. 1945* (Praha: Svoboda, 1951); Bartošek and Pichlík, *Američané v západních Čechách*.
42 Bartošek and Pichlík, *Hanebná role amerických okupantů v západních Čechách v r. 1945*.
43 "Návrh rezoulce plenárního zasedání univerzitní organizace Československého svazu mládeže na Pedagogické fakultě Karlovy univerzity v Praze," in *Majáles 1956: Nevydarená revolta československých studentů*, ed. John P. C. Matthews (Brno: Prius, 2000), 22–29.
44 In Czechoslovakia, de-Stalinization began later than, for example, in Hungary or in Poland and proceeded only hesitantly, as the Communist Party of Czechoslovakia was reluctant to admit any failures or to acknowledge the existence of the personality cult in the early 1950s.
45 Bernhard Giesen, *Kollektive Identität: Die Intellektuellen und die Nation* (Frankfurt am Main: Suhrkamp, 1999), 17.
46 Paulina Bren, *The Greengrocer and His TV: The Culture of Communism After the 1968 Prague Spring* (Ithaca: Cornell University Press, 2010), 62.
47 Jan C. Behrends, "Erfundene Feindschaft und exportierte Erfindung: Der spätstalinistische Antiamerikanismus als sowjetische Leiterzählung und polnische Propaganda," in *Antiamerikanismus im 20. Jahrhundert: Studien zu Ost- und Westeuropa*, eds. Jan C. Behrends, Árpád von Klimó and Patrice G. Poutrus (Bonn: Dietz, 2005), 185.
48 In an opinion poll conducted in Slovakia in May 1968, the vast majority of the respondents approved of Czechoslovakia's foreign policy and its cooperation

with the Soviet Union. Only 4 percent were dissatisfied with the foreign policy orientation. But about 60 percent said that the Czechoslovak media concealed deficiencies in the Soviet Union. About a half of the respondents claimed that they had seen more problems while visiting the Soviet Union than expected. "O našich a sovietskych vzťahoch," *Svet socializmu* 17.24 (1968): 2.

49 See, for example, Jindřich Pecka, *Spontánní projevy Pražského jara 1968–1969* (Brno: Doplněk, 1993); Jan Drda, "Hodina pravdy," *Literární listy*, August 28, 1968; Jiří Seydler, "Naše místo," *Reportér* 3.38 (1968): 15.

50 For an overview of the images of the US, see Jozef Švéda, *Země zaslíbená, země zlořečená: Obrazy Ameriky v české literatuře a kultuře* (Příbram: Pistorius, 2016).

51 Hájek, *Wilsonovská legenda*, 16–17; Čestmír Vejdělek, "Socialisticky vychováme československou mládež: Projev člena předsednictva ÚV ČSM Čestmíra Vejdělka," *Rudé Právo*, June 9, 1950, 7.

52 Ofer Zur, "The Love of Hating: The Psychology of Enmity," *History of European Ideas* 13.4 (1991): 345–369.

53 See, for example, a collection of Czechoslovak Peace Committee posters: "Dokumentace I.," box 34 (Československý výbor obranců míru), Národní archiv Praha.

54 "Zpráva o reakci občanstva na poslední události na vnitřním a mezinárodním foru." Coll. Krajský výbor Obránců míru Karlovy Vary, box 115, unit 525, Státní oblastní archiv Plzeň.

55 "Zápis 1. schůze předsednictva Zpč. KV KSČ ze 14.5.1968. K bodu: Návrh krajské skupiny spolupracovníků ÚD KSČ na řešení některých aktuálních historických otázek." Coll. KV KSČ, box 176, unit 1336, 33–36.

56 Aleida Assmann, *Erinnerungsräume: Formen und Wandlungen des kulturellen Gedächtnisses* (München: Beck, 2003); Mathias Berek, *Kollektives Gedächtnis und die gesellschaftliche Konstruktion der Wirklichkeit: Eine Theorie der Erinnerungskulturen* (Wiesbaden: Harrassowitz, 2009).

57 Michael Schudson, "The Present in the Past versus the Past in the Present," *Communication* 11 (1989): 105–112; Barry Schwartz, "Social Change and Collective Memory: The Democratization of George Washington," *American Sociological Review* 56.2 (1991): 221–236.

11 Constructing Memoirs of the October Revolution in the 1920s

Oksana Klymenko

"The October Revolution as a Memory Project"[1]

History is everywhere a means of controlling the present and the future through the interpretation of the past, and the Soviet Union of the 1920s is no exception. A new historical concept was indeed developed: The meaning of the past was to be understood through the lens of class. The October Revolution was at the center of this concept, and the Bolsheviks used it to legitimize their power. Moreover, for the Bolsheviks 1917 marked a new world era as the first step toward the "world proletarian revolution." The implementation of the new concept was part of the formation of the "new Soviet person" who would believe in the revolutionary ideals and in the party, and be able to sacrifice his or her life for them. The first year that celebrations of the revolution's anniversary began to take place in the territories controlled by the Bolsheviks was 1918; it also became one of the Soviet Union's state holidays.

In what follows, I will deal with the "recollection" of the October Revolution. It was a "memory project" primarily involving the gathering of memoirs from revolutionary participants, such as famous Bolsheviks, members of the Communist Party, workers and poor peasants. However, it was aimed not at "restoring" historical memory, but at establishing certain frameworks for "remembering."[2] In the process of redacting the material, a particular interpretation of revolutionary events was developed. The Bolsheviks tried to show that what had occurred in October of 1917 was a revolution, not a coup. The aim was to demonstrate that all actions taken by the Bolsheviks in Petrograd and other cities and towns were revolutionary and for a good cause. The word "revolution" emphasized the legitimacy of Soviet power. In addition, the Bolsheviks identified themselves with revolutionary episodes of previous eras, such as the revolt of Spartacus and the Paris Commune.[3]

However, other terms were also used, among them "the October Uprising" and "the October." These terms are used very consistently in the memoirs of participants in the revolution. Originally, "October Uprising" was used to describe the events that took place in Petrograd in 1917, but armed insurrections and the establishment of the Soviet regime at the local level, which continued to take place after 1917, were referred to as "the October Uprising" as well. "The October Revolution" and "the October" were used synonymously. The term "uprising" was widespread during the 1920s, especially in the first years following the Petrograd events. However, the term "revolution" gradually superseded both of these, as can be seen in its predominance in memoirs published on the eve of the tenth anniversary of the event. Such a transition was unlikely to have been spontaneous, and in fact, the Bolsheviks' claim that the "revolution" marked a new beginning is more convincing than it would be if called an "uprising." Moreover, an "uprising" inadequately designated the kind of event that could legitimize a new authority; it suggested local changes, while the Bolsheviks wanted to emphasize the world proletarian revolution. They underlined its exceptionalism. The revolutionaries claimed to be builders of a "new," "fair," "peaceful" and "perfect" world.[4] This is most probably what lies behind the substitution of the new term.

The term "the October" was disseminated together with the other terms starting in 1917 and used throughout the entire history of the USSR. It offered the advantage of not conveying a meaning as strong as "revolution" did, and it avoided the contradictory connotations of the term "uprising." In Soviet historiography, these three terms ("October Revolution," "the October Uprising" and "the October") were used interchangeably. However, the "October Revolution" was the principal name for the "revolutionary events," and it dominated the reminiscences of the 1920s.

The special Committee on the History of the October Revolution and of the Communist Party (*Komisiia z vyvchennia istorii Zhovtnevoi revoliutsii ta istorii Komunistychnoi partii*—whose acronym is Istpart) supervised the soliciting and publication of memoirs of the October Revolution and, consequently, the construction of Bolshevik history in the 1920s. The committee consisted of a wide network of departments throughout the USSR. It established historical archives, museums and libraries, mounted exhibitions and organized "evenings of reminiscences" and lectures on topics related to the revolution.[5] Istpart created groups of individuals, groups of participants in revolutionary events and "grassroots circles," especially for collecting October Revolution memoirs. Local activists, teachers, pupils and students could work in these groups.

The Ukrainian department of Istpart, whose activity will be at the focus of this study, was under the control of the Central Istpart. The tasks of Istpart territorial divisions were identical throughout the whole of the Soviet Union, and the Ukrainian division's task was primarily to demonstrate that the October Revolution also took place on Ukrainian territory—revolutionaries there had fought against not only the Russian Provisional Government but also against the local authority: The Central Council of Ukraine. A rule was established in the Ukrainian Istpart division to hire not only Russian but also ethnic Ukrainian researchers for territorial departments.[6] Such a requirement was part of the Bolsheviks' *korenizatsiya*,[7] policy of the 1920s, which was called *ukrainizatsiya* on Ukrainian territory. Here it meant the promotion of the Ukrainian language and culture in various spheres of political life.

The activities of the commission were analyzed in the works of Soviet and post-Soviet scientists: Galina Alekseeva, Nikolaj Andrukhov, Nina Komarenko, Vitaly Sarbej and others.[8] What they did, however, was to interpret the memoirs collected and published by Istpart as merely factual material. Different views can be found in the works of Jochen Hellbeck and Frederick Corney.[9] Corney characterized the memoirs of "the October" collected in the 1920s as the first Soviet "memory project."[10] He pointed out that it was implemented not only through the campaign of collecting memoirs by the revolution's participants but also visual means, including the renaming of streets and squares throughout the USSR, the decoration of buildings and squares on "the October" anniversary, the holding of demonstrations and the staging of performances that illustrated the course of the revolution.

It should be noted that the construction of new monuments was also a part of the "correct remembering" of the October Revolution: Monuments of the Russian Empire were destroyed (for example, monuments to tsars), and new monuments were established and dedicated, primarily to Vladimir Lenin, the "leader" of the revolution. Photos of the Bolshevik leaders were printed in magazines and newspapers, and films were made about the revolution, among others Sergei Eisenstein's *Battleship "Potemkin"* (1925), *October: Ten Days That Shook the World* (1928)[11] and Boris Barnet's *Moscow in October* (1927), the plot of which was agreed to by Istpart.[12] This unit also organized and managed archives, exhibitions and museums related to the history of the revolution. Aleida Assmann summed up the importance the Bolsheviks accorded to the archives by emphasizing that "the archive was not only a place where documents from the past were stored, but also a place where the past was constructed, created."[13] She also pointed out the crucial role of control:

> Control over the archive is control over the memory. The composition of the archive was changed after the change of political authority: a new hierarchy of values of importance was created (what had been a secret became open to the public).[14]

In the words of Jacques Derrida, quoted by Assmann, "There could not be political authority without control over archives."[15]

One of the first exhibitions organized by the Central Istpart was on the history of the Communist Party. It opened on the eve of the Tenth Congress of the Russian Communist Party (Bolsheviks) (1921) in the House of Soviets. Books, brochures, documents of the tsarist police, pictures and posters were among its exhibits. Following the example of Moscow, local exhibitions and museums were organized.[16] They also became the basis for a Museum of the Revolution. The idea of the creation of such a museum was announced in 1919 in Petrograd, and in the same year, it opened its gates to the public.[17] German historian Stefan Plaggenborg notes that the museums of the revolution performed the important function of mediator between politicians and the people, and they reflected the self-esteem of the new regime.[18] Describing museums of the 1920s, Plaggenborg emphasizes the political factor of the accountability of revolutionary history museums to Istpart.[19] Istpart interpreted the museums of the revolution as "keepers of revolutionary sites and as cultural and educational institutions."[20]

The objective of this chapter is to analyze the practices of constructing memoirs of the October Revolution in the 1920s or, more precisely, the period from 1920 to 1928 in which Istpart conducted its activities. I examined texts published in Soviet newspapers and magazines, primarily by Istpart press agencies, such as *Proletarskaya revolyutsiya* [Proletarian Revolution] and *Letopis revolyutsii* [The Chronicles of Revolution], as well as the collections of memoirs prepared by Istpart local departments. Recently established research approaches to memory and "remembering" of the past were adopted in this study.[21] The research methodology of ego-documents offered by Irina Paperno (interpretation of ego-documents)[22] and Jochen Hellbeck (changes in the text) was applied to the interpretation of diaries and memoirs of the 1920s to the 1930s.[23]

Earlier researchers were concerned to use the memoirs merely as sources of information on the described events rather than as objects reflecting Ispart's policy and its goal of teaching the "new Soviet man" how to "remember" the "Revolution" "in a proper way." As mentioned earlier, creating an image of the October Revolution and its history occurred both through its portrayal in Soviet films and in literature. These were also elements of the first Soviet "memory project," though the basis of the overall campaign was the memoirs. When people wrote them, they were "learning" to write "like Bolsheviks," demonstrating thus that they were "new Soviet people," loyal to authority and were not among the "subversive elements."

Istpart highlighted the importance of collecting the memoirs: "One of the primary tasks is the creation of sources such as memoir literature and literature of mixed memoir and monographic character."[24] There was a reason that stress was laid on the idea that the sources *were created*. The focus was not primarily on the already written material, but on the writing of new sources about the past. The 1921 Istpart work plan outlined the aim of memory collection as follows:

> To reanimate the memoir literature. This genre of literature should not have the same character as the old literature. Rather, it should differ in its, so to speak, degree of emphasis. In other words, memoirs ought to illustrate this particular period in our party's history rather than represent the author.[25]

In fact, the guideline of "reanimating the memoir literature" actually meant "creating a new literature." And the new literature was shorn of the genre's primary characteristic; that is, the author's personality was pushed to the sidelines, and the event or events became central.

Istpart sent requests for written memoirs to particular individuals, famous participants of the revolution and party leaders. These requests provided detailed instructions on what and how to write. Special schemes designed for memoir writing ensured that memoirs were written "correctly." Memoirs were checked in the central and local departments of Istpart and in publishing houses. The final stage of memoir collecting was their publication, mainly in the form of collective volumes. It should be noted that very often Istpart departments did not get answers to their requests. Even two to five reminders could remain unanswered.[26] It is impossible to determine from how many people Istpart requested memoirs and how many answered. The materials regarding Istpart's work are incomplete and located in the archives of different countries.

The Ispart Guidelines

The first special memoir guidelines were published in the *Byulleten Istparta* [Ispart Newsletter] and *Iz epohi "Zvezdy" i "Pravdy"* [From the Era of "Star" and "Truth"] in 1921 in an article titled "The Basic Outline for Memoirs" (*Konspekt-minimum dlya vospominanij*).[27] The author of this rough scheme was Nikolai Baturin (1877–1927), a Bolshevik, a social and political activist and one of the founders of Istpart. This "Basic Outline" listed 14 points. They were more than just simple recommendations; they were instructions. The authors were not supposed to focus on personal experiences; instead, they were to write about the Bolshevik organizations. They were asked about the size of the organization, how they were formed and financed and about their involvement in the work of different sectors of society (peasants, soldiers, women, students).

Most questions were related to the character of the Bolshevik organizations' work: the dissemination of illegal and foreign literature, the carrying out of propaganda, the relationship between the local organization and the Central Committee with foreign centers and neighboring cities and regions. Attention was paid to mass mobilization: "Were demonstrations and mass meetings organized? What were their themes and slogans? Who spoke at them?"[28] The next group of questions was about the leaders of the organization's activities, such as, "With which party members and propagandists of communist ideas did you cooperate? Were there professional revolutionaries in your organization? How did they work?"[29] The third group of questions was connected with the characteristics of the author:

> If you took part in a certain party congress, what were your reminiscences about it? What were your impressions of the talks and meetings

with famous leaders of the party? Describe your activities before February 1917, after the February Revolution, and during and after the October Revolution.[30]

Answers to these questions made clear to the reader what kind of Bolshevik the author was, but they left out the author's personal qualities.

Similar recommendations were worked out at the local level. For example, one of the local departments on Ukrainian territory prepared its own "Basic Outline" for memoir writing based on the 1921 outline. It contained questions on the content and nature of the party's activities; its propaganda among the rural population, workers and women; and the curricula vitae of the authors, their participation in historical events, etc.[31]

In 1925, entire methodological essays on what and how to write memoirs were published, the most important of which was "How to Write Memoirs" (*Kak nado pisat' vospominaniya*) by Istpart member Joseph Gelis, published in the magazine of Central Istpart, *Proletarskaya revolyutsiya*.[32] He wrote that the main task of memoirs was to recount facts. This involved very detailed narrations of revolutionary events in particular cities. Gelis divided the memoirs into categories depending on the author's participation in certain events: as organizer, participant, witness or simply as one who lived in that period.[33] This view presupposed that everybody would learn how to write equally: both party members and workers. Gelis severely criticized memoirs in which the author spoke a lot about himself or herself: "Such memoirs mostly do not reflect reality, but serve to put the 'central' person in a favorable light. These memoirs are harmful to the younger generation as they influence and hypnotize them."[34] In studying workers' diaries of the 1930s, Jochen Hellbeck notes that these ego-documents mostly recounted major campaigns such as collectivization and industrialization, and, as with the memoirs of the revolution, personal experience here too was secondary, and events were told in a daily-chronicle style.[35] In both cases, we may say that the Soviet memoirs were not only the act of producing the "right version of history" but also producing the "right revolutionary subject."

Gelis's article prescribed the kind of things that should and should not be written about. The time and place of revolutionary events and the social groups, political parties and organizations that took part in them were to be precisely indicated; political leaders clearly characterized; events described; and consequences of victory or defeat clearly specified. According to Gelis, it was not necessary to write about external events when not closely related to the main topic. He, of course, recommended that the authors avoid describing their role in revolutionary events:

> There is no need to mix the activity of the organization and one's personal involvement in its work for the sake of historical credibility, as it always leads to the substitution of the role of the party and general public by one's personal role as a "hero" of one's time. It is extremely

important in historical terms to bring to light the genuine meaning of the events that took place and their venue. Social phenomena in their essence cannot be restricted to one or several individuals. The general public is always influenced by social events.[36]

A person in history is only an external sign of an internal movement of the masses. So, it is harmful to reduce mass movement to some person's individual experience.[37]

Memoir guidelines had to contribute to the construction of "appropriate" memoirs and, respectively, Bolshevik history as a whole. The leitmotif of all guidelines was to describe the revolution and the particular organization that had participated in it, with the result that the author's personality was eclipsed. This was, in fact, one of the features of writing "appropriately," "like Bolsheviks."

Survey Questionnaires for Participants in the Revolution

Another way of constructing memoirs was through the use of surveys. The first one of these was worked out in 1920 together with the Istpart Central Committee of the Russian Communist Party (Bolsheviks) and was addressed "To All Members of the Party" (*Ko vsem chlenam partii*).[38] Istpart hoped that "the mass poll would result in credible factual material, filling the gaps in official documentation."[39] But the appropriate formulating of questions, in fact, required an "appropriate" answer and the avoidance of raising undesirable issues. Their distribution was carried out in 1920 simultaneously with the memoirs' writing campaign. These were two instruments used to teach the population how to write "correctly" about themselves as Soviet citizens. It was also an effective way to gather information about the party members and other citizens. It is probable that the information collected in the surveys was also used by the authorities during the purges of 1937–1938.

Soviet Marxist historian Mikhail Pokrovsky prepared the survey used to solicit memoirs from participants in the 1905 revolution and published it in 1925. It might at first seem unrelated to the October Revolution memoirs, but the two projects applied the same methods of memoir collection. An examination of this survey reveals how it was influenced by the surveys designed for the October Revolution participants.

Istpart did not require complete answers for the survey on 1905. There was only a list of things desirable to remember. The survey was given to those in charge of memoirs' collection, not to those writing them.[40] It consisted of 17 question blocks. Each block consisted of 2 to even as many as 12 questions. We can only mention some of them here. For instance,

> Were there any strikes in your area in 1905? Did you have any party in your area in 1904? What was the population's attitude toward the

declaration of war against Japan? What was the reaction to the events of 9 January? How did the labor movement manifest itself in 1905? What was the attitude towards the "Potemkin" uprising? How was the student movement organized? How active were the trade unions? How was the peasant movement organized?

—along with other questions.[41] Again, this survey did not focus on the personal attitudes of the individuals and their participation. The main focus was on the organizations, events and population as a whole. We can also see parallels between this survey and "The Basic Outline for Memoirs"— namely, in the quantity of questions, answers to which would describe, first of all, the events that had taken place as well as the activity of the Bolshevik organizations and of their supporters. In addition, the main feature of this survey was the emphasis placed on the class division of society, which would emerge from the author's reading of history.

On the eve of the tenth anniversary of the 1917 Revolution, Istpart worked out "The Survey for the October Overturn Participant" (*Anketa uchastnika Oktyabrskogo perevorota*), which was sent to 1,500 individuals, including former members of the Bolshevik fraction of the Central Executive Committee of Councils 1917, members of the Petrograd Military Revolutionary Committee, the Central Committee of the Party, delegates to the Second Congress of Soviets and other activists of the revolution.[42] Around 350 completed surveys came back.[43] With such a low rate of return, it was decided not to publish them in the magazine *Proletarskaya revolyutsiya* as had been planned.[44] Among the completed surveys, there were 35 concerning events that had occurred on Ukrainian territories, including Kyiv, Odessa, Katerynoslav, Zaporizhia, Mykolaiv, Kherson, etc.[45]

The survey consisted of three main sections: 1) your work from February to October 1917, 2) the workplace and character of work during the last period before and at the time of the "October Overturn" and 3) work during the first days after the establishment of Soviet rule.[46]

It can be assumed from the headings of the three main sections of the survey that those filling it out were, first of all, expected to demonstrate their own work during the events of the revolution. However, it also assumed that their own personal work should continuously be portrayed in relation to the activities of the Bolshevik organization. Moreover, the texts of the surveys often resembled chronicles of events, as they simply narrated the developments of a certain period, sticking to the questions of the particular section.[47]

In preparation for the tenth anniversary of the October Revolution, a survey was projected for the participants of local revolutionary events. For example, in Kyiv, it would involve the participants in the Arsenal Uprising against the Central Council of Ukraine, which took place in January 1918. The survey dealt with the place and time of the event's onset, its causes, the organization in charge, etc.[48] In 1926, in Kyiv, Istpart disseminated a printed version of "The Survey for the Participant of the October Revolution and Civil War in Kyiv, the Kyiv Region and Other Places" (*Ankety uchastnika Oktyabrskoy revolyutsii i grazhdanskoy voynyi v Kieve, na Kievshchinie i v drugih mestah*) throughout the region. It suggested that the internal order of each account correspond to Ispart's list.[49] However, the results of the survey's preparation, dissemination and responses remain unknown. Apparently, it shared the fate of "The Survey for the October Overturn Participant."[50]

Thus the memoirs of the October events were to be written in the same way that the history of "the October" was constructed. More precisely, the memoirs were used for such a construction.

The Level of Compliance with the Recommendations

During the 1920s, several dozen memoirs were published in the magazine *Letopis revolyutsii*. Almost all of them were written according to the given rules. In most cases, the authors of memoirs were famous Bolsheviks and members of the party. Reminiscences of ordinary revolutionaries, mainly workers, were included in special collections of memoirs and local newspapers such as *Dneprostroy* [Dneprostroi Dam], *Zmychka* [The Union] and others. Comparison of the memoirs of party leaders and simple workers reveals some differences: Despite the instructions provided, party leaders and workers wrote in different ways. The Bolshevik leaders followed Istpart's recommendations more exactly than workers did. Many points of the "Basic Outline for Memoirs" were absent in the workers' memoirs, as simple workers sometimes did not know all the details and thus could not answer all of the questions.

Memoirs published by *Letopis revolyutsii* were carefully checked and corrected by the editorial office before publication. However, there were cases in which they were severely criticized only after publication. A discussion of this appeared in the section "Letters to the Editors" (*Pis'ma v redaktsiyu*). The third issue of the magazine in 1925 contained a correspondence between the author Volodymyr Aussem (1879–1936) and the editor. The author was dissatisfied with the alterations in his memoirs and claimed that the text and, consequently, the meaning was distorted. His memoirs addressed the activity of Yevgenia Bosch (1879–1925), the first national secretary of internal affairs of the Ukrainian People's Republic of Soviets.[51] The discussion came to a stalemate: The editors denied and refuted all the accusations. Volodymyr Aussem, a party member and Soviet military leader, was expelled from the party in 1927, charged with supporting "Trotskyism."

Memoirs published in newspapers represent a separate group of recollections of the October Revolution. For the purpose of analysis, I looked at local publications in a newspaper form devoted directly to the topic of "the October" and spread throughout a certain area of the Ukrainian Soviet Socialist Republic or separate institutions (for example, factories). I analyzed one-day newspapers, released on the eve of the tenth anniversary of the October Revolution, and wall newspapers at factories, such as *Desiat rokiv Zhovtnia* [Ten Years since October], *Krasnyi pechatnik* [The Red Typographer], *Zmychka* and others. Considering the fact that Istpart's plenipotentiaries were at the factories, they must have also participated in the preparation of newspaper materials, especially the wall newspapers. As historian Catriona Kelly points out, the wall newspaper was the means of administrative control, a point explicitly enunciated by the Thirteenth Congress of the Russian Communist Party (Bolsheviks) in 1924, according to which a wall newspaper as a means of propaganda had to be under the control of party centers and the Komsomol.[52]

Newspaper issues dedicated to the October Revolution also paid great attention to memoirs of the revolution's participants. Special attention was paid to the factories at the time of the revolution. The titles of the memoirs speak for themselves: "The Baltic Shipyard in the Days of the Revolution (The Reminiscences of a Participant)" (*Baltijskij zavod v oktyabr'skie dni (vospominaniya uchastnika)*) "How We Saved a Factory from Devastation" (*Kak my ohranyali fabriku ot razgroma*) and others.[53]

Memoirs were characterized by the division between "us" and "them," such as "Mensheviks are not our allies."[54] Soldiers of the Ukrainian National Army (*petlyurivtsi*) and the soldiers of the Volunteer Army (*denikintsi*) were also often described as "them."[55] Sometimes, it was already evident from the title who was considered an enemy: "Barbarities Committed by Kolchak" (*Zverstva Kolchaka*),[56] "Struggle Against Antonov's Gangs" (*Borot'ba z bandami Antonova*).[57]

The other object of analysis is the dating and chronology of events. Newspapers talked not only about October 1917. They also mentioned the February Revolution and the "underground revolutionary movement" in general.[58] Similar tendencies were also visible in Istpart's publications of memoirs. The revolution was interpreted there as carefully prepared and not spontaneous, and the vast majority of attention in the newspapers focused on the "Civil War." The Ispart memoirs mostly associated "the October" with the first Bolshevik actions; however, the newspaper memoirs were not so clear. In the newspapers, "the October" meant either the events in Moscow and Saint Petersburg (for example, in memoirs "The First Clashes with Junkers" (*Pervye boi s yunkerami*) by Drozhyn[59] and "The Past" (*Byloe*) by N. Belman)[60] or the first Bolshevik uprisings on different territories and the final seizure of power by them (for example, "October memoirs" placed in the newspaper *Zmychka*, encompassed the years 1918–1919 in the southern governorates of Ukraine and described the periods of "hetmanate" rule, "Petlyura rule" or "Denikin rule," which resulted in the establishment of Bolshevik government).[61]

Thus the selection of events is one of the main differences between the memoirs published in newspapers and by Istpart. Moreover, this problem is closely related to the next one: Many newspaper memoirs did not provide the dates and locations of the described events. This is the case, for example, with "The Memoirs" (*Vospominaniya*) by Drobytko,[62] "In the Days of Struggle—The Reminiscences" (*V dni bor'by. Vospominaniya tov. Stepanova*) by Stepanov and others.[63]

Further, another major difference should be pointed out: The author could be at the center of his or her own reminiscences in the memoirs published in the newspapers, which is very uncommon in Istpart publications. In addition, newspaper memoirs about the revolution were often connected to stories about the author's family. This meant that in the official memoirs, emphasis was placed on the public sphere—the collective and the political—while those published in the newspapers to some extent brought in the private sphere—the individual and the personal.

It is thus evident that Istpart was unable to control the process of the October Revolution's "remembrance" in society completely. If Istpart had problems with its own staff, it was even more difficult to keep all newspapers under complete control. Sometimes local departments of Istpart consisted of only one or two people. As a result, not all the points from the "Basic Outline for Memoirs" and the methodological essay by Joseph Gelis were fully implemented.

Nonetheless, from Istpart's point of view, newspaper articles about the revolution could not be simply labeled "wrong" because all of them were about certain revolutionary events, which the authors called the October Revolution. The authors wrote about the revolution's participants and movements. Here we can see the influence of Gelis's article. The instructions did in fact affect the writing style of the newspaper articles, but their compliance could only be partial because these instructions were primarily intended for memoirs published in Ispart magazines, such as *Letopis revolyutsii* and *Proletarskaya revolyutsiya*, and in memoir collections.

Conclusions

It must be remembered that the "memory project" dedicated to 1917 was the first Bolshevik attempt at memory policy. This October "recollection" campaign was one of the new power's first projects in the cultural sphere. The October Revolution played a key role in the new Bolshevik version of history: It was both reference point and culmination of their political activity.

The enforcement of Ispart's rules and methodology differed in various publications. Therefore, the Soviet Union of the 1920s can still not be called "The Empire of Memory."[64] The authority only took the first steps in this direction, and control over its practical implementation was minimal—"the October" was not always "correctly" described in the reminiscences. Nevertheless, this project, despite the weaknesses in its implementation, established a model for future campaigns to propagate the desired manner of writing history and launched the writing of new Soviet "ego-documents." The first "memory project" became the basis for future Soviet memorial practices, which later did indeed transform the Soviet Union into the "Empire of Memory."

During the Stalin period, more precisely from the end of the 1920s to the mid-1930s, another "memory project" was carried out. It was dedicated to writing the history of factories: Workers wrote reminiscences about their participation in "building socialism." A new commission was established in 1931. It was called The Commission on the History of the Factories (*Komissiya s istorii fabrik i zavodov*). Some of its tasks were similar to those of Istpart. The memoir-gathering methods were similar to those used in the previous project—for example, in the issuing of special instructions for writing reminiscences. After World War II, the memoir-collection plan established in the 1920s became the basis for the campaign of "remembering" the war. In addition, detailed reviews of the memoirs by Istpart's editors contributed to the transformation of memoirs into a literary genre.

Notes

1 I refer to the title of Frederick C. Corney's article "Rethinking a Great Event: The October Revolution as Memory Project," *Social Science History* 22.4, Special Issue: *Memory and the Nation* (1998): 389–414.
2 Corney, "Rethinking a Great Event," 401.
3 Serhy Yekelchyk, *Imperiia pamiati: Rosiisko-ukrainski stosunky v radianskii istorychnii uiavi* (Kyiv: Krytyka, 2008), 35.
4 Stefan Plaggenborg, *Revolyutsiya i kultura: kulturnyie orientiry v period mezhdu Oktyabrskoy revolyutsieyi epohoy Stalinizma*, trans. from the German Irina Kartasheva (Sankt-Petersburg: Zhurnal "Neva," 2000), 7.
5 Vitaly Sarbei, "Istparty ta yikh mistse v rozvytku istorychnoi nauky na Ukraini," *UIZh* 1 (1967): 3–4.
6 The Central State Archive of Public Organizations of Ukraine (further: TsDAHOU)—F. 1—Op. 20—Spr. 2021.—Ark. 13.
7 *Korenizatsiya*, in Russian "putting down roots," that is, promoting identities of ethnic groups within the Soviet Union.
8 Galina Alekseeva, "Istpart: osnovnye napravleniya i ehtapy deyatel'nosti," *Voprosy istorii* 9 (1982): 17–29; Nikolaj Andruhov, *U istokov istoriko-partijnoj nauki (Kratkij ocherk deyatel'nosti Istparta: 1920–1928)* (Moskva: Izdatelstvo "Znanie," 1979); Nina Komarenko, "Vysvitlennia borotby za peremohu vlady rad na Ukraini v zhurnali *Litopy srevoliutsii*," *UIZh* 1 (1967): 130–137; Sarbei, "Istparty ta yikh mistse v rozvytku istorychnoi nauky na Ukraini."
9 Jochen Hellbeck, "Fashioning the Stalinist Soul: The Diary of Stepan Podlubnyi, 1931–1939," in Jochen Hellbeck, *Revolution on My Mind: Writing a Diary Under Stalin* (Cambridge and London: Harvard University Press, 2006): 77–115; Corney, "Rethinking a Great Event," 389–414.
10 Corney, "Rethinking a Great Event," 389–414.
11 Corney, "Rethinking a Great Event," 400.
12 M. S. Volin, "Istpart i sovetskaya istoricheskaya nauka," in *Velikij Oktyabr': Istoriya: Istoriografiya: Istochnikovedenie* (Moskva: Nauka, 1978), 194.
13 Aleida Assmann, *Prostory spohadu: Formy transformatsii kulturnoi pamiati*, trans. from the German Kseniia Dmytrenko, Larysa Doronicheva and Oleksandr Iudin (Kyiv: Nika—Tsentr, 2012), 30.
14 Assmann, *Prostory spohadu*, 361.

15 Assmann, *Prostory spohadu*.
16 Andruhov, *U istokovistoriko-partijnoj nauki*, 61.
17 Plaggenborg, *Revolyutsiya i kultura*, 274.
18 Plaggenborg, *Revolyutsiya i kultura*, 274.
19 Plaggenborg, *Revolyutsiya i kultura*, 282.
20 TsDAHOU—F. 1—Op. 20—Spr. 2710—Ark. 32.
21 Aleida Assmann, *Cultural Memory and Western Civilization: Functions, Media, Archives* (Cambridge: Cambridge University Press, 2012); Maurice Halbwachs, *The Collective Memory*, trans. from the French Francis J. Ditter, Jr. and Vida Yazdi Ditter (New York: Harper and Row, 1980); Pierre Nora, *Realms of Memory: Rethinking the French Past*, vol. 1: *Conflicts and Divisions*, trans. Arthur Goldhammer, ed. Lawrence D. Kritzman (New York: Columbia University Press, 1996); Paul Connerton, *How Societies Remember* (Cambridge: Cambridge University Press, 1989); Paul Ricoeur, *Memory, History, Forgetting*, trans. Kathleen Blamey and David Pellauer (Chicago: University of Chicago Press, 2004); Reinhart Koselleck, *Futures Past: On the Semantics of Historical Time*, trans. and introduction Keith Tribe (New York: Columbia University Press, 2004).
22 Irina Paperno, "What Can Be Done with Diaries?" *Russian Review* 63.4 (2004): 561–573.
23 Jochen Hellbeck, "Working, Struggling, Becoming: Stalin-Era Autobiographical Texts," *Russian Review* 60.3 (2001): 340–359; Hellbeck, "Fashioning the Stalinist Soul," 77–115.
24 V. A. Peresvetov, "Deyatel'nost' Istparta po sobiraniyu vospominanij ob Oktyabr'skoj revolyucii i grazhdanskoj vojne," *Voprosy istorii* 5 (1981): 114.
25 "Plan raboty Komissii po istorii RKP," *Iz ehpohi "Zvezdy" i "Pravdy"* 1 (1921): 184.
26 Evgeniya Adamovich, "Doklad Istparta CK KP(b)U na konferencii Istpartov vo vremya 12 s'ezda partii," *Letopis' revolyutsii* 4 (1923): 322–323.
27 Nikolai Baturin, "Konspekt-minimum dlya vospominanij," *Byulleten' Istparta* 1 (1921): 11–12.
28 Baturin, "Konspekt-minimum dlya vospominanij."
29 Baturin, "Konspekt-minimum dlya vospominanij."
30 Baturin, "Konspekt-minimum dlya vospominanij."
31 Diana Shchedrina, "Deyatel'nost' Istparta CK KP(b)U i ego mestnyh organov po sozdaniyu istochnikovoj bazy istoriko-partijnoj nauki (1921–1929 gg.)" (Dis. kand. ist. nauk, Kyiv, 1974), 152.
32 Joseph Gelis, "Kak nado pisat' vospominaniya (Metodologicheskij ocherk)," *Proletarskaya revolyutsiya* 7 (1925): 197–212.
33 Gelis, "Kak nado pisat' vospominaniya," 203.
34 Gelis, "Kak nado pisat' vospominaniya," 202.
35 Hellbeck, "Working, Struggling, Becoming," 350.
36 Gelis, "Kak nado pisat' vospominaniya," 207.
37 Gelis, "Kak nado pisat' vospominaniya," 207.
38 Shchedrina, *Deyatel'nost' Istparta CK KP(b)U*, 148.
39 Shchedrina, *Deyatel'nost' Istparta CK KP(b)U*, 158.
40 Mihail Pokrovskiy, "Prilozhenie k state Pokrovskogo M. N.: Proekt ankety po revolyucii pyatogo goda," *Proletarskaya revolyutsiya* 11 (1924): 14.
41 "Prilozhenie k state Pokrovskogo M.N.," 14–18.
42 Peresvetov, "Deyatel'nost' Istparta po sobiraniyu vospominanij," 119.
43 Peresvetov, "Deyatel'nost' Istparta po sobiraniyu vospominanij," 119.
44 Gennadiy Strel'skij, *Memuary kak istochnik izucheniya istorii Velikogo Oktyabrya na Ukraine* (Kyiv: Vyshcha shkola, 1978), 22.
45 Strel'skij, *Memuary kak istochnik izucheniya istorii Velikogo Oktyabrya na Ukraine*, 22–23.

46 R. Lavrov, V. Loginov, V. Stepanov and Z. Tihonov, *Ot Fevralya k Oktyabryu (Iz anket uchastnikov Velikoj Oktyabr'skoj socialisticheskoj revolyucij)* (Moskva: Gosudarstvennoe Izdatelstvo Politicheskoy Literary, 1957), 7–10.
47 The collected surveys were partially published in a separate edition on the eve of the fortieth anniversary of the October Revolution in 1957. However, the edition contained only 71 completed surveys, including 6 written by those whose activity was connected to Ukraine. Because of their very limited publication, it is impossible to compare the surveys of different periods. These surveys are difficult to analyze since their published texts are incomplete. Thus some events are subject to fragmented description. Sometimes, entire sections are missing. The surveys provide partial information about the authors; the description of the authors' work follows certain set frameworks and, at times, does not allow for the analysis of the causes and consequences of some events in the lives of those filling out such surveys.
48 TsDAHOU—F. 1—Op. 20—Spr. 2021—Ark. 163.
49 Shchedrina, *Deyatel'nost' Istparta CK KP(b)U*, 172.
50 The survey was a part of broader attempt to preserve the memory of the Arsenal Uprising. Films were produced about the Kyiv factory: *Arsenaltsi* (1925, directed by Les Kurbas) and *Arsenal* (1927, directed by Alexander Dovzhenko). The first monuments dedicated to this uprising appeared at the beginning of the 1920s, before the anniversaries of the October Revolution in 1923 and 1927.
51 "Pis'mo v redakciyu," *Letopis' revolyutsii* 3 (1925): 248; "Otvet redakcii," *Letopis' revolyutsii* 3 (1925): 248–250.
52 Catriona Kelly, "'A Laboratory for the Manufacture of Proletarian Writes': The *Stengazeta* (Wall Newspaper), *Kulturnost'* and the Language of Politics in the Early Soviet Period," *Europe—Asia Studies* 54.4 (2002): 579.
53 Smirnov, "Baltijskij zavod v oktyabr'skie dni (vospominaniya uchastnika)," *Krasnyj provod*, November 5, 1927, 1; Tihtenko, "Kak my ohranyali fabriku ot razgroma," *Zavarka*, November 7, 1927, 5.
54 Gromov, "To, chto ostalos' v pamyati," *Dneprostroj*, November 7, 1927, 4.
55 Hnat Taran, "Spomyny z partyzanskoho zhyttia 1919 roku Hnata Onysymovycha Tarana," *Desiat rokiv Zhovtnia*, November 7, 1927, 1; S. Oprishko, "K desyatoj godovshchine Oktyabrya," *Zavarka*, November 7, 1927, 6.
56 Nezhnaya, "Zverstva Kolchaka," *Krasnaya dzhutovka*, November 7, 1927, 3.
57 Lushenko, "Borot'ba z bandami Antonova," *Desyat' rokiv borot'by ta budivnictva*, November 7, 1927, 5.
58 Nezabyt'ko, "V podpol'i," *Zavarka*, November 7, 1927, 5.
59 Drozhzhin, "Pervye boi s yunkerami," *Dneprostroj*, November 7, 1927, 4.
60 N. Bel'man, "Byloe," *Krasnaya dzhutovka*, November 7, 1927, 2.
61 Kherniak, "Zhovtnevi spohady," *Zmychka*, November 7, 1927, 1.
62 Drobit'ko, "Vospominaniya," *Zavarka*, November 7, 1927, 4.
63 Stepanov, "V dni bor'by. Vospominaniya tov. Stepanova," *Krasnaya dzhutovka*, November 7, 1927, 1.
64 See Yekelchyk, *Imperiia pamiati*.

Contributors

Walter Baier is an economist. He received his doctorate at the Vienna University of Business and Economics. He is the political coordinator of transform! europe, a research network of 32 associations, journals and foundations in 21 European countries, also recognized by the Party of the European Left as the political foundation associated with it. He was national chairman of the Communist Party of Austria (KPÖ) from 1994 to 2006 and chief editor of the Austrian weekly *Volksstimme*. His current research is focused on nationalism and European integration, the radical left in Europe and the history of the socialist left in Austria. His latest publications include *Linker Aufbruch in Europa?* (Wien: Edition Steinbauer, 2016); "Europe on the Precipice: The Crisis of the Neoliberal Order and the Ascent of Right-Wing Populism," *New Labor Forum* 25.3 (2016): 48–55; and *Das kurze Jahrhundert: Kommunismus in Österreich. KPÖ 1918 bis 2008* (Wien: Edition Steinbauer, 2009).

Monica Ciobanu is a professor of criminal justice at Plattsburgh State University of New York. She received her PhD in sociology at the Graduate Faculty of Political and Social Science of the New School for Social Research in New York in 2005. Her research is focused on issues of democratization, memory, truth and justice in post-socialism and especially in Romania. Some of her most recent articles include "Remembering the Gulag: Religious Representations and Practices," in *Justice, Memory and Redress in Romania: New Insights*, eds. Lavinia Stan and Lucian Turcescu (Newcastle upon Tyne: Cambridge Scholars Publishing, 2017), 214–234; "Pitești: A Project in Re-education and Its Post-1989 Interpretation in Romania," *Nationalities Papers. The Journal of Nationalism and Ethnicity* 43.4 (2015): 615–633; and "Reconstructing the History of Early Communism and Armed Resistance in Romania," *Europe—Asia Studies* 66.9 (2014): 1452–1481.

Stanislav Holubec holds a PhD in sociology and in social history from the Charles University in Prague. From 2010 to 2016, he was a researcher at Friedrich Schiller University in Jena, Germany. Since 2017, he has been the associate professor at the University of České Budějovice, Czech Republic. His most recent monograph *Ještě nejsme za vodou. Obrazy druhých a historická paměť v období postkomunistické transformace* (Praha: Scriptorium, 2015) examines the Czech post-communist discourses on Otherness and historical memory. He has edited three volumes and has published numerous articles on social history, history of the left and historical memory. Together with Włodzimerz Borodziej and Joachim von Puttkamer, he has co-authored the volume *Mastery and Lost Illusions: Space and Time in the Modernization of Eastern and Central Europe* (München: De Gruyter Oldenbourg, 2014).

Thorsten Holzhauser is a doctoral candidate and teaches modern history at the University of Mainz, Germany. His PhD thesis analyzes the public discourse on German post-communists and their political integration in the united Germany. His recent publications include an article on the strategic relationship between German Social Democrats and Socialists, 1990–1998 ("Niemals mit der PDS?," *Vierteljahrshefte für Zeitgeschichte* 62.2 (2014): 285–308), which was named the journal's "article of the year 2014."

Antony Kalashnikov is a doctoral student at Nuffield College, University of Oxford. His current project is titled "Stalinist Monumental Art and Architecture, and the 'Immortalization of Memory.'" It seeks to demonstrate that the intended audience of Stalinist monumental art and architecture was, at least in part, posterity. The project investigates the motives behind this circumstance and its effect on style and form. His recent publications include "Strength in Diversity: Multiple Memories of the Soviet Past in the Russian Communist Party (CPRF), 1993–2004," *Nationalities Papers. The Journal of Nationalism and Ethnicity* 45.3 (2017): 370–392; and "Interpellation in the Late Soviet Period: Contesting the De-Ideologization Narrative," *Canadian Slavonic Papers* 58.1 (2016): 23–48.

Csilla Kiss holds a PhD in political science from McGill University and has been a teaching fellow at the University of Aberdeen, Scotland. Her research interests focus on the twentieth-century European politics and history, transitional justice, the politics of memory and history and individual accounts of European history, including memoirs and life writings. She has contributed a number of entries to the *Encyclopedia of Transitional Justice* (Cambridge University Press, 2013). Her publications include "Divided Memory in Hungary: The House of Terror and the Lack of a Left-Wing Narrative," in *Life Writing and Politics of Memory in Eastern Europe*, ed. Simona Mitroiu (New York: Palgrave Macmillan, 2015), 242–259; "Historical Memory in Post-Cold War Europe," *The European Legacy: Toward New Paradigms* 19.4 (2014): 419–432; and "We Must Remember Thus: Transitional Justice in Service of Memory in

Hungary," *Studia Universitatis Cibiniensis. Series Historica* 11 (2014): 71–87.

Ekaterina V. Klimenko received her candidate of sciences degree in cultural studies at the Saint Petersburg State University of Culture and Arts in 2010. For several years, she taught at various state universities in Saint Petersburg. In 2016, she held a Wayne S. Vucinich Fellowship at Stanford University. Her research interests are ethnicity and nationalism, nation-building and national identity, political use of history and diversity management; her research focus is on contemporary Russian Federation. She has published a number of articles and book chapters, both in Russian and in English. Her publications include "Izobretenie 'Chuzhogo' i Konstruirovanie Granic: 'Integracija Migrantov' v Rossijskoj Presse (Na Materialah *Rossijskoj Gazety*)," *Politeia* 81.2 (2016): 77–88; "Integracija I Razlichija: O Grazhdanskoj Nacii v Rossii," *Polis* 6 (2015): 131–143; and *Fostering Tolerance towards Migrants: Efforts of the State. The Polish Experience and the Case of Russia* (Warszawa: Instytut Spraw Publicznych, 2014). She is currently a doctoral candidate at the Polish Academy of Sciences in Warsaw.

Oksana Klymenko is a PhD student in the department of history of the National University of Kyiv-Mohyla Academy. Her research interests include the twentieth-century history of Ukraine, politics of memory in the USSR and Soviet political celebrations. Her recent research focuses on the campaign on writing the history of factories, which was held in the USSR in 1920s–1930s, with particular interest in the case study of the Dnieper Hydroelectric Station. Her recent publications include "Soviet Ideology in Workers' Memoirs of the 1920s–1930s (A Case Study of John Scott's and Borys Weide' Memoirs)," *Kyiv-Mohyla Humanities Journal* 3 (2016): 37–55; and "Obraz 'novoi liudyny' u spohadakh radianskykh robitnyts 1920-kh—1930-kh rr.," *Naukovi zapysky NaUKMA* 182 (2016): 35–40.

Aleksandra Kuczyńska-Zonik is an assistant professor at the Institute of East-Central Europe, independent research institute in Lublin, Poland. She holds PhD degrees from the Faculty of Political Science at the Maria Curie-Skłodowska University in Lublin (2015) and from the Faculty of Sociology and History at the University of Rzeszów (2013). Her recent research focuses on politics and security in East-Central Europe and the post-Soviet space, Russian diaspora and Soviet heritage. Her recent publications include "Monument Wars in the Baltic States," *New Eastern Europe* 6 (2016): 165–169; and "Sowjetische Denkmäler in den baltischen Staaten—Nationale Konflikte und internationale Auseinandersetzungen," *Europäische Rundschau* 4 (2016): 95–99.

Agnieszka Mrozik has been an assistant professor at the Institute of Literary Research of the Polish Academy of Sciences since 2012. She holds a

PhD in literary studies (2012) and an MA in American studies (2005). Her research interests include women, gender and generations in state socialist and post-socialist Eastern Europe; female communists in twentieth-century Poland: their history, biography and literature; feminist criticism and women's literature in post-1989 Poland; and critical analysis of media discourse and popular culture. She is the author of the book *Akuszerki transformacji. Kobiety, literatura i władza w Polsce po 1989 roku* (Warszawa: Wydawnictwo IBL PAN, 2012). She has co-authored and co-edited the volumes. . . *czterdzieści i cztery. Figury literackie. Nowy kanon* (Warszawa: Wydawnictwo IBL PAN, 2016), *Encyklopedia gender* (Warszawa: Czarna Owca, 2014) and *PRL—życie po życiu* (Warszawa: Wydawnictwo IBL PAN, 2013).

Jakub Szumski is a research assistant and a PhD candidate at the Graduate School at Friedrich Schiller University of Jena, Germany; the School specializes in the German Democratic Republic (GDR) and the European dictatorships after 1945. He studied history and philosophy at the University of Warsaw and at the University of Konstanz. His research focuses on late socialism in Poland and the GDR. He is currently working on his PhD thesis on political corruption and the fight against it in the Eastern Bloc. His publications include "The Party, Solidarity or Both? Transformation of Political Identities in 1980–81 Poland," in *Post-1945 Poland: Modernities, Transformations and Evolving Identities. Working Papers*, eds. Mikołaj Kunicki, Katarzyna Jeżowska and Hubert Czyżewski (Oxford: St. Antony's College, 2016), 160–172; and "Między radykalizmem a stabilizacją. Polska emigracja górnicza w Belgii 1918–1939," *Neerlandica Wratislaviensia* 25 (2015): 19–37.

Darina Volf is a post-doctoral researcher in the research unit Cooperation and Competition in the Sciences located at the University of Munich and funded by the German Research Foundation. She completed doctoral studies at the Graduate School for East and Southeast European Studies and obtained her PhD from the University of Munich in 2016. Her recent research focuses on the history of Soviet-American cooperation in space. Her further research interests include cultural history and memory studies. She is the author of the book *Über Riesen und Zwerge: Tschechoslowakische Amerika- und Sowjetunionbilder 1948–1989* (Göttingen: Vandenhoeck & Ruprecht, 2017).

Index

Agárdi, Péter 30, 37n7
Allende, Salvador 10, 75, 86, 131, 133, 135
Althusser, Louis 83
Angyal, István 34, 40n44
Anketa uchastnika Oktyabrskogo perevorota [The Survey for the October Overturn Participant] 267–268; see also Istpart
anti-Americanism 51, 253–254
anti-communism 12–14, 22, 36, 46, 52–53, 56–57, 110, 135–137
anti-Stalinism 48
anti-totalitarianism 48, 58–59
Antonescu, Ion 228, 231
Apostol, Gheorghe 226, 233–235, 240n37, 241n44, 241n49, 241n51; see also Letter of the Six (Romania)
Arendt, Hannah 80, 95n31
Arsenal Uprising (Kiev) 267, 273n50; see also October Revolution of 1917
Artner, Annamária 30, 37n7
Ashworth, Gregory J. 102–103, 116nn9–12
Aster Revolution (Hungary) 26; see also Károlyi, Mihály
Austro-Hungarian Monarchy 25, 38n14, 254

Bârladeanu, Alexandru 224, 233–235, 240n37, 241n48, 241n50; see also Letter of the Six (Romania)
Baturin, Nikolai 264, 272nn27–30; see also *Konspekt-minimum dlya vospominanij* [The Basic Outline for Memoirs]
Bauer, Otto 77, 80, 95n30
Beria, Lavrentiy 47, 144
Berlinguer, Enrico 84–85

Berlin Wall 56, 58, 124
Bertinotti, Fausto 88–90, 94n17, 96n53
Bisky, Lothar 45, 52, 64n42
Bolshevik revolution 13, 101, 248–249, 260; see also Bolsheviks; October Revolution of 1917
Bolsheviks 3–6, 199, 216n23, 260–263, 266, 268–269; see also Bolshevik revolution; October Revolution of 1917
Brezhnev, Leonid 5, 11, 47, 49, 53, 146, 173, 189n47
Brucan, Silviu 223, 233–235, 240n37, 241n52; see also Letter of the Six (Romania)
Bukharin, Nikolai 12; see also Great Purge
Butovo (Russia) 149, 155, 161nn73–74; see also Memorial Day for the Victims of Political Repression (Russia)

Carillo, Santiago 84–85, 96n45; see also Eurocommunism
Carl Zeiss factory (Jena) 125–126, 130
Ceaușescu, Nicolae vi, 9, 17n34, 29, 90, 131, 221–227, 233–238, 238n2, 238n5, 240n37, 241n47
Černý, David 107–108; see also monuments, communist and Soviet
Chernyakhovsky, Ivan 104–105; see also monuments, communist and Soviet
Chiocchetti, Paolo 78, 94n24, 95n39
Cold War 1, 49, 52, 56–59, 71n159, 82–83, 91, 168–169, 183, 188n31, 244, 250
collective memory vi, 41–43, 62n10, 111, 113, 141–142, 145, 158n5,

167, 169, 186nn6–7, 191n107, 218n51, 241n56, 241n60, 255, 259n57, 272n21; *see also* historical memory
Cominform 82, 96n40; *see also* Comintern (Communist International)
Comintern (Communist International) 3–6, 30, 79–82, 200, 216n23, 226–228, 234; *see also* Cominform
Communist League (Germany) 79; *see also* Engels, Friedrich; Marx, Karl
Communist Party of Austria (KPÖ) 17n29, 86, 96n54, 274
Communist Party of China (CPC) 169
Communist Party of Czechoslovakia (KSČ) 96n40, 124, 169, 213n5, 243, 247, 255, 256n5, 257n7, 257n11, 258nn36–38, 258n44, 259n55
Communist Party of France *see* French Communist Party (PCF)
Communist Party of Germany (KPD) 4, 66n74, 73n195; *see also* German Communist Party (DKP)
Communist Party of Greece *see* Greek Communist Party (KKE)
Communist Party of Italy 95n36; *see also* Italian Communist Party (PCI)
Communist Party of Poland (CPP) 193, 196, 198–201, 206, 215n19, 216n28, 216n38, 217n41, 219n66; *see also* Communist Workers' Party of Poland (CWPP)
Communist Party of the Russian Federation (CPRF) v, 13, 41–48, 50, 53–57, 59–60, 60nn1–3, 62n7, 62n11, 62n14, 67n94, 68n105, 69n132, 71n153, 96n56, 160n36, 275
Communist Party of the Russian Soviet Federative Socialist Republic (CPRSFSR) 43
Communist Party of the Soviet Union (CPSU) 5, 10, 12, 43–44, 47, 55–56, 80, 82, 84, 87, 96n40, 192, 207; *see also* Twentieth Congress of the CPSU of 1956
Communist Party of Ukraine (CPU) 14
Communist Refoundation Party (PRC) (Italy) 86, 88–89, 96n52, 96n54
Communist Workers' Party of Poland (CWPP) 199; *see also* Communist Party of Poland (CPP)

counterrevolution 13, 31, 45, 184, 186n3
Courtois, Stéphane 18n53, 83; *see also* Maoism
Czechoslovak coup d'état of 1948 *see* Victorious February

Day of People's Unity (Russia) 152
Day of Reconciliation and Cohesion (Russia) 152
Declaration of Independence of 1964 (Romania) 230, 235–236; *see also* Gheorghiu-Dej, Gheorghe
de-communization 102, 111, 115; *see also* de-Sovietization
de-Sovietization 101; *see also* de-communization
de-Stalinization 9, 82, 171, 187n23, 192–193, 206, 213n3, 229, 234, 253, 258n44; *see also* Thaw
Deutscher, Isaac 80, 95n28
DIE LINKE (Germany) 13, 18n50, 60, 61n4, 73n204, 88, 91, 127, 139n43; *see also* Party of Democratic Socialism (PDS)
Dimitrov, Georgi 6, 135, 227
Dobrynin, Konstantin 150
Doftana Prison (Romania) 226, 231–232, 240n29; *see also* Gheorghiu-Dej, Gheorghe
Dzerzhinsky, Felix 198–199, 215n23, 216n28; *see also* Dzerzhinsky, Felix, monument to (Moscow)
Dzerzhinsky, Felix, monument to (Moscow) 145, 156; *see also* Dzerzhinsky, Felix

Eastern Bloc 1, 5, 9–10, 13, 15, 41, 49, 74, 101, 109, 122, 135–136, 227, 277
ego-documents 263, 265; *see also* Istpart
Ellenstein, Jean 85, 96n44
Engels, Friedrich i, 2–3, 5, 13, 16n7, 79, 93n2, 94n23, 94n25, 95nn26–27, 133, 203, 218n53
Eurocommunism 76, 84–86, 96n45; *see also* Carillo, Santiago
European Anti-Capitalist Left 89; *see also* Trotskyism
European Left Party 90, 96n51; *see also* Party of the European Left
European Social Forum 88–89; *see also* World Social Forum

February Revolution of 1917 3, 265, 269; see also Russian Revolution of 1917
Fidesz (Hungary) 21–23, 30–33, 35; see also Orbán, Viktor
First Czechoslovak Republic 136, 243, 248–249, 254, 257n23; see also Masaryk, Tomáš Garrigue
Fourth International 83; see also Trotsky, Leon
French Communist Party (PCF) 7–8, 79, 83–85, 87, 96n40, 96n54
French Revolution 2, 4, 9, 12
Fučík, Julius 136

Gelis, Joseph 265, 270, 272nn32–34, 272nn36–37; see also Istpart; *Kak nado pisat' vospominaniya* [How to Write Memoirs]
Georgescu, Teohari 226, 229; see also Doftana Prison (Romania)
German Communist Party (DKP) 86; see also Communist Party of Germany (KPD)
German Democratic Republic (GDR) i, 9, 15, 16n10, 45, 48–53, 58, 60, 64n43, 66n71, 69n121, 71n173, 73n204, 75, 122–124, 126–127, 129–131, 134–137, 138n12, 140n58, 246, 253, 277
Gheorghiu-Dej, Gheorghe vi, 9, 221–223, 225–227, 229, 231, 233, 235, 237, 239nn16–17, 240n25, 240nn31–32, 240n34, 241n39, 241n41, 241nn43–44, 241nn48–51, 241n55, 241n63
Gierek, Edward 165, 172, 174–175, 181–182, 187n25, 188n33, 194
Glucksmann, André 83; see also Maoism
Gomułka, Władysław 171, 188nn33–34, 192–194, 196, 200–201, 208–209, 212n3, 216n27, 220n75
Gorbachev, Mikhail 11–13, 45, 47, 49–51, 54, 75, 87, 143–144, 184, 223, 233
Gottwald, Klement 1, 9, 130–132, 134–135, 139n27, 139n32, 243, 246–248, 267n10, 257n21
Gramsci, Antonio 77
Great Patriotic War i, 6, 10–11, 47, 54, 105, 146, 152, 154, 157
Great Purge 12; see also Stalinist purges of the 1930s

Greek Communist Party (KKE) 87, 90
Green Bridge (Vilnius) 106, 114, 117n34; see also monuments, communist and Soviet
Grivița strikes of 1933 (Romania) 231–232, 240n29; see also Gheorghiu-Dej, Gheorghe
Grūtas Park (Lithuania) 112; see also museums
Gulag i, 9, 14, 27, 47, 55–56, 155–156, 236, 274; see also Perm-36; State Museum of the History of Gulag (Moscow)
Gysi, Gregor 45, 52, 57, 61n4, 64n33, 64n35, 67n77–78, 69nn117–118, 69nn124–126, 69n128, 72nn174–175, 72n178, 72n189, 75, 93n6
Gyurcsány, Ferenc 22, 29, 31–35, 39n37, 39n39, 39n41

Hajdú, Tibor 26, 38n20
Hájek, Jiří 246–247, 249–250, 257nn13–14, 257nn18–19, 258n29, 259n51
Havel, Václav 133; see also Velvet Revolution
heritagization 101; see also objects of memory; places of memory
Hiller, István 29, 39n26
historical memory i–iii, v, 1–3, 15, 18n48, 45, 48, 57, 60, 61n4, 74, 149, 155, 169, 186n8, 187n21, 260, 275; see also collective memory
Hobsbawm, Eric J. 26, 38n16, 216n33, 242, 256n1
Hoffmann, Werner 80
Honecker, Erich 75
Horn, Gyula 32, 34
Horthy, Miklós 26, 28–31, 33, 36, 37n9, 39n35
House of Terror Museum (Budapest) 13, 23, 30–31, 275; see also museums
Hungarian Communist Party (HCP) 21, 26–28
Hungarian Socialist Party (HSP) 12, 21–24, 26, 29–35, 37, 39n38
Hungarian Socialist Workers' Party (HSWP) 21, 96n40, 168, 187n19
Hungarian Soviet Republic (*Magyarországi Tanácsköztársaság*) 24, 26–30, 36
Hungarian Uprising of 1956 i, 24, 31, 33–34, 39n34, 40n44, 49, 168–169,

186n17, 187n19; *see also* Soviet invasion of Hungary in 1956
Hungarian Working People's Party (HWPP) 168
Husák, Gustáv 130, 169

Iliescu, Ion 224–225, 236–237, 239n7, 240n37; *see also* Romanian Revolution of 1989
Il-sung, Kim 10
Independence Day of the Russian Federation 145
internationalism 25, 27, 81–83, 88, 195, 197–198, 200–201, 205, 217n41, 246, 257n20
Istpart 261–271, 271n5, 271n8, 271n12, 272n24, 272nn26–27, 272n31, 272nn38–39, 272nn42–43, 273n49; *see also* memory project
Italian Communist Party (PCI) 8, 12, 76, 79, 84–88, 96n40, 96n47; *see also* Communist Party of Italy
Iwanów, Zbigniew 176–177, 189n55

Jaruzelski, Wojciech 35, 144, 166, 170–173, 176–185, 186n5, 190n69, 190n73, 191n80, 191n82, 191n86; *see also* Martial law of 1981 (Poland)
Jobbik (Hungary) 26, 31
John Paul II 127, 133

Kádár, János 24, 27, 31, 33–34, 168
Kaganovich, Lazar 47
Kak nado pisat' vospominaniya [How to Write Memoirs] 265, 272nn32–34, 272nn36–37; *see also* Gelis, Joseph; Istpart
Kamenev, Lev 12; *see also* Great Purge
Kania, Stanisław 172–174, 176
Károlyi, Mihály 26–28, 30; *see also* Aster Revolution (Hungary)
Katyn massacre i, 7, 12, 144–145, 148–149, 160n36
Khrushchev, Nikita 8–12, 47, 49, 80, 120n87, 192, 206, 229, 234–235
Kohl, Helmut 51, 53, 56, 71nn166–167
Kommunarka (Russia) 155, 161n74; *see also* Memorial Day for the Victims of Political Repression (Russia)
Komsomol 269
Konspekt-minimum dlya vospominanij [The Basic Outline for Memoirs] 264, 267–268, 270, 272nn27–30; *see also* Baturin, Nikolai

Korean War 250, 252, 255
Kreisky, Bruno 85
Kun, Béla 27–29; *see also* Hungarian Soviet Republic (*Magyarországi Tanácsköztársaság*)

Lenin, Vladimir Ilyich vi, 1, 4–6, 8, 10–14, 16n10, 55, 63n19, 65n55, 70n146, 70n151, 79, 94n19, 95n28, 101, 107, 112, 118n39, 118n43, 122–123, 125, 127, 129–131, 133–135, 137, 139n34, 199, 231, 262; *see also* Lenin Shipyard in Gdańsk (Poland); *Leninopad* [Lenin fall]
Leninopad [Lenin fall] 107; *see also* Lenin, Vladimir Ilyich
Lenin Shipyard in Gdańsk (Poland) 86, 171, 188n33; *see also* Lenin, Vladimir Ilyich
Letopis revolyutsii [The Chronicles of Revolution] journal (USSR) 263, 268, 270, 272n26, 273n51; *see also* Istpart
Letter of the Six (Romania) 222, 224, 233–234, 241n46; *see also* Apostol, Gheorghe; Bârlădeanu, Alexandru; Brucan, Silviu; Mănescu, Corneliu; Pîrvulescu, Constantin; Răceanu, Ion Grigore
Liberal Democratic Party of Russia (LDPR) 50
Liebknecht, Karl 4–5, 16n10, 57, 75, 130, 135–136
Lieu(x) de mémoire 3, 5, 113, 120n82, 231; *see also* places of memory
Luca, Vasile 227–229, 232; *see also* Pauker, Ana
Lukács, György 29
Lumumba, Patrice 10, 135
Luxemburg, Rosa 4–5, 16n10, 57, 71n173, 73n195, 75, 135–136, 199, 210, 216n30

Magri, Lucio 11, 18n43, 18n46, 76, 85, 94nn11–13, 96n47
Mănescu, Corneliu 224, 233–234, 241n51; *see also* Letter of the Six (Romania)
Manifesto of Ventotene (Italy) 87; *see also* Rossi, Ernesto; Spinelli, Altiero
Maoism *see* Zedong, Mao
March, Luke 60–61n3, 62n9, 62nn11–13, 64n44, 67n92, 69n131, 70nn137–138, 71nn153–155, 78, 93n1, 94nn22–23

Marchais, Georges 8, 87; see also French Communist Party (PCF)
Marshall Plan 82, 244, 250
Martial law of 1981 (Poland) vi, 35, 86, 110, 165–166, 170–171, 173, 177–185, 186n3, 187n23, 191n107; see also Jaruzelski, Wojciech
Marx, Karl i, vi, 2–5, 13, 16nn6–7, 26, 38n13, 74–76, 78–80, 93n2, 93n6, 94n23, 94n25, 95nn26–27, 95n33, 122–123, 125, 127, 129, 131–133, 135–137, 139nn39–40, 139nn43–44, 202–203, 217n44, 218n53, 231
Marxism 2, 16n4, 64nn34–36, 64nn40–41, 67nn88–89, 72n180, 76, 93n7, 183, 187n29, 188n35, 226
Marxism-Leninism 45, 49, 79–80, 139n26, 200
Masaryk, Tomáš Garrigue 1, 9, 128–129, 132–134, 136, 140n48, 249, 254, 257n24, 257n28; see also First Czechoslovak Republic
Maurer, Gheorghe 235, 240n37, 241nn53–54
May Day 3, 11, 16n8
Medgyessy, Péter 31–32
Mednoje (Russia) 155, 161n75; see also Memorial Day for the Victims of Political Repression (Russia)
Medvedev, Dmitry 149, 152, 160n50
Memorial (NGO, Russia) 46, 154, 162n77, 162n82
Memorial Day for the Victims of Political Repression (Russia) 144, 149; see also Butovo (Russia); Kommunarka (Russia); Mednoje (Russia)
memory forging vi, 165–167, 170, 185, 186nn7–8
memory project 157, 260, 262–263, 270, 271, 271n1; see also Istpart
Minh, Ho Chi 10
Molnár, Erik 27, 38n22
monuments, communist and Soviet v, 4, 10, 73n195, 101–102, 105–106, 109–115, 116n21, 118n49, 119n54, 120n77, 120n79, 130–131, 135, 156, 170, 262, 273n50; destruction 101, 104, 107–109, 111, 114, 116n18, 118n41, 118n47, 119n68, 121n94, 132, 134, 145; see also Dzerzhinsky, Felix, monument to (Moscow); Green Bridge (Vilnius); Leninopad [Lenin fall]; objects of memory; socialist realism

Moro, Aldo 85
Moschonas, Gerassimos 77, 92, 94n16, 97n64
Munich Agreement 249–250, 252, 254, 258nn30–31
museums 4, 13, 23, 104, 106, 109, 112–114, 116n6, 130, 135, 143, 154–156, 161n71, 231, 233, 237, 261–263; see also Grūtas Park; House of Terror Museum (Budapest); Perm-36; State Museum of the History of Gulag (Moscow)

Nagy, Imre 33–34, 169
National Salvation Front (FSN) (Romania) 221, 223–225, 233–234, 236–237, 239n7
Nejedlý, Zdeněk 246, 257nn10–11
Neubert, Harald 75–76, 93nn9–10
Niculescu-Mizil, Paul 224, 235, 239n11, 240n28, 241n53, 241n58
Nostalgia 1, 16n2, 33, 36, 43–46, 51, 59, 64nn44–45, 65n46, 118n45, 215n14, 224; see also Ostalgie
Nowa Huta (Krakow) 135

objects of memory 109–110; see also monuments, communist and Soviet
October Revolution of 1917 i, vi, 4–5, 8–9, 11–12, 26, 50, 56, 77, 87, 193, 195–199, 213n5, 216n25, 218n56, 248, 260–263, 265–270, 271n1, 273n47, 273n50; see also Bolshevik revolution; Russian Revolution of 1917
October Uprising of 1917 (Russia) 260–261; see also October Revolution of 1917
operaismo 86
Orbán, Viktor 23, 27, 31–32, 35, 38n23, 39n34; see also Fidesz (Hungary)
Ostalgie 46, 51, 64n43; see also Nostalgia

Pan-Slavism 254; see also Slavic Unity
Paris Commune 2–3, 5–6, 16n5, 75, 260
Party of Democratic Socialism (PDS) v, 12, 41–46, 48–49, 51–53, 56–60, 60n2, 61n4, 62n7, 63n29, 64nn30–40, 64n42, 66–67n74, 67n75, 67nn77–83, 68n106, 68n108, 68n110, 68nn112–114, 69nn118–119, 69n127, 71n161, 71nn164–165, 71nn168–169, 71nn171–172, 72n175, 72nn181–184,

Index   283

72nn186–187, 72nn189–191, 72nn193–194, 73n195, 73n197, 73nn203–204, 88, 96n54, 127, 132, 139n43, 275; see also DIE LINKE Party of the European Left 74, 96n55, 274; see also European Left Party
Pătrăşcanu, Lucreţiu 228–229, 231, 236, 240n23, 240n35
Pauker, Ana 213n5, 226–229, 232, 239n20, 240n24, 240n36; see also Luca, Vasile
Perm-36 (Russia) 155; see also Gulag; museums
Pieck, Wilhelm 131
Pîrvulescu, Constantin 228, 233–234; see also Letter of the Six (Romania)
places of memory 105, 111, 131, 140n56; see also Lieu(x) de mémoire
Podemos (Spain) 35, 74, 78, 90
Pokrovsky, Mikhail 266
Polish United Workers' Party (PUWP, PZPR) vi–vii, 96n40, 165–168, 170–185, 186n5, 186nn14–16, 187nn27–28, 188n33, 189n37, 189nn53–54, 190n58, 190nn61–62, 190nn66–68, 190n70, 190n74, 190nn76–77, 191n88, 191n90, 191n106, 192, 194, 196, 214nn9–10, 215nn20–21, 220n75, 216n27; see also Polish Workers' Party (PWP, PPR)
Polish Workers' Party (PWP, PPR) 196, 201, 214n10, 215n19, 217n41, 219n69, 220n75; see also Polish United Workers' Party (PUWP, PZPR)
politics of history 1–2, 5, 10, 12–14, 22–24, 33, 36–37, 37n3, 275; see also politics of memory
politics of memory vi, 16n2, 24, 31, 37, 37n3, 57–58, 66n70, 107, 114–115, 136–137, 154, 170, 186n13, 221–223, 337, 275–276; see also politics of history
Popescu, Dumitru 224, 231, 235, 239n11, 241n53
Prague Spring of 1968 (Czechoslovakia) i, 49, 84, 107, 118n41, 122, 129–130, 187n20, 255–256, 258n46; see also Warsaw Pact invasion of 1968
Presidential Commission of the Russian Federation to Counter Attempts to Falsify History to the Detriment of Russia's Interest (Russia) 153; see also Putin, Vladimir

Presidential Council for Civil Society and Human Rights (Russia) 149; see also Putin, Vladimir
Program for Perpetuating the Memory of Victims of the Totalitarian Regime and on National Reconciliation (Russia) 149; see also Putin, Vladimir
Proletarian Democracy (*Democrazia Proletaria*, Italia) 86
Proletarskaya revolyutsiya [Proletarian Revolution] journal (USSR) 263, 265, 267, 270, 272n32, 272n40; see also Istpart
Putin, Vladimir 54, 60, 147, 149, 152–155, 159nn19–21, 160nn35–36, 162n85

Quaderni rossi journal (Italia) 86; see also operaismo

Răceanu, Ion Grigore 233–234; see also Letter of the Six (Romania)
Răceanu, Mircea 234, 241n45; see also Răceanu, Ion Grigore
Rákosi, Mátyás 27, 29
Red Army 7, 101–102, 108–113, 116nn20–21, 118n41, 123, 128, 131–132, 148, 188n31, 252, 254–255; see also Soviet Army
Rehabilitation of victims of political repression (Russia) 143–144
Reunification of Germany 124
revisionism 8, 15n2, 49, 55, 182, 207
Revolution of 1905 (Russia) 4, 195, 198–199, 266–267
Ripp, Zoltán 32, 37nn8–9, 38n19, 39n32, 39n38, 40n42, 40n45, 40n48
Romanian Communist Party (PCR) 221–229, 231–234, 236–237
Romanian Revolution of 1989 222–223, 238, 238n4, 238n6
Rossi, Ernesto 87, 96n49; see also *Manifesto of Ventotene* (Italy)
Russian Communist Party (Bolsheviks) 216n23, 262, 266, 269; see also Bolsheviks
Russian Historical Society 153, 155
Russian Military-Historical Society 153, 155
Russian Revolution of 1917 4, 6, 16n13, 80; see also Bolshevik revolution; February Revolution of 1917; October Revolution of 1917
Russian Social Democratic Labor Party (Bolsheviks) (RSDLP(B)) 199; see also Bolsheviks

Sartre, Jean-Paul 83
Schröder, Gerhard 56, 69n117
Second International 25
Sfetcu, Paul 235, 241nn53–54
Slavic Unity 245–246, 257n10; see also Pan-Slavism
Social Democratic Party of Germany (SPD) 56, 59, 66n67, 71n161, 72n175, 72n190, 73n195, 73n204, 75
Social Democratic Party of Hungary (HSDP) 21, 25, 38n13
Social Democratic Workers' Party of Austria (SDAPÖ) 81
Social Democratic Workers' Party of Cisleithania see Social Democratic Workers' Party of Austria (SDAPÖ)
socialist realism 114, 120n85, 120n87, 121n88; see also monuments, communist and Soviet
Socialist Unity Party of Germany (SED) 43–45, 48–49, 52, 56, 58, 63n29, 64nn31–33, 64n36, 64n38, 66n67, 66nn73–74, 67n75, 67n78, 67nn81–82, 71n161, 72n191, 75–76, 96n40, 124, 132
Solidarity trade union (Solidarność) 11, 86, 111, 165–166, 170–181, 183–185, 185nn1–2, 186n3, 187n23, 189n37, 189n44, 190n57, 191n107, 222, 277
Soros Foundation 51
Soviet Army 104, 108, 113, 120n77, 120n79; see also Red Army
Soviet invasion of Hungary in 1956 8, 12; see also Hungarian Uprising of 1956
Spanish Civil War 1, 29, 75, 195, 227, 232
Spinelli, Altiero 87, 96n49; see also Manifesto of Ventotene (Italy)
Stalin, Joseph i, 1, 4–6, 8–10, 12–13, 17n20, 18n39, 18n51, 27, 29, 44, 47–49, 53, 63n16, 63n19, 65nn55–56, 68n104, 70n146, 70n150, 70n152, 72n176, 79–82, 84, 95n28, 101, 104, 107, 120n87, 129–131, 143–144, 147–148, 150–151, 156, 162nn79–81, 171, 192, 196, 200, 206–208, 213n5, 219n66, 228–229, 271n9, 272n23
Stalinism i, 2, 6, 8, 12–14, 17n30, 18n49, 40n44, 44, 48–49, 57–58, 66n74, 79–80, 85, 90, 95n32, 123, 128, 133, 150, 155, 192, 204, 208–209, 212, 239nn16–17

Stalinist purges of the 1930s 27, 29, 193, 206–207, 215n17, 219n60, 219n64, 219n66, 227, 266; see also Great Purge; Stalinist purges of the 1950s
Stalinist purges of the 1950s 213n5, 228; see also Stalinist purges of the 1930s
Stasi 52, 69n124, 69n127, 133–134, 137
State Museum of the History of Gulag (Moscow) 155–156; see also Gulag; museums
Synaspismos (Greece) 88, 96n54
Syriza (Greece) 13, 18n50, 74, 90, 92
Szanyi, Tibor 34
Szydlak, Jan 174–175, 181

Tamás, Gáspár Miklós 26, 33–34, 38n17, 39n40, 40n49
Thälmann, Ernst 131, 135–136, 140n56
Thaw 8, 192, 209, 213n3, 213n5; see also de-Stalinization
Tito, Josip Broz 82, 227
Togliatti, Palmiro 80, 84, 95n29, 96nn42–43; see also Italian Communist Party (PCI)
totalitarianism 35, 58, 124, 134
Transformation of 1989 13, 25, 42, 51, 101–104, 110, 115, 122–124, 126–127, 133, 194, 219n64, 221; see also Transition of 1989
Transition of 1989 25, 30, 32, 34, 37n1, 37n5, 39n38, 41, 44, 46, 51–54, 62n5, 102, 107, 110, 221; see also Transformation of 1989
Traverso, Enzo 75–76, 93nn7–8, 94n14, 97n65
Treaty of Trianon 28, 36
Trotsky, Leon 6, 12, 47, 80
Trotskyism 80, 268; see also Trotsky, Leon
Tsipras, Alexis 90–91; see also Syriza (Greece)
Twentieth Congress of the CPSU of 1956 82, 207, 229; see also Communist Party of the Soviet Union (CPSU)

Ukrainian Soviet Socialist Republic (UkSSR) 268; see also October Revolution of 1917
Ulbricht, Walter 49, 137n4
Uprising of 1953 in East Germany 49, 58

Vajnai, Attila 35, 40n46
Velvet Revolution of 1989 (Czechoslovakia) 1, 133, 140n48; see also Havel, Václav
Victorious February 130, 243, 246, 250

Wagenknecht, Sahra 45, 49, 64n41, 67nn87–90, 72n176
Wall of Sorrow (Moscow) 156, 162n76; see also objects of memory
Warsaw Pact invasion of 1968 (Czechoslovakia) 81, 254–256; see also Prague Spring of 1968 (Czechoslovakia)
Wasilewska, Wanda 193, 208, 214n9, 220n73
Weimar Republic 136

Wilson, Thomas Woodrow 243, 246–249, 257n17, 257n20, 257–258n28
World Social Forum 77, 88–89, 94n20; see also European Social Forum

Yeltsin, Boris 12, 47, 49–50, 53–54, 65n50, 69nn130–131, 143–145, 152, 155

Zedong, Mao 10, 18n38, 90
Zinoviev, Grigory 12; see also Great Purge
Ziuganov, Gennadii 44, 54, 63nn25–26, 65nn52–54, 67n97, 68n98, 68nn101–103, 70nn137–139, 70n145, 70nn147–148, 70nn150–151